NORTH CAROLINA
STATE BOARD OF COMMUNITY COLLEGES
LIBRARIES
SAMPSON TECHNICAL COLLEGE

P9-CMP-498

Mechanical and Electrical Systems in Building

TH
6010
D3

Mechanical and Electrical Systems in Building

373-82

Frank R. Dagostino

Dean of Engineering Technology
Trident Technical College
Charleston, South Carolina

Reston Publishing Company, Inc.
Reston, Virginia
A Prentice-Hall Company

18498

Library of Congress Cataloging in Publication Data

Dagostino, Frank R.
   Mechanical and electrical systems in building.

   Includes index.
   1. Buildings—Mechanical equipment.   2. Buildings—
Electric equipment. I. Title.
TH6010.D3   696   81-11981
ISBN 0-8359-4312-7   AACR2

Copyright © 1982 by Reston Publishing Company, Inc.
A Prentice-Hall Company
Reston, Virginia 22090

All rights reserved. No part of this book may
be reproduced in any way, or by any means, without
permission in writing from the publisher.

10   9   8   7   6   5   4   3   2   1

Printed in the United States of America

Contents

Chapter 3: Plumbing Drainage   56

Chapter 4: Storm Drainage   78

Chapter 5: Private Sewage Disposal   92

Chapter 6: Comfort   107

Chapter 7: Heat Loss and Heat Gain   123

Chapter 8: Heating and Air Conditioning Systems   199

Chapter 9: Forced Air Systems and Design   207

Chapter 10: Hot Water Heating Systems and Design   241

Chapter 11: Electric Heating Systems and Design   267

Chapter 12: Solar Energy and Heat Pumps   277

Chapter 13: Electrical Systems and Design   294

Chapter 14: Lighting Systems and Design   339

Chapter 15: System Installation   368

Appendix A   383

Appendix B   384

Index   385

Preface

This text is geared for use by the entire construction industry—from those interested in the actual design of the systems to those who realize they must know and understand the mechanical systems in order to successfully design, draw, or build a building or project.

The mechanical equipment covered in this book is an integral part of the design and construction of all buildings and projects built. Its successful integration into the designs depends upon the close cooperation of the designer, the draftsmen, the mechanical systems designer, the general construction contractor, and each of the contractors who may install a portion of the mechanicals.

To be successful, each of these people or groups of people must be familiar with the requirements of the mechanical systems. Each should at least be familiar with the basic design procedures used, flexibilities in each system, space required, and the time at which such work must be done on the job so it is fully coordinated. The basic format of this text is to discuss the chapter topic, describe the material available, and then show, step-by-step, how to approach a design problem.

Frank R. Dagostino

Chapter 1
Water Supply

1-1 Water

Basically, water may be *potable* (suitable for human drinking) or *nonpotable* (not suitable for human drinking). While an abundant supply of water is vital to a prosperous economy, on an individual basis a supply of potable water is even more important to survival than food. This potable water must be supplied, or be available, for drinking and cooking. Nonpotable water may be used for flushing water closets (toilets), watering grass and gardens, washing cars and irrigating farms, and for any use other than drinking or cooking.

At this time potable water is commonly used for many activities that could be done with nonpotable water. As potable water becomes scarcer and as the cost of treating nonpotable water to make it potable increases, the use of potable water where nonpotable water will adequately serve is clear evidence of waste. Already in some communities the cost of potable water is so high that many residents use water from shallow wells to water their lawns and gardens and to wash their cars.

1

1-2   Water Sources

Rain is the source of most of the water available for our use, and it is classified as *surface water* or *groundwater*. Surface water is the rain that runs off the surface of the ground into streams, rivers, and lakes. Groundwater is the water that percolates (seeps) through the soil, building the supply of water below the surface of the earth.

Surface water readily provides much of the water needed by cities, counties, large industry, and others. However, this source is dependent on rain, and during a drought, the flow of water may be significantly reduced. Most surface water will probably have to be treated to provide the potable water required. Where non-potable water is required, such as for irrigating farms, no treatment of the water may be necessary.

Also classified as surface water is rain which may be collected in a small reservoir or tank (cistern) (Fig. 1-1) as it drains from the roof of a building.

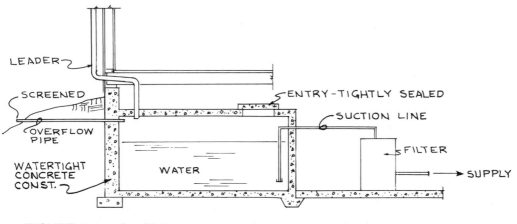

FIGURE 1-1   /   Cistern

This water is then pumped into the supply line of the building for use. The need for water is so critical on certain islands that the government has covered part of the land surface (usually the side of a mountain or a hill facing the direction from which the rains usually come) with a plastic so that rain may be collected and stored for later use.

As groundwater percolates through the soil, it forms a water level below the surface of the earth. This water level is referred to as the *water table*. The distance from the ground surface to the water table (referred to as the *depth* of the water table) varies considerably; generally the more rainfall an area gets, the higher the water table will be. During a dry spell the water table will usually go down, while during a rainy season it will probably rise.

Since the water table is formed by an accumulation of water over an impervious stratum (a layer of earth, usually rock, that the water cannot pass through), the flow of the water follows the irregular path of the stratum, sometimes moving close to the surface while dropping off nearby (Fig. 1-2). This underground supply of water flows horizontally, and if it reaches a low spot in the ground surface, it may flow as a spring or seep out creating a swampy area.

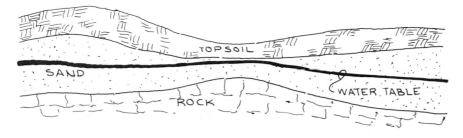

FIGURE 1-2 / Water table

Or, if the flowing water becomes confined between impervious strata, enough pressure may be built up in the water that if opened (by drilling through the top stratum or by a natural opening in the stratum), it will create an artesian well.

Groundwater may require treatment to provide potable water, but often it does not. When treatment is required, it is generally less than that required to make surface water potable.

The increased use (and misuse) of our potable water supply has forced the development of additional sources of water. This need for potable water has led to the desalination (taking the salt out) of water from the oceans and the purification of waste (sewage) water to be returned to the water system for reuse. To date, these methods involve a great deal of additional cost compared with the use and treatment of surface and groundwater.

1-3 Impurities

All water sources contain some impurities. It is the type and amount of these impurities which may affect the water's suitability for particular use.

As surface water runs over the ground, it may pick up various organic matter such as algae, fungi, bacteria, vegetable matter, animal decay and wastes, garbage wastes, and sewage.

As groundwater percolates down through the soil, it dissolves minerals such as calcium, iron, silica, sulphates, fluorides, and nitrates, and it may also entrap gases such as sulfide, sulphur dioxide, and carbon dioxide. It may also pick up contamination from public or private underground garbage and sewage wastes. Generally, as it percolates, it will filter out any organic matter which may have been accumulated at the surface or in the ground.

The impurities in the water may be harmful, of no importance, or possibly even beneficial to a person's health. To determine what is in the water it must be tested.

1-4   Tests

All potable water supplies should be tested before being put in use and periodically checked during their use. It is assumed that whatever agency of a city, municipality, etc., controls the supply of water to a community regularly tests its water to be certain it is potable. Private water supplies, such as wells and streams, should always be checked before the water system is put into use and periodically thereafter. Such tests are usually performed free of charge, or at a very low cost, by the local governmental unit in charge of public health. The governing unit (town hall, city hall, county health department) will put you in touch with the proper authorities, or it will refer you to a private testing laboratory.

The test for potable water provides a chemical analysis of the water, indicating the parts per million (ppm) of each chemical found in the water. A separate test is made for bacteriological quality, providing an estimate of the density of bacteria in the water supply. Of particular concern in this test is the presence of any coliform organisms which indicate that the water supply may be contaminated with human wastes (perhaps seepage from a nearby septic tank field). Since the test reports mean little to most people, a written analysis of the test or a standardized form is included with the test results stating whether the water is potable or not.

Water may have an objectionable odor and taste, even be cloudy and slightly muddied or colored in appearance, and yet the test may show it to be potable. This may not mean you *want* to drink it, but it does mean that it is drinkable. Such problems are often overcome by use of water-conditioning equipment, such as filters. As any traveler can quickly tell you, water varies considerably from place to place, depending on the water source of the area, the chemical and bacteria contents of the water, and the amount and type of treatment given the water before it is put into the system.

1-5   Water Systems

The design of any water supply begins with a check of the water system from which the water will be obtained. Basically, water is available through systems which serve the community or through private systems.

Community Systems

Systems which provide water to a community may be government owned, as in most cities, or privately owned, such as in a housing development where the builder or real estate developer provides and installs a central supply of water to serve the community. The water for these systems may have been obtained from any of the water sources listed in Sec. 1-2, and quite often it is drawn from more than one source. For example, part of the water supply may be taken from a river, and the rest supplemented by deep wells.

Before proceeding with the design of the water supply, the following information should be obtained:

1. What is the exact location of the water main (pipe) in relation to the property being built on?
2. If the main is on the other side of the street from the property, what procedures must be followed to get permission (in writing) to cut through the street, set up barricades, and patch the street? Also, what permits are required from local authorities, how much do the permits cost, and who will inspect the work and when? If available, obtain the specifications (written requirements) concerning the cutting and patching of the street.
3. If the water main does not run past the property, can it be extended from its present location to the property (Fig. 1-3), and who pays for the extension?
4. Is there a charge to connect (tap) onto the community system? Many communities charge just to tap on, and the charge is often hundreds of dollars.

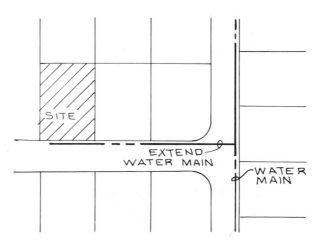

FIGURE 1-3 / Water main location

5. What is the pressure in the main at the property? If it is too low for a resi-
    dence [less than 30 psi (pounds per square inch)], a storage tank and pump
    may be required to raise the pressure. Such a system is often used on com-
    mercial and industrial projects where the pressure may have to be quite high
    to meet the water demands. Water pressure that is too high (above 60 psi for
    a residence) will probably require a pressure-reducing valve in the system to
    cut the pressure to an acceptable level.

    Since plumbing fixtures are manufactured to operate efficiently with
    water pressures from about 30 to 60 psi, higher pressure may result in poor
    operation of the fixtures, rapid wearing out of the washers and valves, and
    noises in the piping. Low pressure may cause certain fixtures to operate
    sluggishly, especially dishwashers, showers, flush valve water closets (toi-
    lets), and garden hoses. The required water pressure at various fixtures and
    the water pressure from the main to the fixtures are discussed in detail in
    Sec. 2-10.

6. What is the cost of the water? Typically, a water meter is installed, either out
    near the road or somewhere in the project, and there is a charge for the
    water used. After determining what the charges are, a cost analysis may
    show that it is cheaper to put in a private system. Some areas do not allow
    private systems for potable water, but quite often it will be desirable to put
    in a well to provide nonpotable water for sprinkling the lawn and garden
    and for washing the car. Where costs for potable water are extremely high, it
    may be feasible to use separate potable and nonpotable water supply sys-
    tems within the project (especially industrial and commercial projects).

Private Systems

Private systems may also use any of the water sources discussed in Sec. 1-2. Large
industrial and commercial projects may draw all of their supply from one source,
or they may draw part of their supply from one source (such as a stream) and
supplement the supply with another source (such as a well). Such systems often
include treatment plants, water storage towers, and sometimes even lakes or reservoirs to store the water.

Small private systems, such as those used for residences, usually rely on a
single source of water to supply potable water through the system. Installing a
well is the most commonly used method of obtaining water, and springs may be
used when one is available.

Experts, usually consulting mechanical engineers, soil engineers, or water
supply and treatment specialists, should be consulted early in the planning stages
of any large project requiring its own private water system. Such specialists can
make tests, interpret what the tests mean to the project, and make recommendations concerning the quality and amount of water available.

1-6 Wells

Most private water systems use wells to tap the underground water source. Wells are classified according to their depth and the method used to construct the well.

DEPTH	CONSTRUCTION METHOD
Shallow (25 ft or less)	Dug Driven Drilled
Deep (in excess of 25 ft)	Drilled Bored

The depth of the well is determined by the depth of the water table and the amount of water which can be pumped. This flow of water is considered the *yield* or capacity of the well. Once the water *demand* (the amount of water required) has been calculated (Sec. 1-9), it can be determined whether one well is enough or whether other wells will be needed to provide the required water for the project. Where the water table is high, it may not be necessary to go 25 ft deep, but it is not unusual for wells to be 100 ft deep, and in some areas well depths of several hundred feet are required to provide an adequate supply of water.

Dug wells (Fig. 1-4) should be 3 to 5 ft in diameter and not more than 20 to 25 ft deep. To minimize the chances of surface contamination, the well should

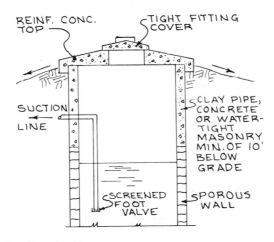

FIGURE 1-4 / Dug well

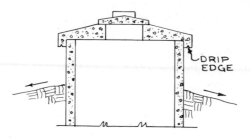

FIGURE 1-5   /   Dug well—top above ground

have a watertight top and walls. The top should be either above the ground (Fig. 1-5) or sloped so that surface water will run away from it and not over it. The watertight walls should extend at least 10 ft down. The walls may be concrete block, poured concrete, clay tile, precast concrete tile, or curved masonry units referred to as *manhole block* (Fig. 1-6).

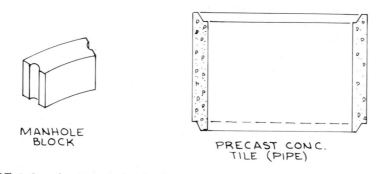

MANHOLE
BLOCK

PRECAST CONC.
TILE (PIPE)

FIGURE 1-6   /   Manhole block

The water will flow into the well through the bottom of the well, and will rise to about the level of the water table. Some wells also allow water to seep through the walls by use of porous construction near the bottom of the wall. This porous construction may be concrete block or manhole block placed without mortar (normally used to hold the blocks together and make them watertight).

The placing of washed gravel in the bottom of the well, and on the sides of the well when porous walls are used, will reduce the sand particles or discoloration in the well water. Washed gravel is gravel (stone) that has been put through a wash (water sprayed over the stone) to remove much of the sand or clay. To further protect the water from possible contamination, tightly seal around the suction line pipe where it passes through the wall. And don't take water out with a bucket or other container since it may have contamination on it, and by dipping such a container into the water, the contaminant is transferred to the water supply.

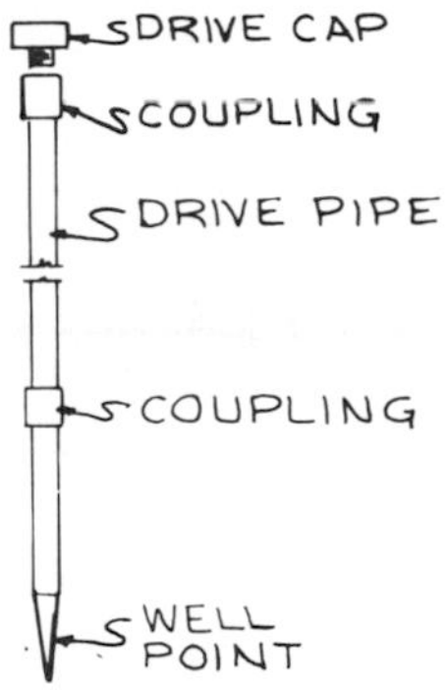

DRIVE CAP

COUPLING

DRIVE PIPE

COUPLING

WELL
POINT

FIGURE 1-7   /   Shallow well materials

Shallow wells may also be driven. To drive a well, first attach a well point to a drive pipe and drive cap (Fig. 1-7). Then, by means of an impact loading device such as a small pile driver or even a sledge hammer for very shallow wells in soft, sandy soil, the well point is driven into the ground until it is into the water table. The well point has holes or slots in the side, allowing water to be sucked up to the surface by a shallow well pump (Sec. 1-7). As the point is driven, additional lengths of pipe may be attached (usually 5-ft lengths are used) by the use of a coupling (Fig. 1-7). Driven wells will not pass through rock formations, and the maximum diameter commonly available is 2 in.

Shallow wells may have to be drilled if it is necessary to pass through rock to get to the water table.

Drilling and boring methods are used for deep wells. A well-digging rig (Fig. 1-8) is used to form the well hole. Drilled and bored wells differ in that drilled wells have the holes formed by using rotary bits (Fig. 1-9) and spudders, while bored wells have the holes formed by using augers (Fig. 1-10). Only the drilling method is effective in passing through rock.

FIGURE 1-8   /   Well-drilling rig

FIGURE 1-9   /   Rotary bit

FIGURE 1-10   /   Auger

As the hole is formed, a casing (pipe) is lowered into the ground. This steel or wrought-iron pipe (usually 3 to 6 in. in diameter) protects the hole against cave-ins where unstable soil conditions are encontered and keeps out surface drainage and possible surface or underground contamination. To further protect against surface drainage and contamination, a concrete apron, sloping away from the well, is poured around the casing at the surface (Fig. 1-11).

Well location and construction are often controlled by governmental regulations that set minimum distances between the well and any possible ground contaminant. When certain types of construction methods are used, these regulations may even require that licensed well drillers install the well. Various authorities and governmental regulations require different minimum distances, and no single set of standards is used. The table in Fig. 1-12 shows minimum distances required in one locale. It is important that local regulations be checked for each project.

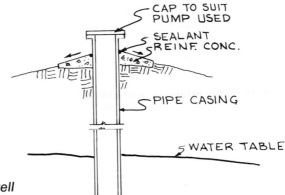

FIGURE 1-11 / Drilled well

FIGURE 1-12 / Well locations

Type of system	Distance from well
Building sewer	50'
Septic tank	50'
Distribution box	50'
Disposal field	100'
	100'
	50'

Well contamination from an underground flow of contaminants through rock formations which allow free-flowing groundwater to travel long distances is always possible, especially through strata of eroded limestone. Constant testing of water quality is required wherever there is a possibility of such contamination. For the well contaminated in this manner, three methods used to eliminate the problem are water treatment, relocation of the well, and elimination of the source of contamination.

Before planning the well, local conditions should be checked to provide some background information. For example, existing local wells should be checked for depth and yield of water. This information can be obtained from local well drillers and governmental agencies and, if possible, verified by testing existing or just completed wells.

Where insufficient information on well yields is available, and especially where large projects will require substantial water supplies, it may be necessary to have test wells made so that the yield can be checked. The well(s) should be tested by the driller to determine the yield, and a sample should be taken so that the quality of the water can be analyzed. It is important that this be done at an early stage in the design so that the size of the water storage tank can be determined (Sec. 1-9) and so that any water treatment equipment required can be designed and space allowed in the design of the project to locate the tank and equipment.

When a large supply of water is required for the continuous operation of the project, it may be necessary to put in other wells to be certain that the water yield will be sufficient to meet the projected demand (Sec. 1-9). For example, if one well provides adequate water, it may be a good investment to have a second well put in to act as a "back-up" in case the first well should fail in some way. This is not usually done for residences, but may be wise for industries or businesses that need water to operate (such as a car wash, farm, or apartment complex).

When more than one well is used, they must be spaced so that the use of one well will not lower the water table in the other well. Generally, deep wells must be 500 to 1,000 ft apart, while shallow wells must be 20 to 100 ft apart. Due to soil variables, the minimum distance between wells can be determined only by testing (usually trial and error).

Many industries and businesses which draw their water from community systems have private systems that can be put into operation in case of a water shortage due to a breakdown in the system or a prolonged drought. As an example, during a recent drought in Raleigh, N.C., a local ordinance was passed prohibiting the washing of cars. This meant that all car washes served by the community system had to close down. Imagine the relief of one owner who had a well as an alternate source of water; he was in business while all the other car washes closed. The local newspaper even carried a story on it, providing the owner with free advertising.

1-7   Pumps

Pumps used to bring well water to the surface are referred to as *shallow well* and *deep well*, depending on the type of well.

Shallow-well pumps are located above the ground, and a suction line extends into the well below the water table (Fig. 1-13). The pump cannot lift or pull

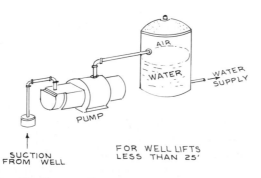

FIGURE 1-13   /   Shallow-well pump

the water up more than about 25 ft, so any well with the water table deeper than 25 ft is considered a deep well, and a deep-well pump is used. The shallow-well pumps commonly used are the shallow-well jet, rotary, and reciprocating piston pumps.

The deep-well pumps most commonly used are the jet and submersible pumps. Jet pumps are located above ground, either directly over or offset from the well (Fig. 1-14). Submersible pumps have a waterproof motor and are placed in the well below the water table.

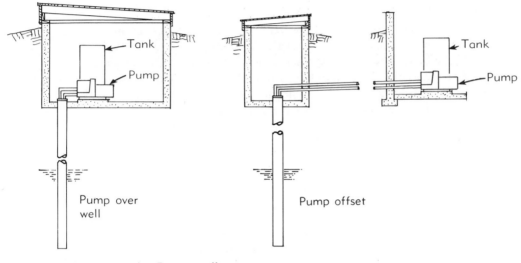

FIGURE 1-14   /   Deep-well pump

1-8   Plumbing Fixtures

The plumbing fixtures may be selected by the designer of the plumbing system, the architect, the owner, or a combination of these people. It is important that the designer of the plumbing system know what fixtures will be used (and even the manufacturer and model number, if possible) in order to do as accurate a job as possible in the design.

The fixtures are the only portion of the plumbing system that the owners or occupants of the building will see regularly since most of the plumbing piping is concealed in walls and floors. All fixtures should be carefully selected since they will be in use for years, perhaps for the life of the building.

The available sizes for each fixture should be carefully checked in relation to the amount of space available. Most manufacturers supply catalogs which show the dimensions of the fixtures they supply.

Whoever selects the fixtures should check with the local supplier to be certain that those chosen are readily available; if not, they may have to be ordered far in advance of the time they are required for installation. In addition, most of the fixtures are available in white or colors, so the color must also be selected.

Fixtures are grouped according to their use: water closets; urinals; bidets; bathtubs; showers; lavatories; kitchen sinks; and service sinks.

Water Closets

Water closets are made of solid vitrified china cast with an integral trap (Fig. 3-3 and Sec. 3-3). Water closets are available as flush tank or flush valve fixtures.

A flush tank water closet (Fig. 1-15) has a water tank as a part of the fixture. As the handle (or button) is pushed, it lifts the valve in the tank, releasing the water to "flush out" the bowl. Then, when the handle is released, the valve drops and the tank fills through a tube attached to the bottom of the tank. This type of fixture cannot be effectively flushed again until the tank is refilled. There are several types of flushing action available on water closets, as illustrated in Fig. 1-16.

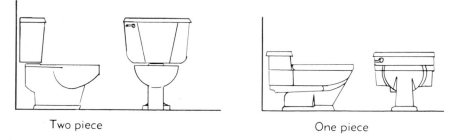

Two piece   One piece

FIGURE 1-15   /   *Typical flush tank water closets*

Flush tank models range from those having the tank as a separate unit set on the closet bowl to those having a low tank silhouette with the tank cast as an integral part of the water closet. Generally, this low-slung appearance is preferred by clients, but it is considerably more expensive.

Flush valve water closets (Fig. 1-17) have no tank to supply water. Instead, when the handle is pushed, the water to flush the bowl comes directly from the water supply system at a high rate of flow. When used, it is important that the water supply system be designed to supply the high flow required. While most of the fixtures operate effectively at 20 psi pressure, the manufacturer's specifications should be checked, since higher pressure is often required and must be considered in the design.

20014267

Washdown
Least expensive
Least efficient
Noisiest

Reverse trap
Efficient
Moderately noisy

Siphon jet
Efficient
Fairly quiet

Siphon jet
Quietest
Most expensive

FIGURE 1-16 / Types of flushing action

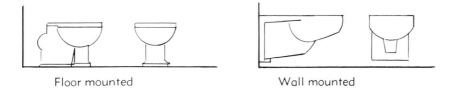

Floor mounted

Wall mounted

FIGURE 1-17 / Flush valve water closets

Water closets may be floor or wall mounted, as shown in Figs. 1-17 and 1-18. The floor-mounted fixture is much less expensive in terms of initial cost, but the wall-mounted fixture allows easier and generally more effective cleaning of the floor. Wall-mounted fixtures are considered desirable for public use, and some codes even require their use in public places. When wall-mounted fixtures are used in wood stud walls, a 2-in. × 6-in. stud will be required instead of the 2-in. × 4-in. stud sometimes used with floor-mounted fixtures.

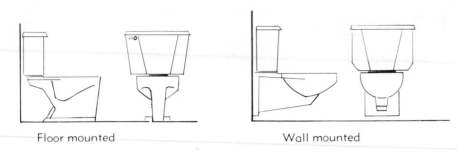

Floor mounted   Wall mounted

FIGURE 1-18   /   Floor- and wall-mounted water closets

Urinals

Urinals are commonly used in public restrooms where it is desirable to reduce any possible contamination of the water closet seats. They are commonly available in vitreous china and sometimes in enameled iron. They may be flush tank or flush valve and are available in three basic styles—wall, stall, and pedestal—as shown in Fig. 1-19.

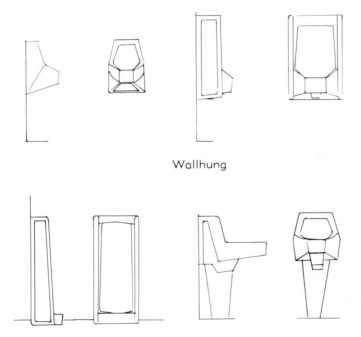

Wallhung

Stall   Pedestal

FIGURE 1-19   /   Urinals

Bidets

Bidets (Fig. 1-20) are designed to wash the perineal area after using the water closet. The bidet is used extensively in Europe and South America and is enjoying increased usage in Canada and the United States. It is designed for use by the entire family and is installed beside the water closet. The user sits on the fixture facing the wall (and the water controls) and is cleansed by a rinsing spray. It is available in vitreous china.

FIGURE 1-20 / Bidets

Bathtubs

Bathtubs are available in enameled iron, cast iron, or fiberglass. Tubs are available in quite a variety of sizes, the most common being 30 or 32 in. wide; 12, 14, or 16 in. high; and 4 to 6 ft long.

Enameled iron tubs (formed steel with a porcelain enamel finish) are generally available in lengths of 4½ and 5 ft, widths of 30 to 31 in., and typical depths of 15 to 15½ in.

Fiberglass bathtubs have been in widespread use since about 1968. The only length commonly available is 5 ft, and it takes 34 to 36 in. of width to install. Generally, the units are cast in a single piece which includes three walls (eliminating the need for ceramic tile around the tub). It is this single-piece feature, with no cracks or sharp corners to clean, which makes the fiberglass tub so popular with clients. The size of the unit makes it almost impossible to fit it through the standard bathroom door; it must therefore be ordered and delivered early enough to be set in place before walls and doors are finished. In wood frame buildings, these units are usually delivered to the job and put in place before the plaster or gypsum board is put on the walls or the doors installed. When selecting fiberglass tubs, be certain to specify only manufacturers who are widely known and respected, with long experience in the plumbing fixture field. Off-brands often give unsatisfactory results in that the fiberglass "gives" as it is stepped on, making a slight noise. In addition, some may be far more susceptible to scratching and damage.

Bathtub fittings may be installed on only one end of a tub, and the tub is designated by the end at which they are placed. As you face the tub, if the fittings are placed on the left, it is called a *left-handed* tub, and, if placed on the right, it is *right-handed*.

Showers

Showers (Fig. 1-21) are available in units of porcelain enameled steel or fiberglass. They may be built in with a base (bottom) of tile, marble, cement, or molded compositions, and walls may be any of these finishes or porcelain enameled steel. Showers have overhead nozzles which spray water down on the bather. Shower fittings may be placed over bathtubs instead of having a separate shower space; this is commonly done in residences, apartments, and motels. However, it is important that when a shower head is used with a bathtub fixture, the walls be of an impervious material (one that will not absorb water).

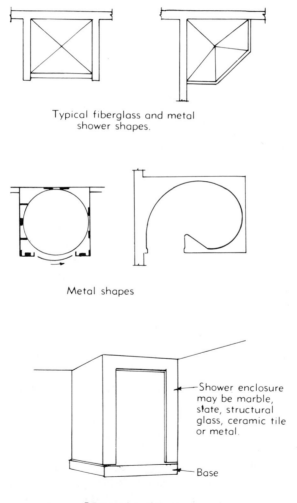

Typical fiberglass and metal
shower shapes.

Metal shapes

Shower enclosure
may be marble,
slate, structural
glass, ceramic tile
or metal.

Base

Base and enclosure

FIGURE 1-21   /   Showers

Showers of tile, concrete, or marble may be built to any desired size or shape. Preformed shower stall bases are most commonly available in sizes of 30 in. × 30 in. and 30 in. × 36 in.; other sizes may be ordered. Steel showers are usually available in sizes of 30 in. × 30 in. and 30 in. × 36 in.; special sizes may also be ordered. Fiberglass showers are commonly available in sizes of 36 in. × 36 in. and 36 in. × 48 in.

Special showers available include corner units and gang head units. Gang head showers are commonly used in institutions, schools, factories where workers must shower after work, and other situations where large numbers of people must shower.

Lavatories

Lavatories (Fig. 1-22) are generally available in vitreous china or enameled iron, or they may be cast in plastic or a plastic compound with the basin and integral part of the countertop. They are available in a large variety of sizes, and the shapes are usually square, rectangular, round, or oval (and even shell shaped).

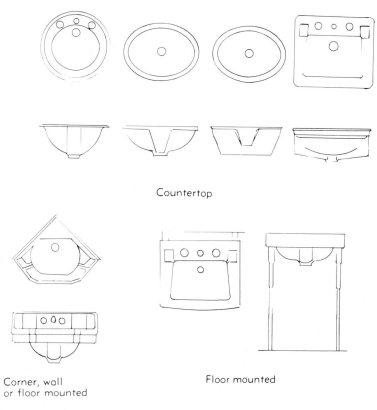

Countertop

Corner, wall
or floor mounted

Floor mounted

FIGURE 1-22   /   Lavatories

The lavatory may be wall hung, set on legs or on a stand, or built into a cabinet (Fig. 1-22). Lavatory styles are usually classified as flush-mount, self-rimming, under-the-counter, or integral, or as units which can be wall hung or supported on legs.

Special fittings for lavatories include foot controls (often used in institutions such as hospitals and nursing homes), and self-closing faucets, which are commonly used in public facilities (especially on hot water faucets) to conserve water.

Kitchen Sinks

Kitchen sinks are most commonly made of enameled cast iron or stainless steel. Sinks are usually available in a single- or a double-bowl arrangement; some even have a third bowl which is generally much smaller. Quite often a garbage disposal is connected to one of the sinks. Kitchen sinks are generally flush mounted into a plastic laminate (such as Formica®) or into a composition plastic counter.

Service Sinks

Service sinks are made of enameled cast iron or vitreous china, and they are often called *slop sinks*. Most service sinks have high backs, and there may be two or as many as three bowl compartments. Other sinks commonly used are laundry trays, pantry sinks, bar sinks, and surgeon's sinks.

Minimum Requirements

The codes generally set the minimum number of fixtures that must be installed on a project according to the type of occupancy (Fig. 1-23). For example, a theatre with 350 seats must have four water closets for men, four water closets for women, three urinals, and three lavatories. When designing any commercial, industrial, or institutional project, this minimum fixture chart must be checked.

1-9   Water Demand Design

The amount of water required for the operation of the fixtures installed in a project will depend on the number and kind of fixtures installed and on the probable simultaneous use of the fixtures (for example, it would be highly unlikely that every sink, dishwasher, water closet, bathtub, shower, clothes washer, and garden hose in a residence would be used at one time). The amount of water required is referred to as a *demand load.* This demand is measured in *fixture units* (f.u.), and the fixture-unit ratings for various commonly used plumbing fixtures are shown in Fig. 1-24. The fixture unit provides a means of comparing the water supply de-

Type of Building or Occupancy[2]	Water Closets		Urinals	Lavatories		Bathtub or Showers	Drinking Fountain[3]
Dwelling or Apt. House[4] [10]	1 for each Dwelling or Apartment Unit		....	1 for Each Apartment or Dwelling Unit.		1 for Each Apartment or Dwelling Unit.	
Schools[5]	Male	Female					
Elementary	1 per 60	1 per 35	1 per 30 Male	1 per 60 Persons.			1 per 75 Persons.
Secondary	1 per 100	1 per 45	1 per 30 Male	1 per 100 Persons.			1 per 75 Persons.
College— Academic	Male 1 per 100	Female 1 per 60	1 per 110 Male	Male 1 per 150	Female 1 per 100		1 per 75 Persons.
Office or Public Buildings[11] or Institutions (other than for patient use)	No. of Persons 1-15 16-35 36-55 56-80 81-100 101-150 1 Fixture for each 40 Additional Persons	No. of Fixtures M. F. 1 1 2 2 3 4 4 5 5 6 6 8	Wherever urinals are provided for men or women, one water closet less than the number specified may be provided for each urinal installed except that the number of water closets in such cases shall not be reduced to less than 2/3 of the minimum specified for men and 3/4 of the minimum specified for women.	No. of Persons 1-15 16-35 36-60 61-90 91-125 1 Fixture for Each 45 Additional Persons.	No. of Fixtures 1 2 3 4 5		1 for Each 75 Persons.
Manufacturing, Warehouses, Workshops, Loft Buildings, Foundries and similar Establishments[6] [11]	No. of Persons 1-9 10-24 25-49 50-74 75-100 1 Fixture for Each Additional 30 Employees	No. of Fixtures M. F. 1 1 2 2 3 4 4 5 5 6	Same substitution as above.	1-100 Persons 1 Fixture for Each 10 Persons. Over 100, 1 for Each 15 Persons.[7] [8]		1 shower for each 15 persons exposed to excessive heat or to skin contamination with poisonous, infectious, or irritating material.	1 for Each 75 Persons.

General. In applying this schedule of facilities, consideration must be given to the accessibility of the fixtures. Conformity purely on a numerical basis may not result in an installation suited to the need of the individual establishment. For example, schools should be provided with toilet facilities on each floor having classrooms.

Temporary workingmen facilities:

        1 water closet and 1 urinal for each 30 workmen.
        24-in. urinal trough — 1 urinal   48-in. urinal trough — 2 urinals
        36-in. urinal trough — 2 urinals   60-in. urinal trough — 3 urinals
                72-in. urinal trough — 4 urinals

FIGURE 1-23 / Minimum fixtures

mands for the fixtures since they are "relative to each other," meaning that a private bathtub with faucet rated at 2 fixture units requires twice as much water as a private lavatory with faucet which is rated at 1 fixture unit.

As the table in Fig. 1-24 shows, the type of occupancy of the building (public or private use) has an effect on the fixture-unit value since the greater use of the fixtures in public buildings increases the amount of simultaneous use.

Step-by-Step Approach

1. The first step in determining the demand load is to list the plumbing fixtures required on the project.
2. Next, the demand load for each plumbing fixture is listed (Fig. 1-24).
3. The demand for water in gallons per minute (gpm) can now be determined by using the large chart in Fig. 1-25 for fixture-unit loads up to 3,000 or the enlarged chart in Fig. 1-26 for fixture-unit loads up to 250. Also, note that the top line (line 1) in both Fig. 1-25 and Fig. 1-26 is to be used for any system which has predominantly flush valve water closets, and line 2 is used for any system which has predominantly flush tank water closets.

Fixture	Number of Fixture Units	
	Private Use	Public Use
Bar sink	1	2
Bathtub (with or without shower over)	2	4
Dental unit or cuspidor	—	1
Drinking fountain (each head)	—	1
Hose bibb or sill cock (standard type)	3	5
House trailer (each)	6	6
Laundry tub or clotheswasher (each pair of faucets)	2	4
Lavatory	1	2
Lavatory (dental)	1	1
Lawn sprinklers (standard type, each head) . . .	1	1
Shower (each head)	2	4
Sink (bar)	1	2
Sink or dishwasher	2	4
Sink (flushing rim, clinic)	—	10
Sink (washup, each set of faucets)	—	2
Sink (washup, circular spray)	—	4
Urinal (pedestal or similar type)	—	10
Urinal (stall)	—	5
Urinal (wall)	—	5
Urinal (flush tank)	—	3
Water closet (flush tank)	3	5
Water closet (flushometer valve)	6	10

Water supply outlets for items not listed above shall be computed at their maximum demand, but in no case less than

3/8 inch	1	2
1/2 inch	2	4
3/4 inch	3	6
1 inch	6	10

The given weights are for total demand. For fixtures with both hot and cold water supplies, the weights for maximum separate demands may be taken as 3/4 of the listed demand for the supply.

Extracted from American Standard National Plumbing Code (ASA A 40.8 - 1955) with permission of the publisher, The American Society of Mechanical Engineers.

FIGURE 1-24 / *Equivalent fixture units (including combined hot and cold water demand)*

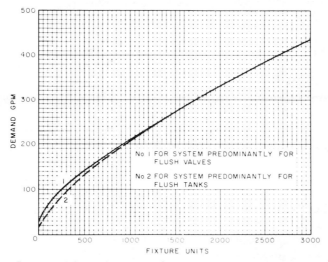

Extracted from American Standard National Plumbing Code
(ASA A 40.8 - 1955) with permission of the publisher, The
American Society of Mechanical Engineers.

FIGURE 1-25   /   Water demand load

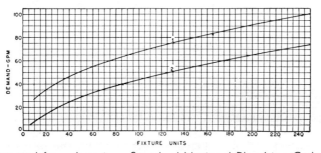

Extracted from American Standard National Plumbing Code
(ASA A 40.8 - 1955) with permission of the publisher, The
American Society of Mechanical Engineers.

FIGURE 1-26   /   Enlarged water demand load

Example:

Now, calculate the fixture units for the entire apartment building (Appendix A):

Total fixture units per floor:
2 flush tank water closets	3 f.u. × 2 = 6 f.u.
2 tubs with shower	2 f.u. × 2 = 4 f.u.
2 lavatories	1 f.u. × 2 = 2 f.u.
2 kitchen sinks	2 f.u. × 2 = 4 f.u.
	16 f.u. per floor

It should be noted at this point that the apartment building being sized for a water system has a repetitive floor plan for each floor. This allows the entire apartment to be serviced from a single water pipe (riser) going up the building.

Total fixture units on this riser:

16 f.u. (per floor) × 4 (floors) = 64 f.u.

Total additional fixture units:

2 hose bibbs (first floor) 3 f.u. × 2 = 6 f.u.

Total fixture units on this project:

64 f.u. (on riser) + 6 f.u. (hose bibbs) = 70 f.u.

Demand in gpm

70 f.u., flush tank, 36 gpm

1-10   Water Reuse System

At this time, there are experimental houses being built throughout the world in order to study and analyze the new products and technology available and to examine the possibility of preserving our natural resources by using these new materials. One such project is the Tech House, the NASA Technology Utilization House in Hampton, Virginia. One portion of the design involves the possibility of processing household waste water for reuse.

In the design of the system a typical family of four is used with typical household appliances. The water from the bathtub or shower and the washing machine is run into a collection tank instead of going into the sewer lines. From the collection tank the water is filtered and chlorinated and then reused as water to flush the toilets. A schematic illustrating the flow of the water is shown in Fig.

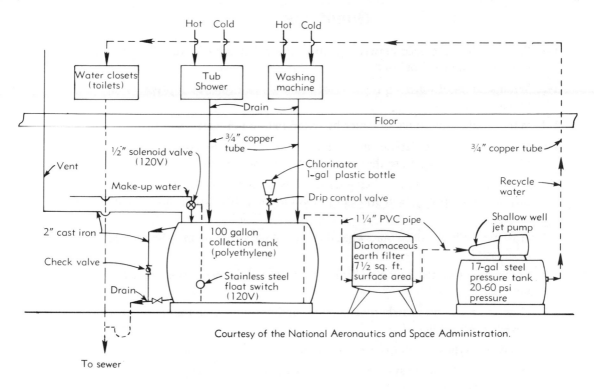

Courtesy of the National Aeronautics and Space Administration.

FIGURE 1-27 / Water reuse system

1-27. This water reuse system cuts water consumption by one-half. Of course, the potable water system is kept completely separate from the reuse portion of the system, and all waste from water closets goes directly into the sewer.

In another experiment all of the household water, except for that from the garbage disposal and water closets, is processed for multiple reuse in the system. This results in savings of up to 70% of overall household water consumption.

Of course, the real significance of this type of reuse system is the reduced amount of water required. The savings from such a system result in:

1. Smaller community or private sewer systems.
2. Smaller community treatment plants required to treat sewage.
3. Smaller community treatment plants needed to treat supply water (when required).
4. Smaller community water supply systems required (distribution system).
5. Smaller water supply (wells, reservoirs, etc.) needed.

Questions

1-1. What is the difference between potable and nonpotable water? For what purposes may each be used?

1-2. What sources of water supply may be available to a city? To a private individual?

1-3. Why should any source of water be tested before the water is used?

1-4. What is the basic difference between a community and a private water supply system, and what are the advantages and disadvantages of each?

1-5. When a project (building) being designed is going to connect to a community water supply system, what information about the system must be obtained?

1-6. How are wells classified, and what methods of construction may be used for each type?

1-7. Show with a sketch how a well may be protected from surface water contaminants.

1-8. How are wells protected from possible underground contamination from sewage disposal fields?

1-9. What two types of pumps are used, and what are the limitations of each?

1-10. What is a water reuse system, how does it work, and why might such a system be desirable?

Chapter 2
Water Supply Systems

2-1   Introduction

Plumbing systems are used to perform the two primary functions of water supply and waste disposal. The water supply portion of the system consists of the piping and fittings which supply hot and cold water from the building water supply to the fixtures in the building or project, such as lavatories, bathtubs, water closets, dishwashers, clothes washers, and sinks. Only water supply is included in this chapter. The waste disposal portion of the system, which consists of the piping and fittings required to take water supplied to the fixtures out of the building and into the sewer line or disposal field, is discussed in Chapter 3.

2-2   Codes

Building codes are the regulations governing the private actions of those who build or modify buildings. They are intended to protect public health, safety, and welfare. The codes establish certain minimum requirements for the construction and subsequent occupancy of buildings.

Plumbing codes may be a part of the general building code or, more commonly, a separate code. The code in force in any locale is determined by the municipality involved (each individual area, or governmental unit, selects its own code). The most commonly used codes are the national, regional, and state codes which may be used intact (complete) or with changes to meet the local needs and requirements. It should be noted that the governmental unit also has a right to decide to have no code at all.

Since the code in a given locale is a law, it must be complied with in all of the buildings constructed under its jurisdiction. For this reason, it is important that all of the people involved in the planning, design, and construction phases of the project become familiar with the code in effect in the locale in which the building will be constructed.

The *National Plumbing Code* has been used as a basis for this text since this is the code most often used, referred to, or adapted from. But it is important for anyone using the text and learning about the construction industry to find out what code is used in your locale and to get a copy. You will probably find it very much in agreement with the *National Plumbing Code* which should also be a part of your library.

In general, plumbing codes limit the types of materials and the sizes of pipe used in the system. The codes generally also form the basis for regulating installation methods.

Multiple Governing Codes

A proposed project may be regulated by several codes, covering the same items at the same time. This situation occurs quite often when the government, or a governmental agency, is providing some or all of the financing on a project and has certain "rules" or "guidelines" which must be followed. This situation may also occur when doing business with large corporations. In such cases, the designers involved will have to become familiar with all of the applicable codes and regulations and, when they are in conflict, use the more stringent requirements.

Administration

Where codes are in force, there will probably be some form of Building Department or Department of Building in the government. The local administration and enforcement of the codes are performed by a building inspector or an engineer who usually reviews the proposed contract documents (drawings and specifications) for compliance with the codes and then checks for compliance during construction. It is important to know just what work must be inspected. Inspections should be scheduled so that work which must be inspected will not be covered prematurely; otherwise, the inspector may require it to be uncovered so it can be checked.

Such responsibilities require qualified personnel—those who are experienced, informed, and objective. Many levels of government offer courses for the inspectors to provide them with great experience and to make the latest technical information available to them.

2-3   Parts of the System

The parts of a typical water supply system are shown in Fig. 2-1. They include the building main, riser, horizontal fixture branch, fixture connection, and a meter in community systems.

Building main: Connects to the community or private source and extends into the building to the furthest riser. The building main is typically run (located) in a basement, crawl space, or below the concrete floor slab.

Riser: Extends from the building main vertically in the building to the furthest horizontal fixture branch. It is typically run vertically in the walls.

Horizontal fixture branch: Extends horizontally from the riser to the furthest fixture to be connected. It is usually run in the floor or in the wall behind the fixtures.

Fixture connection: Extends from the horizontal fixture branch to the fixture.

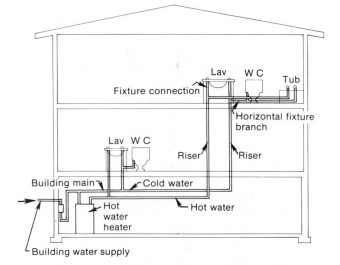

FIGURE 2-1   /   *Parts of a typical water supply system*

Meter: Required by most community water supply systems to measure and record the amount of water used. It may be placed in a meter box located in the ground, near the street or inside the building.

2-4   Piping Materials

Only piping used for water supply is included in this section. Drainage, waste, and vent piping are covered in Sec. 3-3. Piping most commonly used for water supply includes copper, wrought-iron, steel, plastic, and occasionally brass.

Copper is one of the most popular water supply pipes. The pipe types available are K, L, and M, with K having the thickest walls, then L, and finally M with the thinnest walls of this group. (DWV copper tubing is used for drainage, waste, and vent piping.) The thin walls of copper pipe are usually soldered to the fittings. This allows all of the pipes and fittings to be set into place before joints must be "finished" (in this case, by soldering). This advantage generally allows faster installation of copper pipe. Compared with iron or steel pipe, copper pipe also has the advantage of not rusting and of being highly resistant to any accumulation of scale (particles) in the pipe.

Type K copper tube is available either rigid (hard temper) or flexible (soft temper). It is used primarily for underground water service in water supply systems. Soft temper tubing 1 in. and smaller is usually available in coils 60 or 100 ft long while 1¼ and 1½ in. tubing is available in 40- or 60-ft coils. Hard temper is available in 12- and 20-ft straight lengths. Type K copper tubing is color coded in green for quick visual identification.

Type L copper tube is also available in either hard or soft temper in coils and straight lengths. The soft temper tubing is often used as replacement plumbing because the flexibility of the tube allows easier installation. Hard temper tubing is often used for new installations, particularly in commercial work. Type L copper tubing is color coded blue. This type of tubing is most popular for use in water supply systems.

Type M copper tube is made in hard temper only and is available in straight lengths of 12 and 20 ft. It has the thinnest wall and is used for branch supplies where water pressure is not too great, but it is not used for risers and mains. It is also used for chilled water systems, exposed lines in hot water heating systems, and drainage piping. Type M copper tubing is color coded red.

Copper tubing has a lower friction loss per 100 ft than wrought-iron or steel, providing the designer with an additional advantage. Also, the outside dimensions of the fittings are smaller which makes a neater, better-looking job. With wrought-iron and steel pipe the bigger outside dimensions of the fittings sometimes require that wider walls be used in the building.

Red brass piping, consisting of 85% copper and 15% zinc, is also sometimes used as water supply piping. The pipe is threaded for fitting connections, but this requires thicker walls to accommodate the threading, making installation and handling more difficult than for copper. In addition, its relatively higher total cost, installed on the job, limits its usage.

Plastic pipe is also available for water supply systems. Its economy and ease of installation make it increasingly popular, especially on projects such as low-cost housing or apartments, where "cost economy" is most important. Available in 10-ft lengths, it is lighter than steel or copper and requires no special tools to install. While many plumbing subcontractors, engineers, and architects still prefer copper, the use of plastic pipe will continue to increase. It is important to check the plumbing code in force in your locale since some areas still do not allow the use of plastic pipe for water supply systems. This dates back to early concern about possible toxicity (poisoning) resulting from the use of plastic pipe; this concern has long since been proved groundless. Plastic pipe used for water supply should carry the NSF (National Sanitation Foundation) seal. However, not all plastic pipe available should be used for water supply; much of it has been manufactured for use in the drainage portion of the plumbing system. The chart in Fig. 2-2 shows plastic pipe materials and their usual use in the water supply system.

Type	Cold water	Hot water
Polyethylene (PE)	●	
Polyvinyl Chloride (PVC)	●	
Acrilylonitrile Butadiene Styrene (ABS)	●	●
Polyvinyl Dichloride (PVDC)	●	
Chlorinated Polyvinyl Chloride (CPVC)	●	●

FIGURE 2-2 / Plastic pipe use

Wrought-iron pipe is available in diameters from ⅛ in. to 24 in. Lightweight wrought-iron pipe, designated standard (or schedule 40), is the type most commonly used for water supply systems. The wrought-iron pipe used is most commonly galvanized to add extra corrosion resistance. Quite often it is used as the service main from the community main to the riser. Wrought-iron pipe is threaded for connection to the fittings, and it can be identified by a red spiral stripe on the pipe. The higher cost of wrought-iron pipe limits its increased use. Wrought-iron pipe also has a higher friction loss per 100 ft than copper.

Steel pipe is available in diameters from ⅛ in. to 12 in. Plain steel pipe is usually used only when the water is not corrosive. Galvanized steel pipe is moderately corrosion resistant and suitable for mildly acid water. It is not used extensively in water supply systems; most plumbers and engineers prefer copper tubing because of its superior resistance to corrosion. Steel pipe is connected to its fittings with threaded connections. Steel pipe also has a higher friction loss per 100 ft than copper.

2-5   Fittings

A variety of fittings must be used to install the piping in a project and make all the pipe turns, branch lines, joinings on the straight runs, and stops at the end of the runs. Fittings for steel and wrought-iron pipe are threaded and made of malleable iron and cast iron. The fittings for plastic, copper, and brass pipe are made of the same materials as the pipe being connected. Typical fittings for the various materials are shown in Figs. 2-3, 2-4, and 2-5.

90°
Elbow

45°
Elbow

Tee

Reducing
tee

FIGURE 2-3   /   *Copper tubing and fitting*

FIGURE 2-4   /   *Plastic fittings*

Coupling   Reducer   Union

FIGURE 2-5   /   *Wrought-iron fittings*

The 45° and 90° elbows are used to change the direction of the pipe. Unions and couplings are used to join straight runs of pipe. A clamping piece on the coupling allows it to be more easily disengaged for uncoupling of the pipes when future piping revisions are expected at a given point. Tees are used when branch lines must be made; the reducing tee allows different pipe sizes to be joined together. Adapters are used where threaded pipe is being connected to copper or plastic. Adapters have one end threaded to accommodate the steel pipe.

2-6   Valves

Valves are used to control the flow of the water throughout the system. There are usually valves at risers (vertical pipe serving the building), branches (horizontal pipe serving the fixtures), and any pipes to individual fixtures or equipment. The proper location of valves simplifies repairs to the system, fixtures, or equipment being serviced.

The *globe valve* (Fig. 2-6) is a compression-type valve, commonly used where there is occasional or periodic use, such as lavatories (faucets) and hose connections (called hose bibbs). This type of valve usually closes the flow of water and is partially or fully opened only periodically to allow the water to flow. In reviewing Fig. 2-6, the handle is turned and a washer on the bottom of the stem is forced against the metal seat which stops the flow of water. To allow the water to flow, the handle is turned and the washer separates from the seat; the more flow desired, the more the valve is opened. The design of the globe valve is such that the water passing through is forced to make two 90° turns, which greatly increases the friction loss in this valve compared with that in a gate valve.

The *angle valve* (Fig. 2-7) is similar in operation to the globe valve, utilizing the same principle of compressing a washer against a metal seat to cut the flow of water. It is commonly used for outside hose bibbs. The angle valve has a much higher friction loss than the gate valve and about half the friction loss of the globe valve.

The *gate valve* (Fig. 2-8) has a wedge-shaped leaf which, when closed, seals tightly against two metal seats which are set at slight angles. This type of valve is usually used where the flow of the water is left either completely opened or closed for most of the time. Because the flow of water passes straight through the valve, there is very little water pressure lost to friction. The gate valve is usually used to shut off the flow of water to fixtures and equipment when repairs or replacement must be made.

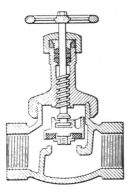

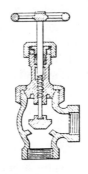

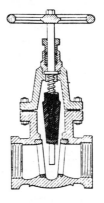

FIGURE 2-6   /
Globe valve

FIGURE 2-7   /
Angle valve

FIGURE 2-8   /
Gate valve

The *check valve* (Fig. 2-9) has a hinged leaf which opens to allow the flow of water in the direction desired (indicated by an arrow in the illustration). But the leaf closes if there is any flow of water in the other direction. This eliminates any possible flow of water in a direction other than that desired, or required, by the designer. The check valve works automatically so there is no need for a handle. This valve is used in such places as the water feed line to a boiler (heating unit) where the water from the boiler might pollute the system if it backed up. The inside of the valve is made accessible for repairs by removing the cover (see Fig. 2-9).

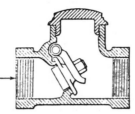

FIGURE 2-9   /   Check valve

Valves referred to as *standard weight* will withstand pressures up to 125 psi; high-pressure valves are also available. Most small valves used have bronze bodies, while large valves (2 in. and larger) have iron bodies with noncorrosive moving parts and seats which may be replaced. They are available threaded or soldered to match the pipe or tubing used.

2-7   Water Shock

Water pressure surges from the quick closing of water valves (faucets) may cause the water system to be noisy. This abrupt closing of the valve causes the fast-flowing water to stop quickly and make the pipes rattle. A length of pipe, installed above the water connection, will act as a cushion or shock absorber as it controls the pressure surge of the water (Fig. 2-10). Special shock absorbers are also available (Fig. 2-11). Oftentimes the noise in the system is referred to as *water hammer*.

2-8   Expansion Allowances

No matter what type of pipe is used in the water supply system, some expansion in the pipe will occur, and this expansion must be considered in the design of the system. The amount of expansion will depend on the type of piping used and the range of temperatures to which the pipe will be subjected.

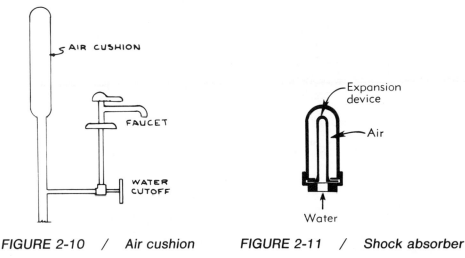

FIGURE 2-10 / Air cushion   FIGURE 2-11 / Shock absorber

The piping for hot water will have to withstand a temperature range from about 70°F, the average indoor temperature, to about 180°F, the temperature of the water. This range will vary, sometimes considerably, on projects and must be checked. Cold water piping will be subjected to a much smaller temperature range, usually with a low of 40°F and a high of 75°F. This range may vary if the piping is placed very close to the hot water line, heating line, or other heat source that may raise the temperature.

The amount of expansion of pipe and tubing which will occur due to temperature change is shown in Fig. 2-12. A review of the expansion figures shows that it would be minimal in the average residence, but it must be considered in large homes and commercial projects. The expansion is allowed for in the system by using one of the methods shown in Fig. 2-13.

Elongation in inches per 100 ft of pipe or tube

Increase in Temperature, Deg. F	Steel pipe	Wrought iron pipe	Copper tubing
120	.91	.95	1.35
20	.15	.16	.22
40	.30	.31	.44
60	.45	.47	.67
80	.60	.63	.90
100	.76	.79	1.12

FIGURE 2-12 / Pipe and tubing expansion

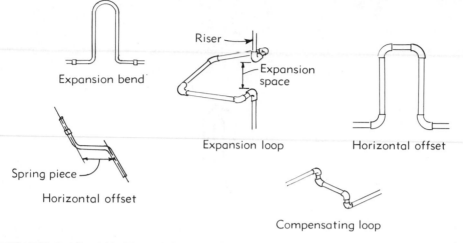

FIGURE 2-13   /   Expansion allowance

2-9   Water Supply Systems

The two basic types of water supply system used inside the building or project are the *upfeed* and the *downfeed* systems.

Since the water pressure in community mains averages about 50 to 60 psi, which is also considered about the upper limit for private systems, this places limits on how far the water can be moved in an *upfeed* system (Fig. 2-14). The 50–60 psi pressure will be used up in friction losses as the water passes through the building main pipe, the meter, and the various fittings. In addition, part of the pressure is used to overcome *static head*—the pressure required to push water up

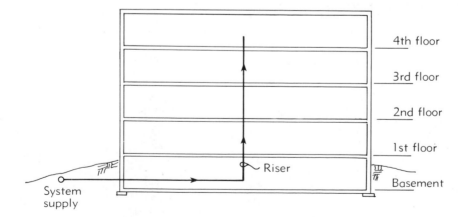

FIGURE 2-14   /   Upfeed system

vertically (up the riser). Also, sufficient pressure must be left at the top floor to provide proper operation of the fixtures (a shower requires 12 psi, a bathtub 5 psi, etc.).

It requires 0.434 psi to push the water up 1 ft. Pushing the water up 20 ft will require 20×0.434 psi $= 8.68$ psi. Even if the entire 50 psi were available for static head, the maximum height would be 50 psi $\div$ 0.434 psi per ft $= 115.2$ ft. (It should be noted that 0.434 psi per ft is the same as saying 1 psi can raise water 2.3 ft and 50 psi $\times$ 2.3 ft of head per psi $= 115$ ft.) Depending on the exact floor-to-floor height, this would raise the water 10 to 15 stories (floors) *if there were no friction loss or fixture operation to consider.* Practical limitations set about 60 ft as the usual maximum height, and 40 ft is the preferred height.

In buildings which cannot be adequately serviced to the top floor by an up-feed system, the water is pumped to elevated storage tanks in, or on, the building, and the water is fed down into the building by gravity. This gravity system, fed from the upper stories to the lower, is called a *downfeed* system (Fig. 2-15).

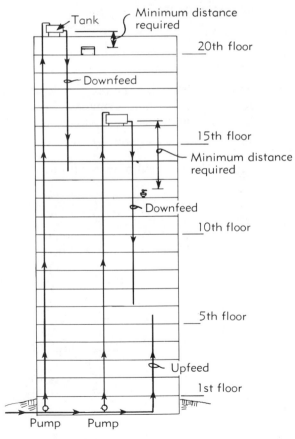

FIGURE 2-15 / Downfeed system

2-10   Upfeed System Design

Water supply pipes must be of sufficient size to provide adequate pressure to all fixtures in the system at a reasonable cost. Selection of economical sizes for the piping and the meter is based on the total demand for water (Sec. 1-9); this process must take into account the available water pressure (street main pressure), the pressure loss due to static head (pressure loss to raise the water up the pipe), the pressure loss due to friction in piping and fittings, and the pressure required to operate the fixture requiring the most pressure on the top floor.

Street main pressure must be adequate to supply:

Required fixture flow pressure

+

Static head

+

Friction in pipe and meter

Step-by-Step Approach

1.   The first step in sizing the supply is to determine the pressure losses. The pressure loss due to static head is figured by multiplying 0.434 psi per ft times the vertical distance of the riser from the service main into the building to the top branch water line (Fig. 2-16).

Static head loss = 0.434 psi × Vertical rise of water (in ft)

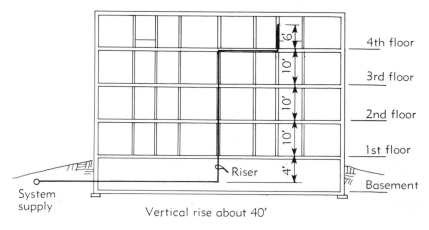

FIGURE 2-16   /   Vertical riser

2.   Next, find the pressure required to operate the fixture on the top floor re-
      quiring the most pressure. The rate of water flow and the required pressure
      to properly operate various fixtures are shown in Fig. 2-17.

Fixture	Flow Pressure (a) psi	Flow rate gpm
Ordinary basin faucet	8	3.0
Self-closing basin faucet	12	2.5
Sink Faucet - 3/8 in.	10	4.5
Sink Faucet - 1/2 in.	5	4.5
Bathtub faucet	5	6.0
Laundry tub cock - 1/2 in.	5	5.0
Shower	12	5.0
Ball-cock for closet	15	3.0
Flush valve for closet	10-20	15-40 (b)
Flush valve for urinal	15	15.0
Garden hose, 50 ft. and sill cock	30	5.0

(a) Flow pressure is the pressure in the pipe at the
    entrance to the particular fixture considered.
(b) Wide range due to variation in design and type
    of flush-valve closets.

FIGURE 2-17 / *Fixture flow pressure and flow*

3.   The pressure loss due to friction in the main and riser pipes, the fittings, and
      the meter must be found next. Add the static head and the pressure required
      for the top fixture; then subtract the total from the available street main
      pressure to find the pressure left, which is the maximum amount that can be
      lost to friction.

4.   Sizing the piping is often a matter of trial and error, even for experienced
      engineers; the process involves first selecting a pipe size for the building
      main which runs from the water system to the riser(s) and then determining
      the friction loss for the pipe used from the charts in Figs. 2-18, 2-19, and
      2-20. The chart used will depend on the type of pipe used.
          Since these charts have many lines and numbers, use them with care.
      Before beginning the selection, review what information is on each chart.
      Along the left and right is the flow in gallons per minute (gpm), and along
      the bottom and top is the friction loss in the pipe per *100 ft of length*. The
      heavy, solid lines running diagonally on the chart represent the diameters of
      pipe which may be used; the long-short-long lines going perpendicular (at a
      90° angle) to the pipe diameter lines represent the velocity of the water in a
      pipe of a given size. Be certain that you do not confuse the diagonal lines.

5.   Since all friction losses are given per 100 ft of pipe length, the distance from
      the street main (or point of service, such as a storage tank) to the base of the
      riser must be checked on the plot plan.

6.   The next step is to determine the pressure loss as the water passes through
      the meter (if one is required; if not, this step is eliminated). The chart in Fig.
      2-21 gives the pressure loss for various meter sizes with the flow in gpm
      along the bottom and the pressure loss on the left.

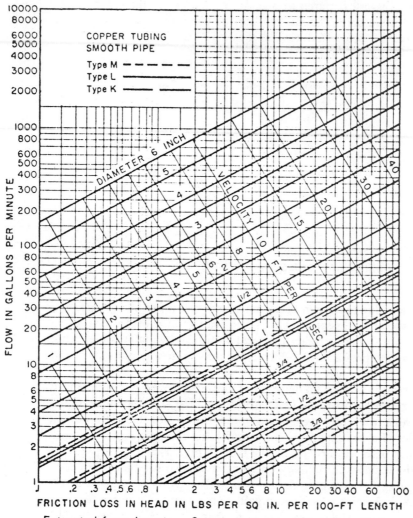

FIGURE 2-18 / Friction loss (smooth pipe)

Extracted from American Standard National Plumbing Code
(ASA A 40.8 - 1955) with permission of the publisher, The
American Society of Mechanical Engineers.

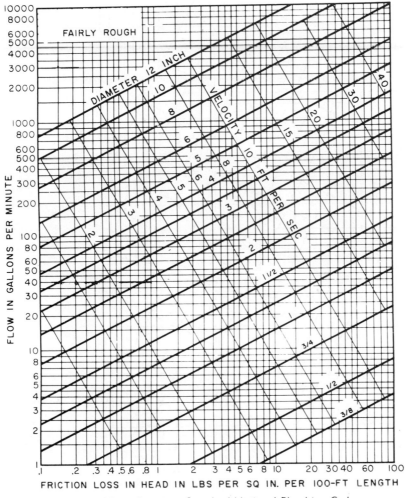

FAIRLY ROUGH

Extracted from American Standard National Plumbing Code
(ASA A 40.8 - 1955) with permission of the publisher, The
American Society of Mechanical Engineers.

FIGURE 2-19 / Friction loss (fairly rough pipe)

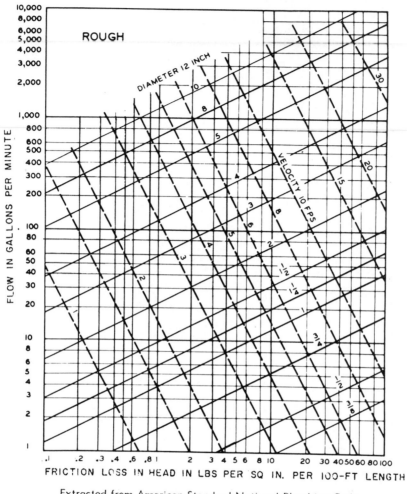

Extracted from American Standard National Plumbing Code (ASA A 40.8 - 1955) with permission of the publisher, The American Society of Mechanical Engineers.

FIGURE 2-20   /   Friction loss (rough pipe)

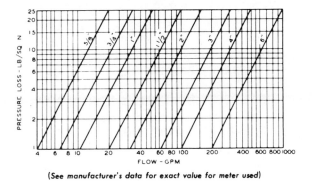

(See manufacturer's data for exact value for meter used)

Extracted from American Standard National Plumbing Code
(ASA A 40.8 - 1955) with permission of the publisher, The
American Society of Mechanical Engineers.

FIGURE 2-21   /   Meter pressure loss

**Allowance in equivalent length of pipe for friction loss
in valves and threaded fittings.***

Diameter of fitting (inches)	Equivalent length of pipe for various fittings						
	90° standard elbow	45° standard elbow	standard T 90°	Coupling or straight run of T	Gate valve	Globe valve	Angle valve
	Feet	Feet	Feet	Feet	Feet	Feet	Feet
⅜	1	0.6	1.5	0.3	0.2	8	4
½	2	1.2	3	6	.4	15	8
¾	2.5	1.5	4	.8	.5	20	12
1	3	1.8	5	.9	.6	25	15
1¼	4	2.4	6	1.2	.8	35	18
1½	5	3	7	1.5	1	45	22
2	7	4	10	2	1.3	55	28
2½	8	5	12	2.5	1.6	65	34
3	10	6	15	3	2	80	40
4	14	8	21	4	2.7	125	55
5	17	10	25	5	3.3	140	70
6	20	12	30	6	4	165	80

*Allowances based on non-recessed threaded fittings. Use one-half (½) the allowances for recessed threaded fittings or streamline solder fittings.

Extracted from American Standard National Plumbing Code
(ASA A 40.8 - 1955) with permission of the publisher, The
American Society of Mechanical Engineers.

FIGURE 2-22   /   Equivalent length in fittings

7.   The next step will be to select the possible pipe sizes for the riser. Using the
     friction-loss pipe chart (Fig. 2-18), find the gpm on the left; the friction-loss
     readings are then taken. Once again, note that the friction losses are given
     per 100 ft of pipe length. This means that the vertical distance from the main
     to the highest and most remote fixture must be estimated. On some projects
     this may mean a meeting with the architects to be certain of ceiling heights
     and thickness of the floor construction, or of the floor-to-floor height. In
     such piping there is an additional friction loss for fittings. When the entire
     system has been designed and all pipes sized and fittings located, it is possi-
     ble to determine the friction loss for the fittings. An example of how to cal-
     culate fittings is given later in this section. In reviewing Fig. 2-22 in order to
     determine the friction loss for fittings, the table lists the fitting across the top,
     the diameter required along the left, and the equivalent length of pipe for
     each type and size. This equivalent length of pipe means that, for example,
     when water passes through a 2-in.–diameter standard 90° ell, the same fric-
     tion loss occurs as when water passes through 7 lineal ft of 2-in. pipe. So the
     equivalent length of the 2-in.–diameter 90° ell is 7 ft.

     Since, during this stage of the design, the fittings have not been determined,
it is common practice to allow an additional 50% of the piping length to account
for the friction loss in the fittings.

     Another approach to finding riser pipe size is often used. In this approach,
once a main size has been tentatively selected, the riser may be more directly selected from the chart in Fig. 2-18. The following formula will convert the psi left
for friction loss and the equivalent length of riser into the friction loss per 100 ft
using a 100-ft constant, so that the chart in Fig. 2-18 may be used more easily.

$$\frac{\text{Available psi} \times 100 \text{ ft}}{\text{Equivalent length}} = \text{psi loss per 100 ft}$$

2-11   Downfeed System Design

Step-by-Step Approach

1.   The first step in the design is to list all the information about the project.
2.   In order to determine the main, meter, and riser sizes for the system, the next
     step is to determine the fixture units per floor and the total fixture units in
     the building.
3.   The next step is to determine the demand load for water in gpm (from Fig.
     1-25).

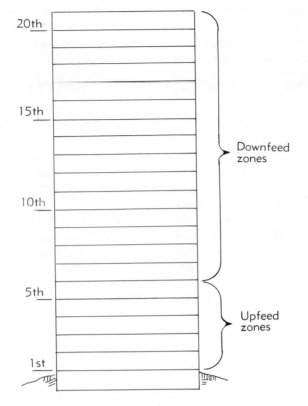

FIGURE 2-23   /   Water supply zoning

4. Typically, the bottom floors of the building will be serviced by upfeed zones (Fig. 2-23) and the upper floors by downfeed zones.

    The first step will be to make a preliminary decision on how many floors each zone will supply and the number of zones required. The upfeed zone (refer to Sec. 2-10) is limited to a practical maximum height of about 60 ft. With a floor-to-floor height given as 11 ft, the upfeed system will serve five to six floors (stories), depending on how deep the community main is (a deep main would limit the zone to five floors).

5. Downfeed zones also have maximum heights (distances they can serve) without using special pressure reducing and control valves. First, since the water is stored in the tank, it has no pressure in the riser as it leaves the tank. As the water leaves the tank and travels down the riser, the water pressure begins to build at a rate of 0.434 psi per ft (without considering friction loss). This means that the highest fixtures, those nearest the tank, will receive the least pressure.

6. The zoning for the downfeed systems is determined next. Since the water pressure is increasing as it goes down the downfeed riser, the vertical distance that a zone can service is limited to the maximum amount of pressure that can be put on the lowest fixture and still have it operate properly. This maximum pressure varies with the type and manufacturer of the fixtures being used; the allowable pressure may range from about 45 to 60 psi.

7. Next, the top downfeed zone will be sized. First, the accumulated information should be tabulated. Since the downfeed system is served from the top, the accumulated fixture units and the greatest gpm required are at the top (just the opposite of upfeed systems). Thus, large risers are used at the top floors in a downfeed zone to keep friction loss at a minimum, since the water tank should be no higher than necessary and since the pressure required to operate the fixtures at the top floors is critical.

8. The vertical riser distance is 40 ft with a horizontal branch to the fixture plus any horizontal run from the tank to the riser. Assume that the equivalent length of fittings will add 50% to the actual length and calculate the total equivalent length. Determine maximum pressure drop available (converted to psi per 100 ft for easy use of chart in Fig. 2-18).

9. From Fig. 2-18, the pipe size selected for the run from the tank to the top fixture is selected.

10. At the 19th floor, the water pressure has increased 11 ft × 0.434 psi per ft = 4.78 psi.

11. From Fig. 2-18, select the possible pipe sizes for the 18th floor riser, based on gpm and friction loss.

12. The pressure below the 18th floor is no longer critical; for each floor the pressure (due to static head) will increase at a rate of 0.434 psi per ft, and all of this psi can be used to overcome friction loss in the riser (and branch) pipes.

13. Another approach to designing downfeed systems involves the same principle—using tanks to hold the water supply and feeding down the system—with one difference. Instead of limiting the downfeed system pressure to a maximum of about 50 psi (as in the problem just completed), zones as large as 300 ft with static pressures up to 120 psi are used. To design such a system requires the use of pressure-reducing valves and control valves on the fixtures to reduce the pressure. This type of design would service the entire building just designed with one downfeed system.

2-12   Hot Water

By piping part of the water in the building main (Fig. 2-24) into a heating device, the hot water required on the project can be supplied. The heating device may be a direct or an indirect heater and may operate on oil, gas, electricity, or the sun (solar heat). Direct heaters (Fig. 2-25) are designed solely to provide the hot water required. Indirect heaters (Fig. 2-26) use some type of boiler (heater) to heat the hot water and also to provide heat or steam to the heating system of the project.

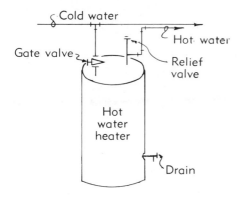

FIGURE 2-24   /   Hot water heater

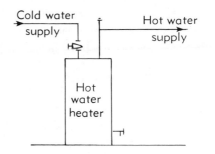

FIGURE 2-25   /   Direct heater

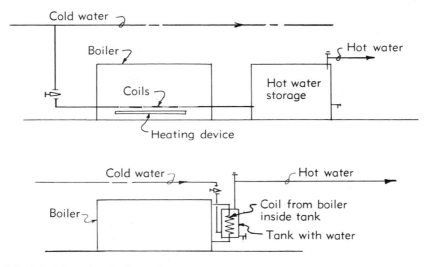

FIGURE 2-26   /   Indirect heaters

Direct heaters come in a variety of sizes and capacities that allow them to be located in the basement, crawl space, or closet; in a cabinet under the counter; or as units which look similar to clothes washers. For projects such as apartments, cold water is often run to a direct heater (usually electric) in each apartment, instead of using one large hot water heating unit. This also allows for each individual apartment to be on a separate electric meter and for each resident to pay for the electricity he uses. Residences commonly use a direct heater, and in large homes two units are sometimes used (one near the kitchen–laundry and one near the bathrooms) to cut down the amount of hot water piping required and to provide almost instant availability of hot water when a faucet is turned on. (The hot water in a pipe will cool off when not used for awhile.)

Indirect heaters use the same heating unit to provide hot water or steam to the heating system and to heat the hot water required for use at the fixtures. The same water used in the heating system is not used for the fixtures; instead, a separate compartment or coil containing the water is fed through the unit to be heated. Such units have been used in residences as well as commercial projects. This method is more commonly used in colder climates where the heating system is in operation for more months of the year. Often it is not an economical solution because during the warmer months, the heating system (boiler or furnace) will have to go on to provide hot water when no heating is required. Indirect heaters usually have tanks to store the heated water, or they may have a high-capacity coil capable of providing hot water very quickly.

Some projects use a combination of direct and indirect hot water heaters (Fig. 2-27) whereby the cold water is piped through the indirect heater and then to the direct heater. When the indirect heater is being used for heating, it will provide fully or partially heated water to the direct heater. This means that at times the direct heater will have little or no additional heating to do.

The cold water supply should have a cutoff valve so that the water supply to the heater can be cut off if necessary. This allows for easier repair or replacement of the heater if required. The hot water pipe exits off the top of the tank and should have a relief valve to allow escape of any excess pressure built up in the system. Heaters which operate on oil or gas will require ventilation (Fig. 2-28) to the exterior, usually through a chimney, to get rid of poisonous gases. Electric and solar units do not require venting to the exterior.

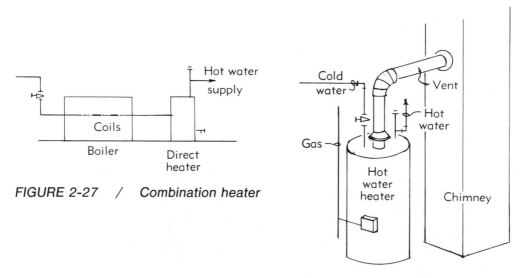

FIGURE 2-27   /   Combination heater

FIGURE 2-28   /   Water heater exhaust

2-13   Hot Water Requirements

The first step in sizing hot water equipment is to estimate the amount of hot water that will be used during a 24-hour time period, the maximum amount used during the hour the demand will be heaviest, and the length of time this maximum (of peak) demand will last. Using this information, the heating capacity of the unit and the size of the storage tank may be selected.

The hot water consumption for typical residences, apartments, office buildings, and schools is shown in Fig. 2-29. Other information required includes the maximum hourly demand, the duration of peak load, the amount of storage capacity suggested, and the heating capacity of the hot water heater. This heating capacity gives the suggested rating of the heater in terms of the gallons per hour (gph) that the heater can heat to the desired temperature. (The values given in Fig. 2-29 are conservative and allow for some extra hot water when used in calculations.)

Hot Water Demands and Use for Various Types of Buildings

Type of Building	Maximum Hour	Maximum Day	Average Day
Men's Dormitories	3.8 gal/student	22.0 gal/student	13.1 gal/student
Women's Dormitories	5.0 gal/student	26.5 gal/student	12.3 gal/student
Motels: No. of Units*			
20 or less	6.0 gal/unit	35.0 gal/unit	20.0 gal/unit
60	5.0 gal/unit	25.0 gal/unit	14.0 gal/unit
100 or more	4.0 gal/unit	15.0 gal/unit	10.0 gal/unit
Nursing Homes	4.5 gal/bed	30.0 gal/bed	18.4 gal/bed
Office Buildings	0.4 gal/person	2.0 gal/person	1.0 gal/person
Food Service Establishments:			
Type A—Full Meal Restaurants and Cafeterias	1.5 gal/max meals/hr	11.0 gal/max meals/hr	2.4 gal/avg meals/day*
Type B—Drive-Ins, Grilles, Luncheonettes, Sandwich and Snack Shops	0.7 gal/max meals/hr	6.0 gal/max meals/hr	0.7 gal/avg meals/day*
Apartment Houses: No. of Apartments			
20 or less	12.0 gal/apt.	80.0 gal/apt.	42.0 gal/apt.
50	10.0 gal/apt.	73.0 gal/apt.	40.0 gal/apt.
75	8.5 gal/apt.	66.0 gal/apt.	38.0 gal/apt.
100	7.0 gal/apt.	60.0 gal/apt.	37.0 gal/apt.
200 or more	5.0 gal/apt.	50.0 gal/apt.	35.0 gal/apt.
Elementary Schools	0.6 gal/student	1.5 gal/student	0.6 gal/student*
Junior and Senior High Schools	1.0 gal/student	3.6 gal/student	1.8 gal/student*

*Per day of operation.
* Interpolate for intermediate values.

Reprinted with permission from ASHRAE, Systems Handbook, 1976

FIGURE 2-29   /   Hot water requirements

2-14   Hot Water Distribution Systems

Hot water systems make use of upfeed zones to provide the water, under pressure, throughout the project. In taller buildings, the heaters are fed cold water from the tanks supplying water to the downfeed systems (Fig. 2-30). This allows the water from the tank to build up sufficient pressure, as it feeds down to the heater, to create an upfeed zone.

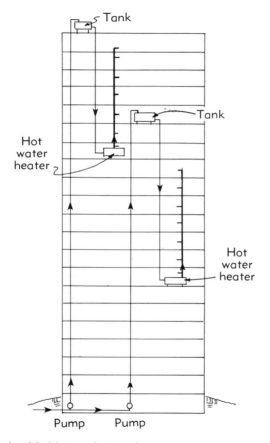

FIGURE 2-30   /   Multistory hot water zones

When designing hot water piping systems, the best solution is one which requires the hot water to travel as short a distance as possible from the heater to the point at which it will be used. The longer the supply pipe, the less efficient the system because as the water stays in the pipe, it quickly loses its heat to the surrounding air, even if the pipe is insulated.

For example, review the situation shown in Fig. 2-31, in which the bathroom faucet is about 75 ft from the heater. This means that if the water has had time to cool in the pipe (say, during the night), when the faucet is turned on, cool water will come from the faucet until the 75 ft of cool water has flowed through the faucet. Only at that time will hot water come out of the faucet. Then, once the faucet has been shut off, there is 75 ft of hot water in the pipe which begins to lose its heat. Back at the heater, as the hot water is drawn out, cold water begins to enter and be heated, and enough extra hot water must be heated to fill the 75-ft supply pipe again. This process is repeated over and over, several times a day every day.

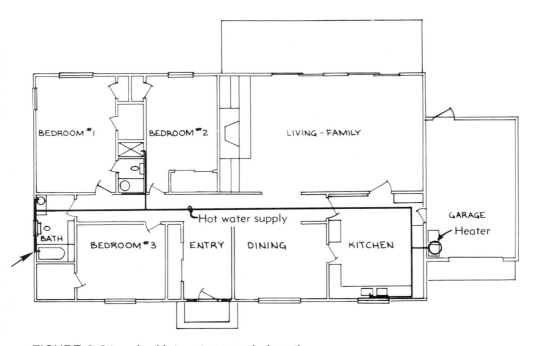

FIGURE 2-31 / Hot water supply length

One solution to this problem, in projects such as apartment buildings, is to provide each apartment with a direct-type water heater which can be located as conveniently as possible. Typical locations include under the bathroom sink, in a kitchen cabinet, and in a closet.

In large residences, it is quite common to put in two (or perhaps more) heaters to reduce the distance from heater to source of use. Quite often, one heater will be located near the kitchen with another in the bedroom area. These units are commonly located in a crawl space, basement, or closet, or in a kitchen or bathroom closet.

Most plumbing installations have a noncirculating, direct supply layout, similar to that shown in Fig. 2-32 and discussed in this section. But when the rapid delivery of hot water becomes part of the design requirements and it is not practical to provide small direct heaters throughout the project, a system which circulates the hot water through the supply piping and back to the heater for reheating is used (Fig. 2-33). Circulating systems have a continuous riser going from the tank, through the project and back to the tank; the fixtures being serviced are fed by a direct branch supply off the riser. The only hot water which stays in the pipe and may cool off is that which is in the branch piping. The hot water will circulate through the system by gravity flow as the hot water rising to the top of the system forces the cooler water back toward the tank.

The circulating system may be upfeed, downfeed, or a combination upfeed-and-downfeed system. A check valve keeps the water flowing in the proper direction. A pump may be required for circulation of the water where the tank is not located below the lowest fixture being served.

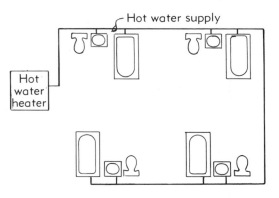

FIGURE 2-32   /
Noncirculating hot water

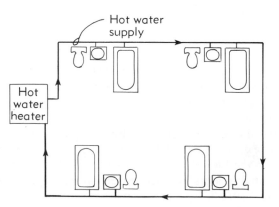

FIGURE 2-33   /
Circulating hot water

2-15   Testing the System

In many larger cities and municipalities, a separate plumbing permit must be taken out. Oftentimes building departments will even review the drawings to see if the design conforms to the code in force; others may simply require a brief written description of the system.

Also, depending on the locale, once the plumbing is roughed in, the municipal plumbing inspector will check all installed work, particularly the waste portion of the system, for conformance with the code. This inspection should be made before any pipes are covered, and most inspectors will not approve a system unless a complete inspection can be made. It is far better to find a leak in the system before the walls, ceilings, and floor are finished than after.

Tests on a system are made to be certain that it will perform satisfactorily and not solely for inspectors or because it is required. The water supply system is checked by sealing all openings in the system, filling it with potable water, and then pressurizing it (up to the normal operating pressure). Such a check of the system will show any leaks in the fittings.

There are still many areas which do not have inspectors and do not enforce the building codes. These codes are designed to protect human life and to ensure that the completed system will fulfill the function it was designed for. Tests should be made on any system, whether it is inspected or not.

2-16   Solar Hot Water

Solar hot water heating systems are no longer a dream of the future. Development continues on systems which capture the heat from the sun to heat water for use in the home or project. The final chapter cannot yet be written on these systems as experimentation continues and as millions of dollars from government and private enterprise are poured into further research and development. Meanwhile, many dependable and cost-effective hot water heating systems are now available for purchase.

The most successful solar hot water heater, in the author's opinion, is the solar flat-plate absorber/collector; the principles of operation are shown in Fig. 2-34. In many areas, the solar heating unit is supplemented with an electric heating coil to provide hot water in case of prolonged cloudiness that limits the amount of solar energy available to heat water. This is not to imply that the solar heater cannot be designed to provide all of the hot water required—just that it is most efficient costwise to design the solar system to provide 85% to 90% of the hot water required during a year. Designing the system to definitely provide *all* of the hot water required will mean the solar system will have to be about 25% to 33% larger (this is also true in solar heating, Chapter 12).

The cost of the unit *must* be analyzed and the purchase of such a system viewed as an investment of money. Whether it is a good investment or not de-

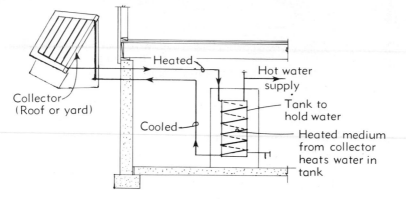

Tank—This tank could be used to just hold water heated by the collector medium or it could be a direct hot water heater used to supplement the collector during times when the collector cannot provide all of the hot water required.

FIGURE 2-34 / Solar hot water system

pends on whether it will give a good return. Naturally, the economics of the system will vary according to the geographic location, the total amount of hot water required, and the current cost of hot water. There is no doubt that an installed solar hot water heating system will cost significantly more than a fuel-burning hot water heating system—in general about 8 to 10 times as much. But a determination on cost is not based on "8 to 10 times as much." It is based on a careful examination of dollars and cents.

Questions

2-1. What are plumbing codes, and why are they used?

2-2. What is meant by *multiple governing codes,* and why must the designer be aware of them?

2-3. Who is most likely to enforce the plumbing code?

2-4. What materials are most commonly used for the pipes and tubing in a water supply system?

2-5. How and where are the following values used in the system?
   a. Globe
   b. Angle
   c. Gate
   d. Check

2-6. What is *water shock,* and how can it be reduced in the system?

2-7. How may expansion be allowed for in the system, and what type of pipe expands the most?

2-8. What are the two basic types of water supply systems used, and what determines which will be used?

2-9. What is meant, in water supply systems, by *static head?*

2-10. What is the difference between a direct and an indirect water heater?

2-11. Why is more than one hot water heater sometimes used in larger residences?

2-12. What is the difference between circulating and noncirculating hot water systems, and when would the circulating system most likely be used?

2-13. Briefly, describe and sketch how a solar hot water heating system might work.

2-14. What factors affect whether or not it might be economical to use a solar hot water heating system?

2-15. Why are supplemental heating units often installed in solar hot water heating systems?

Chapter 3
Plumbing Drainage

3-1 Drainage Principles

In Chapter 2, hot and cold water supply systems were described, with pipes to provide sufficient running water to all of the fixtures throughout a building or project. Following the flow of the water through the system, the next step will be to dispose of the waste matter, both fluid and organic, which is accumulated. The wastes will come from almost all sections of the building—bathrooms, kitchens, and laundry areas, and, in commercial projects, even the equipment being serviced. Because all of the wastes tend to decompose quickly, one of the primary objectives of the plumbing system is to dispose of decaying wastes quickly, before they cause objectionable odors or become hazardous to health.

Water is used to transport the wastes into the drainage piping and to the point where they will enter a community sewer line leading either to a community sewage treatment plant or to a private sewage treatment system. The sewage from residences, apartments, motels, office buildings, and other similar types of buildings is referred to as *domestic sewage*. Special sewage from laboratories and many industrial plants requires special handling and such treatment is not discussed here. However, it is important to note that such wastes should not be put into a community sewage system without first getting approval from the community.

3-2   Plumbing Codes

The *National Plumbing Code* is used as the basis for the plumbing discussed in this text. Increasingly, all plumbing codes are being modeled after this code with only minor revisions to meet the requirements of specific geographic locations. References in this portion of the text relate to the *National Plumbing Code,* and everyone who is learning about plumbing, its design and its requirements, should have a current copy available. In addition, any relevant state or local plumbing codes should be made a part of your library for future reference.

3-3   The Drainage System

In this section the terminology and function of each of the parts of the drainage system are explained. The basic parts of the system are illustrated in Fig. 3-1.

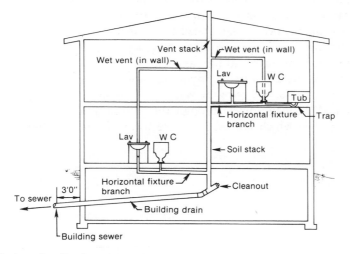

FIGURE 3-1   /   Drainage system

Traps

A *trap* (Fig. 3-2) is a device which catches and holds a quantity of water, thus forming a seal which prevents the gases resulting from sewage decomposition from entering the building through the pipe. Traps are installed at each fixture as bent pipes unless the fixture is designed with the trap as an integral part of it (as in the case of the water closet in Fig. 3-3).

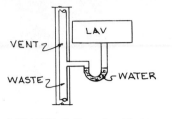

FIGURE 3-2 / Traps

FIGURE 3-3 / Integral trap

Traps may be made of copper, plastic, steel, wrought iron, or brass, with brass most commonly used. Traps in water closets are made of vitreous china and are cast right into the fixture.

The trap is located as close to the fixture as possible, usually within 2 ft of it. Occasionally, more than one fixture is tied to one trap. Quite often a laundry tray and a kitchen sink, a dishwasher and a kitchen sink, or two kitchen sinks may be connected to a single trap, provided all fixtures are close to one another. There should never be more than three closely located fixtures (such as lavatories) on a single trap, or the trap may not operate properly (it may lose its *water seal,* also called *trap seal*). Since the trap may occasionally need to be cleaned, either there should be a plug in the bottom which may be removed (Fig. 3-4), or the trap should have screwed connections on each end for easy removal (Fig. 3-5).

In locations where the fixtures are infrequently used, care must be taken or the water in the traps may evaporate, and once the water seal is gone, gases may back up from the sewer and drainage pipes through the fixture and into the building. Floor drains (Fig. 3-6) which are used to take away the water after

FIGURE 3-4 / Trap cleanout

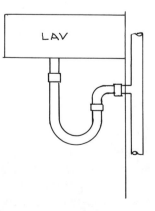

FIGURE 3-5 / Trap connection

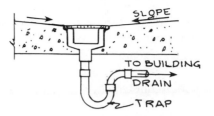

FIGURE 3-6 / Floor drain

washing floors or which may be used only in case of equipment malfunctions or repairs present the most serious possibility of losing the water seal. When these floor drains are connected to the drainage system, the possibility of a serious gas problem exists. The designer of the system can avoid such a situation by *not* tying the floor drain into the drainage system. Instead, the floor drains should be tied into a drywell (Fig. 4-2) from which there will be no gases. Many building departments and plumbing codes prohibit the connection of floor drains to the sewage drainage system.

The water seal may also be broken if there is a great deal of air pressure turbulence in the pipes. To reduce the turbulence and to tend to equalize the pressure throughout the system, it is opened to the outside at the top and sufficient air is supplied throughout the system through *vent pipes*.

Vents

Vent pipes allow gases in the sewage drainage system to discharge to the outside and sufficient air to enter the system to reduce the air turbulence in the system. Also, without a vent, once the water discharges from a fixture, the moving waste tends to siphon the water from other fixture traps as it goes through the pipes. This means that the vent piping must serve the various fixtures, or groups of fixtures, as well as the rest of the sewage drainage system. The vent from a fixture or group of fixtures ties in with the main vent stack (Fig. 3-7) or the stack vent (Fig. 3-8) which goes to the exterior. Vent piping may be copper, plastic, cast iron, or steel.

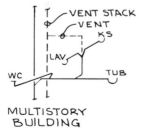

FIGURE 3-7 / Vent to vent stack

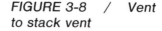

FIGURE 3-8 / Vent to stack vent

A *stack vent* is that portion of the vertical sewage drainage pipe (which may be a soil or waste stack) which extends above the highest horizontal drain that is connected to it (Fig. 3-9). It extends through the roof to the exterior of the building.

A *vent stack* is used in multistory buildings where a pipe is required to provide the flow of air throughout the drainage system. The vent stack begins at the soil or waste pipe, just below the lowest horizontal connection, and may go through the roof (Fig. 3-10) or connect back into the soil or waste pipe not less than 6 in. above the top of the highest fixture.

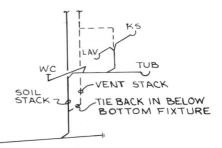

MULTISTORY

FIGURE 3-10 / Vent stack to soil stack

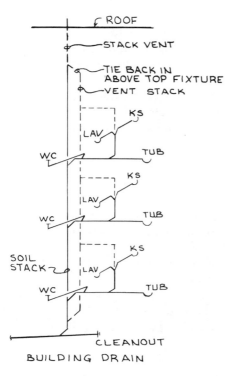

FIGURE 3-9 / Vent stack to stack vent

Fixture Branches

The fixtures at a floor level are connected horizontally to the stack by a drain called a *fixture branch* (Fig. 3-1). Beginning with the fixture farthest from the stack, the branch must slope ⅛ to ½ in. per ft for proper flow of wastes through the branch. Branch piping which serves urinals, water closets, showers, or tubs is usually run in the floor (Fig. 3-11). When these fixtures are not on the branch, the piping may be run in the floor or in the wall behind the fixtures (Fig. 3-12). Branch piping may be copper, plastic, galvanized steel, or cast iron.

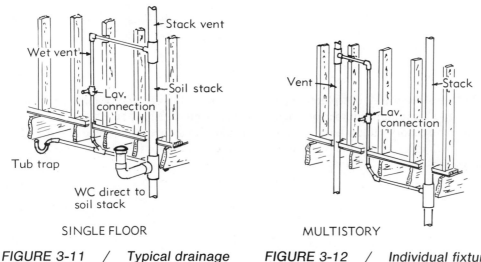

FIGURE 3-11 / Typical drainage piping

FIGURE 3-12 / Individual fixture drainage

Soil and Waste Stacks

The fixture branches feed into a vertical pipe referred to as a *stack*. When the waste that the stack will carry includes human waste from water closets (or from fixtures which have similar functions), the stack is referred to as a *soil stack*. When the stack will carry all wastes *except* human waste, it is referred to as a *waste stack*. Soil and waste stacks may be copper, plastic, galvanized steel, or cast iron. These stacks service the fixture branches beginning at the top branch and go vertically to the building drain (Fig. 3-13).

In larger buildings, the point where the stack ties into the building drain rests on a masonry pier or steel post so that the downward pressure of the wastes will not cause the piping system to sag. In addition, the stack must be supported at 10-ft intervals to limit movement of the pipe. When a stack length is greater than 80 ft, horizontal offsets are used to reduce free fall velocity and air turbulence. Connections to fixture branches and the building drain should be angled 45° or more to allow the smooth flow of wastes.

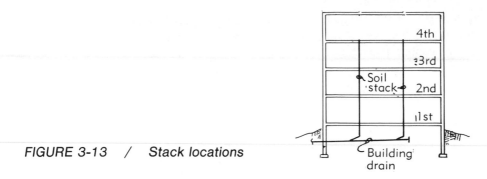

FIGURE 3-13   /   Stack locations

Most designers try to lay out plumbing fixtures to line up vertically floor after floor so that a minimum number of stacks will be required. Many times a central core of a multistory building will be used as a plumbing core, and a *pipe chase,* a space which is left to put the pipes in, runs from the first floor to the roof of the building (Fig. 3-14).

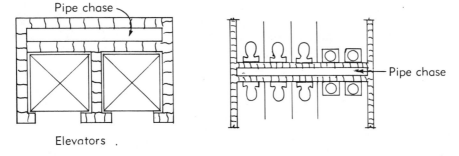

FIGURE 3-14   /   Pipe chase

Building Drains (Also Called House Drains)

The soil or waste stacks feed into a horizontal pipe referred to as the *building drain.* The building drain slopes ⅛ to ¼ in. per ft as it feeds the waste into the building sewer outside the building. By definition, the building drain extends to a point 3 ft *outside* the wall of the building (Fig. 3-13).

Provision is made to allow cleaning of the building drain by putting a *clean-out* at the end of the drain (Fig. 3-13). Another cleanout is sometimes placed just inside the building wall in case it is necessary to clean the building drain or sewer line. Cleanouts should also be placed no more than 50 ft apart in long building drains.

Location of the building drain in the building depends primarily on the location (elevation) below grade of the community sewer. Ideally, all of the plumbing wastes of the building will flow into the sewer (whether it is a community or a private sewer system) by gravity. Typically, the drain is placed below the first floor (Fig. 3-13) or below the basement floor (Fig. 3-15). If the height of the sewer requires the drain to be placed above the lowest fixtures (Fig. 3-16), it will be necessary for the low fixtures to drain into a sump pit. When the level in the sump pit rises to a certain point, an automatic float or control will activate a pump which raises the waste out of the pit and into the building drain.

Building drains are usually made of plastic, copper (for above the floor), or extra-heavy cast iron (for below the floor) pipe.

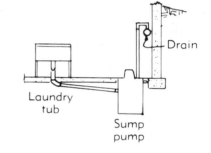

FIGURE 3-16 / Sump pump

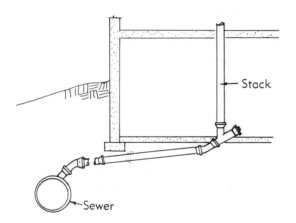

FIGURE 3-15 / Underfloor building drain

Building Traps (Also Called House Traps) and Fresh Air Inlets

Some codes may require a *building trap* on the building drain near the building wall (Fig. 3-17). This trap acts as a seal to keep gases and vermin (rats and mice) from entering the sewage system from the sewer line. The *National Plumbing Code* and most regional and state codes do not feel a building trap is necessary; instead it is felt that this trap will impede the flow of wastes in the system. However, when required by local, state, or regional codes, it must be put in the system. When a building trap is used, a *fresh air inlet* (Fig. 3-17) is required to allow fresh air into the system to be certain that the trap seal is not siphoned through. The fresh air inlet must be a minimum of 4 in. or one-half the diameter of the building drain, whichever is larger.

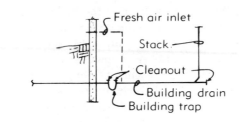

FIGURE 3-17   /   Building trap

Building Sewers (Also Called House Sewers)

The *building sewer* (Fig. 3-1) begins 3 ft out from the building wall and extends to the community sewer or the private sewage disposal tank. The building sewer slopes ⅛ to ¼ in. per foot and should never be smaller in diameter than the building drain. Building sewers are usually made of cast iron or plastic (not less than 6 in. in diameter). Vitrified clay pipe is occasionally used, but there is the possibility that roots from shrubs or trees may penetrate through the mortar joints and obstruct the flow of the wastes.

3-4   Pipes and Fittings

Drainage lines and vents make use of most of the same types of piping used in the water supply system, except that vitrified clay tile may be used in the building sewer line. Copper tubing, type DWV, is very commonly used in drainage piping but is *not* used in water supply. The *DWV* on the tubing means it can be used for drainage, waste, and venting on the job. Type M copper may be used above grade and type L copper below grade. Plastic piping is used extensively in drainage systems because of its low cost and speedy installation. Other piping sometimes used in the building sewer line includes concrete, asbestos–cement, and bituminous pipes. Fittings used in drainage systems are shown in Fig. 3-18.

3-5   Plumbing Drainage Design

Step-by-Step Approach

1.   The first step will be to sketch an isometric of the drainage piping. It will be easiest to follow if you first locate the stack on the plan (Fig. 3-19). Then sketch the vertical stack (Fig. 3-20), and beginning at the top floor, sketch the fixture branch and then the connection at each fixture. Now, add the

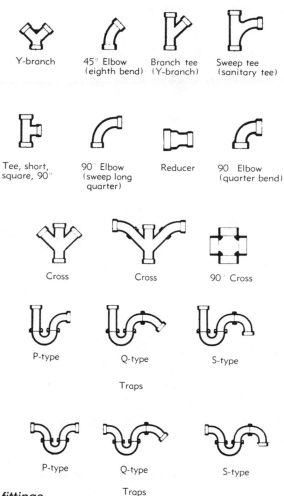

Y-branch 45° Elbow (eighth bend) Branch tee (Y-branch) Sweep tee (sanitary tee)

Tee, short, square, 90° 90° Elbow (sweep long quarter) Reducer 90° Elbow (quarter bend)

Cross Cross 90° Cross

P-type Q-type S-type

Traps

P-type Q-type S-type

Traps

FIGURE 3-18 / Drainage fittings

vent stack from a point just below the bottom fixture branch to a point above the top fixture and the building drain.

2. Next, the minimum trap size for each fixture is selected from Fig. 3-21, and the trap size is noted on the schematic pipe layout.

3. The fixture branch is the first drainage pipe to be sized. The first portion of the branch to be sized is from the fixture farthest from the stack to the next fixture. Begin by determining the fixture units that this short piece of pipe will serve.

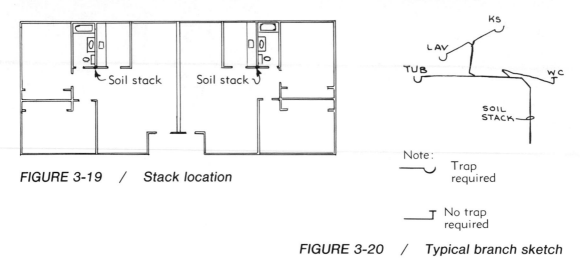

FIGURE 3-19   /   Stack location

FIGURE 3-20   /   Typical branch sketch

4. Next, select the branch size to serve the bathtub from the table of sizes in Fig. 3-22. Be sure to check the figures for horizontal fixture branches and stacks each time you use Fig. 3-22. The left row of numbers gives the various diameters of pipe which may be used. The rest of the columns list the maximum number of fixture units which can be connected to a given pipe size. Each of the fixture-unit columns defines the type of piping being selected.

5. For all fixtures, there is a maximum horizontal distance between the fixture trap and a vent. The distance depends on the pipe size being used and is listed in Fig. 3-23.

6. Now, size that portion of the pipe which serves the next fixture or group of fixtures.

7. Continue to size the horizontal fixture branch until all fixtures have been connected.

8. The stack size is selected next. Because this stack handles human waste, it is a *soil* stack. The stack must be selected and sized for the total fixture units that it must handle.

9. The vent stack is sized next, using the table in Fig. 3-24. To use the table, it is necessary to know the maximum size of the soil stack (left column) and the fixture units connected to the vent stack; the maximum length of vent stack is noted in ft. The developed length of the vent stack is the lineal ft of pipe required from the lowest point where it connects with the soil stack to the point where it terminates outside the building.

FIXTURE UNITS PER FIXTURE OR GROUP

Fixture Type	Fixture-Unit Value as Load Factors	Minimum Size of Trap[2] Inches
1 Bathroom group consisting of water closet, lavatory and bathtub or shower stall.	Tank water closet 6 Flush-valve water closet 8	
Bathtub[1] (with or without over-head shower)	2	1 1/2
Bathtub[1]	3	2
Bidet	3	Nominal 1 1/2
Clothes washer (domestic)	3	2
Combination sink and tray	3	1 1/2
Combination sink and tray with food disposal unit	4	Separate traps 1 1/2
Dental unit or cuspidor	1	1 1/4
Dental lavatory	1	1 1/4
Drinking fountain	1/2	1
Dishwasher, domestic	2	1 1/2
Floor drains[2]	1	2
Kitchen sink, domestic	2	1 1/2
Kitchen sink, domestic with food waste grinder	3	1 1/2
Lavatory[3]	1	Small P.O 1 1/4
Lavatory[3]	2	Large P.O. 1 1/2
Lavatory, barber, beauty parlor	2	1 1/2
Lavatory, surgeon's	2	1 1/2
Laundry tray (1 or 2 compartments)	2	1 1/2
Shower stall, domestic	2	2
Showers (group) per head	3	
Sinks:		
Surgeon's	3	1 1/2
Flushing rim (with valve)	8	3
Service (trap standard)	3	3
Service (P trap)	2	2
Pot, scullery, etc.	4	1 1/2
Urinal, pedestal, syphon jet, blowout	8	Nominal 3
Urinal, wall lip	4	1 1/2
Urinal stall, washout	4	2
Urinal trough (each 2-ft. section)	2	1 1/2
Wash sink[2] (circular or multiple) each set of faucets	2	Nominal 1 1/2
Water closet, tank-operated	4	Nominal 3
Water closet, valve-operated	8	3

[1]A shower head over a bathtub does not increase the fixture value.
[2]Size of floor drain shall be determined by the area of surface water to be drained.
[3]Lavatories with 1 1/4 or 1 1/2-inch trap have the same load value; larger P.O. plugs have greater flow rate.

Extracted from American Standard National Plumbing Code (ASA A 40.8 - 1955) with permission of the publisher, The American Society of Mechanical Engineers.

FIGURE 3-21 / Drainage fixture units and trap sizes

Diameter of Pipe	Maximum No. of Fixture Units That May Be Connected To:			
	Any Horizontal[1] Fixture Branch	One Stack of 3 Stories in Height or 3 Intervals	More Than 3 Stories In Height	
			Total for Stack	Total at One Story or Branch Interval
Inches				
1¼	1	2	2	1
1½	3	4	8	2
2	6	10	24	6
2½	12	20	42	9
3	20[2]	30[3]	60[3]	16[2]
4	160	240	500	90
5	360	540	1,100	200
6	620	960	1,900	350
8	1,400	2,200	3,600	600
10	2,500	3,800	5,600	1,000
12	3,900	6,000	8,400	1,500
15	7,000	. . . .	. . . .	. . . .

[1]Does not include branches of the building drain.
[2]Not over two water closets.
[3]Not over six water closets.

Extracted from American Standard National Plumbing Code (ASA A 40.8 - 1955) with permission of the publisher, The American Society of Mechanical Engineers.

FIGURE 3-22   /   *Horizontal fixture branches and stacks*

Size of Fixture Drain Inches	Distance Trap to Vent
1¼	2 ft. 6 in.
1½	3 ft. 6 in.
2	5 ft. 0 in.
3	6 ft. 0 in.
4	10 ft. 0 in.

Extracted from American Standard National Plumbing Code (ASA A 40.8 - 1955) with permission of the publisher, The American Society of Mechanical Engineers.

FIGURE 3-23   /   *Distance from fixture trap to vent*

The next step is to determine the size and location of the main (vent) stack. The code requires that every building "shall have at least one main stack." This main stack must be sized to handle the total fixture units on the system.

SIZE AND LENGTH OF VENTS

Size of Soil or Waste Stack	Fixture Units Connected	DIAMETER OF VENT REQUIRED (INCHES)								
		1¼	1½	2	2½	3	4	5	6	8
		MAXIMUM LENGTH OF VENT (FEET)								
Inches										
1¼	2	30								
1½	8	50	150							
1½	10	30	100							
2	12	30	75	200						
2	20	26	50	150						
2½	42		30	100	300					
3	10		30	100	200	600				
3	30			60	200	500				
3	60			50	80	400				
4	100			35	100	260	1000			
4	200			30	90	250	900			
4	500			20	70	180	700			
5	200				35	80	350	1000		
5	500				30	70	300	900		
5	1100				20	50	200	700		
6	350				25	50	200	400	1300	
6	620				15	30	125	300	1100	
6	960					24	100	250	1000	
6	1900					20	70	200	700	
8	600						50	150	500	1300
8	1400						40	100	400	1200
8	2200						30	80	350	1100
8	3600						25	60	250	800
10	1000							75	125	1000
10	2500							50	100	500
10	3800							30	80	350
10	5600							25	60	250

Extracted from American Standard National Plumbing Code (ASA A 40.8 - 1955) with permission of the publisher, The American Society of Mechanical Engineers.

FIGURE 3-24 / Vent size and length

The developed length is found by using the table in Fig. 3-24 to size the stack; find the soil stack size and then move horizontally to the right to check the fixture-unit column. The plumbing code states that the main vent and vent stack shall be sized in accordance with the table "and be not less than 3 in. in diameter." In addition, it states that the size of the vent stack must not be reduced all the way through the roof. So in this design, the minimum vent stack size of 3 in. is used.

Code requirements also stipulate that the vent and vent stack will terminate no less than 6 in. above the roof (Fig. 3-25), and if the roof is to be used for other than weather protection (for example, as a terrace or balcony), the vent stack must run at least 5 ft above the roof. Most codes require at least a 3-in. vent through the roof (Fig. 3-25).

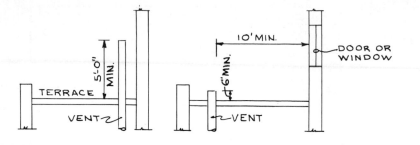

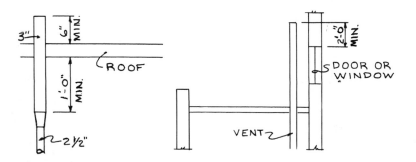

Most codes require at least
a 3" vent through the roof
beginning at least one foot
below the roof.

FIGURE 3-25 / Vent termination

10. The next step in the design is to size the building drain. At this point, review the basic system being designed. The building drain must be sized for the total amount of fixture units connected to the point at which the main vent is connected. Building drains are sized from the table in Fig. 3-26.

11. The plumbing drainage system has now been designed, with the exception of checking the location of the vent in relation to the fixtures. As the fixture branch sizes were being selected, the maximum distance from the trap to a vent was also tabulated. While an experienced designer would make a tentative decision as to vent locations early in the design, it has been left to the end here so that a more thorough explanation of the various methods of venting and possible venting solutions may be given.

If fixtures are so spread out that one or more fixtures are beyond the maximum horizontal distance, there are two options:

| Diameter of Pipe | Maximum Number of Fixture Units That May Be Connected to Any Portion[1] of the Building Drain or the Building Sewer | | | |
| | Fall per Foot | | | |
	1/16 Inch	1/8 Inch	1/4 Inch	1/2 Inch
Inches				
2			21	26
2½			24	31
3		20[2]	27[2]	36[2]
4		180	216	250
5		390	480	575
6		700	840	1,000
8	1,400	1,600	1,920	2,300
10	2,500	2,900	3,500	4,200
12	3,900	4,600	5,600	6,700
15	7,000	8,300	10,000	12,000

[1] Includes branches of the building drain.
[2] Not over two water closets.

Extracted from American Standard National Plumbing Code (ASA A 40.8 - 1955) with permission of the publisher, The American Society of Mechanical Engineers.

FIGURE 3-26 / *Building drains and sewers*

a. Increase the size of the horizontal fixture branch which automatically increases the allowable horizontal distance.

b. Add more vents. Instead of trying to service a group of fixtures with one vent, perhaps a vent should be added to service any fixtures which are beyond the allowable distance. A variety of venting solutions for various groups of fixtures is shown in Figs. 3-27 through 3-30.

The size of the wet vent is selected from Fig. 3-24. But a little explanation is needed. First, a review of the sketch in Fig. 3-27 shows that the portion of the vent referred to as a *wet vent* is actually a part of the drainage system for the lavatory and the kitchen sink. Because it acts as both a *vent* and a *drainage* pipe, it is referred to as a *wet vent*. For single bathroom groups, selection of the wet vent is based on the number of fixture units that the wet vent serves. A careful check of the code requirements for wet venting a multistory bathroom group (Fig. 3-29) indicates that a wet vent and its extension must be 2 in. in diameter and can serve the kitchen sink, lavatory, and bathtub. Fig. 3-30 states that "each water closet below the top floor is individually back vented" unless wet vented as illustrated in Fig. 3-30. When the minimum size of the vent is larger than the waste sizes previously selected, the larger size must be used.

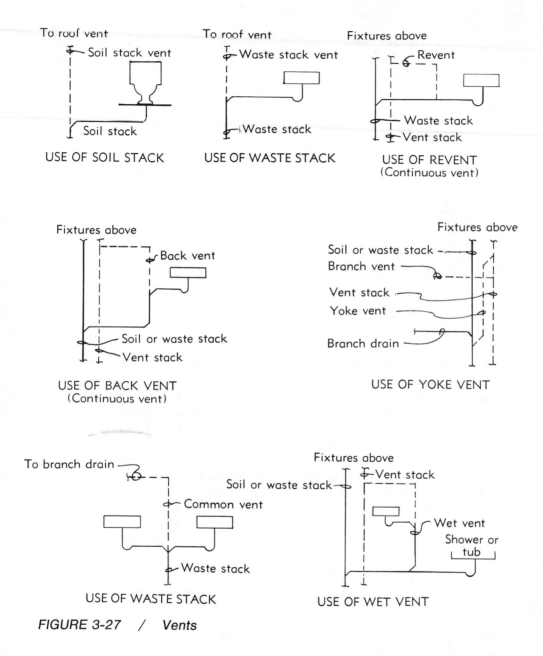

To roof vent
Soil stack vent
Soil stack
USE OF SOIL STACK

To roof vent
Waste stack vent
Waste stack
USE OF WASTE STACK

Fixtures above
Revent
Waste stack
Vent stack
USE OF REVENT
(Continuous vent)

Fixtures above
Back vent
Soil or waste stack
Vent stack
USE OF BACK VENT
(Continuous vent)

Fixtures above
Soil or waste stack
Branch vent
Vent stack
Yoke vent
Branch drain
USE OF YOKE VENT

To branch drain
Common vent
Waste stack
USE OF WASTE STACK

Fixtures above
Vent stack
Soil or waste stack
Wet vent
Shower or tub
USE OF WET VENT

FIGURE 3-27 / Vents

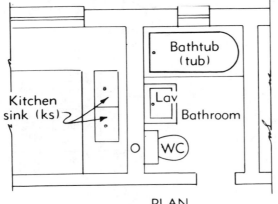

PLAN

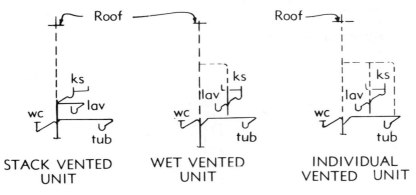

STACK VENTED
UNIT

WET VENTED
UNIT

INDIVIDUAL
VENTED UNIT

FIGURE 3-28 / Vent for a one-family dwelling

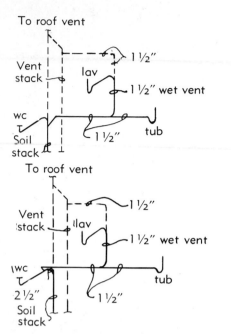

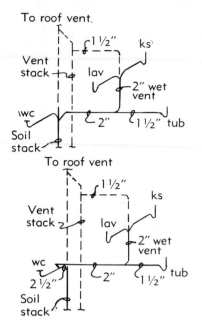

To roof vent

Vent stack

lav

1½"

1½" wet vent

wc

Soil stack

1½"

tub

To roof vent.

Vent stack

ks

1½"

lav

2" wet vent

wc

Soil stack

2"

1½" tub

To roof vent

Vent stack

lav

1½"

1½" wet vent

wc

2½"

Soil stack

1½"

tub

To roof vent

Vent stack

ks

1½"

lav

2" wet vent

wc

2½"

Soil stack

2"

1½"

tub

Wet vented single bathroom and single bathroom and kitchen fixture group on a stack or at the top floor of a stack serving multistory bathroom groups.

FIGURE 3-29 / Wet venting—top floor

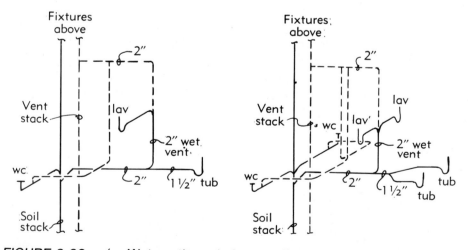

Fixtures above

Vent stack

lav

2"

2" wet vent

wc

Soil stack

2"

1½" tub

Fixtures above

Vent stack

wc

lav

lav

2"

2" wet vent

wc

Soil stack

2"

1½"

tub

tub

FIGURE 3-30 / Wet venting—below top floor

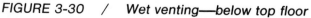

WET VENTING

Single Bathroom Groups—A single bathroom group of fixtures may be installed with the drain from a back-vented lavatory, kitchen sink, or combination fixture serving as a wet vent for a bathtub or shower stall and for the water closet, provided that: (1) not more than one fixture unit is drained into a 1½-inch diameter wet vent or not more than four fixture units drain into a 2-inch diameter wet vent, and (2) the horizontal branch connects to the stack at the same level as the water closet drain or below the water-closet drain when installed on the top floor. It may also connect to the water-closet bend.

Multistory Bathroom Group—On the lower floors of a multistory building, the drain from one or two back-vented lavatories may be used as a wet vent for one or two bathtubs or showers provided that: the wet vent and its extension to the vent stack is 2 inches in diameter;

each water closet below the top floor is individually back vented; and the vent stack is sized in accordance with the following table:

SIZE OF VENT STACKS

Number of wet-vented fixtures	Diameter of vent stacks in inches
1 or 2 bathtubs or showers....	2
3 to 5 bathtubs or showers....	2½
6 to 9 bathtubs or showers....	3
10 to 16 bathtubs or showers..	4

In multistory bathroom groups, wet vented in accordance with the paragraph above, water closets below the top floor group need not be individually vented if the 2-inch wet vent connects directly into the water-closet bend at a 45-degree angle to the horizontal portion of the bend and in the direction of flow.

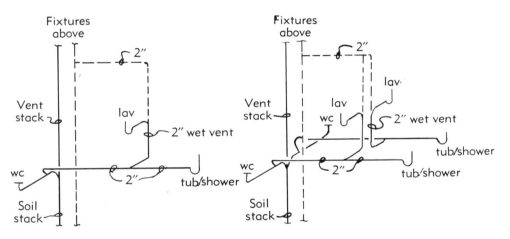

FIGURE 3-30 / Wet venting—below top floor (continued)

3-6   Plumbing Economy

Economies in plumbing are possible through the careful planning and location of
fixtures in clusters, back-to-back, or otherwise grouped to form as few wet walls
(walls in which the plumbing pipes are located) as possible.

In multistory construction, locating fixtures above each other saves considerable money since a minimum amount of piping and the smallest sizes possible
may be used for both supply and disposal.

In residences designed with low cost as a primary objective, it is even possible to use the same wet-wall for a back-to-back bathroom and kitchen (Fig. 3-31).
For middle-priced and custom-designed residences, the primary concern is the location of fixtures where they will best suit the plan. Most designers find no problem in planning and designing a building so that a certain amount of economy is
achieved at no sacrifice to the overall plan.

While the plumbing designer is not an architect (and, typically, he will be
working on a layout designed by the architect), he should not hesitate to make
suggestions that might save money for the client or provide for more effective use
of the space. The designer should also check the plans to be certain that the fixtures will fit properly in the space and that there are at least the minimum clear-
ances required.

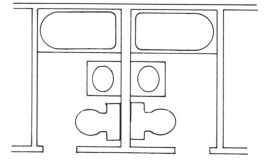 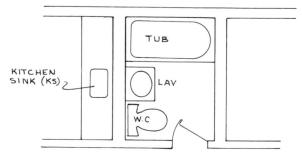

FIGURE 3-31   /   Plumbing back to back

3-7   Testing the System

Plumbing permits and inspection are also discussed in Chapter 2. Once again, any
inspections should be made after the system is roughed in and before it is covered.

The inspectors always pay close attention to the waste system to be certain
that the layout conforms with the code. The system must also be checked to be

certain it is watertight. The watertight test involves introducing an air pressure of 5 psi into the system. If it holds the pressure for 15 minutes, it is considered watertight. The system can also be checked with a water test, in which all openings are plugged, the system is filled with water, and is then inspected for leaks.

Questions

3-1. What is a *trap,* where is it located, and how does it work?

3-2. Why are vents required on the waste system? Where are they located in reference to the fixture?

3-3. What is a *wet vent,* and how does it differ from other types of vents?

3-4. What is the difference between a *stack vent* and a *vent stack?* Using a sketch, show the location of a stack vent and a vent stack in a multistory design.

3-5. What is the difference between a *soil stack* and a *waste stack?*

3-6. Sketch and locate the house (building) drain and the sewer.

3-7. What provisions must be made to provide drainage for fixtures located below the level of the building drain and the sewer?

3-8. Why are sketches of the drainage piping made by the designer?

3-9. Sketch a typical drainage piping design for a residence having a single bathroom with a kitchen sink on the other side of the wall.

3-10. What is the difference between a *flush tank* and *flush valve* water closet?

Chapter 4

Storm Drainage

4-1 Types of Systems

Whenever it rains, the drainage and runoff from roofs, courtyards, and paved areas (such as parking lots) must be carried away from the building and properly disposed of. This water may be directed to drains in the building roofs, parking areas, courtyards, and the like, and then be directed into:

1. A community storm sewer line.

2. A private storm sewer and drywell, or be run off onto a low portion of the client's land or into a creek, stream, lake, or pond.

3. A community sewer line.

4-2 Community Storm Sewer

If the water is directed to a community storm sewer system, the only concern will be that the elevation of the sewer line is low enough that the private storm line can run into it (Fig. 4-1). Many communities have such systems which are also used to drain rainwater from the streets and safely away.

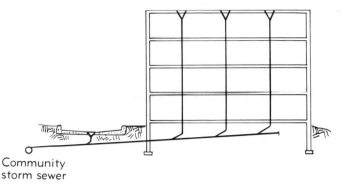

FIGURE 4-1 / *Community storm sewer*

4-3 Private Storm Sewer—Drywell

If the water is collected into a private storm sewer line, the line can:

1. Be directed into drywells (Fig. 4-2) which allow the water to be absorbed into the ground.

2. Be run so that it will empty into an area of low elevation on the plot.

3. Be run into a nearby creek or stream.

4. Be run into a public or private lake or pond.

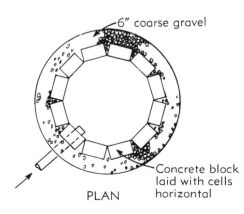

PLAN

SECTION

FIGURE 4-2 / *Drywell*

If the line serves a large area, the force of the water, after a rain, may cause considerable damage where it runs out the end of the line. This should be carefully considered by an engineer with experience in drainage.

Running the private line into a creek, stream, or lake may require a permit and may not be allowed in some areas. Usually, before approval, the design of the system will be checked to be certain there is no possibility of sewage wastes (chemical, human, or industrial wastes) getting into the storm sewer line and contaminating a lake, stream, or creek.

Many times on large projects, the storm water is run into a pond so that the water will be available for nonpotable uses such as watering lawns and gardens and circulating in fountains.

4-4   Community Sewer Line

In many cities, especially in the more urban sections, storm sewers from city streets and from private buildings, driveways, and parking areas all run into the city sewer line which is used for sewage waste; this is called a *combined sewer*. This should be done only if no other solution is available and if the city allows storm lines to be tied into its sewage lines. Storm water creates a tremendous excess work load for the city, county, or municipality sewage treatment plant. This unnecessary burden often requires that the sewage treatment plants be much larger than they would be if only sewage were to be treated. In cities which presently have such systems, the cost of separating the storm and sewage lines would be prohibitive. However, many cities have separate storm and sewage lines, and it is illegal to tie storm drainage lines into sewage lines. Cities with only sewage lines may or may not allow storm water to be introduced into the sewage lines, and this should be carefully checked with local authorities.

When designing drainage for driveways, parking lots, and surrounding ground, the site plan of the project must be checked to determine what effect the existing and revised contours will have on the flow of the surface water after a rain. It is most important that the flow of water be away from the building and not toward it (Fig. 4-3). On large projects (usually not individual residences), the ground should be contoured so water will flow toward the storm sewer system (usually a catch basin for collecting the water, Fig. 4-4). On projects without a storm sewer system, the water should be directed away from buildings, driveways, and parking lots.

The detail for the construction of driveways and parking lots should also be checked. When the water is simply being allowed to run off onto the surrounding ground, the driveway and any curbs should be constructed higher than the surrounding ground (Fig. 4-5) so that the water will run off and onto the ground. When a storm sewer system will be used to collect and carry away the water, the driveway and curbs may be set lower than the surrounding ground (Fig. 4-6) and should be generally pitched toward the catch basins which collect the water. When this detail is used and there is no storm sewer system, the driveways and parking lots become shallow "swimming pools."

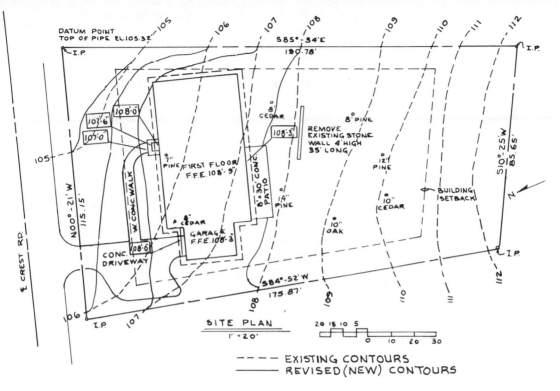

SITE PLAN
1" = 20'

20 15 10 5
0   10   20   30

---- EXISTING CONTOURS
—— REVISED (NEW) CONTOURS

FIGURE 4-3   /   Slope of land

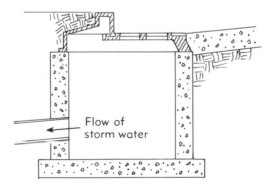

Flow of
storm water

FIGURE 4-4   /   Catch basins

FIGURE 4-5   /   High driveways

81

4-5   Roof Drainage Design

The water from the roof may be taken into consideration by any of three methods:

1.   Install roof drains.

2.   Install gutters.

3.   Allow the water to run off without drains or gutters.

Roof drains (Fig. 4-7) are commonly placed in "flat" or built-up roofs to be certain that the water will not stay on the roof after a rain. Because it is generally considered detrimental to the roofing materials to have water left on the roof, the roof should not be flat but have at least a small pitch (slope) to it.

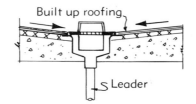

Built up roofing

Leader

FIGURE 4-7   /   Roof drain

When placed in a flat roof, it is very important that the roof surface be pitched toward the drain to be certain that *all* the water is drained off the roof. This slope may be accomplished on a "flat" roof deck by the use of a layer of lightweight concrete or asphalt. When the deck is made of poured gypsum or concrete, the slope is put in as the deck is poured.

Properly installed roof drains are quite effective in draining a roof. The drains connect to pipes (called *leaders*) which carry the water away from the drain and into a horizontal storm drain (Fig. 4-8) or to the exterior of the building (Fig. 4-9). The leaders may be concealed in the walls or columns (Fig. 4-10) if the sight of an exposed pipe is objectionable. However, once enclosed, it is more expensive to make necessary repairs. Leaders are usually made of cast iron, galvanized steel, galvanized wrought iron, copper, brass, lead, or plastic pipe. The method used to size roof drain leaders and horizontal storm drains is described later in this section.

If the leader runs to the outside of the building and empties, precautions must be taken so that the water will be directed away from the building. Immediately adjacent to the building, a concrete pad or splashblock (Fig. 4-11) or other similar device is required so that the water coming from the end of the pipe will not hit the soil with such force that it will wash it away, causing soil erosion and permitting the possibility of wet foundation walls. Undermining of the construc-

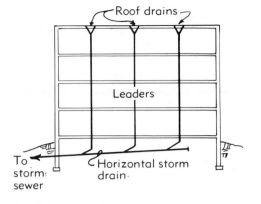

FIGURE 4-8 / Storm leader to drain

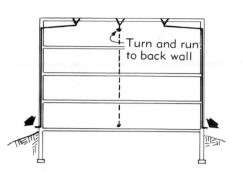

FIGURE 4-9 / Leader through wall

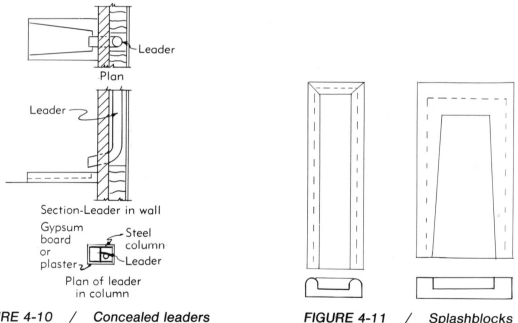

FIGURE 4-10 / Concealed leaders

FIGURE 4-11 / Splashblocks

tion is even possible in extreme cases. Minor problems such as staining the building may also occur. Once the water is directed away from the building in some manner, be certain that the surrounding contours keep the water moving *away* from the building.

In locales where the leaders can be tied into the sewage system, the system is referred to as a *combined* sewer. Figure 4-12 illustrates how the leader might be tied into the building drain (discussed in Sec. 4-4). In this situation, most codes require a trap on the leader (storm sewer systems seldom require traps, mainly with combined sewers), and they may specify that the trap shall be a minimum of 10 ft from any stack. Sizing of the leader for a combined sewer and its effect on the building drain are discussed in Sec. 4-6.

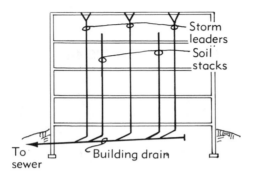

FIGURE 4-12   /   Leaders and soil stacks to building drain

The water may also be directed off the roof into gutters. The roof surface should be pitched to direct the flow of water toward the gutter. The gutters are tied to leaders (often called *downspouts*) or which may be tied to a storm sewer line (either community or private) or which may empty outside the building onto a pad, splashblock, or other means of dispersing the water (Fig.4-13).

FIGURE 4-13   /   Leader and splashblock

Another possible solution is to run the leader into a small catch basin or disposal area filled with gravel (Fig. 4-14). This may be effectively used on smaller buildings, such as residences, but it is important that the catch basin be located at least 10 ft from the foundation walls to reduce any chance for wet walls from the water.

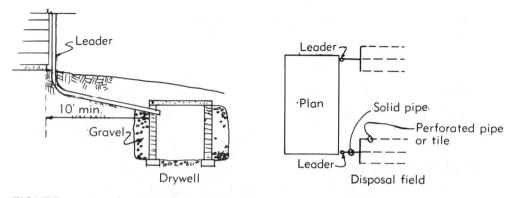

FIGURE 4-14   /   *Leaders to drywell and disposal field*

Gutters and leaders commonly used may be made of copper, steel, aluminum, or vinyl. Vinyl gutters can be made in one piece (without seams), but if the gutters are properly installed, seams are no problem (too often they are not properly installed). It is most important that the gutters be installed with a definite slope toward the leaders.

Sizing Roof Drains and Leaders

1.   Determine the area of the roof in square feet.
2.   Determine number of roof drains and the roof area each drain must serve.
3.   Select leader size from Fig. 4-15, based on square footage of roof area each leader must handle.

Example

Size the leaders for the roof of an apartment building with a roof area of 3200 square feet. If three roof drains are used, each will serve 1,067 square feet of roof area. The leader size selected from Fig. 4-15 is 2½ inches.

> *Note:*   Figures 4-15, 4-16 and 4-21 are based on an average rainfall of 4 inches per hour and the square foot area is adjusted proportionally based on the rainfall in the design area.

Size of Leader or Conductor[1] Inches	Maximum Projected Roof Area Square Feet
2	720
2½	1,300
3	2,200
4	4,600
5	8,650
6	13,500
8	29,000

[1]The equivalent diameter of square or rectangular leader may be taken as the diameter of that circle which may be inscribed within the cross-sectional area of the leader.

NOTE: See footnote to Fig. 4-25.

Extracted from American Standard National Plumbing Code (ASA A 40.8 - 1955) with permission of the publisher, The American Society of Mechanical Engineers.

FIGURE 4-15   /   Vertical leader sizes

Sizing Roof Gutters and Leaders

Gutters are sized based on the square foot area they serve and on the slope of the gutter toward the leader. To make an accurate determination of this information it is often necessary to sketch out exactly what the gutter and leader layout will be.

1. Select leader size from Fig. 4-15, based on the square footage of roof area served by the portion of gutter that empties into the leader.

2. Determine the square foot area which each portion of the gutter serves and decide on the slope of the gutter. Select the gutter size from Fig. 4-16.

Diameter of Gutter[1]	Maximum Projected Roof Area for Gutters of Various Slopes			
	1/16-In. Slope	1/8-In. Slope	1/4-In. Slope	1/2-In. Slope
Inches	Square Feet	Square Feet	Square Feet	Square Feet
3	170	240	340	480
4	360	510	720	1,020
5	625	880	1,250	1,770
6	960	1,360	1,920	2,770
7	1,380	1,950	2,760	3,900
8	1,990	2,800	3,980	5,600
10	3,600	5,100	7,200	10,000

[1]Gutters other than semicircular may be used provided they have an equivalent cross-sectional area.

Extracted from American Standard National Plumbing Code (ASA A 40.8 - 1955) with permission of the publisher, The American Society of Mechanical Engineers.

FIGURE 4-16   /   Gutter sizes

Example

Determine the gutter and leader sizes for a roof, assuming the roof is sloped (Fig. 4-17). The roof area is 3200 square feet and the sketch of the gutters and leaders (Fig. 4-18) shows four leaders, each serving 800 square feet (3200 square feet ÷ 4). The leader size from Fig. 4-15 is 2½ in. Each segment of the gutter serves 400 square feet, has a ¼-in. slope per foot, and a 5-inch diameter is selected from Fig. 4-16.

FIGURE 4-17 / Sloped roof

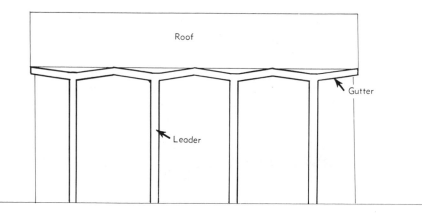

FIGURE 4-18 / Gutters and leaders

Sizing the Horizontal Storm Drain

Once the roof drains or gutters and leaders have been selected and sized, the next step is to size the horizontal storm drain (if one is to be used).

1. The horizontal storm drain is sized from Fig. 4-19; its size depends on the square footage being served and the slope at which the pipe is installed. The

Diameter of Drain	Maximum Projected Roof Area for Drains of Various Slopes		
	1/8-In. Slope	1/4-In. Slope	1/2-In. Slope
Inches	Square Feet	Square Feet	Square Feet
3	822	1,160	1,644
4	1,880	2,650	3,760
5	3,340	4,720	6,680
6	5,350	7,550	10,700
8	11,500	16,300	23,000
10	20,700	29,200	41,400
12	33,300	47,000	66,600
15	59,500	84,000	119,000

Figs. 4-15 and 4-19 are based on a maximum rate of rainfall of 4 inches per hour. If in any state, city, or other political subdivision, the maximum rate of rainfall is more or less than 4 inches per hour, then the figures for roof area must be adjusted proportionately by dividing the figure by 4 and multiplying by the maximum rate of rainfall in inches per hour.

Extracted from American Standard National Plumbing Code (ASA A 40.8 - 1955) with permission of the publisher, The American Society of Mechanical Engineers.

FIGURE 4-19   /   *Horizontal storm drain sizes*

pipe may be increased in size as it collects the leaders, so the first step will be to make a sketch of the system. Next, add the square footage that each leader serves and the slope selected for the horizontal drain to the sketch.

2.   Using this information, the drain is sized from Fig. 4-19.

4-6   Sizing a Combined Sewer

If the roof leaders (from Sec. 4-5) are to be connected to the building drain (Fig. 4-20), it will be necessary to convert the roof area into an equivalent number of fixture units so that the building drain can be sized to reflect the increased load.

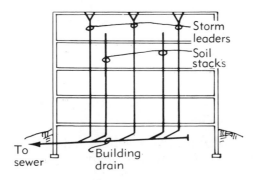

FIGURE 4-20   /   *Combined sewer*

(Building drains were sized for sewage waste from the stacks in Sec. 3-5). Few communities allow combined sewers.

1. First, a schematic sketch of the stacks, leaders, and building drain should be made so that the relationship of the stacks and the leaders to the building drain can be seen.

2. Next, the fixture units served by each stack must be converted into equivalent square feet. The code sets up a ratio of f.u. and equivalent square feet (Fig. 4-21). The equivalent square feet, based on the code, for the first 256 f.u. is 1,000 square feet.

$$256 \text{ f.u.} = 1,000 \text{ sq. ft.}$$

Any additional f.u. are converted into equivalent square feet on the basis that 1 f.u. equals 3.9 square feet.

3. Add the equivalent square feet to the roof area being collected for the total area being served by the building drain and size the drain using Fig. 4-22.

4. The equivalent square feet are based on a rainfall of 4 inches per hr. A check of the local weather service will indicate whether the rainfall in the proposed building location is a greater or lesser amount. If so, then the equivalent square feet must be adjusted proportionally.

When the total fixture unit load on the combined drain is less than 256 fixture units, the equivalent drainage area in horizontal projection shall be taken as 1000 square feet.

When the total fixture unit load exceeds 256 fixture units, each fixture unit shall be considered the equivalent of 3.9 square feet of drainage area.

If the rainfall to be provided for is more or less than 4 inches per hour, the 1000 square foot equivalent and the 3.9 shall be adjusted by dividing by 4 and multiplying by the rainfall per hour to be provided for.

Extracted from American Standard National Plumbing Code (ASA A 40.8 - 1955) with permission of the publisher, The American Society of Mechanical Engineers.

FIGURE 4-21   /   Roof area to fixture units

| Diameter of Pipe | Maximum Number of Fixture-Units that may be Connected to Any Portion[1] of the Building Drain or the Building Sewer[3] | | | |
| | Fall Per Foot | | | |
	1/16 Inch	1/8 Inch	1/4 Inch	1/2 Inch
Inches				
2			21	26
2½			24	31
3		20[2]	27[2]	36[2]
4		180	216	250
5		390	480	575
6		700	840	1,000
8	1,400	1,600	1,920	2,300
10	2,500	2,900	3,500	4,200
12	3,900	4,600	5,600	6,700
15	7,000	8,300	10,000	12,000

[1]Includes branches of the building drain.
[2]Not over two water closets.
[3]No building drain or sewer shall be less than 4 inches in size
Extracted from American Standard National Plumbing Code
(ASA A 40.8 - 1955) with permission of the publisher, The
American Society of Mechanical Engineers.

FIGURE 4-22   /   *Building drains and sewers*

4-7   Foundation Drains

Many times drains are placed around the foundation of a building (Fig. 4-23) to direct water away from the building (usually after a rain). These footing drains may be of hard fibrous materials with holes, of plastic pipe with holes, or of clay tile spaced about ¼ in. apart with the upper half of the joint covered. The pipes are laid on a layer of gravel, with the holes toward the bottom, and then gravel is placed over the pipe or tile. The drain must be installed at a slope so the water will run to a low point and then run into a drywell or storm sewer.

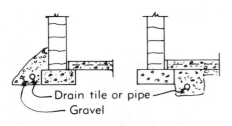

FIGURE 4-23   /   *Foundation drains*

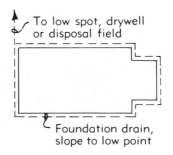

Questions

4-1. What methods may be used to dispose of the water from roofs, courtyards, and parking lots?

4-2. What is a *combined sewer,* and under what conditions should this system of storm drainage be used?

4-3. What methods are commonly used for roof drainage?

4-4. Why should flat roofs be avoided?

4-5. When the roof drainage water is run into roof drains or gutters, what solutions may be used to disperse the water at the end of the leader?

Chapter 5
Private Sewage Disposal

5-1   Types of Systems

Whenever possible, the sanitary drainage system should connect to a community (public) sewer, but when no community sewer is available, a private sewage disposal system must be installed. This is particularly true in suburban and rural areas and is one of the initial items that the designer should check. The information contained in this chapter is based on the *National Plumbing Code,* but the codes in force in the geographic area of construction should always be checked *before* the system is designed. In some areas, the municipality will not only specific exactly where on the site the system will be placed but will also simply state the size of all equipment required and the installation method. In addition, many areas limit the minimum lot size on which a private sewage disposal system might be placed (often one-half acre) and the minimum size if both a sewage disposal system and a well are required (often about one acre). Most of these requirements are established because of the type of soil in the area and because there is always a concern that the potable water supply might be contaminated by a sewage disposal system (either the system serving this project or a neighbor's sewage system).

5-2 Private Systems

Private sewage disposal systems (Fig. 5-1) usually consist of the building sewer which leads from the project into a septic tank and then the line into a distribution box which feeds the fluid (effluent) into the disposal or leach fields. There are variations on this design: as shown in Fig. 5-2, the septic tank may feed into a seepage pit(s), and the packaged unit in Fig. 5-3 is designed to serve larger complexes.

The watertight septic tank is placed underground where it receives the sewage from the building and holds it for about a day while the suspended solids settle to the bottom and putrefy. The liquids pass out of the tank at the other end into the distribution box. Septic tanks may be concrete, of rectangular shape (Fig. 5-4), or asphalt-protected steel, usually round (Fig. 5-5).

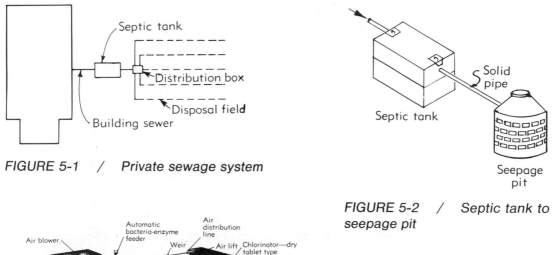

FIGURE 5-1 / Private sewage system

FIGURE 5-2 / Septic tank to seepage pit

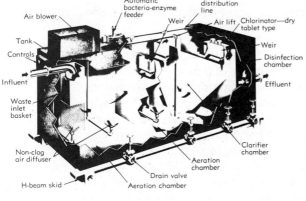

Courtesy of Demco

FIGURE 5-3 / Package sewage unit

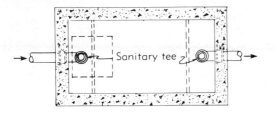

PLAN

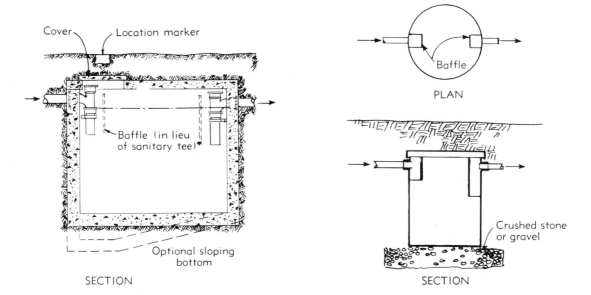

FIGURE 5-4 / Rectangular septic tank   FIGURE 5-5 / Steel septic tank

It is the size of the septic tank that will be one of the first considerations in private sewage disposal design. For individual residences, the tank design is based on the number of bedrooms and the maximum number of persons served and on whether a garbage disposal is used (Fig. 5-6); for institutional and commercial projects, it is based on the estimated sewage flow in gallons per day (Fig. 5-7).

A three-bedroom home which will have five people living in it will require a septic tank size of 600 gal minimum (Fig. 5-6). When a garbage disposal is being installed, the code requires an additional 50% to be added to the tank size, so a 900-gal tank is required. Also listed in Fig. 5-6 are *recommended* inside dimensions of the tank. It should be noted, however, that the tank need only be *approximately* the dimensions shown. In many locales the tank sizes available may be limited, and it may be necessary to use a larger tank than the minimum. Using a larger tank will not interfere with the operation of the system. If a larger capacity is

MINIMUM CAPACITIES FOR SEPTIC TANKS SERVING AN INDIVIDUAL DWELLING

Number of Bedrooms	Maximum Number of Persons Served	Nominal Liquid Capacity of Tank	Recommended Inside Dimensions			
			Length	Width	Liquid Depth	Total Depth
	Persons	Gallons	Ft. In.	Ft. In.	Ft. In.	Ft. In.
2 or less	4	500	6 0	3 0	4 0	5 0
3	6	600	7 0	3 0	4 0	5 0
4	8	750	7 6	3 6	4 0	5 0
5	10	900	8 6	3 6	4 6	5 6
6	12	1,100	8 6	4 0	4 6	5 6
7	14	1,300	10 0	4 0	4 6	5 6
8	16	1,500	10 0	4 6	4 6	5 6

NOTE: Liquid capacity is based on number of bedrooms in dwelling. Total volume in cubic feet includes air space above liquid level.

Add 50% to requirements when a garbage disposal is used.

Extracted from American Standard National Plumbing Code (ASA A 40.8 - 1955) with permission of the publisher, The American Society of Mechanical Engineers.

FIGURE 5-6   /   Residential septic tank requirements

In general, the plans will be examined on the basis of the sewage flows in the following table:

Type of Establishment	Gallons per person per day
Multiple-family dwellings (apartments)	75
Boarding houses	65
Additional kitchen wastes for nonresident boarders	10
Hotels	65-75
Restaurants (toilet and kitchen wastes per patron)	7-10
Tourist courts or mobile home parks	50
Resort camps	65-75
Day camps	15-20 .
Day schools	15-20
Boarding schools	75-100
Day workers (per shift)	15-35
Hospitals (per bed)	250-350
Institutions other than hospitals	75-125
Picnic parks (gallons per picnicker)	5
Swimming pools and beaches with bathhouses	10
Country clubs (per member)	25
Motels (per person)	50-75
Drive-in theaters (per car space)	5
Movie theaters (per seat)	3
Airports (per passenger)	3-5
Self-service laundries (gallons per machine per day)	400
Stores (per toilet room)	400
Camp sites (per site)	100
Place of public assembly (per person)	3-10

FIGURE 5-7   /   Commercial flow requirements

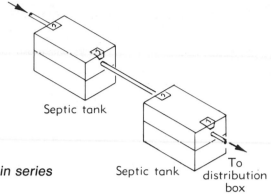

FIGURE 5-8   /   *Septic tanks in series*

required than is available in one tank (for example, if 900 gal is required and only 600-gal tanks are available), two 600-gal tanks may be connected (Fig. 5-8). The tanks should be set close enough together that a single length of pipe (with no joints) can be used to join the outlet of the first tank to the inlet of the second.

Many municipalities require tanks larger than those recommended by the *National Plumbing Code*. It is the designer's responsibility to know or find out local requirements *before* designing the system. When the designer is working in an area where he is not familiar with local codes and requirements, he must visit the local authorities and discuss the design, obtain local requirements in writing, or perhaps call to determine what codes are in effect in the locale.

The code also sets minimum distances for the location of the various parts of the private sewage disposal system (Fig. 5-9); the septic tank must be a minimum of 50 ft from any well or suction line (Fig. 5-10), and when possible, the tank is put even farther away. Many local codes require longer distances and therefore must be checked; in general, about 100 ft is the preferred distance, but this is not always feasible. These distances greatly reduce the danger of contaminating drinking water if leaks should occur in the tank or pipes (lines).

The depth of the tank will be determined by the depth of the sewer line from the building to the tank. It is important that the sewer line be sloped gradually toward the tank (about ⅛ to ¼ in. per ft). Too much slope will cause the sewage to flow into the tank too rapidly and disturb the natural action in the tank. Too little slope may cause the sewer line to become clogged. The top of the tank is usually located 12 to 36 in. below the ground surface so it can be serviced as required.

Institutions and commercial projects base their sewage treatment system sizes on the expected flow of sewage from the project in a day. The table in Fig. 5-7 lists various types of building uses and the gallons per person per day the system must be designed for. The septic tank is sized using the calculated gallons per day and Figure 5-22.

Type of System	Distance						
	Well or Suction Line	Water Supply Line (Pressure)	Stream	Dwelling	Property Line	Disposal Field	Seepage Pits
	Feet	Feet	Feet	Feet	Feet	Feet	Feet
Building sewer	50	10	. . . .	. . . .	. . . .	. . . .	. . . .
Septic tank	50	. . . .	. . . .	. . . .	. . . .	. . . .	. . . .
Distribution box	50	. . . .	. . . .	. . . .	. . . .	. . . .	. . . .
Disposal field	100	. . . .	25	10	10	. . . .	. . . .
Seepage pit	100	. . . .	50	20	10	20	20
Dry well	50	. . . .	. . . .	10	. . . .	. . . .	. . . .
Cesspool	150	. . . .	50	20	15	15	15

This separation may be reduced to 50 ft when the well is provided with an outside watertight casing to a depth of 50 ft or more.

Not recommended as a substitute for a septic tank. To be used only when approved by the Administrative Authority.

Extracted from American Standard National Plumbing Code (ASA A 40.8 - 1955) with permission of the publisher, The American Society of Mechanical Engineers.

FIGURE 5-9 / Sewage disposal system distances

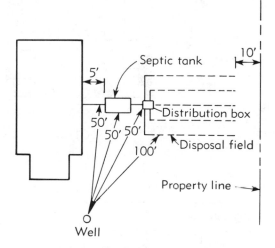

FIGURE 5-10 / Private disposal system distances

The *distribution box* receives the effluent from the septic tank and distributes it equally to each individual line of the disposal field (as illustrated in Fig. 5-11). Distribution boxes are not used when one seepage pit is used (Fig. 5-12). The box is connected to the septic tank with a tight sewer line.

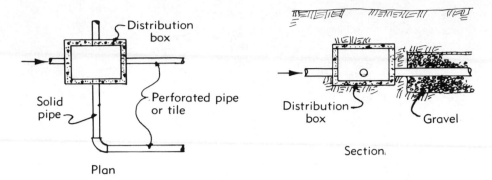

FIGURE 5-11   /   Distribution box

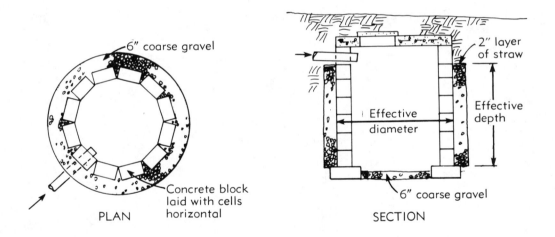

ABSORPTION AREAS						
Diam.	Depth					
	4'	5'	6'	7'	8'	10'
4'	62.8	75.3	87.9	100.5	113	138.1
5'	82.4	97.8	113.5	129.2	144.9	176.3
6'	103.7	122.5	141.4	160.2	179	197.9
8'	150.7	175.8	200.9	226	251.3	276.3

FIGURE 5-12   /   Typical seepage pit

Disposal or tile fields are the preferred method for distributing the effluent. They consist of rows (called *lines*) of pipe through which the effluent passes. The lines may be made of clay tile (usually 12 in. long), bituminized pipe, or plastic pipe. The clay tile is laid with about ¼ in. of space between them (Fig. 5-13) to allow the effluent to be absorbed into the gravel fill the tile is placed on. The top portion of the ¼-in. space (Fig. 5-13) is covered with a piece of felt so that soil will not fall into the pipe and clog or stop the flow of effluent. Most fields installed today use the bituminized or plastic pipes which have holes in them. These pipes are installed much faster and do not have any open joints to be covered with felt as the tile does. These pipes are installed with the holes down, and as the effluent flows through the pipes, it is absorbed into the gravel.

The tile or pipe is set into a trench which varies from 18 to 30 in. in depth and 24 to 36 in. in width (Fig. 5-14). Trenches must be sloped in the direction of flow; the code limits the maximum slope to 6 in. in 100 ft so that the effluent will not simply flow to the end of the line and then back up. The bottom of the trench is filled with a layer of filter material not less than 6 in. deep below the pipe line, extending the full width of the trench and a minimum of 2 in. above the pipe, and covered with a layer of straw. The code also limits any individual line to a length of 100 ft and sets the minimum separation between lines at 6 ft. The disposal field may take any of a number of shapes (Fig. 5-15), depending on the contours (slope) of the ground, the size of the lot, and the location of any well or stream on the property. The minimum distance between the field and the building is 10 ft, between field and property line 10 ft, between field and stream 25 ft, and between field and well 100 ft. If the well has an outside watertight casing which extends down to a depth of 50 ft or more, the minimum separation between field and well may be reduced to 50 ft.

The length of line required in the disposal field depends on the ability of the soil to absorb sewage. The subsurface conditions are checked first by digging a hole about 5 ft below final grade to observe the type of soil encountered and

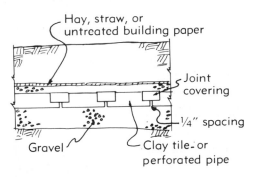

FIGURE 5-13 / Clay tile disposal field

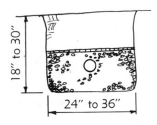

FIGURE 5-14 / Disposal field trench

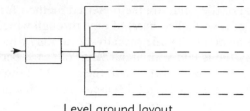

Level ground layout

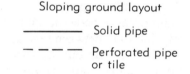

Sloping ground layout

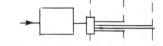

Solid pipe

Perforated pipe
or tile

FIGURE 5-15   /   Disposal field
patterns

whether any groundwater is evident. Next, a soil percolation test is made to measure the ability of the soil to absorb sewage. The procedure for making the soil
percolation test is:

1. Dig a hole about 12 in. in diameter and 30 in. deep, keeping the sides of the
    hole vertical (Fig. 5-16)

2. Presoak the hole by filling it with water and allowing it to completely seep
    away. The hole should be presoaked several hours before the test and again
    at the time of the test.

3. After presoaking, remove any loose soil that might have fallen in from the
    sides of the hole.

4. Carefully fill the hole to a depth of 6 in. with clean water with as little
    splashing at possible.

5. Record the time (in minutes) that it takes for the water level to drop 1 in.
    (from 6 in. to 5 in.).

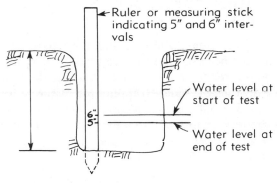

Ruler or measuring stick indicating 5" and 6" intervals

Water level at start of test

Water level at end of test

FIGURE 5-16 / Percolation pit

6.   Now, repeat the test a minimum of three times until the time it takes the water to drop 1 in. for two successive tests is approximately the same. Then take the last test as the stabilized rate of percolation; it is the time recorded for this test which will be used to size the disposal field.

Individual residences are sized from Fig. 5-17 which lists the time required for the water to drop 1 in. and the square feet of trench required *per bedroom* for the various times.

ABSORPTION AREAS FOR
INDIVIDUAL RESIDENCES

Time Required for Water to Fall 1 Inch (Minutes)	Effective Absorption Area Required in Bottom of Disposal Trenches (Square Feet per Bedroom)
2 or less	50
3	60
4	70
5	80
10	100
15	130
30	180
60	240
Over 60	(1)

1Special design
NOTE: A minimum of 150 sq. ft. should be provided for each dwelling unit."
Extracted from American Standard National Plumbing Code (ASA A 40.8 - 1955) with permission of the publisher, The American Society of Mechanical Engineers.

FIGURE 5-17 / Residential absorption rate

Example

Assuming a soil percolation time of 4 minutes, from Fig. 5-17, the square feet required per bedroom is 70. For a three-bedroom residence, a total of 70 sq ft (per bedroom) × 3 bedrooms = 210 sq ft is required. Using a trench width of 3 ft, find the lineal feet of line required by dividing the square feet required by the width of the trench; in this design, 210 sq ft ÷ 3 = 70 lineal ft is the minimum length of line.

Institutional and commercial projects are sized from Fig. 5-18 which lists the time required for percolation in minutes and the absorption of the soil for tile fields and seepage pits in *gallons per square foot per day*.

Example

For a four-story apartment building with a sewage flow of 2250 gpd, assuming a soil percolation time of 4 minutes, from Fig. 5-18, the amount that the soil can absorb is 2.4 gal per sq ft per day. To determine the amount of square footage required, divide the sewage flow by the absorption rate. In this design, divide 2250 gpd by 2.4 gal per sq ft and 938 sq ft of absorption area are required. Using a trench width of 3 ft, 313 lineal ft of line are required.

Seepage pits (also referred to as *leaching pits* and illustrated in Fig. 5-12) may be used instead of tile fields. They are preferable where the soil becomes more porous below a depth of 2 or 3 ft and where the property does not have sufficient space for all buildings, driveways, parking areas, and the drain field. They cannot be used in areas with high water tables since the bottom of the pit must be at least 2 ft above the water table.

The seepage pit is usually made of concrete block or is a precast concrete unit (Fig. 5-19). Typically, 8-in. thick block are used, and they are laid with the cells (holes) placed horizontally (Fig. 5-12) to allow the effluent to seep into the ground. The tapered cells of the block are set with the widest area to the outside to reduce the amount of loose material behind the lining that might fall into the pit.

Sewage Application Rate, gal./sq. ft./day		
Time for 1" Fall (Minutes)	Tile Fields	Seepage Pits
0-5	2.4	3.2
6-7	2.0	2.8
8-10	1.7	2.3
11-15	1.3	1.8
16-20	1.0	1.5
21-30	0.8	1.1
Over 30	QUESTIONABLE SUITABILITY	
Over 60	— — — UNSUITABLE — — —	

FIGURE 5-18   /   *Commercial absorption rate*

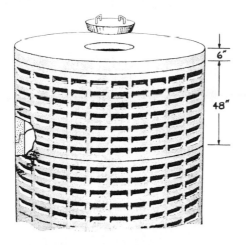

FIGURE 5-19 / Precast seepage pit

The typical precast concrete seepage pit shown in Fig. 5-19 is the same unit used for drywells (Sec. 4-3). The bottom of the pit is lined with coarse gravel a minimum of 1 ft deep before the block or concrete is placed. Between the block or concrete and soil is a minimum of 6 in. of clean crushed stone or gravel. Straw is placed on top of the gravel to keep sand from filtering down and reducing the effectiveness of the gravel. The top of the pit should have an opening with a watertight cover to provide access to the pit if necessary. The construction of the pit above the inlet pipe should be watertight.

When more than one seepage pit is used, the pipe from the settling tank must be laid out so that the effluent will be spread uniformly to the pits. To provide equal distribution, a distribution box with separate laterals (Fig. 5-20)—each lateral feeding no more than two pits—provides the best results. The distance between the outside walls of the pits should be a minimum of 3 pit diameters and not less than 10 ft.

The size of the seepage pit is based on the outside area of the walls plus the area of the bottom of the pit. The areas for pits of various diameters are given in Fig. 5-12. Many designers exclude the bottom area of the pit from the absorption area required to allow for a safety factor, while others calculate the total area available and then size the system to allow some safety factor. The latter approach is used in this text.

Seepage pits for individual residences are sized from Fig. 5-21 which lists the type of soil on the left and the absorption area required *per bedroom* on the right. Based on an on-site inspection on this project, assume a fine sand soil and 30 sq ft of absorption area required per bedroom. For a three-bedroom residence, a total of 30 sq ft × 3 bedrooms = 90 sq ft is required. The size of the pit required is then selected from Fig. 5-12. In this problem, a pit 4 ft in diameter and 7 ft deep, providing 100.5 sq ft of absorption area, is selected.

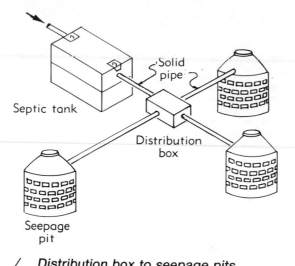

FIGURE 5-20   /   Distribution box to seepage pits

Soil structure:	Effective Absorption Area Required per Bedroom[1] (Square Feet)
Coarse sand and gravel	20
Fine sand	30
Sandy loam or sand clay	50
Clay with considerable sand and gravel . .	80
Clay with small amount of sand and gravel . .	160

Extracted from American Standard National Plumbing Code
(ASA A 40.8 - 1955) with permission of the publisher, The
American Society of Mechanical Engineers.

FIGURE 5-21   /   Seepage pit absorption areas

Seepage pits for institutional and commercial projects are sized from Fig. 5-18 which lists the time required for percolation; the absorption of the soil is listed under "Seepage Pits" as gallons per square foot per day. For a four-story apartment building with a sewage flow of 2250 gpd, assuming a soil percolation of 4 minutes, from Fig. 5-18, the soil can absorb 3.2 gal per sq ft per day. To determine the amount of absorption area required, divide the sewage flow by the absorption rate.

2250 gpd ÷ 3.2 gal per sq ft = 703 sq ft

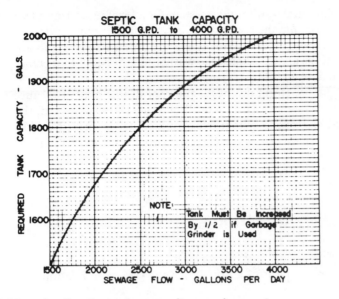

FIGURE 5-22   /   *Septic tank capacity requirements*

The size of the pits to be used is selected from Fig. 5-12, and four seepage pits 6 ft in diameter and 8 ft deep are selected. Other combinations, such as three 8-ft diameter, 8-ft deep pits or six 6-ft diameter, 5-ft deep pits may be used, depending on the area required to place the pits, the sizes available locally, whether precast concrete is used, and the designer's own preference.

5-3   Sewage Problems

The uncertainty of exactly how much the soil will actually absorb is reflected in the values given in the various tables and charts. Even so, many designers prefer to oversize the system slightly to allow for poor absorption and also to allow for future increased amounts of effluent either because more people are using the facility than anticipated or because of an addition to the individual residence or an addition of various water-using fixtures which may not have been included in the original design.

One of the most wasteful uses of the private system is the connection of a washing machine to it. Many times the tying-in of a washing machine to an older system has resulted in more water flow than the ground could handle through the system installed. It is suggested that when a washing machine is installed (especially where there are several children in the family), a drywell should be installed. Problems may also occur if all of the family washing is done on one day.

This puts a tremendous additional flow into the system for a brief period, and as a result, the system may back up into the house. One of the simplest solutions to this is to spread the washing out over several days, giving the ground a chance to absorb the water. Other solutions are to connect the washer to a drywell, to increase the size of the disposal field, or to add a seepage pit.

The connection of gutters, storm drainage, and roof drains may also cause periodic overloads on the private sewage system. When these are connected, the designer must increase the size of the system to accommodate the periodic additional flow. Most designers prefer to run such connections into drywells if no storm drain system is available.

Questions

5-1. When are private sewage systems generally used?

5-2. Draw a sketch of the major parts of a private sewage system in relation to a residence.

5-3. Why do most codes set minimum distances between the parts of the sewage system and wells and streams?

5-4. What is the function of a distribution box?

5-5. How is the ability of the soil to absorb sewage determined?

5-6. What are *seepage pits,* and when are they used?

5-7. Why should the designer consider not connecting pipes carrying certain waste water (such as water from washing machines) to the private sewage system?

5-8. How would the reuse water system discussed in Sec. 1-10 and illustrated in Fig. 1-27 affect sewage treatment system designs, both private and community?

Chapter 6
Comfort

6-1 Comfort

Comfort means different conditions to different people. Inside any room it means being able to carry on a desired activity without being either chilly or too hot. Most people don't care what combination of factors cause them to be comfortable as long as they feel comfortable.

6-2 Transfer of Body Heat

Since we are concerned here with people, a short study of the body, its heat, and how it is transferred is required. Body heat is transferred to the surrounding air and surfaces by three natural processes which usually occur at the same time. These natural processes are convection, radiation, and evaporation.

Convection

The process of heat transfer by convection is based on two fundamental principles:

1. Heat flows from a hot to a cold surface.
2. Heat rises.

   Applying these principles to the body (Fig. 6-1):

1. As the body gives off heat, it will flow to the surrounding cooler air.
2. As the surrounding air warms, it moves in an upward direction.
3. As the warm air moves upward, cooler air is pulled in behind it; then the cooler air heats and flows upward and more cool air moves in as the cycle of convection continues.

Radiation

The process of heat transfer by radiation is based on one fundamental principle (Fig. 6-2):

   Heat flows from a hot to a cold surface.

But radiation is different from convection in one respect: no air movement is required to transfer the heat. In the process of radiation *heat rays* transfer the heat from the heat source, just as the sun's rays heat any surface they touch. The only difference is that, in this case, people are the heat source.

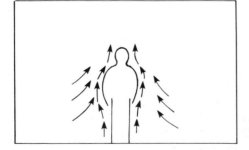

FIGURE 6-1   /   Convection

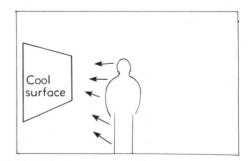

FIGURE 6-2   /   Radiation

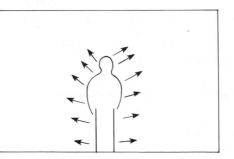

FIGURE 6-3 / Evaporation

Evaporation

The process of heat transfer by evaporation is based on one fundamental principle (Fig. 6-3):

Moisture evaporates from a warm surface.

The evaporation of moisture from a warm surface removes heat from the surface and cools it. As moisture is given off through the pores of the skin, it evaporates, removing heat from the body.

Air Temperature and Body Heat

The amount of body heat given off is affected by the air temperature surrounding it in the following ways:

1. *Convection.* Cool air increases the rate of heat loss by convection while warm air slows the rate.
2. *Radiation.* Cool air will lower the surface temperature of the surroundings, increasing the rate of heat loss by radiation; warm air raises the temperature of the surfaces, lowering the rate of heat loss due to radiation.
3. *Evaporation.* Generally, cool air increases the rate of evaporation while warm air reduces the rate; however, the rate of evaporation also depends on the relative humidity (the amount of moisture in the air) and the amount of air movement.

6-3   Space Conditions Affecting Comfort

The conditions within a space (room) which affect the comfort of the occupant, because they affect the rate of heat loss from the body, are:

1.   Room air temperature (also called dry-bulb temperature).

2.   Humidity or moisture content of the room.

3.   Surface temperatures of surrounding surfaces in the room (also called mean radiant temperature or MRT).

4.   Rate of air motion.

The occupant will feel comfortable when each of these is within a certain range.

The room air temperature affects the rate of convective and evaporative body heat losses. Since the room temperature will be below the body temperature of 98.6 °F, there will be convective heat loss from the body. Generally, the body feels most comfortable in a temperature range of 72° to 78 °F in the winter and 72° to 76 °F in the summer. Of course, the range of comfortable temperatures varies with each individual and is also affected by what the person is wearing and how active he is.

The humidity (moisture content) of the air affects the rate of evaporative heat loss from the body. A high humidity (often occurring in the summer) will cause the surrounding air to absorb less heat from the body, making the occupant feel warmer. A low humidity (often occurring in the winter) allows the air to absorb greater quantities of body heat, making the occupant feel cooler. As discussed later in the text, part of the design problem may be to lower the summer humidity and increase the winter humidity.

The surface temperatures of surrounding surfaces affect the radiant heat loss from the body. The surface temperatures in the room may vary widely. Windows and exterior walls will probably be cooler in the winter than interior walls and the furniture. The temperatures of the floors and ceilings will depend on the air temperature on the other side of the construction. In the winter, comfort can be increased by directing the flow of warm air over the colder surfaces. This is why most heating elements (registers, baseboard heaters) are located under a window.

The rate of air motion affects the transfer of body heat by convection and evaporation. In the summer increased air motion increases the evaporation rate of heat from the body to help keep it cool. This is why buildings without air conditioners use fans to increase the movement of the air on hot days. In the winter a slower rate of air motion is desired, or the occupants will feel cool due to evaporative heat loss. But even in the winter it is desirable to have a flow of air to keep the air from becoming stagnant.

6-4   Comfortable Environment

The building occupant will feel comfortable within certain ranges of air temperature, humidity, surface temperatures of surrounding surfaces, and air motion.

Experiments were made by ASHRAE (The American Society of Heating, Refrigerating and Air Conditioning Engineers) to determine the ranges of these variable conditions which feel comfortable to the occupants. The results were then tabulated and displayed in the "comfort chart" shown in Fig. 6-4. Generally, the results show that there is a definite link between humidity and air temperature when both air movement and surface temperatures remain constant. This air temperature-to-humidity relationship shows that to produce comfort, as the temperature increases, the humidity should decrease. This means that in the winter, it would be most economical to provide comfort with lower air temperature and higher humidity.

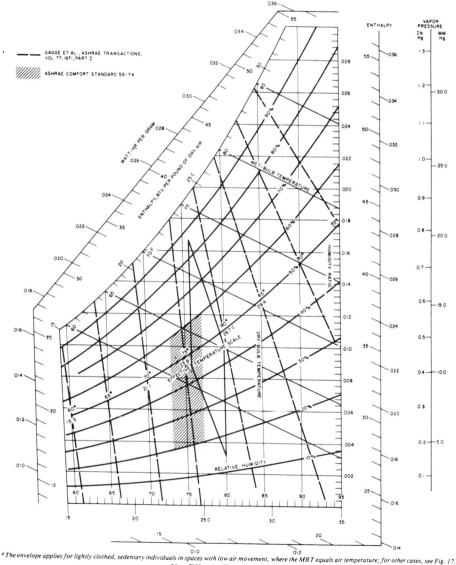

^aThe envelope applies for lightly clothed, sedentary individuals in spaces with low air movement, where the MRT equals air temperature; for other cases, see Fig. 17.

New Effective Temperature Scale (ET*)

Reprinted with permission from ASHRAE, Fundamentals Handbook, 1977

FIGURE 6-4 / Comfort chart

While the experiments and chart were done for central heating systems and have other design limitations noted by ASHRAE, they do show the important humidity/air temperature relationships. But first an explanation of how to read the chart will be helpful. The chart has five basic parts listed here and identified in Fig. 6-4:

1. Dry-bulb temperature (along the bottom).

2. Wet-bulb temperature (along the curve on the upper left side).

3. Relative humidity in percent (diagonally across the chart from the lower left to the upper right, with percentages in the upper right).

4. Effective temperature (ET)—the combination of dry-bulb and wet-bulb temperatures and humidity. It is this effective temperature which was measured to determine the comfort range of occupants in a space. (The effective temperature lines run from the upper left toward the lower right.)

5. The shaded and diamond-shaped areas show the range of conditions in which most people will feel comfortable. Such tests have indicated a 77° ET is most comfortable for lightly dressed, sedentary people (Fig. 6-5).

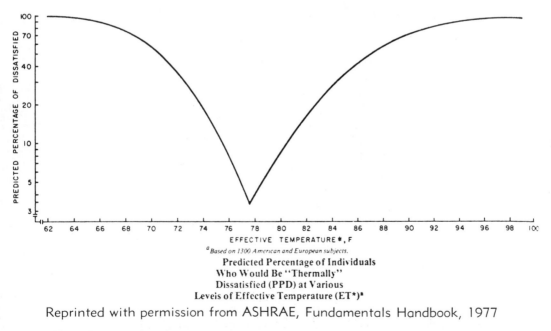

a Based on 1300 American and European subjects.

Predicted Percentage of Individuals
Who Would Be "Thermally"
Dissatisfied (PPD) at Various
Levels of Effective Temperature (ET*)ᵃ

Reprinted with permission from ASHRAE, Fundamentals Handbook, 1977

FIGURE 6-5 / Effective temperature

6-5   Winter Comfort

Use of the comfort chart to determine winter comfort is shown in Fig. 6-6.

1. Determine the most likely dry-bulb temperature for the space along the bottom of the chart.

2. From the dry-bulb temperature move up into the comfort areas on the chart.

3. Determine the range of relative humidity and effective temperature which will provide comfort to the most occupants.

It is this effective temperature that will be used to determine the various combinations of dry-bulb temperature and relative humidity which will provide comfort and still provide an effective temperature of about 75° to 77°F.

Using an effective temperature of 77°F and a dry-bulb (room air) temperature of 76°F, what relative humidity would be required? Use of the chart to determine various dry-bulb to humidity relationships is shown in Fig. 6-6.

1. Find the 76°F dry-bulb temperature along the bottom of the chart (point 1).

2. From point 1 move vertically up to the point where the 76°F dry-bulb line intersects the 77°F effective temperature line (point 4).

3. Read the relative humidity off as between the 49% and 50% lines, or about 50%.

So, with a winter heating condition and a 76°F dry-bulb reading, it is necessary to have about 50% relative humidity for the highest percentage of occupants to feel comfortable. Using a 73°–79°F dry-bulb temperature, about 45% relative humidity is necessary.

Homes with no humidity control will tend to have low relative humidity in the winter. For these homes the chart might best be used as follows: find the relative humidity in the house, follow along the relative humidity line to the 77°F effective temperature line and read off the required dry-bulb temperature. A thorough review of the chart and the relationship quickly shows that a lower room temperature is required when humidity is kept high. The monetary savings from a 5°F temperature reduction throughout a heating season are significant.

The approximate humidity inside a building can be found by putting a hygrometer (Fig. 6-7) in the space; it will show the percentage of humidity just as a thermometer shows temperature. Also, the chart in Fig. 6-8(a) shows the relationship of outside air temperature and relative humidity to heated interior air. For example, with an outside temperature of 45°F and a relative humidity of 80%, the indoor relative humidity will be only 30%. At 13% relative humidity, the chart in Fig. 6-6 indicates that a temperature of 78°F is required to feel comfortable.

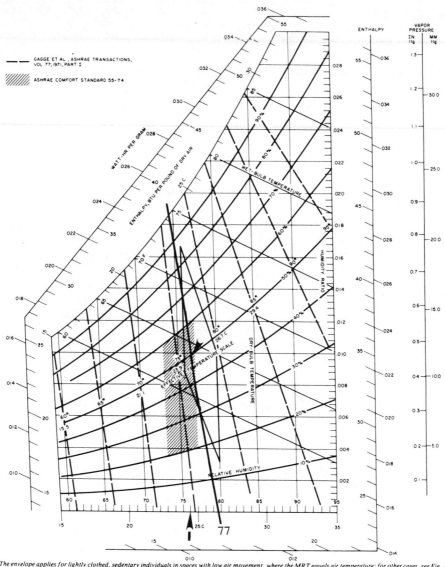

a The envelope applies for lightly clothed, sedentary individuals in spaces with low air movement, where the MRT equals air temperature; for other cases, see Fig. 17.

New Effective Temperature Scale (ET*)

Reprinted with permission from ASHRAE, Fundamentals Handbook, 1977

FIGURE 6-6 / Winter comfort

FIGURE 6-7 / Hygrometer
(humidity meter)

INDOOR RELATIVE HUMIDITY CONVERSION CHART

OUTDOOR RELATIVE HUMIDITY	−20°	−10°	−5°	0°	+5°	+10°	+15°	+20°	+25°	+30°	+35°	+40°	+45°	+50°
100%	2%	3%	4%	6%	7%	9%	11%	14%	17%	21%	26%	31%	38%	46%
95%	2%	3%	4%	5%	7%	8%	10%	13%	16%	20%	24%	30%	36%	44%
90%	2%	2%	4%	5%	6%	8%	10%	12%	15%	19%	23%	28%	34%	41%
85%	2%	2%	4%	5%	6%	8%	9%	12%	15%	18%	22%	27%	32%	39%
80%	2%	2%	4%	5%	6%	7%	9%	11%	14%	17%	20%	25%	30%	37%
75%	2%	2%	3%	4%	5%	7%	8%	10%	13%	16%	19%	23%	28%	36%
70%	1%	2%	3%	4%	5%	6%	8%	10%	12%	15%	18%	22%	26%	32%
65%	1%	2%	3%	4%	5%	6%	7%	8%	11%	14%	17%	20%	25%	30%
60%	1%	2%	3%	3%	4%	5%	7%	8%	10%	13%	15%	19%	23%	28%
55%	1%	1%	2%	3%	4%	5%	6%	8%	9%	12%	14%	17%	21%	25%
50%	1%	1%	2%	3%	4%	4%	6%	7%	9%	10%	13%	16%	19%	23%
45%	1%	1%	2%	3%	3%	4%	5%	6%	8%	9%	12%	14%	17%	21%
40%	1%	1%	2%	2%	3%	4%	4%	6%	7%	8%	10%	12%	15%	18%
35%	1%	1%	2%	2%	3%	3%	4%	5%	6%	7%	9%	11%	13%	16%
30%	1%	1%	1%	2%	2%	3%	3%	4%	5%	6%	8%	9%	11%	14%
25%	1%	1%	1%	1%	2%	2%	3%	3%	4%	5%	6%	8%	10%	12%
20%	+%	1%	1%	1%	1%	2%	2%	3%	3%	4%	5%	6%	8%	10%
15%	+%	+%	1%	1%	1%	1%	2%	2%	3%	3%	4%	5%	6%	7%
10%	+%	+%	+%	1%	1%	1%	1%	1%	2%	2%	3%	3%	4%	5%
5%	+%	+%	+%	+%	+%	+%	1%	1%	1%	1%	1%	1%	2%	2%
0%	0%	0%	0%	0%	0%	0%	0%	0%	0%	0%	0%	0%	0%	0%

OUTDOOR TEMPERATURE

To find indoor relative humidity when outside air is heated to 70 degrees, find outdoor RH at left and outdoor temperature along the bottom. Indoor RH that results in where lines cross.

FIGURE 6-8a / Humidity conversion

It becomes obvious that it is often necessary to add moisture to the air in the winter. Humidity can be introduced into the space by installing humidifiers in the ducts of forced air systems and by placing large portable humidifiers in spaces with water, steam, or electric baseboard or panel heat.

6-6   Summer Comfort

Summer comfort ranges can also be found on the comfort chart (Fig. 6-4).

1.   Determine the most likely dry-bulb temperature for the space along the bottom of the chart.

2.   Follow the dry-bulb line from that point on the chart where it enters the comfort areas.

This is the effective temperature at which the largest percentage of occupants feel comfortable, and it is used to determine the various comfortable combinations of dry-bulb temperature and relative humidity.

As in the winter, a range of about 45% relative humidity (Fig. 6-8b) and a dry-bulb range of 76° to 80°F is required for the highest percentage of occupants to feel comfortable. As the relative humidity increases above 45%, lower dry-bulb temperatures are needed for comfort. At 75%, the maximum dry-bulb would be about 77°F (Fig. 6-9).

During the summer, homes with no humidity control will tend to have high relative humidity. Yet during the summer, a low humidity will make higher temperatures feel comfortable and save cooling costs (where used). However, humidity control is often more expensive than cooling the air.

6-7   Overall Comfort

The overall comfort will still vary from person to person, as well as with air velocity, types of heating and cooling systems, and types and materials of construction.

Women will generally prefer higher effective temperatures than men. Similarly, older people prefer higher effective temperatures, as do people who live in southern climates. Of course, whether a person will be comfortable or not also depends on the type of clothing the individual wears and how active he is. A person with a sweater on who is cleaning the house will need a lower effective temperature than someone with a short-sleeved shirt or blouse on who is watching television.

The suggested inside winter dry-bulb temperatures for a wide variety of spaces are shown in Fig. 6-10. Those spaces in which people will be relatively inactive, such as classrooms and hospital rooms, will require higher temperatures than spaces in which people will be active.

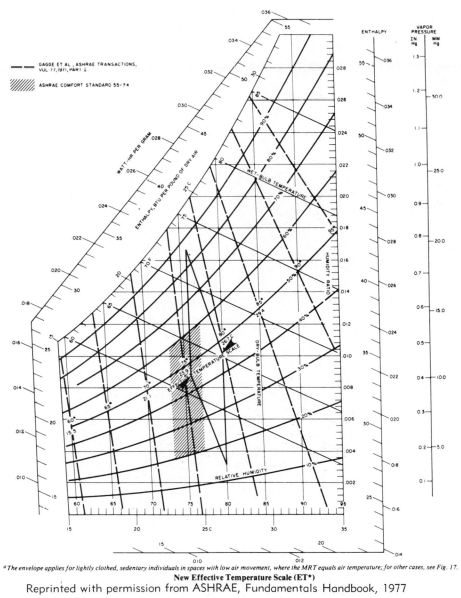

^a The envelope applies for lightly clothed, sedentary individuals in spaces with low air movement, where the MRT equals air temperature; for other cases, see Fig. 17.

New Effective Temperature Scale (ET*)

Reprinted with permission from ASHRAE, Fundamentals Handbook, 1977

FIGURE 6-8b / Humidity limits

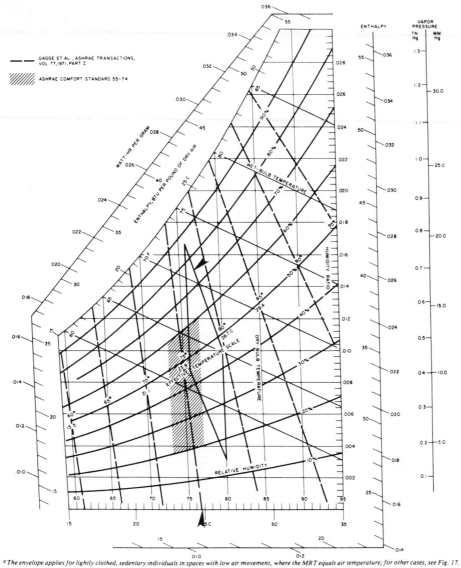

a The envelope applies for lightly clothed, sedentary individuals in spaces with low air movement, where the MRT equals air temperature; for other cases, see Fig. 17.

New Effective Temperature Scale (ET*)

Reprinted with permission from ASHRAE, Fundamentals Handbook, 1977

FIGURE 6-9   /   Summer comfort

Type of Building	F
SCHOOLS—	
Classrooms.	72–74
Assembly rooms.	68–72
Gymnasiums.	55–65
Toilets and baths.	70
Wardrobe and locker rooms.	65–68
Kitchens.	66
Dining and lunch rooms.	65–70
Playrooms.	60–65
Natatoriums.	75
HOSPITALS—	
Private rooms.	72–74
Private rooms (surgical).	70–80
Operating rooms.	70–95
Wards.	72–74
Kitchens and laundries.	66
Toilets.	68
Bathrooms.	70–80
THEATERS—	
Seating space.	68–72
Lounge rooms.	68–72
Toilets.	68
HOTELS—	
Bedrooms and baths.	75
Dining rooms.	72
Kitchens and laundries.	66
Ballrooms.	65–68
Toilets and service rooms.	68
HOMES.	73–75
STORES.	65–68

FIGURE 6-10 / Inside winter dry-bulb temperatures

In the summer, comfort is also greatly affected by the relationship of indoor–outdoor temperatures. This is especially true in spaces which people occupy for short periods of time. A person who is in his residence or office for a long period of time becomes used to a 75 °F temperature and is comfortable in it. But when a person occupies a space for short durations, generally up to 1 hr, he will be most comfortable if there is just a 10° to 15 °F difference between the outside and the inside temperatures. So, if it is 95 °F outside, it should be about 80 °F inside stores and shops for a person to feel comfortable. The common practice in stores, shops, grocery markets, etc., of setting their cooling at a 68° to 70 °F inside temperature does not make for comfortable conditions. This is obvious when you see the number of people who must take sweaters into grocery stores, fast food restaurants, and other stores and shops during the summer. Also, notice that the customers who didn't bring sweaters are almost always shivering. Yet, it is comfortable to some of those working there since it is likely that there is a low temperature/high humidity relationship.

Also, no matter how much heat is introduced into a space, it is very difficult for the occupant to feel comfortable if he is sitting next to a very cold surface, such as a window. The combination of the body heat loss on the side of the body nearest the window and the cold air coming through any cracks around the window makes a difficult situation. In one case, the temperature in a person's office was turned up to 76 °F and he still felt uncomfortable. By rearranging the office so that there was an interior wall at his back instead of a window, he felt comfortable at 72 °F.

6-8   Air Conditioning

Whenever the term *air conditioning* is used, almost everyone automatically thinks of a cool building on a hot day. However, in a technical sense, air conditioning means exactly what it implies—conditioning the air inside a space; this means heating, cooling, humidity control, ventilation, filtering, and any other conditioning that may be required. While realizing that manufacturers will continue to sell air coolers as air conditioners and that when a client says he wants (or doesn't want) air conditioning, he means cooling, the technician and the engineer must be aware of the real meaning of the term.

Modern building design has increased the need for air conditioning since there is an increased tendency to build glass buildings which don't have a window that opens (no operable sash). Even in northern states, which have only short periods of warm weather, total air conditioning is often required since there are no windows to open for fresh air and ventilation.

6-9   Ventilation

Many times it is necessary to ventilate (introduce outside air into a space) in order for the occupants to be comfortable. This is particularly true in any spaces where smoking is permitted and where dust or fumes are present.

Ventilation requirements, as set by ASHRAE, are shown in Fig. 6-11, and many times the codes in force also have ventilation requirements. Rooms with exterior exposures, windows, and exterior doors and with low occupancy may get all the ventilation they need through air leakage around the windows and doors. Rooms without exterior exposures commonly need ventilation so they will not become stale with cigarette smoke and other odors.

VENTILATION DESIGN CRITERIA

Functional Area	Air Changes per Hour	Cfm/ Person	Functional Area	Air Changes per Hour	Cfm/ Person
Anesthesia, hospital	8-12	—	Kitchens	10-30	—
Animal room	12-16	—	Laundries	10-60	—
Auditorium	10-20	10	Libraries	15-25	10
Autopsy, hospital	8-12	10	Locker room	2-15	—
Bakery	20-60	—	Machine shop	8-12	—
Bowling alley	15-30	30	Mechanical equipment	8-12	—
Churches	15-25	5	Media room, hospital	6-10	—
Cystoscopy, hospital	8-10	20	Nursery	10-15	—
Classroom	10-30	40	Offices	6-20	10
Conference	25-35	—	Operating room, hospital	10-15	—
Corridors	3-10	—	Ozalid room	8-12	—
Delivery room, hospital	8-12	—	Paint finishing	18-22	—
Dairies	5-15	—	Radiology	6-10	—
Dishwashing	30-60	—	Restaurant (dining room)	6-20	10
Drycleaning	20-40	—	Retail stores	18-22	10
Foundries	5-20	—	Residences	5-20	—
Gymnasiums	—	1½ sq ft	Telephone equipment	6-10	—
Garages	6-30	—	Traffic and flight cont.	18-22	10
Hydrotherapy, hospital	6-10	—	Toilets	8-20	—
Isolation ward	6-10	—	Transmitter, receiver and electronic	10° rise	—
Janitor and cleaning	8-12	—	Welding	18-22	—

NOTE—Individual design conditions may cause variation in these values of considerable magnitude.

FIGURE 6-11 / Ventilation

Many buildings with forced air systems leave the fan on even when the heating and cooling system is not operating. This provides ventilation throughout the building and reduces the possibility of stagnant air layers in a room.

Questions

6-1. Sketch and label the three natural processes by which body heat is transferred.

6-2. Briefly describe the three natural processes by which body heat is transferred and how they affect comfort.

6-3. In what ways does the surrounding air temperature affect the amount of body heat given off?

6-4. What are the three space conditions which affect the comfort of the occupant of the space?

6-5. What effect does humidity have on the comfort of a body?

6-6. What is meant by *effective temperature* in a relation to comfort?

6-7 What are the components used to determine the effective temperature, and how are these components related to each other in the summer and in the winter?

6-8. Why is humidity control important in most homes during the heating season?

6-9. How may humidity be increased in a building?

6-10. What effect does humidity have on summer comfort?

Chapter 7
Heat Loss and Heat Gain

7-1   Heat Loss

The amount of heat lost from the building to the surrounding air will determine the size of the heating plant, the size of the heat convectors (radiators, ducts, etc.), and the heating cost per year. The amount of heat loss is measured in BTU (British Thermal Units); a BTU is defined as *the amount of heat required to raise 1 pound of water 1 degree Fahrenheit.* Heat loss will depend on the type of construction assembly, the types of doors and windows used, and the climate in the geographical area where the building is being constructed.

7-2   Factors in Calculating Heat Loss

Heat is lost from a space by transmission, infiltration and ventilation.

1.   Before the heat loss for a building can be calculated, the places at which the losses occur must be identified. Since the heat inside will flow to colder areas, the heat will pass through walls, floors, ceilings, doors, and windows.

2.   The heat loss is calculated separately for each room. Therefore, it is neces-
     sary to determine each type of assembly of materials used.

3.   For each room, the area of each type of material assembly which has one
     side exposed to the inside of the room and the other side exposed to a lower
     temperature space—such as the exterior, attic, basement, or crawl space or a
     colder room such as a garage or enclosed porch which is not heated—must
     be calculated. This heat loss is referred to as *heat transmission.* Calculations
     for heat transmission loss are shown in this chapter.

4.   In every building, no matter how well constructed, there is a certain amount
     of cold air which leaks into the building, referred to as *infiltration heat loss,*
     and an equal amount of hot air which leaks out. Most commonly infiltration
     will occur around doors and windows. The tight construction of the building
     will save the building owner a considerable amount of money over the life of
     the building. Some suggestions to reduce infiltration heat loss are discussed
     in Sec. 7-9; calculations for infiltration heat loss are also shown in Sec. 7-9.

5.   *Ventilation* is the introduction of fresh air into the building, or parts of the
     building, at a controlled rate. Many times the air used to ventilate the build-
     ing is heated before it is introduced into the building, and this must be con-
     sidered in the design of the system.

7-3   Resistance Ratings

Since heat passes through different materials at different rates, each material is
considered to have a certain resistance to the flow of heat through it. In general,
the heavier and denser the material, the less resistance it has to the flow of heat
through it and the lower its resitance (R) value is; for lighter, less dense materials,
the higher the R value, the better its insulating value. For example, a 6-in.-thick
poured concrete wall has an R value of about 0.48 while a 1-in. thickness of cork
has an R value of about 3.70. Increasing the thickness of the material also affects
the insulating value of the material in proportion to its original value. For example, doubling the 6-in. concrete wall to 12 in. will double the R value from 0.48 to
0.96. Doubling the cork thickness from 1 in. to 2 in. will double its R value from
3.70 to 7.40. To determine the heat flow of an assembly of materials (U value), it is
first necessary to find the R value for each material and total them.

The resistance listings for most materials can be found in Fig. 7-58 and 7-63.
In addition, the U values for some of the assemblies of materials commonly used
in construction are also listed in Fig. 7-63. When materials not listed here are encountered, the heat flow characteristics will have to be determined from the manufacturer.

There are four values used to measure the heat resistance of a material; they
are the U, R, C, and k values. Each of the values is related, and the designer must
understand the relationships:

1. The k value of the material used in the construction measures heat flow conductance in terms of how effective it is *per inch of thickness* (t).

2. The C (conductance) value of the material measures the material's ability to conduct heat in terms of how effective it is for the *thickness being used.* The more effective the material, the lower the C value ($C = k \div t$).

3. The R (resistance) value of the material measures heat flow resistance in terms of how effective it is for the *thickness being used.* (This term is inversely related to the C value.) The more effective the material, the higher the R value ($R = 1 \div C$).

4. The U value of the entire assembly of materials measures heat flow resistance in terms of how effective it is for the type and thickness of the materials used in the total assembly ($U = 1 \div R$).

Example

To show the relationship of the values we will use a 2-in.-thick piece of polystyrene foam insulation (Fig. 7-1). Polystyrene foam has a k value of 0.26 per inch of thickness. Since it is 2 in. thick, its insulating value is given as a C value as 0.13 (or one-half the k value). These values are directly proportional to each other, based on the thickness of material used. The *lower* these values, the better the material is as a heat insulator. The R value is equal to 1 divided by the C value. So for the 2-in.-thick polystyrene foam, $R = 1/C = 1 \div 0.13 = 7.7$. This indicates the resistance value of that particular material.

It is quite unlikely that a wall would be built only of 2-in. polystyrene foam; this insulating material is often used with other materials, such as metal facings, masonry, and concrete. For this example, assume that the wall is made of 6-in. poured concrete, gravel aggregate, 2-in. polystyrene foam and ⅜-in. gypsum board (Fig. 7-2). From Fig. 7-58, the resistance values listed are:

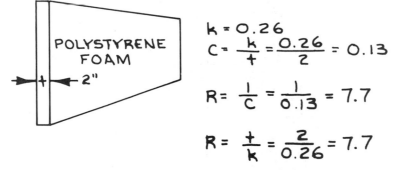

FIGURE 7-1   /   Heat flow terms

⅜-in. gypsum board	0.32
6-in. concrete, gravel (0.08 per in.)	0.48
2-in. polystyrene foam (3.45 per in.)	7.70
Outside air film (see Sec. 7-4)	0.17
Inside air film (see Sec. 7-4)	0.68
	———
Total resistance R	9.35

Heat flow from the interior of the building to the cooler exterior is determined by multiplying the heat flow characteristics of a given assembly of materials (referred to as the U *value*) times the area (A) of the material involved times the difference between the inside temperature desired and the average low temperature on the other side of the construction (referred to as ΔT and given in °F). In equation form:

$$U \times A \times \Delta T = BTU/hr\ (Btuh)$$

In the above equation, the U value is the most important item since it can vary so much, depending on the material assembly used. With any given A and ΔT, the number of Btuh required will vary in direct relationship with the U value for the assembly of materials used. The U value is determined by adding the R

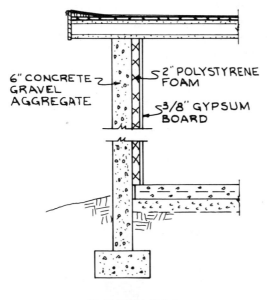

6" CONCRETE
GRAVEL
AGGREGATE

2" POLYSTYRENE
FOAM

3/8" GYPSUM
BOARD

SECTION

FIGURE 7-2   /   *Wall section*

values of each material plus the resistance to heat flow caused by the flow of air inside and outside the building and then dividing 1 by the total R ($U = 1 \div R = 1/R$).

$$U = 1/R = 1 \div 9.35 = 0.107 \text{ (use 0.11)}$$

The U value must be determined for walls, floors, and ceilings and for each material or assembly of materials used in the construction.

The area used in the formula is the *net exposed area* of the material assembly being considered. If a room has two different material assemblies (Fig. 7-3), each must be considered separately since each has a different U value. Likewise, the area of windows and doors must be deducted from the total area to obtain the net exposed wall area of the particular material assembly being considered. Assuming that the room being designed has two exposed walls 8 ft high (Fig. 7-4) with a total of 36 lineal ft, this would give a gross square footage of 288. Deduct the two 3 ft × 4 ft windows for a net exposed wall area of 288 sq ft − 24 sq ft = 264 sq ft.

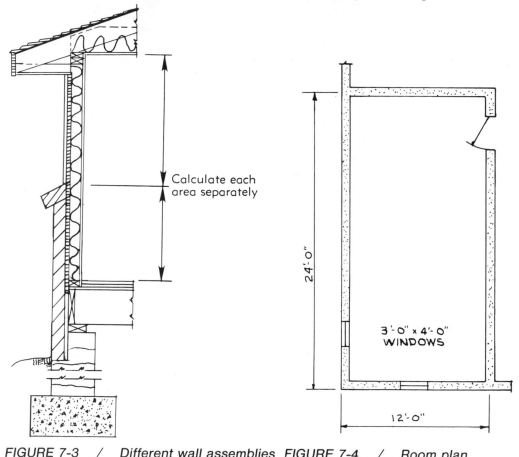

Calculate each area separately

24'-0"

12'-0"

3'-0" x 4'-0" WINDOWS

FIGURE 7-3 / Different wall assemblies FIGURE 7-4 / Room plan

The ΔT is the difference between the inside temperature desired and the temperature on the cold side of the construction in °F. If the cold side of the construction is the outside air, then the average low temperature expected during the year is used. This varies considerably, depending on the geographical area of construction. Some typical outside design temperatures for various areas are listed in Fig. 7-66. Assuming an indoor design temperature of 70°F, if the building is being built in Rutland, Vermont, with an outside design temperature of −10°F, the ΔT will be 80°F (Fig. 7-5). If the same building is constructed in Raleigh, North Carolina, the outside design temperature is 20°F and the ΔT will be 50°F. Assuming that similar buildings are being built in Raleigh and Rutland, the heat loss for the walls in that one room would be:

Raleigh $U \times A \times \Delta T = 0.11 \times 264 \times 50 = 1{,}452$ Btuh

Rutland $U \times A \times \Delta T = 0.11 \times 264 \times 80 = 2{,}323$ Btuh

It is important that the designer become proficient in calculating U values for various assemblies of materials. The flow of heat through any barrier—in this case, the construction of the walls—is resisted by the materials used for the construction, the inside and outside air films, and any air spaces left. It is, therefore, important that the designer carefully review the drawings, especially wall sections and details, to determine what materials will be used on the project. In addition, he should check to be certain that the materials that he is *told* are being specified actually *are*. For example, the wall section (Fig. 7-6) may show 2 in. of rigid insulation. The designer must also know exactly what type of rigid insulation is going to be used. Then he must also be certain that the material he based his calculations on is actually specified on the project and, even further, that no material substitution is allowed. This is because if the rigid insulation in Fig. 7-6 is urethane, it is about twice as effective as polystyrene foam insulation.

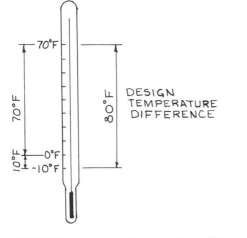

FIGURE 7-5   /   Calculating ΔT

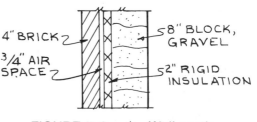

FIGURE 7-6   /   Wall section

Example

Problem: Determine the resistance values for each of the materials in the wall section shown in Fig. 7-7.

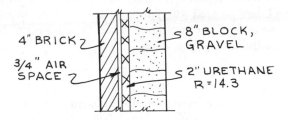

4" BRICK

3/4" AIR SPACE

8" BLOCK, GRAVEL

2" URETHANE R = 14.3

FIGURE 7-7 / Wall section

First, list all of the materials of construction; then list their resistance values next to them. When necessary, convert the C and k values to R values.

$$R = 1/C \quad \text{and} \quad R = t/k$$

(t = thickness of the material, in inches)

The materials and R values for the wall section shown in Fig. 7-7 are indicated in Fig. 7-8.

```
4" BRICK              0.44
8" BLOCK,GRAVEL       1.11
2" URETHANE          14.30
```

FIGURE 7-8 / Material R values

7-4   Air Films

Both inside a room and outside the building, there is a movement of air over the surfaces, creating a film of air which causes the air and wall to exchange convective heat. This air film helps resist the flow of heat through the construction. The air film's resistance value depends first on whether it is an *inside* air film (inside the room) or an *outside* air film (on the outside of the wall).

The resistance values of inside air films are shown in Fig. 7-59. These values are based on still air (no wind), and proper selection from the table is based on:

1.   Surface position or orientation. (Is it a vertical wall, horizontal ceiling or floor?)

2.   Direction of heat flow—for a wall, horizontal; for a ceiling, upward; for a floor over a basement, downward. (In what direction is the heat flowing in the room in which the heat loss is being calculated?)

3.   Surface emissivity. (Is the surface reflective or not? Most surfaces used in buildings, such as gypsum board painted with flat paint and concrete block, are not reflective. Use the nonreflective or reflective value, depending on the wall finish to be used in the building.) (Fig. 7-62)

Example

Given: For the wall section in Fig. 7-7, the interior wall is gypsum board which will be nonreflective (from Fig. 7-62, an emissivity value of 0.90).

Problem: Using Fig. 7-59, find the resistance value of the air film.

The resistance value of this inside air film—which is for a vertical, nonreflective wall, with horizontal heat flow—is taken from Fig. 7-59 as $R = 0.68$. This value is included with the tabulation of material resistance values from Fig. 7-8 and combined here (Fig. 7-9):

4" BRICK	0.44
8" BLOCK, GRAVEL	1.11
2" URETHANE	14.30
→ INSIDE AIR FILM	0.68

FIGURE 7-9   /   *Inside air film resistance*

The resistance values of exterior air films are shown in Fig. 7-60. Proper selection of the R value is based on:

1.   Winter: 15 mph air velocity; use $R = 0.17$.

2.   Summer: 7½ mph air velocity; use $R = 0.25$.

This value is now included with the tabulation of resistance values for materials and inside air film (Fig. 7-9) and combined here (Fig. 7-10):

4" BRICK	0.44
8" BLOCK, GRAVEL	1.11
2" URETHANE	14.30
INSIDE AIR FILM	0.68
→ OUTSIDE AIR FILM	0.17

FIGURE 7-10   /   *Outside air film resistance*

7-5 Air Spaces

Many times an assembly of materials will have an air space left between the materials. For example, there is usually an air space between the brick veneer on a building and the material behind it. A review of the wall section in Fig. 7-7 shows that it calls for a ¾-in. air space. These air spaces also resist the flow of heat and have an R or a C value.

The resistance values of air spaces are shown in Fig. 7-61. Proper selection of an R value from the table is based on:

1. Position of air space (horizontal, 45° slope, vertical—for this wall, it is vertical).

2. Direction of heat flow (up, horizontal, down—for this wall, the heat flow is horizontal).

3. Air space thickness (thicknesses other than those listed may be interpolated from the values given; for thickness greater than 3.5 in., use the 3.5-in. value).

4. Value of E (emissivity) (Are the surfaces on each side of the wall space reflective or not? For nonreflective materials, use $E = 0.82$; for reflective materials, such as aluminum foil, use $E = 0.05$. In this case, there are only nonreflective surfaces.).

Example

For the ¾-in. air space in the wall section (Fig. 7-7), with a vertical air space, horizontal flow of heat, and nonreflective surfaces, the resistance value R is 0.94. This value is included in the tabulation of material resistance values from Fig. 7-10 and combined here (Fig. 7-11):

```
4" BRICK              0.44
8" BLOCK, GRAVEL      1.11
2" URETHANE          14.30
INSIDE AIR FILM       0.68
OUTSIDE AIR FILM      0.17
→ 3/4" AIR SPACE      0.94
```

FIGURE 7-11 / Air space resistance

7-6 Total Resistance Values

With all of the materials, air films, and air spaces listed with their appropriate R values, the next step is to total the R values of the wall and convert this total to the equivalent U value. The total resistance value of the wall is 17.60 with a U value of 0.057, as calculated and shown in Fig. 7-12:

$$
\begin{array}{ll}
\text{4" BRICK} & 0.44 \\
\text{8" BLOCK, GRAVEL} & 1.11 \\
\text{2" URETHANE} & 14.30 \\
\text{INSIDE AIR FILM} & 0.68 \\
\text{OUTSIDE AIR FILM} & 0.17 \\
\text{3/4" AIR SPACE} & \underline{0.94} \\
\text{TOTAL R} & 17.64
\end{array}
$$

$$
U = \frac{1}{R} = \frac{1}{17.64} = 0.057
$$

FIGURE 7-12   /   Calculate total R and U values

7-7   Calculating *R* and *U* Values

The method described in Secs. 7-3 through 7-6 of combining the *R* values for each separate material, for the inside and outside air films, and for any air spaces gives the total *R* value of the assembly. It is this total *R* of the assembly which is used to calculate the *U* value for the particular assembly and is used in the basic heat loss formula:

$$
U \times A \times \Delta T = \text{Btuh}
$$

To become proficient in the use of the tables and to be certain that the basic relationships of the various *R* values are understood, examples for floors and ceilings are given next. Keep in mind that:

1.   The higher the *R* value, the more effective the material at resisting the flow of heat.
2.   The higher the *R* value, the lower the heat loss. The lower the heat loss, the less expensive the entire installation in terms of the yearly fuel bills.

Example

Problem: Calculate the *R* and *U* values for the wall assembly shown in Fig. 7-13.

The tabulations are shown in Fig. 7-14.

Example

Problem: Calculate the *R* and *U* values for the roof assembly shown in Fig. 7-15.

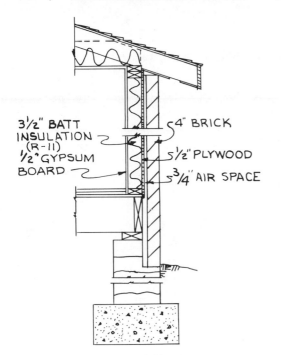

3½" BATT
INSULATION
(R-11)
½" GYPSUM
BOARD

4" BRICK

½" PLYWOOD

¾" AIR SPACE

FIGURE 7-13 / *Wall assembly*

½" PLYWOOD	0.62
4" BRICK	0.44
3½" BATT INSUL.	11.00
½" GYPSUM BOARD	0.45
INSIDE AIR FILM	0.68
OUTSIDE AIR FILM	0.17
¾" AIR SPACE	0.94
TOTAL R	14.30

$$U = \frac{1}{R} = \frac{1}{14.30} = 0.07$$

FIGURE 7-14 / *R and U calculations*

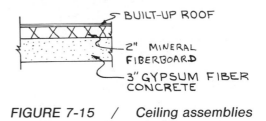

BUILT-UP ROOF

2" MINERAL FIBERBOARD

3" GYPSUM FIBER CONCRETE

FIGURE 7-15 / *Ceiling assemblies*

The tabulations are also shown in Fig. 7-16. Note that the *R* values for the inside and outside air films are different from those used for the wall assembly and that there is no air space.

3" GYP. CONC.	1.80
2" FIBERBOARD INSUL.	5.88
BUILT-UP ROOF	0.33
OUTSIDE AIR FILM	0.17
INSIDE AIR FILM	0.61
TOTAL R	8.79

$$U = \frac{1}{R} = \frac{1}{8.79} = 0.114$$

FIGURE 7-16 / *Ceiling R and U calculations*

Example

Problem: Calculate the *R* and *U* values for the floor assembly shown in Fig. 7-17.

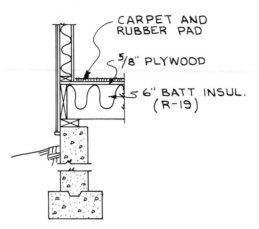

FIGURE 7-17 / *Floor assembly*

Note that the tabulation (Fig. 7-18) shows *R* values for outside and inside air films different from those used for the wall and roof assemblies.

CARPET, RUBBER PAD	1.23
5/8" PLYWOOD	0.77
6" BATT INSUL.	19.00
INSIDE AIR FILM	0.92
OUTSIDE AIR FILM	0.92
TOTAL R	22.84

$$U = \frac{1}{R} = \frac{1}{22.84} = 0.044$$

FIGURE 7-18 / *Floor R and U calculations*

In reviewing the various assemblies, it becomes obvious that as more and better insulation is used, the *R* values of the other materials in the assembly become relatively less important.

Example

In Fig. 7-12, the total *R* value is 17.64 with a *U* value of 0.057. If the concrete block were changed to lightweight block, the *R* value of the block would change from 1.11 to 2.00. This would cause the total *R* to change from 17.64 to 18.53 and the *U* value to change from 0.057 to 0.054. In terms of real savings, this is extremely little and unnecessary.

The designer must be able to see that small changes in the *R* value will have little effect on overall *R* value, on *U* value, and on subsequent heat loss of the building. This is particularly important when reading technical "sales sheets" and talking to materials salesmen. As an exammple of what is meant, on one residential project, it was proposed to use ½-in.-thick asphalt-impregnated fiberboard instead of ½-in.-thick plywood over the 2 × 4 studs because the fiberboard has a higher insulation value. A review of Fig. 7-58 quickly shows that:

½-in. sheathing (vegetable fiberboard)	*R* = 1.32
½-in. plywood	*R* = 0.62

Now, while the point could be made that the impregnated sheathing is twice as resistant as the plywood, it must be judged in relation to the entire wall.

A review of the tabulations (Fig. 7-14) indicates that the wall with ½-in. plywood has an *R* of 14.30; if ½-in. impregnated sheathing were used, the *R* value would increase by 0.69 (1.32 − 0.63) to 15.00 (Fig. 7-19)—about a 5% increase in the total *R*. There may be other reasons to use the impregnated sheathing (because it is less expensive, for example), but not because it is a better insulation.

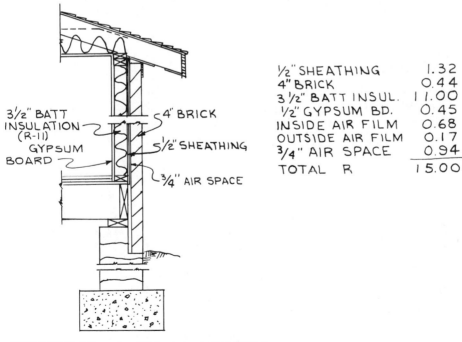

½" SHEATHING	1.32
4" BRICK	0.44
3 ½" BATT INSUL.	11.00
½" GYPSUM BD.	0.45
INSIDE AIR FILM	0.68
OUTSIDE AIR FILM	0.17
¾" AIR SPACE	0.94
TOTAL R	15.00

FIGURE 7-19 / *Material comparisons*

The designer (as well as the architect, engineer, and owner) is subjected to this type of logic much of the time, and newspapers, magazines, television, and direct mailings send this type of logic into every household and business.

There is one other type of R value information that the designer should be aware of. To illustrate the type of analysis required, the following example has been prepared (this is a fictitious example and not taken from any manufacturer's brochure or data sheet):

Heat flow: Horizontal
R value:
¾-in. to 4-in. air space + ½-in. impregnated fiber sheathing board = 2.24

Now, this in itself is not misrepresentation since the R value would be 2.24. But the R value of the board is 1.32 and the air space is about 0.92, so any comparison of materials should be based on the R of the 1.32, not 2.24. Also, the designer who is familiar with construction would realize that in the brick veneer construction shown in Fig. 7-20, the air space would easily be available; but the wood frame construction, with plywood panel facing, shown in Fig. 7-21 would not have an air space at the sheathing unless special construction methods were used. This is because R-11 insulation is 3½ in. thick, filling the entire space of the 2 x 4 studs; the sheathing is attached to the studs and the exterior finish material attached to the sheathing and studs. The only way there would be a ¾- to 4-in. air space is to use 2¼-in.-thick batt insulation which as an R of about 7.

7-8   *U* Value Selection

The U values for several wall, ceiling (roof), and floor assemblies are already calculated and are listed in Fig. 7-63. Once the designer understands the relationship of the R values that make up the assembly, he should make use of the tables to save time. It is important to understand this basic relationship in order to under-

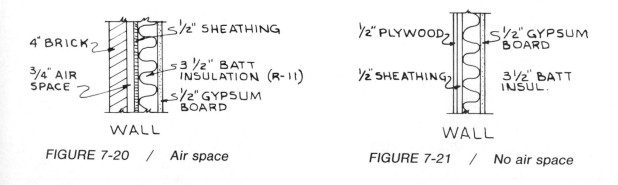

FIGURE 7-20   /   Air space   FIGURE 7-21   /   No air space

stand what happens as materials are substituted and to understand what others in the trade, especially salesmen, architects, draftsmen, and engineers, are talking about.

In using the tables for U values, be certain that the proper table is selected and that the U value used is for the assembly of materials being used. The U values for various assemblies of materials are often provided by manufacturers in their catalogs and engineering data sheets. The designer often makes use of such information, but he must check the origin of the tests to determine if the values listed are reputable. Even so, the designer should carefully review the material assembly to be certain that it is the same as that being used on the project. A typical example of this type of information is shown in Fig. 7-22. In this case, the manufacturer of an insulation for use in the cores of block has presented U values in the sales brochure. Since the material, in this form, is new to the market, there are no tabulated data in ASHRAE publications or elsewhere on the use of materials. So the company had tests run at a university in accordance with approved testing procedures (American Society for Testing and Materials, ASTM C236-66). The values shown are straightforward and easy to read.

Test results.

Thermal conductance (C) measurements were made by means of the guarded hot box test (ASTM designation C236-66) at the University of Rhode Island Department of Chemical Engineering.

The tests showed that lightweight concrete masonry units conductance decreased 58% when KORFIL insulation was used.

Coefficient of transmission through masonry walls

Type of wall	U-factors BTU/hr-ft^2-°F	
	No KORFIL insulation	KORFIL insulation
8" two-core lightweight block	0.33	0.16
8" two-core med. weight block	0.43	0.17
12" two-core lightweight block	0.31	0.14
12" two-core med. weight block	0.38	0.15
4" face brick plus 1" air cavity and 8" lightweight block	0.26	0.13

FIGURE 7-22 / U values   Courtesy of Korfil International

7-9   Infiltration Heat Loss Factors

Air leaks into a building through cracks around windows and doors, between the foundation wall and the sill plate, and at many of the connections between walls made of different types of materials. This air leakage is caused by a combination of the wind pressure on the building and the difference in temperature between the inside and the outside. As the wind velocity increases, the amount of air leakage also increases.

The infiltration heat loss will be calculated by multiplying the lineal feet (*LF*) of window and door infiltration cracks or crackage (as outlined in this section) times *Q*, the air volume (in cubic feet per hour, cfh) times 0.018 times the design temperature difference (Δ*T*).

$$\text{Btuh} = LF \times Q \times 0.018 \times \Delta T$$

Window air infiltration is determined primarily by the type of window. The lineal feet of infiltration through which air leaks occur is measured by finding the total length of crackage in the window parts for the type of window used. For example, a double-hung window (Fig. 7-23) is made so that both the top and bottom sash open, and this means that air can infiltrate around the entire perimeter of the window as well as the space where the stiles meet. For a 3-ft-wide x 5-ft-high double-hung wood window, the lineal feet of infiltration will be three times the width (*w*) plus two times the length (*l*) or

$3w + 2l = 3(3 \text{ ft}) + 2(5 \text{ ft}) = 9 \text{ ft} + 10 \text{ ft} = 19$ lineal ft of infiltration cracks

There are two general guidelines to be followed regarding what is measured:

1. For a room with *one wall* of exterior exposure, list the totals for each type of window and door *separately*. Since different types of windows and doors have different infiltration factors (IF), it is important to list each type separately.

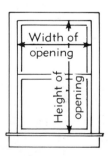

FIGURE 7-23   /   Infiltration dimensions

2. For a room with *two or more* exterior walls, only the wall with the most infiltration is used. Since the infiltration factor (amount of infiltration) will vary considerably for different types of doors and windows, it will be necessary to total the infiltration for each wall separately. The amount of infiltration loss will be taken as the total loss of the wall having the most loss *or* one-half of the total infiltration, whichever is more.

This approach to two or more exposed walls is taken because as air infiltrates into a building it must also be leaving at the same rate (otherwise, the building would blow up like a balloon). So, while a portion of the crackage allows air to infiltrate, the air is escaping through other cracks. Typically, the cold air infiltrates on whatever side the wind is blowing.

The air volume (Q) is a measure of the amount of outdoor air entering the building per lineal foot of crack. This value will vary considerably, depending on the type and material of the windows and doors, whether they fit well or poorly, and whether they are weatherstripped or not. Typical air volume values are listed in Fig. 7-64, and the appropriate values will be used in the infiltration loss formula (Btuh = $LF \times Q \times 0.018 \times \Delta T$).

For the 3-ft-wide x 5-ft-high double-hung wood window with 19 lineal feet of crackage (calculated earlier in this section), assuming a 15-mph wind velocity from Fig. 7-64, the air volume (Q) is taken as 14 cfh. The total infiltration Btuh for the window (assuming $\Delta T = 60$) is:

$$19 \times 14 \times 0.018 \times 60 = 288 \text{ Btuh}$$

In new construction, it is natural to assume that the windows will be tight fitting. This may or may not be the case since it depends a great deal on the window being used. Usually the more expensive the window, the better it fits, but for a window that has the sash slide (such as a double-hung window), a good fit would be considered average since if it is too tight, it will not open. Many of the better-quality windows also have built-in weatherstripping, and it is important to check the specifications to determine whether it is actually called for or not.

Door fit may also be considered average or poor. This depends to a great extent on the builder (or worker) who installs the door. All exterior doors should be weatherstripped since it is difficult to get a good fit on doors. The weatherstripping can then fill the cracks and reduce the air infiltration tremendously. The designer must check the building specifications to be certain that all exterior doors will get weatherstripping.

When designing a heating system for an existing building, the designer can see what is actually used on the building and the fit is more easily checked. In addition, the visual inspection shows if any of the cracks are larger than usual; if this is the case, it will be necessary to allow for the increased infiltration, and this must be considered in the calculations. For such a situation, values two, three or four times the values in Fig. 7-64 are used. Many times the designer will recommend storm windows, sealing of cracks with a sealant, weatherstripping, and perhaps even new windows. But it is important that a heating system design based on these recommended changes not be implemented until the changes are made. This is because the owner might install the new heating system, not make the recommended changes, and then have a cold building.

Construction cracks many times occur at the connection of different materials in the construction, such as the point where the sill plate of the floor construction attaches to the foundation wall (Fig. 7-24). To seal this crack, a roll of compressible plastic filler may be placed on the top of the foundation wall and then the sill plate put on top of it. In this way, the compressible filler seals the space. This type of situation can occur even more frequently in commercial construction at material junctions, such as the precast concrete plank on the top of the masonry wall (Fig. 7-25). Similar situations can occur throughout the construction of a building. It is the responsibility of the designer to analyze the drawings and specifications and to be familiar enough with the builder to know if his work is of good quality or not and, if an architect or engineer is involved, to know him well enough to determine whether he will insist that the building be built in accordance with the drawings and specifications. If there is any doubt in the designer's mind, he will have to take this information into account as the heating system for the building is designed.

Residential construction cracks most commonly occur between the window and door frames and the wood which forms the openings. To more effectively seal these cracks, a sealant should be applied so that as the window or door frame is installed, it will compress the sealant against the wood construction (Fig. 7-26) and seal the crack. In addition, all exterior wood trim should have two beads (rows) of sealant along the full length of the back of the trim or along the construction material it will be attached to. This further reduces any infiltration of air around the frame. Too often the exterior trim simply covers the cracks between the frame and the construction, and air can still infiltrate.

> *Note:*   As you review various manuals and books, you may find that they contain information on estimating air infiltration based on the air change method. Since this method allows a high possibility of error, it is not covered in this text.

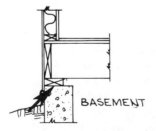

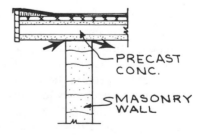

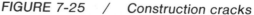

FIGURE 7-24   /   *Construction cracks*   FIGURE 7-25   /   *Construction cracks*

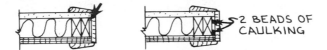

FIGURE 7-26 / /Caulk frames and trim

7-10 Temperatures in Unheated Spaces

To determine the heat loss from a heated room to an unheated room or space, it is first necessary to determine the temperature in the unheated space, after which the ΔT can be calculated. The temperature in the unheated space will fall somewhere between the outside and inside temperatures and will vary depending on the amount of surface area adjacent to heated rooms compared to the amount of surface area adjacent to the exterior.

Temperatures in Spaces other than Attics

All unheated spaces, except attics, use the equation:

$$t_u = \frac{t_i(A_1 U_1 + A_2 U_2 + \ldots) + t_o(A_a U_a + A_b U_b + \ldots)}{(A_1 U_1 + A_2 U_2 + \ldots) + (A_a U_a + A_b U_b + \ldots)}$$

where

t_u = temperature in unheated space (°F)
t_i = indoor design temperature of heated room (°F)
t_o = outdoor design temperature (°F)
$A_1, A_2, A_3, \ldots$ = areas of the surfaces which are exposed to the heated space (sq ft)
$A_a, A_b, A_c, \ldots$ = areas of the surfaces which are exposed to the exterior (sq ft)
$U_1, U_2, U_3, \ldots$ = coefficients of heat transmission for the material assemblies in $A_1, A_2, A_3, \ldots$
$U_a, U_b, U_c, \ldots$ = coefficients of heat transmission for the material assemblies in $A_a, A_b, A_c. \ldots$

Each of the areas involved, and their U values, must be considered in the formula.

Design:

Problem: Calculate the temperature in the cold room.

1. Determine the net area of the cold wall.

2. Determine the U value of the cold wall.

3. Determine the opening area and determine its U value.

4. At this point, all of the areas and U values of the cold wall have been calculated and accumulated. Put this cold wall information into the equation.

5. Next, the areas and U values of the surfaces which are exposed to the outside are determined. Begin by listing each of the material assemblies which must be considered.

    Ceiling
    Wall
    Floor (slab on grade, neglected)
    Door

6. Determine the net area of the exterior wall of the cold room.

7. Determine the U value of the exterior wall. Many times this information is not as readily available to the designer as is the information for the material assembly for the heated portion of the building. Check the drawings and specifications carefully to determine if insulation is required in these walls and, if so, how thick it must be. Quite often insulation is not required in these exterior walls.

8. Determine the area and U value of the ceiling.

9. Determine the wall openings and their U values.

10. Determine the temperature of the unheated space. Gather all of the accumulated information and put it into the equation.

Temperatures in Attics

To calculate the heat loss of the ceiling area of a building which has an uninsulated attic, it is necessary to estimate the temperature in the attic. Attic temperature will fall somewhere between the outside and inside temperatures and will vary depending on the amount of surface area adjacent to heated rooms compared to the amount of surface area adjacent to the exterior.

To estimate the attic temperature use the equation:

$$t_a = \frac{A_c U_c t_i + t_o(A_r U_r + A_w U_w + A_g U_g)}{A_c U_c + A_r U_r + A_w U_w + A_g U_g}$$

where

t_a = attic temperature (°F)
t_i = indoor temperature near top floor ceiling (°F)
t_o = outdoor design temperature (°F)
A_c = area of ceiling (sq ft)
A_r = area of roof (sq ft)
A_w = net area of vertical attic wall surface (sq ft)
A_g = area of attic glass (sq ft)
U_c = coefficient of heat transmission of ceiling
U_r = coefficient of heat transmission of roof
U_w = coefficient of heat transmission of vertical wall surface
U_g = coefficient of heat transmission of glass

Design:

Problem: Calculate the temperature in the attic.

1.   Determine the area and U value of the ceiling.

2.   Determine the area and U value of the roof.

3.   Determine the area and U value of any vertical wall surface (at the gable ends). Many times this information is not as readily available to the designer as is the information for the material assembly for the heated portion of the building. Check the drawings and specifications carefully to determine if insulation is required in these walls and, if so, how thick it must be. Quite often insulation is not required in these exterior walls.

4.   Determine the temperature of the unheated attic. Gather all of the accumulated information and put it into the equation.

What we find in determining unheated attic temperatures is that when the ceiling of the building is very well insulated and when there is no insulation in the roof and vertical walls, the temperature will be quite close to the outside design temperature. The added flow of air through attic vents or louvers will further bring the temperature down. The only times that the unheated attic temperature is significantly above the outside design temperature are when the ceiling of the building is not well insulated, or when the ceiling is well insulated and the roof is insulated also.

Temperatures Below Floors

To calculate the heat loss through the floor area of a building, it is necessary to estimate the temperature in the basement or crawl space below the floor. Since the temperature cannot be readily calculated, the designer should use the following guidelines:

1.   Basements and crawl spaces located almost entirely below ground will normally have a temperature midway between the inside and outside design temperatures being used.

2.   If the basement has windows, the temperature will be lower than if it does not have windows.

3.   If the heating unit (boiler or furnace) is located in the basement, the temperature will be higher than if the heater were located elsewhere.

4.   The crawl space temperature will be affected by the size and number of vents; the presence of heating unit, hot water heater, piping, and ductwork; and the amount of insulation used.

In short, the designer must use his judgment in determining the basement or crawl space temperature to use in the heat loss calculation.

7-11   Designer Responsibilities

The designer of the heating system for a building will have to review carefully all drawings and specifications for the construction. It is important that the designer not simply accept the word of the builder, general contractor, architect, or owner that certain materials, assemblies of materials, details, windows, and glass will be used. Whenever possible, all these things should be properly shown and specified for the designer's review.

In addition, the designer should clearly note on his design proposal the assemblies of materials, insulation, window types, and any other items on which the design is based. This is done because many times changes which may greatly affect the design are made and the designer is never told. Common changes include the type of windows, number of windows, type or thickness of insulation, ceiling height, materials in walls, ceilings, and floors, and type of window glass. Sometimes even room sizes are changed without letting the designer know. For these reasons, it is important that the designer make every attempt to keep in close contact with the others involved in the construction.

The designer has a further responsibility to the others in the sense that he should make recommendations on methods of construction and changes in materials which can reduce heat loss and save money.

7-12   Obtaining Building Dimensions

When calculating the heat loss of a proposed building, the dimensions used are taken from the written dimensions on the drawings of the building. If written dimensions are incomplete, check the scale at which the drawings are made, and then check at least one dimension in each direction to be certain that it is drawn fairly close to scale. Be very careful since in many architectural and engineering offices, once the building has been drawn, if there are any small changes in room or building sizes, they simply change the written dimensions and do not revise the scale drawing. The written dimension takes precedence over any scaled dimension and should be used. Of course, if large discrepancies are found, check with whoever drew the plans to find out what is correct.

Room Measurements

For heat loss calculations, the inside dimensions of a room are used when available. When working from the floor plan, the dimensions given are used. They should be accurate to the nearest foot for walls; for example, a wall 12 ft–8 in. long is considered 13 ft. Ceiling heights should be accurate to the nearest one-half foot; a 7 ft–10 in. ceiling height is considered 8 ft.

When calculating the areas, the following guidelines are used:

1. Any closet is figured as a part of the room that it opens into. Any exposed closet wall, ceiling, or floor is included as part of the heat loss of the room. Dressing rooms and walk-in closets are generally considered separate rooms with their own heat loss and will require heat to be supplied to them.

2. Any cabinets, bookshelves, or other types of pantry or closet areas are ignored when calculating the heat loss of a room. The calculations will be made as if they are not on the walls.

3. When two or more types of wall assemblies are used in one room (Fig. 7-27), the wall areas must be calculated separately since each assembly will have a different heat transmission value.

Many times special care must be taken in calculating the area of a wall, floor, or ceiling because part of the area may be a cold partition, floor, or ceiling. Typical *cold partitions* are found between a heated room and an adjoining unheated space, such as any unheated garage, enclosed porch, attic or cellar stairway, crawl space, basement, or storage area. The area of cold partitions must be carefully separated from the areas of partitions which are exposed to the exterior since they will have different ΔT's.

Cold ceilings are found between a heated room and an unheated attic, storage area, or other unheated space. In a one-story house, all of the rooms have cold ceilings. In some two-story designs (such as Fig. 7-28), the second-story rooms have cold ceilings while some of the first-floor rooms may have full or partial cold ceilings. That area of the ceiling located below an unheated space must be calculated by multiplying the length times the width and then recorded. The ceiling portions of any first-floor rooms that are under heated second-floor rooms have no heat loss since the temperature would be balanced on each side of the ceiling (Fig. 7-29).

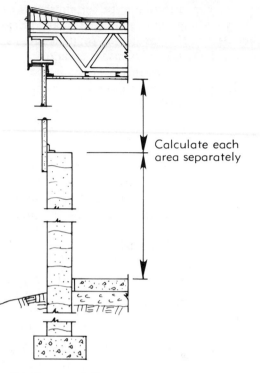

Calculate each
area separately

FIGURE 7-27 　/　 *Wall assemblies*

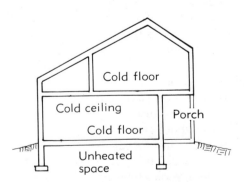

FIGURE 7-28 　/　 *Cold floor and ceilings*

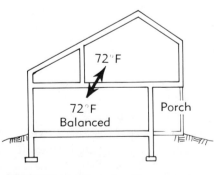

FIGURE 7-29 　/　 *Temperature balance*

Cold floors are found between a first-floor room and an unheated basement or crawl space, and the area of these floors must be calculated. Floors over heated basements are not considered cold floors. If the basement is heated, check to be certain that it is completely heated since quite often only a portion is heated and part is left unheated. Any floor over the unheated portion is considered a cold floor. Cold floors also occur when a second-floor heated room is fully or partially over an unheated, enclosed first-floor space such as an enclosed porch or a garage. The area of the floor exposed to the cold must be calculated also.

When the floor construction is a concrete slab at or near the grade, calculate and record the lineal feet of exposed edge of slab around the building. In addition, the square footage of floor area is calculated and recorded. The heat loss factor for slab construction is given in Fig. 7-65.

Window and Door Measurements

Windows and doors are measured inside the casings (Fig. 7-30), and while they are measured to the nearest inch, they are usually recorded to the nearest 0.1 ft, since it will be necessary to determine their area in square feet. A window 3 ft–4 in. x 5 ft–8 in. would be recorded as 3.3 ft x 5.7 ft. Greater accuracy in recording is not required since the area need be calculated only to the nearest 0.1 sq ft. The area of a 3.3-ft × 5.7-ft window is 18.8 sq ft. The values used in Fig. 7-31 may be used in place of inches as the dimensions are recorded. When totalling up the door and window areas of the room, these measurements should be rounded off to the nearest square foot. If the window area calculated is 38.6 sq ft, use 39 sq ft, while if it is 44.2 sq ft, use 44 sq ft. The door and window areas should be kept separate. Many windows and doors come in stock (standardized) sizes; the commonly used sizes, with the area of window listed, are given in Fig. 7-32.

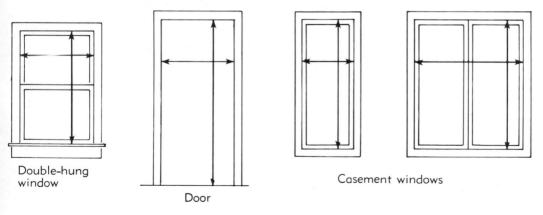

Double-hung window

Door

Casement windows

FIGURE 7-30 / Infiltration dimensions

When recording the area of windows, note whether a storm window (SW) or insulating glass (IG) is specified (Fig. 7-33) since this will greatly affect the heat transmission value of the window. Similarly, note also the type of exterior door used and whether or not there is a storm door.

Actual dimension (in.)	Recorded dimension (ft.)
1	0.1
2	0.2
3	0.3
4	0.3
5	0.4
6	0.5
7	0.6
8	0.7
9	0.8
10	0.8
11	0.9

FIGURE 7-31   /   Dimension conversion

Window Type	Size	Infiltration length (ft.)
Double-hung	2'-0" x 3'-10"	13.7
	2'-0" x 4'-2"	14.3
	2'-4" x 3'-10"	14.7
	2'-4" x 4'-2"	15.3
	2'-4" x 4'-6"	16.0
	2'-8" x 3'-10"	15.7
	2'-8" x 4'-2"	16.3
	2'-8" x 4'-6"	17.0
	3'-0" x 4'-2"	17.3
	3'-0" x 4'-6"	18.0
	3'-0" x 5'-2"	19.3
	3'-4" x 5'-2"	20.3
	3'-4" x 5'-6"	21.0
Casement	2'-0" x 3'-0"	10.0
	2'-0" x 3'-6"	11.0
	2'-0" x 4'-0"	12.0
	2'-0" x 5'-0"	14.0
	2'-0" x 6'-0"	16.0
	2'-4" x 3'-6"	11.7
	2'-4" x 4'-0"	12.7
Awning	3'-0" x 2'-0"	10.0
	3'-0" x 3'-6"	13.0
	4'-0" x 2'-0"	12.0

FIGURE 7-32   /   Infiltration lengths

2-3'-0" x 4'-0" DOUBLE HUNG WOOD WINDOWS, INSULATING GLASS
                    or
2- 3/0 x 4/0 D.H., WOOD, I.G.

FIGURE 7-33   /   Window notation

7-13 Heat Loss Calculations

The actual procedure in estimating heat loss is best illustrated by doing the calculations for a typical building. For this example, the single-story house shown in Appendix B is used. Throughout these calculations, keep in mind that accuracy should be limited to the first three figures since this is an *estimate* of the heat loss, *not* an exact measurement. Similarly, those using calculators should not use such accuracy that the Btuh might be listed as 587.236; instead, 587 or 588, even 590, would be a logical answer.

Step-by-Step Approach

To record the heat loss, some type of form is required; the one shown in Fig. 7-34 is typical. Whatever form is used should be set up to list the rooms separately. Begin the heat loss estimate by putting the name of the project, the date, and the designer's initials on the form and on the sheet of paper which will be used for calculations. Now, the actual heat loss estimate may begin:

1. Select the outdoor design temperature for the geographical area of construction (Fig. 7-66).

2. Select the indoor design temperature for the design.

   Typically this is about 70 °F for all residences or living quarters; occasionally it may vary slightly in an office design.

3. Calculate the design temperature difference. This is the difference between the outdoor and indoor design temperatures.

   Note: Take care; if the outdoor design temperature were −10 °F, then the difference would be 80 °F (Fig. 7-35).

4. Locate and identify the construction of all walls, ceilings, floors, and windows from the drawings.

5. The *U* values of the construction must be found next—either directly from the *U* value tables at the end of the chapter or by totalling up the

Room	Portion considered	Dimensions	Height	Gross area or l.f.	Openings	Opening area	Net area or l.f.	U IF value	ΔT	Heat loss (Btuh)	Room heat loss (Btuh)

FIGURE 7-34 / Typical heat loss form

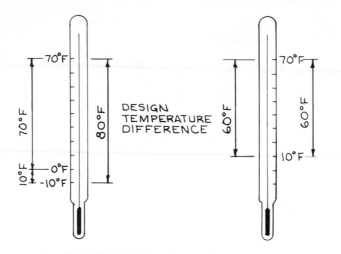

FIGURE 7-35 / Calculating ΔT

resistances of the assembly of materials. Calculations should be made on the plain sheet and then the *U* value recorded in the table under the appropriate column.

6. Next, the infiltration factors for the windows and doors should be determined and then recorded on the table (Fig. 7-64).

7. Next, the gross wall area of each room is calculated and recorded in the table.

8. Calculate the window and door areas for each room separately and record them in the table.

> Sizes are taken from the floor plan(s) and from the window and door schedules of the building. Record the gross area of windows and doors for each room in the table.

9. Calculate the net exposed wall area by subtracting the windows and doors from the gross wall area for each room. Record the net exposed wall area for each room in the table.

10. Calculate the area of any cold partitions, ceiling, and floors (discussed in Sec. 7-12) and record the net area for any such rooms.

11. Calculate the total lineal feet of window and door crackage for each room as outlined in Sec. 7-12. Record the lineal feet of crackage of the windows and doors separately in the table.

12. Calculate the design heat loss for each of the areas of heat loss in the room. For the transmission heat loss, multiply the *U* value times the area times the design temperature difference:

$$U \times A \times \Delta T = \text{Btuh}$$

For infiltration heat loss, multiply the infiltration air volume times the lineal feet of crackage times the design temperature difference:

$$0.018 \times Q \times LF \times \Delta T = \text{Btuh}$$

The design heat losses calculated are recorded in the table.

13. Calculate the total heat loss for each room by adding the design heat losses obtained for each room in Step 12. Each room is totalled separately and recorded in the table.

14. Calculate the total heat loss for the entire building by adding the heat losses of each room together, and record this total in the table. This total heat loss will be used later when the heating unit (furnace) size is being selected; however, this value is *not* the heating unit's size (sizing of heating units is discussed in Sec. 10-7).

The total heat loss for the building in Appendix B is shown in Fig. 7-36.

Caution: There are many manuals and books which have various "short cuts" for calculating heat loss. While they may save a little time for the person learning to calculate heat losses, the short cuts are not as accurate and should not be used. It is important that the designer work through several problems such as the one in this book in order to become familiar with what makes up a *U* value, how *R* values and *U* values are related, and how various materials compare in terms of heat loss characteristics. Whether you intend to design heating systems or work for an architect, contractor, or developer of projects, this information provides the basis for an informed comparison of materials and their relative heat loss values.

The total heat loss calculated for the residence in Appendix B may seem quite low in comparison to calculations in various other reference books and manuals. This large difference is attributed to the thicknesses of insulation used in this text and to the limited amount of window area used. In addition, many of the other references use an air-change method of calculating infiltration which is not readily adaptable to the smaller windows used in this design. Typically, a residence designed according to the Federal Housing Administration (FHA) standards of 1976 would have a heat loss of about twice the amount calculated in this example.

ROSE RESIDENCE 1/8/ —

Room	Portion considered	Dimensions	Height	Gross area or lf	Openings	Opening area	Net area or lf	U IF value	ΔT	Heat loss (Btuh)	Room heat loss (Btuh)
LIVING-FAMILY	EXT.WALL	32.25+7.0	8	314	2-6/0x6/8	80	234	0.07	60	983	
	COLD WALL	12.7	8	104			104	0.076	47	372	
	FLOOR	32.25x18.8		603			603	0.066	35	1393	
	CEILING	32.25x18.8		603			603	0.047	56	1587	
	GLASS	2-6/0x6/8		80			80	0.061	60	2928	
	INF-DOORS	16 8 / 6.7 31/4x2		63			63	(14 x 0.018)	60	953	8216
KITCHEN	EXT.WALL	15.8+7.0	8	183	W2-4.0x3.0	12	171	0.07	60	718	
2x4=8	COLD WALL	10.3	8	82	3.0x6.8	21	61	0.076	47	218	
4x3=12	FLOOR	15.8x17.3		274			274	0.066	35	633	
20 l.f.	CEILING	15.8x17.3		274			274	0.047	56	721	
	GLASS	4.0x3.0	12				12	0.61	60	439	
	INF-GLASS	—	20				20	14 x 0.018	60	302	
	DOOR		21	21			21	0.61	47	602	
Door to garage →	INF-DOOR		20	20			20	7 x 0.018	47	119	3752
DINING ROOM	EXT.WALL	14.5	8	116	6.0x5.0	30	86	0.07	60	360	
6	FLOOR	14.5x13.3		193			193	0.066	35	446	
6x5=30	CEILING	14.5x13.3		193			193	0.047	56	508	
6x2=12	GLASS	6.0x5.0	30				30	0.61	60	1098	
42	INF-GLASS		42				42	14 x 0.018	60	635	3047
ENTRY & HALL	EXT.WALL	7.5+2.5	8	80	6.0x6.8	40	40	0.07	60	168	
NO INF-GLASS,	FLOOR	7.5+2.5x 13.3+3.0x39		289			289	0.066	35	668	
FIXED GLASS	CEILING			289			289	0.047	56	761	
	GLASS	2.8x6.7					19	0.61	60	696	
	DOOR			21			21	0.61	60	769	
	INF-Door			21			21	14 x 0.18	60	302	3364
BEDROOM 3	EXT.WALL	14.5+8+6.8	8	225	4.0x4.0	16	209	0.07	60	878	
	FLOOR	14.5x13.3+ 6.8x6.8		239	—		239	0.066	35	552	
4	CEILING			239	—		239	0.047	56	629	
6x4=24 l.f.	GLASS	4.0x4.0	16	16			16	0.61	60	586	
	INF-GL		24	24			24	14 x 0.018	60	363	3008

FIGURE 7-36 / Total heat loss

152

Room	Portion considered	Dimensions	Height	Gross area or l.f.	Openings	Opening area	Net area or l.f.	U IF value	ΔT	Heat loss (Btuh)	Room heat loss (Btuh)
BEDROOM 1 (INC. 2 CLOSETS)	EXT. WALL	12.7+18.7+ / 2.5	8	272	4.0×4.0 / 3.0×4.0	28	244	0.07	60	1025	
	FLOOR	12.7+18.7+ / 4.0×6.0	1	271	—		271	0.066	35	626	
	CEILING	—		271			271	0.047	56	713	
	GLASS	—		28			28	0.62	60	1025	
	INF.- GL.	—		46			46	14×	60	696	
								0.018	—	—	4085
BEDROOM 2 (INC. 2 CLOSETS)	EXT. WALL	11.5+2.5	8	112	3.0×4.0	12	100	0.07	60	420	
	FLOOR	11.5×18.8+ / 2.5×4.0		226			226	0.066	35	522	
	CEILING	—		226			226	0.047	56	595	
	GLASS	—		12			12	0.62	60	440	
	INF.- GL.	—		22			22	14×	60	333	
								0.018	—	—	2310
BATH	EXT. WALL	10.5		84	2.0×2.0	4	80	0.07	60	336	
	FLOOR	10.5×6.8		72			72	0.066	35	166	
	CEILING	—		72			72	0.047	56	190	
	GLASS	—		4			4	0.62	60	147	
	INF.- GL.	—		8			8	14×	60	121	960
INTERIOR BATH (MAY ADD TO BEDROOM 1)	FLOOR	8.0×5.0		40			40	0.081 / 0.066	35	93	
	CEILING	—		40			40	0.047	56	105	198

TOTAL HEAT LOSS   28,940 BTUH

FIGURE 7-36 / Total heat loss (continued)

153

DESIGN TEMPERATURES

	INSIDE	OUTSIDE	ΔT
EXTERIOR WALLS	70°F	10°F	60°F
COLD WALLS	70°F	23°F	47°F
CEILING	70°F	14°F	56°F
CRAWL SPACE	70°F	35°F	35°F

U VALUES :

EXTERIOR WALL

1/2" PLYWOOD	0.63
4" BRICK	0.44
3 1/2" BATT INSUL.	11.00
1/2" GYPSUM BD.	0.45
INSIDE AIR FILM	0.68
OUTSIDE AIR FILM	0.17
3/4" AIR SPACE	0.94
TOTAL R =	14.30

$$U = \frac{1}{R} = \frac{1}{14.30} = 0.07$$

FLOOR

CARPET	2.08
1/2" PLYWOOD	0.63
3 1/2" BATT INSUL.	11.00
INSIDE AIR	0.61
OUTSIDE AIR	0.92
TOTAL R =	15.23

$$U = \frac{1}{R} = \frac{1}{15.23} = 0.066$$

ROOF

SHINGLES	0.44
BLDG. PAPER	0.06
5/8" PLYWOOD	0.77
INSIDE AIR	0.17
OUTSIDE AIR	0.61
TOTAL R =	2.05

$$U = \frac{1}{R} = \frac{1}{2.05} = 0.48$$

CEILING

1/2" GYPSUM BD.	0.45
6" BATT INSUL.	19.00
INSIDE AIR	0.61
OUTSIDE AIR	0.61
TOTAL R =	21.67

$$U = \frac{1}{R} = \frac{1}{21.67} = 0.047$$

COLD WALL

1/2" GYPSUM BD.	0.45
3 1/2" BATT INSUL.	11.00
1/2" GYPSUM BD.	0.45
INSIDE AIR	0.68
OUTSIDE AIR	0.68
	13.26

$$U = \frac{1}{R} = \frac{1}{13.26} = 0.076$$

GLASS, I.G., 0.1875" AIR SPACE
U = 0.62

DOOR, SAME AS WINDOW

INFILTRATION

DOORS AND WINDOWS,
IF = 14 CFH
KITCHEN DOOR
IF = 7 CFH

FIGURE 7-36 / Total heat loss (continued)

7-14   Sealing the Cracks

It is most important that the space (cracks) between different materials be properly sealed so that air will not infiltrate through them. This is a common problem
in commercial buildings after about 5 years. One of the most common points of
this air infiltration tends to be around the outside frame of a window or door
where it rests against the surrounding wall (Fig. 7-37). Whether the window is operable (opens) or fixed has no effect on this infiltration since it occurs around the
edges of the frame. This tendency can be reduced by any one or a combination of
several methods:

1.   Detail the window and door to rest against a protruding portion of the
     structure or wall, as illustrated in Fig. 7-38. This reduces the chance of frame
     and wall separation which commonly occurs when a detail such as Fig. 7-37
     is used and when the building undergoes expansion and contraction.

2.   When using a detail such as Fig. 7-39, place a compressible filler between
     the wall and the window frame. This filler will reduce the chance of air flow
     as materials contract.

3.   All exterior cracks should be filled with a sealant designed to remain flexible
     so that it will hold to both the frame and the wall during periods of material
     contraction. Sealants should be called for in details, as shown in Fig. 7-39,
     and, when possible, they are used in combination with compressible fillers.
     It is important that caulking not be used since it will eventually dry and
     crack, allowing the air to infiltrate the building. Not only should sealants be
     specified inside and out, but also the designer must be certain that they are
     used on the job and that caulking is not substituted.

These suggestions should be followed whenever different materials meet and at
junctions in the walls, walls and floor, and walls and roof.

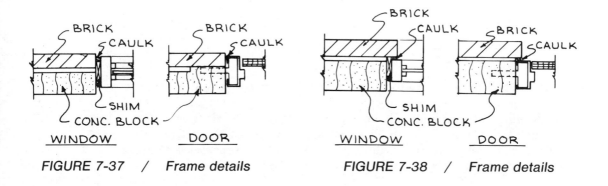

FIGURE 7-37   /   Frame details   FIGURE 7-38   /   Frame details

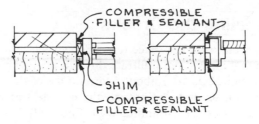

FIGURE 7-39 / Frame details

The importance of such air flow can be verified in any older building. On a cold day, especially if the wind is blowing, the air infiltrating between the frame and wall can be felt by placing your hand at the juncture of materials. This cool flow of air is usually not considered in the design calculations, yet there it is. In some buildings, with large amounts of glass and glass frame, the air infiltration becomes so great on a cold, windy day that it is impossible to heat the space to the design temperature. This can be solved in new construction by the use of the installation methods outlined. In existing buildings, it can be corrected by removing the dried caulking, resealing around the frames with compressible filler, and using a sealant inside and out.

It is important to realize that the designer of the heating system *must* review the drawings, details, and specifications to determine what is being called for on the project. But just as important, the designer has a responsibility to make suggestions for the architect to consider which will improve the heat flow characteristics.

Once the designer has reviewed the drawings and specifications and carefully taken into consideration his experience with the builder, architect, or owner, he must make a decision on how to calculate possible air infiltration through the construction. When the designer feels that typical good construction methods and practices will be used, he has the option of ignoring the infiltration through the construction and calculating only the infiltration around operable windows and doors as outlined in Sec. 7-9. If construction cracks must be considered, the lineal feet of cracks must be determined in the same manner as for windows and doors (Sec. 7-9). The infiltration factor used will be determined largely by the designer and in relation to the IF values given for windows and doors in Fig. 7-64.

7-15   Fireplaces

Since heat rises, a fireplace in a room has a tendency to allow the warm inside air to flow up the chimney. Once that begins, a natural flow of air will occur, continuously drawing warm air up the chimney and pulling in cooler air from the exterior through infiltration (Fig. 7-40). This natural flow of air can be greatly reduced if the fireplace is equipped with a tight-fitting damper that is kept *closed* when the fireplace is not in use. This flow of air increases greatly when there is a fire in the

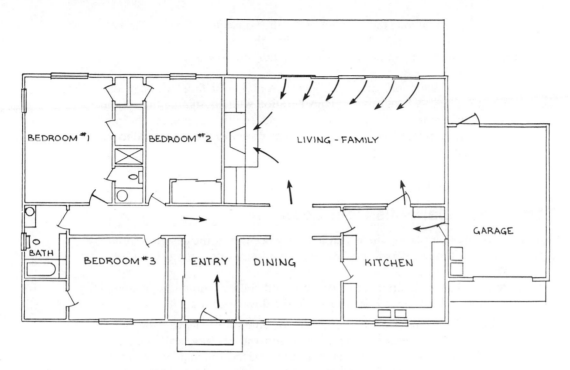

FIGURE 7-40 / Flow of warm air toward fireplace

fireplace, and the constant draft of air up the chimney may result in warm air in adjoining rooms being pulled toward the fireplace; these rooms then become cool as air is pulled into them through infiltration cracks. At the same time, the room with the fireplace will become quite warm, even overheated.

When the fuels used to provide heat were relatively inexpensive, little attention was paid to the heat loss through the fireplace. But the tremendous increases in fuel costs to date, along with even higher costs projected for the future, make it necessary to reduce heat loss as much as possible. This does not mean that fireplaces should no longer be built or used. It does mean that a few precautions must be taken to prevent some of the heat from escaping up the chimney.

1. Be certain that the fireplace has a tight-fitting damper and that the damper is closed when the fireplace is not being used.

2. Consider the use of a glass enclosure in front of the fireplace. This reduces the flow of air up the chimney, thus reducing the heat loss.

3. Consider a "snuff box" to put out the fire instead of leaving the fire to go out by itself. Even if the fire is almost out when you go to bed at night, the fire in the fireplace will probably still have hot ashes or coals in the morning. This

means that all night long the air from inside the house flows up the chimney. The fire can be extinguished with a metal box that is placed over the fire to smother it. Then the damper can be closed and the flow of air reduced.

There are no calculations that a designer can make for fireplace heat loss. The designer must simply take this into consideration while designing the system by providing slightly more heat in surrounding rooms and by keeping the thermostat away from the fireplace, preferably in another room, to reduce the effect of fireplace heat on it.

7-16   Miscellaneous Heat Loss

There are several other places where heat loss may occur that the designer should be aware of, even though he will not calculate the loss in designing the system.

1.   Electrical boxes in exterior (or cold) walls and ceilings should be insulated around and in back (Fig. 7-41) to reduce the flow of cold air.

2.   Medicine cabinets recessed into exterior (or cold) walls leave little or no space for insulation between the cabinet and the exterior wall sheathing (Fig. 7-42). A recessed medicine cabinet should be located in an interior wall when possible. If located in an exterior wall, consider placing a thin sheet of rigid insulation, such as polystyrene, between the cabinet and the sheathing (Fig. 7-43).

3.   The exhaust fan for a cooking area that is vented to the exterior will draw heat out of the space. Consider using a charcoal filter exhaust which cleans the air but blows it back into the room. This way heat from the space is not exhausted to the exterior, and the fact that the heat from the stove and range is put into the room instead of exhausted to the exterior is an extra bonus.

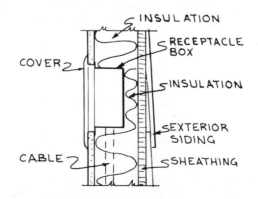

FIGURE 7-41   /   Insulate electrical boxes

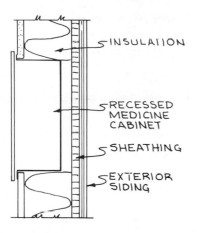

INSULATION

RECESSED
MEDICINE
CABINET

SHEATHING

EXTERIOR
SIDING

FIGURE 7-42 / Recessed medicine cabinet

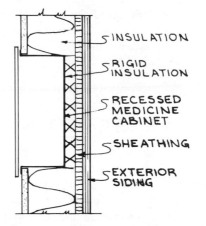

INSULATION

RIGID
INSULATION

RECESSED
MEDICINE
CABINET

SHEATHING

EXTERIOR
SIDING

FIGURE 7-43 / Insulate recessed medicine cabinet

4. Exhaust fans in bathrooms do an excellent job of reducing humidity in the space and are also effective in eliminating odors. Since the air being exhausted is heated, it will increase the heat loss in the building. However, this can be greatly reduced if the fan is on a switch separate from the light switch (Fig. 7-44) so that it can be shut off when no longer needed.

5. All doorways to attics and cellars or other cold areas should have weatherstripping to reduce infiltration.

6. If the attic is reached through an access door or "hatch" in the ceiling of a heated space, be certain that the access door is insulated and weatherstripped to reduce heat loss.

7. Folding stairways into attics from heated spaces should also be insulated and weatherstripped to reduce heat loss.

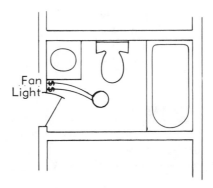

Fan
Light

FIGURE 7-44 / Separate switches

These are just several of the many places that miscellaneous heat loss can occur. Any place that a pipe, duct, or any material passes from a cold to a warm space is a possible location for heat loss, and it should be tightly installed and sealed and compressible filler used.

7-17   Heat Loss Considerations

There is an increased tendency to design buildings with as low a heat loss as possible to conserve fuel and reduce fuel costs. Increasingly, the R values are approaching 20 and sometimes higher, resulting in a 0.05 U factor for the assembly. Similar savings are being realized by increased use of insulating glass and weather-stripping, and use of smaller amounts of glass. While taking all of these factors into account in the sizing of the system, the designer must be particularly careful since the U values for material assemblies used will result in a total system which is much smaller than for designs based on U values of 0.10 to 0.15. Care must be taken so that the system will have sufficient capacity to provide any extra heat (above that calculated) that may be required due to:

1. The possibility that the materials will not be carefully installed. For example, insulation may not be packed in the smaller areas around windows and doors. Similar problems may occur when windows and doors are not installed snugly into the construction, allowing more infiltration than had been calculated.

2. The possibility that the builder (contractor) may use different materials from those on which the designer based his calculations (this may even be done with the architect's approval).

3. The probability that over the years the construction may deteriorate, allowing increased infiltration loss. This is a particular problem in buildings with window frames caulked into the wall similar to the detail shown in Fig. 7-37. If the sealant separates from the frame or the wall as the building settles, or if the sealant dries, cracks, and separates for any reason, the increased infiltration will require substantial extra heat. Obviously, the owner should have the windows resealed, but the initial separation occurs slowly, and the heat loss will slowly increase.

7-18   Degree Days

Degree days are a measure of approximately how much the ΔT is per year, and they are determined by finding the *daily* difference between the 65 °F inside temperature and the average outside temperature during a 24-hour period (not the low temperature but the *average* over the 24 hours). For example, if the average outside temperature is 40 °F, then the ΔT for that day is 65 °F − 40 °F = 25 °F. The ΔT for each day is added for a yearly total which is given as degree days.

Figure 7-67 lists degree days for various cities; if one near your locale is not listed, contact the closest weather bureau for information. From Fig. 7-67, note the variations in degree days based on climate. For example, Albany, N.Y., has 6,875 degree days at the airport and 6,201 in the city, while Raleigh, N.C., has 3,393 degree days at the airport. These degree days show the relative amount of heat and fuel which will be required. Since airports are located in the suburbs, and generally in open areas where they are more exposed to the climate, they have more degree days than the city where the buildings help protect one another and where the buildings and streets store heat during the day which they radiate at night.

7-19 Fuel Cost Comparisons

The amount of fuel required for one year to heat a residence is determined by the following formula:

$$\frac{\text{Heat loss} \times \text{Degree days} \times 24 \text{ (a constant)}}{\text{Overall efficiency of fuel} \times \Delta T \times \text{Heating value of fuel}} = \text{Amount of fuel required in a year}$$

For this example, assume 62,500 Btuh for baseboard, ceiling, or partition electric resistance heat and 75,000 Btuh for all other types of systems. The higher amount allows for an additional heat loss in the heating unit and in the pipes or ducts used to distribute the heat to the rooms.

Using the heating values and efficiency from Fig. 7-45, the amount of fuel required each year for a given residence would be:

Oil

$$\frac{(75,000)\,(3,393)\,(24)}{(0.80)\,(60)\,(140,000)} = 909 \text{ gal}$$

Natural gas

$$\frac{(75,000)\,(3,393)\,(24)}{(0.85)\,(60)\,(100,000)} = 1,198 \text{ ccf (hundred cubic feet)}$$

Propane

$$\frac{(75,000)\,(3,393)\,(24)}{(0.85)\,(60)\,(2,300)} = 52,067 \text{ c.f. or } 521 \text{ ccf}$$

Fuel	Btu	Unit	Efficiency (%)
Oil	140,000	Gal.	65-85
Natural gas	100,000	ccf	70-90
Propane	2,300	cf	70-90
Electricity	3,413	kw	100

cf = cubic feet
ccf = 100 cubic feet

FIGURE 7-45   /   Heating values and efficiencies

Electric forced air

$$\frac{(75,000)\ (3,393)\ (24)}{(1.00)\ (60)\ (3,413)} = 29,824 \text{ kWh}$$

Electric baseboard, ceiling, partition

$$\frac{(62,500)\ (3,393)\ (24)}{(1.00)\ (60)\ (3,413)} = 24,854 \text{ kWh}$$

Now the fuel costs per year can be estimated by multiplying the amount of fuel used times its cost. This is when the designer *must check the fuel costs in the locale where the building will be built since it is these costs which determine which is the most economical system.* Fuel costs vary considerably and are rising, so call and get local prices for comparison purposes.

7-20   Controlling Heat Loss

Basically, all residences should be insulated in all portions of the building which are exposed to colder temperatures. By observing several considerations, the total heat loss of the building is reduced by one-half (and more) in the typical home built before 1976. Basically, the heat loss is reduced by:

1.   6 in. of insulation in the crawl space or basement ($R = 19$).

2.   6 in. of insulation in the exterior walls ($R = 19$). (Use 2-in. x 6-in. studs for framing the walls instead of 2 x 4s).

3.   12 in. of insulation in the ceiling ($R = 38$).

4.   Insulated glass windows.

5. A window area limited to 8% of the floor area. (This does away with the large glass windows and sliding glass doors which have such high heat losses. In the past it is estimated that the average home had windows which totalled 12% of the floor area.)

6. An insulated metal entry door with 1¾-in. polyurethane insulation.

7. Humidity controlled by a humidifier and a dehumidifier.

8. Locating forced air heating ducts in the heated area. (Drop the ceilings in corridors and install ducts along the upper perimeters of interior walls to reduce the heat loss from the ducts.)

Comparative studies of actual homes built in Arkansas show that heat loss can be reduced by much more than one-half. The real significance of this study is that for very little additional money actually spent on a house, significant savings can be realized. The type of construction, together with a solar heating system or with solar-assisted heat pumps, provides a major basis for future energy savings. A full report on "The Arkansas Story," *Report No. 1, Energy Conservation Ideas to Build On* is available through Owens–Corning Fiberglass Corp., Insulation Operating Division, Fiberglass Tower, Toledo, Ohio 43659. This report belongs in your library.

Another interesting investigation of energy conservation ideas, including the use of solar energy, was conducted by NASA (National Aeronautics and Space Administration) with similar results. However, the use of solar energy *and* water conservation techniques makes it doubly interesting. Copies of this study, "Technical support package for Tech. Brief LAR—12134," NASA TECHNOLOGY UTILIZATION HOUSE, are available from Technology Utilization Office, NASA Langley Research Center, Hampton, Virginia 23665.

7-21 Heat Gain

Heat gain deals with the amount of heat which a space will accumulate during warm weather. To adequately cool the air inside the space, it is necessary to estimate the amount of heat which will build up in the space. Many of the heat gain factors are basically the same as those considered in heat loss:

1. Transmission (through walls, ceilings and floors).

2. Infiltration (through windows and doors).

While the terms *transmission* and *infiltration* are the same terms as are used for heat loss, and the general principles the same, there are some important differences in the time of day considered and the method of calculation. And for *total* heat gain, several other factors must also be considered:

1.   Solar radiation.

2.   Heat produced in the space.

3.   Latent heat.

7-22   Sensible and Latent Heat

The heat gain of the building is a combination of *sensible* and *latent* heat, which together give the total heat gain, or total cooling load, of the building.

Sensible heat is heat which a substance absorbs, and while its temperature goes up, the substance *does not change its state*. For example, if some water (at, say, 50 °F) is placed in the sunshine, the water will absorb the heat from the sun and warm up, but it will still be water.

Latent heat is heat which is absorbed or given off by a substance *when changing its state*. As a substance changes from a solid to a liquid or from a liquid to a gas, it *absorbs* heat, and as a substance changes from a gas to a liquid or from a liquid to a solid, it *gives off heat*.

7-23   Transmission

While the greatest heat loss will probably occur at night, the greatest heat gain will occur during a sunny day. Heat gain calculations make use of a heat transfer multiplier (HTM) (Fig. 7-46) which takes into account:

1.   The temperature differential (between the inside of a building and the outside).

2.   The type of construction (considering insulation value, mass of the type of construction, and thermal time lag), and the ability of the construction to hold heat.

Some typical heat transfer multipliers are listed in Fig. 7-46. To determine the heat gain by transmission, simply multiply the area of construction by the HTM for the type of construction. When the HTM for a particular material is not listed in the table, it can be found by multiplying the U value by the equivalent temperature differential (ETD) (Fig. 7-47). If the U value is not given in Fig. 7-63, it may be calculated using the R values of the materials. Summer design conditions are listed in Fig. 7-66.

Outdoor Design Dry-Bulb Temperature	90		95			100		105		110
Daily Temperature Range	Low	Med.	Low	Med.	High	Med.	High	Med.	High	High
WALLS AND DOORS										
1. Frame and Veneer-on-Frame										
(a) Wood sheathing or 1/2'' insulating sheathing	6.0	4.8	7.2	6.0	4.8	7.5	6.0	8.7	7.5	8.7
(b) 25/32'' insulating sheathing or one reflective air space	4.3	3.5	5.1	4.5	3.5	5.4	4.5	6.3	5.4	6.3
(c) Same as (a) or (b) plus either 1'' or 2'' insulation or 2 reflective air spaces	2.9	2.4	3.6	3.1	2.4	3.7	3.1	4.4	3.7	4.4
(d) Same as (a) or (b) plus either more than 2'' insulation, or 3 reflective air spaces	1.8	1.5	2.2	1.9	1.5	2.3	1.9	2.7	2.3	2.7
2. Masonry Walls, 8'' Block or Brick										
(a) Plastered or plain	7.2	5.4	9.7	7.9	5.4	10.4	7.9	12.5	10.4	12.5
(b) Furred, no insulation	4.6	3.4	6.0	4.9	3.4	6.3	4.9	7.9	6.3	7.9
(c) Furred, with less than 1'' insulation, or one reflective air space	3.1	2.3	4.3	3.3	2.3	4.3	3.3	5.4	4.3	5.4
(d) Furred, with 1'' to 2'' insulation, or two reflective air spaces	2.1	1.6	2.8	2.3	1.6	3.0	2.3	3.7	3.0	3.7
(e) Furred, with more than 2'' insulation, or three reflective air spaces	1.4	1.0	1.8	1.5	1.0	1.9	1.5	2.4	1.9	2.4
3. Partitions										
(a) Frame, finished one side only, no insulation	8.5	6.0	11.4	9.1	6.0	12.0	9.1	15.0	12.0	15.0
(b) Frame, finished both sides, no insulation	4.8	3.4	6.6	5.1	3.4	6.9	5.1	8.5	6.9	8.5
(c) Frame, finished both sides, more than 1'' insulation or two reflective air spaces	2.0	1.4	2.7	2.1	1.4	2.8	2.1	3.5	2.8	3.5
(d) Masonry, plastered one side, no insulation	2.6	1.2	4.4	3.0	1.2	4.7	3.0	6.6	4.7	6.6
4. Wood Doors (Consider glass areas of doors as windows)	11.4	9.4	14.0	12.0	9.4	14.0	12.0	17.0	14.0	17.0
CEILING OR ROOFS										
5. Ceilings under naturally vented attic, or vented flat roof										
(a) Uninsulated ... Dark	10.0	9.1	11.0	10.0	9.1	11.4	10.0	12.5	11.4	12.5
Light	8.2	7.2	9.1	8.2	7.2	9.4	8.2	10.4	9.4	10.4
(b) Less than 2'' insulation or reflective air space ... Dark	4.3	3.9	4.8	4.4	3.9	4.9	4.4	5.4	4.9	5.4
Light	3.5	3.1	4.1	3.6	3.1	4.1	3.6	4.6	4.1	4.6
(c) 2'' to 4'' insulation, or two reflective air spaces ... Dark	2.6	2.3	2.9	2.6	2.3	2.9	2.6	3.2	2.9	3.2
Light	2.1	1.9	2.4	2.2	1.9	2.5	2.2	2.8	2.5	2.8
(d) More than 4'' insulation or three or more reflective air spaces ... Dark	1.8	1.6	1.9	1.8	1.6	2.0	1.8	2.2	2.0	2.2
Light	1.4	1.2	1.6	1.4	1.2	1.6	1.4	1.8	1.6	1.8
6. Built-up Roof, No Ceiling										
(a) Uninsulated ... Dark	17.0	16.0	19.0	18.0	16.0	20.0	18.0	22.0	20.0	22.0
Light	14.0	12.5	16.0	14.0	12.5	16.0	14.0	18.0	16.0	18.0
(b) 2'' Roof insulation ... Dark	8.5	7.9	9.7	8.7	7.9	9.7	8.7	11.0	9.7	11.0
Light	6.9	6.3	7.9	7.2	6.3	8.2	7.2	9.1·	8.2	9.1
(c) 3'' Roof insulation ... Dark	6.0	5.4	6.6	6.3	5.4	6.9	6.3	7.5	6.9	7.5
Light	4.9	4.3	5.6	5.1	4.3	5.6	5.1	6.3	5.6	6.3
7. Ceilings under rooms which are not cooled	2.7	1.9	3.6	2.9	1.9	3.8	2.9	4.8	3.8	4.8

FIGURE 7-46   /   Heat transfer multipliers

Outdoor Design Dry-Bulb Temperature	90		95			100		105		110
Daily Temperature Range	Low	Med.	Low	Med.	High	Med.	High	Med.	High	High
FLOORS										
8. Over rooms which are not cooled	3.4	2.4	4.6	3.6	2.4	4.8	3.6	6.0	4.8	6.0
9. Over basement, enclosed crawl space, or concrete slab on ground	0	0	0	0	0	0	0	0	0	0
10. Over open crawl space	4.8	3.4	6.6	5.1	3.4	6.9	5.1	8.5	6.9	8.5
INFILTRATION										
11. Btuh per sq. ft. of gross exposed wall area	1.1	1.1	1.5	1.5	1.5	1.9	1.9	2.2	2.2	2.6
MECHANICAL VENTILATION										
12. Btuh per cfm	16.0	16.0	22.0	22.0	22.0	27.0	27.0	32.0	32.0	38.0

Courtesy of The Hydronics Institute.

FIGURE 7-46 / *Heat transfer multipliers* (continued)

Design Equivalent Temperature Differences

Design Temperature, F	85		90			95			100		105	110
Daily Temperature Range[a]	L	M	L	M	H	L	M	H	M	H	H	H
WALLS AND DOORS												
1. Frame and veneer-on-frame	17.6	13.6	22.6	18.6	13.6	27.6	23.6	18.6	28.6	23.6	28.6	33.6
2. Masonry walls, 8-in. block or brick	10.3	6.3	15.3	11.3	6.3	20.3	16.3	11.3	21.3	16.3	21.3	26.3
3. Partitions, frame	9.0	5.0	14.0	10.0	5.0	19.0	15.0	10.0	20.0	15.0	20.0	25.0
masonry	2.5	0	7.5	3.5	0	12.5	8.5	3.5	13.5	8.5	13.5	18.5
4. Wood doors	17.6	13.6	22.6	18.6	13.6	27.6	23.6	18.6	28.6	23.6	28.6	33.6
CEILINGS AND ROOFS[b]												
1. Ceilings under naturally vented attic or vented flat roof—dark	38.0	34.0	43.0	39.0	34.0	48.0	44.0	39.0	49.0	44.0	49.0	54.0
—light	30.0	26.0	35.0	31.0	26.0	40.0	36.0	31.0	41.0	36.0	41.0	46.0
2. Built-up roof, no ceiling—dark	38.0	34.0	43.0	39.0	34.0	48.0	44.0	39.0	49.0	44.0	49.0	54.0
—light	30.0	26.0	35.0	31.0	26.0	40.0	36.0	31.0	41.0	36.0	41.0	46.0
3. Ceilings under unconditioned rooms	9.0	5.0	14.0	10.0	5.0	19.0	15.0	10.0	20.0	15.0	20.0	25.0
FLOORS												
1. Over unconditioned rooms	9.0	5.0	14.0	10.0	5.0	19.0	15.0	10.0	20.0	15.0	20.0	25.0
2. Over basement, enclosed crawl space or concrete slab on ground	0	0	0	0	0	0	0	0	0	0	0	0
3. Over open crawl space	9.0	5.0	14.0	10.0	5.0	19.0	15.0	10.0	20.0	15.0	20.0	25.0

[a] Daily Temperature Range
    L (Low) Calculation Value: 12   M (Medium) Calculation Value: 20   H (High) Calculation Value: 30
    Applicable Range: Less than 15 deg.   Applicable Range: 15 to 25 deg.   Applicable Range: More than 25 deg.
[b] Ceilings and Roofs: For roofs in shade, eight-hour average = 11 deg temperature differential. At 90 F design and medium daily range, equivalent temperature differential for light-colored roof equals 11 + (0.71)(39 − 11) = 31 deg.

Reprinted with permission from ASHRAE, Fundamentals Handbook, 1977

FIGURE 7-47 / *Equivalent temperature differences*

7-24 Infiltration

Heat gain *infiltration* is calculated in the same manner as heat loss infiltration—by multiplying the lineal feet of crackage by the infiltration factor. However, air leakage into structures is much smaller in the summer than in the winter. This is because winter air leakage is caused by a combination of wind direction and velocity which, when combined with the inside–outside temperature difference, creates a "chimney" effect of heat loss. This type of loss does not occur in the summer, and most localities have lower wind velocities in the summer.

Since there is much less air leakage in the summer, when calculating heat gain, ASHRAE suggests use of the air change or ventilation approach. The air change method is based on the assumption that the average air leakage will occur at a rate of one-half air change per hour. In this case, the heat gain is calculated in terms of Btuh per square foot of gross exposed wall area, using the Btuh per square foot values given in Fig. 7-48.

The room plan shown in Fig. 7-49 would have an outside exposed area of 34 ft x 8 ft or 272 sq ft. Based on the Btuh per square foot values given in Fig. 7-48, the value for a 95°F outside design temperature is 1.5 Btuh per sq ft. Based on this, the heat gain for the room is 272 sq ft x 1.5 Btuh per sq ft = 408 Btuh due to infiltration.

When mechanical ventilation is used, the amount of heat gain is based on the volume of air change in cfm. Assuming one air change per hour (the rate most commonly used), a room 12 ft–3 in. x 18 ft–3 in. x 8 ft high with 1,789 cu ft would ventilate 1,789 cu ft ÷ 60 min = 29.3 cfm. The heat gain is based on the Btuh of sensible heat per cfm of ventilating air shown in Fig. 7-48 and is selected from the table according to the outside design temperature used. With a 95°F outside design temperature, the heat gain would be 22 Btuh per cfm. So the heat gain of this room would be 29.8 cfm x 22 Btuh per cfm = 656 Btuh.

Sensible Cooling Load Due to Infiltration
and Ventilation

Design Temperature, F	85	90	95	100	105	110
Infiltration, Btuh per sq ft of gross exposed wall area	0.7	1.1	1.5	1.9	2.2	2.6
Mechanical Ventilation, Btuh per cfm	11.0	16.0	22.0	27.0	32.0	38.0

Reprinted with permission from ASHRAE, Fundamentals Handbook, 1977

FIGURE 7-48 / Infiltration values

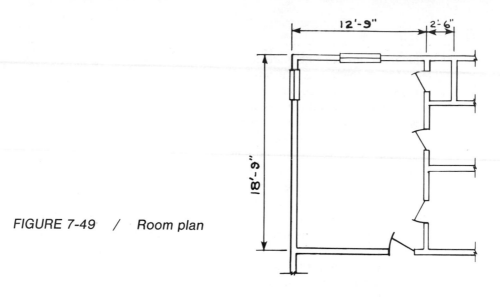

FIGURE 7-49   /   Room plan

7-25   Occupancy Loads

The amount of heat given off by people (Fig. 7-50) and appliances must also be considered in any cooling load considerations. Since the number of occupants and appliances and the amount of appliance use which will occur will vary and cannot be predicted, the cooling load they will create must be estimated.

For residences, the occupant heat is 225 Btuh per occupant. To estimate the number of occupants as accurately as possible, it is necessary to consider how often the owner entertains large groups of people and whether such entertaining occurs during the heat of the day or in the cooler evening. Many times this information is not available, and the designer will simply have to assume that there will be two occupants for each bedroom in the house.

The heat gain from occupants is then distributed equally among the living spaces of the house since during the time when the maximum heat gain will occur, the occupants will be using the living spaces and not the sleeping areas.

Appliance values are generally limited to the kitchen areas of the residence. ASHRAE suggests a heat gain load of 1,200 Btuh for the appliances. The intermittent use of appliances, along with the use of kitchen ventilating fans, makes it difficult to calculate exactly what the heat gain value should be. Appliances which are major sources of latent and sensible heat gain loads must be vented to the exterior. It would be very difficult to provide sufficient cooling to overcome the heat gain which an unvented clothes dryer would produce.

Rates of Heat Gain from Occupants of Conditioned Spaces[a]

Degree of Activity	Typical Application	Total Heat Adults, Male			Total Heat Adjusted[b]			Sensible Heat			Latent Heat		
		Watts	Btuh	kcal/hr	Watts	Btuh	kcal/hr	Watts	Btuh	kcal/hr	Watts	Btuh	kcal/hr
Seated at rest	Theater, movie	115	400	100	100	350	90	60	210	55	40	140	30
Seated, very light work writing	Offices, hotels, apts	140	480	120	120	420	105	65	230	55	55	190	50
Seated, eating	Restaurant[c]	150	520	130	170	580[e]	145	75	255	60	95	325	80
Seated, light work, typing	Offices, hotels, apts	185	640	160	150	510	130	75	255	60	75	255	65
Standing, light work or walking slowly	Retail Store, bank	235	800	200	185	640	160	90	315	80	95	325	80
Light bench work	Factory	255	880	220	230	780	195	100	345	90	130	435	110
Walking, 3 mph, light machine work	Factory	305	1040	260	305	1040	260	100	345	90	205	695	170
Bowling[d]	Bowling alley	350	1200	300	280	960	240	100	345	90	180	615	150
Moderate dancing	Dance hall	400	1360	340	375	1280	320	120	405	100	255	875	220
Heavy work, heavy machine work, lifting	Factory	470	1600	400	470	1600	400	165	565	140	300	1035	260
Heavy work, athletics	Gymnasium	585	2000	500	525	1800	450	185	635	160	340	1165	290

[a]Note; Tabulated values are based on 78 F room dry-bulb temperature. For 80 F room dry-bulb, the total heat remains the same, but the sensible heat value should be decreased by approximately 8% and the latent heat values increased accordingly.

[b]Adjusted total heat gain is based on normal percentage of men, women, and children for the application listed, with the postulate that the gain from an adult female is 85% of that for an adult male, and that the gain from a child is 75% of that for an adult male.

[c]Adjusted total heat value for eating in a restaurant, includes 60 Btuh for food per individual (30 Btu sensible and 30 Btu latent).

[d]For bowling figure one person per alley actually bowling, and all others as sitting (400 Btuh) or standing and walking slowly (790 Btuh).

Also refer to Tables 4 and 5, Chapter 8.
All values rounded to nearest 5 watts or kcal/hr or to nearest 10 Btuh.

Reprinted with permission from ASHRAE, Fundamentals Handbook, 1977

FIGURE 7-50 / *Rates of heat gain from occupants in conditioned spaces*

7-26   Solar Radiation

Solar radiation consists primarily of heat gain through the windows. The window heat gain for both *absorbed solar energy* and *transmitted heat gain* are calculated together by use of a heat gain multiplier. This multiplier (Fig. 7-51) takes into consideration glass orientation (the direction the window faces), type of glass, type of shading, and outside design temperature, and the result is expressed in Btuh per square foot.

Glass which is protected by permanent shading, such as a wide roof overhang, is generally calculated as glass facing north. The overhang probably only protects part of the glass area, and in making the heat gain calculations, it is necessary to separate the square foot of glass which will be shaded from that portion which won't be shaded. The amount of shaded area varies with the direction the window faces, the length of the overhang, and the geographic latitude (in degrees, Fig. 7-52) of the building. The table in Fig. 7-53 lists *shade line factors* which give the distance below the bottom of the fascia which the shadow will cover for every foot of overhang. The shade line factors shown are the average for the 5 hours of

Design Solar Heat Gain Through Windows and Conduction Heat Gain Sensible Cooling Load Due to Transmitted and Absorbed Solar Energy Due to Air-to-Air Temperature Difference, Btuh per sq ft

Outdoor Design Temp.	Regular Single Glass						Regular Double Glass						Heat Absorbing Double Glass					
	85	90	95	100	105	110	85	90	95	100	105	110	85	90	95	100	105	110
No Awnings or Inside Shading																		
North	23	27	31	35	38	44	19	21	24	26	28	30	12	14	17	19	21	23
NE and NW	56	60	64	68	71	77	46	48	51	53	55	57	27	29	32	34	36	38
East and West	81	85	89	93	96	102	68	70	73	75	77	79	42	44	47	49	51	53
SE and SW	70	74	78	82	85	91	59	61	64	66	68	70	35	37	40	42	44	46
South	40	44	48	52	55	61	33	35	38	40	42	44	19	21	24	26	28	30
Draperies or Venetian Blinds																		
North	15	19	23	27	30	36	12	14	17	19	21	23	9	11	14	16	18	20
NE and NW	32	36	40	44	47	53	27	29	32	34	36	38	20	22	25	27	29	31
East and West	48	52	56	60	63	69	42	44	47	49	51	53	30	32	35	37	39	41
SE and SW	40	44	48	52	55	61	35	37	40	42	44	46	24	26	29	31	33	35
South	23	27	31	35	38	44	20	22	25	27	29	31	15	17	20	22	24	26
Roller Shades Half-Drawn																		
North	18	22	26	30	33	39	15	17	20	22	24	26	10	12	15	17	19	21
NE and NW	40	44	48	52	55	61	38	40	43	45	47	49	24	26	29	31	33	35
East and West	61	65	69	73	76	82	54	56	59	61	63	65	35	37	40	42	44	46
SE and SW	52	56	60	64	67	73	46	48	51	53	55	57	30	32	35	37	39	41
South	29	33	37	41	44	50	27	29	32	34	36	38	18	20	23	25	27	29
Awnings																		
North	20	24	28	32	35	41	13	15	18	20	22	24	10	12	15	17	19	21
NE and NW	21	25	29	33	36	42	14	16	19	21	23	25	11	13	16	18	20	22
East and West	22	26	30	34	37	43	14	16	19	21	23	25	12	14	17	19	21	23
SE and SW	21	25	29	33	36	42	14	16	19	21	23	25	11	13	16	18	20	22
South	21	24	28	32	35	41	13	15	18	20	22	24	11	13	16	18	20	22

Reprinted with permission from ASHRAE, Fundamentals Handbook, 1977

FIGURE 7-51 / Solar heat gain

maximum solar intensity which would occur. Windows which face northeast and northwest cannot be effectively protected with roof overhangs, and they are considered to be in full sunshine with no shade.

Example

Given: Using the wall section in Fig. 7-54, *note* that the top of the window is located at the same elevation (level) as the bottom of the fascia. Assume this is a 4-ft wide, 4-ft high, regular double-glass window, facing SE, with draperies, and that the building is located at about latitude 35°.

Problem: Determine the area in shade and the area in sunlight, and then the amount of heat gain through the window. Assume a 95°F design temperature with medium temperature range.

Shade line factor (from Fig. 7-53) = 1.4
Roof overhang (from the wall section in Fig. 7-54) = 2 ft
Shade distance below overhang = 2 ft × 1.4 = 2.8 ft

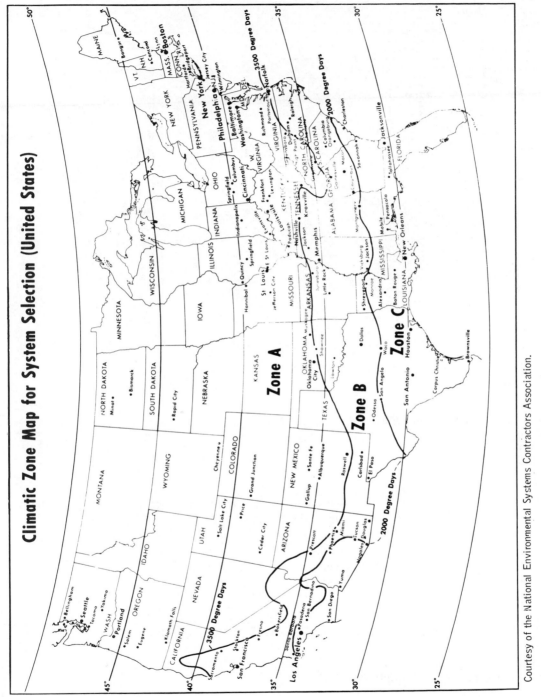

Courtesy of the National Environmental Systems Contractors Association.

FIGURE 7-52 / Summer daily temperature range

171

Shade Line Factors

Direction Window Faces	Latitude, Degrees						
	25	30	35	40	45	50	55
E	0.8	0.8	0.8	0.8	0.8	0.8	0.8
SE	1.9	1.6	1.4	1.3	1.1	1.0	0.9
S	10.1	5.4	3.6	2.6	2.0	1.7	1.4
SW	1.9	1.6	1.4	1.3	1.1	1.0	0.9
W	0.8	0.8	0.8	0.8	0.8	0.8	0.8

Note: Distance shadow line falls below the edge of the overhand equals shade line factor multiplied by width of overhang. Values are averages for five hours of greatest solar intensity on August 1.

Reprinted with permission from ASHRAE, Fundamentals Handbook, 1977

FIGURE 7-53 / Shade line factors

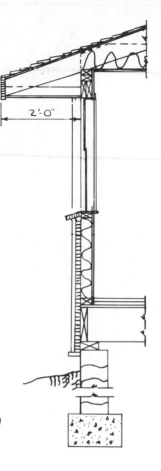

FIGURE 7-54 / Wall section

Since the top of the window lines up with the bottom of the fascia, the top 2.8 ft of the window are considered in shade and calculated as facing N.

Area of window in shade:

$$2.8 \text{ ft} \times 4.0 \text{ ft} = 11.2 \text{ sq ft}$$

Area of window in sun:

$$(4.0 \text{ ft} - 2.8 \text{ ft}) \times 4.0 \text{ ft} = 1.2 \text{ ft} \times 4.0 \text{ ft} = 4.8 \text{ sq ft}$$

Calculate the heat gain based on Fig. 7-51. Using an outdoor design temperature of 95 °F, the heat gain through shaded glass is:

$$11.2 \text{ sq ft (in shade)} \times 17 \text{ Btuh/sq ft (N, draperies)} = 191 \text{ Btuh}$$

The heat gain through unshaded glass is:

4.8 sq ft (in sun) × 40 Btuh/sq ft (SE, draperies) = 192 Btuh

Therefore, the total heat gain through the window is:

191 Btuh + 192 Btuh = 383 Btuh

Example

Given: Using the wall section in Fig. 7-55, *note* that the top of the window is 8 in. below the bottom of the fascia (overhang). Assume that this is a 3 ft–6 in.-wide, 4 ft–6-in.-high single-glass window, facing E, with draperies, and that the building is located at about latitude 35° where the outside design temperature is 95°F.

Problem: Determine the total heat gain through the window.

Shade line factor (from Fig. 7-53)   = 0.8
Roof overhang (from the wall section in Fig. 7-56) = 3 ft
Shade distance below overhang = 3 ft × 0.8   = 2.4 ft

Since the window begins 8 in. (0.67 ft) below the overhang, this distance must be subtracted from the shade distance to determine how much of the window is covered by the shade (Fig. 7-56).

Area of window in shade:

(2.4 ft − 0.67 ft) × 3.5 ft = 1.73 ft × 3.5 ft = 6.1 sq ft

Area of window in sun:

(4.5 ft − 1.73 ft) × 3.5 ft = 2.77 ft × 3.5 ft = 9.7 sq ft

Calculate the heat gain based on Fig. 7-51. Using an outside design temperature of 95°F, the heat gain through shaded glass is:

6.1 sq ft (in shade) × 17 Btuh/sq ft (N, draperies) = 104 Btuh

The heat gain through shaded glass is:

9.7 sq ft (in sun) × 47 Btuh/sq ft (E, draperies) = 456 Btuh

Therefore, the total heat gain through the window is:

104 Btuh + 456 Btuh = 560 Btuh

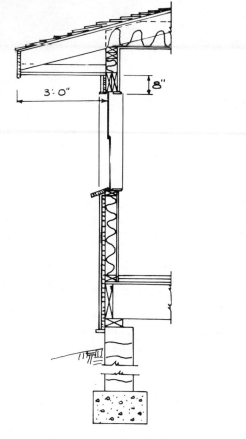

FIGURE 7-55　/　Wall section

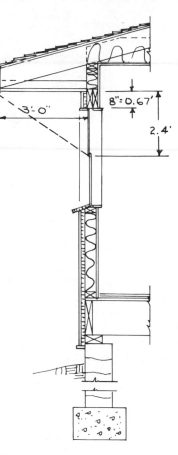

FIGURE 7-56　/　Shade line

7-27　Latent Heat Gain

Heat gain in buildings also occurs due to latent heat. In residential cooling the latent heat is generally estimated to be about 30 percent of the total sensible heat calculated. While this percentage is an approximation, there are numerous moisture sources in a residence. Since it would be very difficult to precisely evaluate the latent heat which will occur, ASHRAE has determined that the 30 percent results in a design system which will be comfortable.

7-28   Total Cooling Load

The total heat gain of the building is the sum of the sensible and latent heat gains. This total cooling load in a residence is calculated as 1.3 times the total sensible heat load.

The sensible heat gain is the total of:

1. The heat transmitted through the floors, ceilings, and walls.

2. The occupants' body heat.

3. The appliance heat, including lights.

4. The heat gain through glass, by both absorption and solar radiation.

5. Infiltration.

7-29   Heat Gain Calculations

Heat gain calculations are similar to heat loss calculations. The heat gain for the residence in Appendix B (the same one for which the heat loss was calculated) is calculated in Fig. 7-57. One major difference that must be considered is that during the summer, roof temperatures outside could be as high as 140–150 °F when the building has a dark roof, making its ΔT value very high compared to that of the walls. This must be taken into account when selecting the HTM value.

```
HTM
MEDIUM  95°F
WALLS  1.9
COLD WALLS  (MEDIUM 90°F) 1.4
CEILINGS  1.8 (DARK)
FLOORS, NO HEAT GAIN
INFILTRATION  1.5 BTUH/SQ.FT GROSS EXPOSED WALL

WINDOWS
DETERMINE SHADE LINE
    LOCATION, 35° LAT.
    ORIENTATION
    FRONT OF HOUSE FACES NORTHEAST, ALL IN SUN
    REAR OF HOUSE FACES SOUTHWEST
ROOF OVERHANG  2'-0"
SHADE LINE FACTOR
    SOUTHWEST  1.4
DRAPERIES –ALL EXCEPT KITCHEN
WINDOW HTM
    NORTHEAST  32 (WITH DRAPERIES)
               51 (WITHOUT DRAPERIES)
    SOUTHWEST  17 (SHADE & DRAPERIES)
               40 (SUN & DRAPERIES)
    SOUTHEAST  40 (SUN & DRAPERIES, NO OVERHANG)

OCCUPANTS
2 @ 225 BTUH IN KITCHEN
4 @ 225 BTUH IN LIVING-FAMILY
```

FIGURE 7-57   /   Heat gain for building

Room	Portion considered	Dimensions	Height	Gross area or l.f.	Openings	Opening area	Net area or l.f.	HTM U value	ETD	Heat gain (Btuh)	Room heat gain (Btuh)
BEDROOM 1 INC. 2 CLOSETS AND BATH	EXTERIOR WALL	12.7+18.7+2.5	8	272	4.0×4.0 ⟩ 3.0×4.0	28	244	1.9		464	
	CEILING	12.7×18.7+		323	—	—	323	1.8		582	
	SM. CLOSET	2.5×4.0+		—	—	—	—				
	CLOS¢ BATH	5.0×14.7		—	—	—	—				
	GLASS, S.W.SUN	4.0×1.2		4.8	—	—	4.8	40		192	
	SHADE	4.0×2.8		11.2	—	—	11.2	17		191	
	S.E. SUN	3.0×4.0		12	—	—	12	32		384	
	INFILTRATION	—	—	272	—	—	272	1.5		408	2221
BEDROOM 2 INC. 1 CLOSET	EXT. WALL	11.5+2.5	8	112	3.0×4.0	12	100	1.9		190	
	CEILING	11.5×18.8+		226	—	—	226	1.8		407	
		2.5×4.0		—	—	—	—				
	INFIL.	11.5+2.5	8	112	—	—	112	1.5		168	
	GLASS,S.W.SUN	3.0×1.2		3.6	—	—	3.6	32		115	
	SHADE	3.0×2.8		8.4	—	—	8.4	17		143	1148
LIVING (4 PEOPLE)	EXT. WALL	32.25+7.0	8	314	2-6.0×6.7	80	234	1.9		445	
	COLD WALL	18.8−7.0	8	95	—	—	95	1.4		133	
	CEILING	18.75×32.25		605	—	—	605	1.8		1089	
	INFIL.	—	—	314	—	—	314	1.5		471	
	GLASS,S.W.SUN	12×3.9		46.8	—	—	46.8	40		1872	
	SHADE	12×2.8		33.6	—	—	33.6	17		571	
	2 PEOPLE	—		—	—	—	—			900	5481
KITCHEN (2 PEOPLE)	EXT.WALL	15.8+7.0	8	183	4.0×3.0	12	171	1.9		291	
	COLD WALL	10.3·	8	82	3.0×6.8	21	61	1.4		86	
	CEILING	15.8×17.3		274	—	—	274	1.8		493	
	INFIL	—		183	—	—	183	1.5		275	
	GLASS,N.E.SUN	—		12	—	—	12	51		612	
	DOOR	—		21	—	—	21	9.4		197	
	APPLIANCES	—								1200	
	1 PERSON	—								450	3604
DINING	EXT.WALL	14.5	8	116	6.0×5.0	30	86	1.9		164	
	CEILING	14.5×13.3		193	—	—	193	1.8		375	
	INFIL	—		116	—	—	116	1.5		174	
	GLASS,N.E.SUN	—		30	—	—	30	32		960	1673

Room	Portion considered	Dimensions	Height	Gross area or l.f.	Openings	Opening area	Net area or l.f.	HTM U value	ETD	Heat gain (Btuh)	Room heat gain (Btuh)
ENTRY (AND HALL)	EXT. WALL	7.5+2.5	8	80	DITSIDELTS.	40	40	1.9		76	
	CEILING	4.0×37.0+ 13.3×(7.5+2.5)		289	6.0×6.8		289	1.8		520	
	INFIL			80			80	1.5		120	
	GLASS, N.E.			20			20	32		640	
	DOOR			20			20	12		240	1596
BEDROOM 3	EXT. WALL	14.5+6.8+ 6.8	8	225	4.0×4.0	16	209	1.9		397	
	CEILING	14.5×13.3		239			239	1.8		430	
	INFIL	6.8×6.8		225			225	1.5		338	
	GLASS, N.E.			16			16	32		512	1677
BATH	EXT. WALL	10.5	8	84	2.0×2.0	4	80	1.9		152	
	CEILING	10.5×6.8		72			72	1.8		130	
	INFIL			84			84	1.5		126	
	GLASS, SW			4			4	32		128	536

CALCULATED SENSIBLE HEAT GAIN   17,936 BTUH
TOTAL HEAT GAIN = SENSIBLE HEAT GAIN × 1.3 (LATENT HEAT)
17,936 × 1.3 = 23,317 BTUH

BEDROOM 1 = 2221 × 1.3 = 2887
BEDROOM 2 = 1148 × 1.3 = 1492
LIVING = 5481 × 1.3 = 7125
KITCHEN = 3604 × 1.3 = 4685
DINING = 1673 × 1.3 = 2175
ENTRY (AND HALL) = 1596 × 1.3 = 2075
BEDROOM 3 = 1677 × 1.3 = 2188
BATH = 536 × 1.3 = 697

FIGURE 7-57 / Heat gain for building (continued)

Thermal Properties of Typical Building and Insulating Materials—(Design Values)[a]

(For Industrial Insulation Design Values, see Table 3B). These constants are expressed in Btu per (hour) (square foot) (degree Fahrenheit temperature difference). Conductivities *(k)* are per inch thickness, and conductances *(C)* are for thickness or construction stated, not per inch thickness. **All values are for a mean temperature of 75 F, except as noted by an asterisk (*) which have been reported at 45 F.** The SI units for Resistance (last two columns) were calculated by taking the the values from the two Resistance columns under Customary Unit, and multiplying by the factor 1/k (r/in.) and 1/C (R) for the appropriate conversion factor in Table 18.

FIGURE 7-58 / *Resistance values*

Notes to Table

[a] Representative values for dry materials were selected by ASHRAE TC4.4, Insulation and Moisture Barriers. They are intended as design (not specification) values for materials in normal use. For properties of a particular product, use the value supplied by the manufacturer or by unbiased tests

[b] Resistance values are the reciprocals of *C* before rounding off *C* to two decimal places.

[c] Also see Insulating Materials, Board.

[d] Does not include paper backing and facing, if any. Where insulation forms a boundary (reflective or otherwise) of an air space, see Tables 1 and 2 for the insulating value of air space for the appropriate effective emittance and temperature conditions of the space.

[e] Conductivity varies with fiber diameter. (See Chapter 20, Thermal Conductivity section, and Fig. 1) Insulation is produced by different densities; therefore, there is a wide variation in thickness for the same *R*-value among manufacturers. No effort should be made to relate any specific *R*-value to any specific thickness. Commercial thicknesses generally available range from 2 to 8.5.

[f] Values are for aged board stock. For change in conductivity with age of expanded urethane, see Chapter 19, Factors Affecting Thermal Conductivity.

[g] Insulating values of acoustical tile vary, depending on density of the board and on type, size, and depth of perforations.

[h] The U. S. Department of Commerce, *Simplified Practice Recommendation for Thermal Conductance Factors for Preformed Above-Deck Roof Insulation,* No. R 257-55, recognizes the specification of roof insulation on the basis of the *C*-values shown. Roof insulation is made in thicknesses to meet these values.

[i] Face brick and common brick do not always have these specific densities. When density is different from that shown, there will be a change in thermal conductivity.

[j] Data on rectangular core concrete blocks differ from the above data on oval core blocks, due to core configuration, different mean temperatures, and possibly differences in unit weights. Weight data on the oval core blocks tested are not available.

[k] Weights of units approximately 7.625 in. high and 15.75 in. long. These weights are given as a means of describing the blocks tested, but conductance values are all for 1 ft[2] of area.

[l] Vermiculite, perlite, or mineral wool insulation. Where insulation is used, vapor barriers or other precautions must be considered to keep insulation dry.

[m] Values for metal siding applied over flat surfaces vary widely, depending on amount of ventilation of air space beneath the siding; whether air space is reflective or nonreflective; and on thickness, type, and application of insulating backing-board used. Values given are averages for use as design guides, and were obtained from several guarded hotbox tests (ASTM C236) or calibrated hotbox (BSS 77) on hollow-backed types and types made using backing-boards of wood fiber, foamed plastic, and glass fiber. Departures of ±50% or more from the values given may occur.

Reprinted with permission from ASHRAE, Fundamentals Handbook, 1977

FIGURE 7-58 / *Resistance values* (continued)

Description	Density (lb/ft³)	Conductivity (k)	Conductance (C)	Resistance[b] (R) Per inch thickness (1/k)	Resistance[b] (R) For thickness listed (1/C)	Specific Heat, Btu/(lb) (deg F)	SI Unit Resistance[b] (R) (m·K) / W	SI Unit Resistance[b] (R) (m²·K) / W
BUILDING BOARD								
Boards, Panels, Subflooring, Sheathing								
Woodboard Panel Products								
Asbestos-cement board	120	4.0	—	0.25	—	0.24	1.73	
Asbestos-cement board.................0.125 in.	120	—	33.00	—	0.03			0.005
Asbestos-cement board.................0.25 in.	120	—	16.50	—	0.06			0.01
Gypsum or plaster board ....0.375 in.	50	—	3.10	—	0.32	0.26		0.06
Gypsum or plaster board ....0.5 in.	50	—	2.22	—	0.45			0.08
Gypsum or plaster board ....0.625 in.	50	—	1.78	—	0.56			0.10
Plywood (Douglas Fir)......................	34	0.80	—	1.25	—	0.29	8.66	
Plywood (Douglas Fir)...............0.25 in.	34	—	3.20	—	0.31			0.05
Plywood (Douglas Fir)..............0.375 in.	34	—	2.13	—	0.47			0.08
Plywood (Douglas Fir)..............0.5 in.	34	—	1.60	—	0.62			0.11
Plywood (Douglas Fir)..............0.625 in.	34	—	1.29	—	0.77			0.19
Plywood or wood panels..........0.75 in.	34	—	1.07	—	0.93	0.29		0.16
Vegetable Fiber Board								
Sheathing, regular density.............0.5 in.	18	—	0.76	—	1.32	0.31		0.23
...........................0.78125 in.	18	—	0.49	—	2.06			0.36
Sheathing intermediate density ....0.5 in.	22	—	0.82	—	1.22	0.31		0.21
Nail-base sheathing.....................0.5 in.	25	—	0.88	—	1.14	0.31		0.20
Shingle backer.....................0.375 in.	18	—	1.06	—	0.94	0.31		0.17
Shingle backer.....................0.3125 in.	18	—	1.28	—	0.78			0.14
Sound deadening board ....0.5 in.	15	—	0.74	—	1.35	0.30		0.24
Tile and lay-in panels, plain or								
acoustic	18	0.40	—	2.50	—	0.14	17.33	
.............................0.5 in.	18	—	0.80	—	1.25			0.22
.............................0.75 in.	18	—	0.53	—	1.89			0.33
Laminated paperboard....................	30	0.50	—	2.00	—	0.33	13.86	
Homogeneous board from								
repulped paper	30	0.50	—	2.00	—	0.28	13.86	
Hardboard								
Medium density	50	0.73	—	1.37	—	0.31	9.49	
High density, service temp. service								
underlay	55	0.82	—	1.22	—	0.32	8.46	
High density, std. tempered	63	1.00	—	1.00	—	0.32	6.93	
Particleboard								
Low density	37	0.54	—	1.85	—	0.31	12.82	
Medium density	50	0.94	—	1.06	—	0.31	7.35	
High density	62.5	1.18	—	0.85	—	0.31	5.89	
Underlayment.....................0.625 in.	40	—	1.22	—	0.82	0.29		0.14
Wood subfloor ....0.75 in.		—	1.06	—	0.94	0.33		0.17
BUILDING MEMBRANE								
Vapor—permeable felt....................			16.70		0.06			0.01
Vapor—seal, 2 layers of mopped								
15-lb felt............................			8.35		0.12			0.02
Vapor—seal, plastic film			—		Negl..			
FINISH FLOORING MATERIALS								
Carpet and fibrous pad			0.48	2.08		0.34		0.37
Carpet and rubber pad			0.81	1.23		0.33		0.22
Cork tile ....0.125 in.			3.60	0.28		0.48		0.05
Terrazzo ....1 in.			12.50	0.08		0.19		0.01
Tile—asphalt, linoleum, vinyl, rubber			20.00	0.05		0.30		0.01
vinyl asbestos						0.24		
ceramic.............................						0.19		
Wood, hardwood finish ....0.75 in.			1.47	0.68				0.12
INSULATING MATERIALS								
BLANKET AND BATT								
Mineral Fiber, fibrous form processed								
from rock, slag, or glass								
approx.[e] 2–2.75 in....................	0.3–2.0		0.143		7[d]	0.17–0.23		1.23
approx.[e] 3–3.5 in....................	0.3–2.0		0.091		11[d]			1.94
approx.[e] 3.50–6.5....................	0.3–2.0		0.053		19[d]			3.35
approx.[e] 6–7 in.....................	0.3–2.0		0.045		22[d]			3.87
approx.[d] 8.5 in.....................	0.3–2.0		0.033		30[d]			5.28
BOARD AND SLABS								
Cellular glass	8.5	0.38		2.63		0.24	18.23	
Glass fiber, organic bonded	4–9	0.25		4.00		0.23	27.72	
Expanded rubber (rigid)......................	4.5	0.22		4.55		0.40	31.53	
Expanded polystyrene extruded								
Cut cell surface.......................	1.8	0.25		4.00		0.29	27.72	
Expanded polystyrene extruded								
Smooth skin surface.....................	2.2	0.20		5.00		0.29	34.65	
Expanded polystyrene extruded								
Smooth skin surface.....................	3.5	0.19		5.26			36.45	
Expanded polystyrene, molded beads.............	1.0	0.28		3.57		0.29	24.74	
Expanded polyurethane[f] (R-11 exp.) ....'........	1.5	0.16		6.25		0.38	43.82	
(Thickness 1 in. or greater)	2.5							

FIGURE 7-58 / Resistance values (continued)

179

Description	Density (lb/ft³)	Conductivity (k)	Conductance (C)	Resistance[b] (R) Per inch thickness (1/k)	Resistance[b] (R) For thickness listed (1/C)	Specific Heat, Btu/(lb) (deg F)	SI Unit Resistance[b] (R) (m·K)/W	SI Unit Resistance[b] (R) (m²·K)/W
Mineral fiber with resin binder	15	0.29	—	3.45	—	0.17	23.91	
Mineral fiberboard, wet felted								
Core or roof insulation.	16–17	0.34	—	2.94	—		20.38	
Acoustical tile.	18	0.35	—	2.86	—	0.19	19.82	
Acoustical tile.	21	0.37	—	2.70	—		18.71	
Mineral fiberboard, wet molded								
Acoustical tile[g].	23	0.42	—	2.38	—	0.14	16.49	
Wood or cane fiberboard								
Acoustical tile[g]. . . . . 0.5 in.	—	—	0.80	—	1.25	0.31		0.22
Acoustical tile[g]. . . . . 0.75 in.	—	—	0.53	—	1.89			0.33
Interior finish (plank, tile)	15	0.35	—	2.86	—	0.32	19.82	
Wood shredded (cemented in preformed slabs).	22	0.60	—	1.67	—	0.31	11.57	
LOOSE FILL								
Cellulosic insulation (milled paper or wood pulp).	2.3–3.2	0.27–0.32	—	3.13–3.70	—	0.33	21.69–25.64	
Sawdust or shavings.	8.0–15.0	0.45	—	2.22	—	0.33	15.39	
Wood fiber, softwoods	2.0–3.5	0.30	—	3.33	—	0.33	23.08	
Perlite, expanded.	5.0–8.0	0.37	—	2.70	—	0.26	18.71	
Mineral fiber (rock, slag or glass)								
approx.[e] 3.75–5 in..	0.6–2.0	—	—		11	0.17		1.94
approx.[e] 6.5–8.75 in..	0.6–2.0	—	—		19			3.35
approx.[e] 7.5–10 in..	0.6–2.0	—	—		22			3.87
approx.[e] 10.25–13.75 in.	0.6–2.0	—	—		30			5.28
Vermiculite, exfoliated.	7.0–8.2	0.47	—	2.13	—	3.20	14.76	
	4.0–6.0	0.44	—	2.27	—		15.73	
ROOF INSULATION[h]								
Preformed, for use above deck								
Different roof insulations are available in different thicknesses to provide the design C values listed.[h] Consult individual manufacturers for actual *thickness of their material.*			0.72 to 0.12		1.39 to 8.33		— —	0.24 to 1.47
MASONRY MATERIALS								
CONCRETES								
Cement mortar.	116	5.0	—	0.20	—		1.39	
Gypsum-fiber concrete 87.5% gypsum, 12.5% wood chips.	51	1.66	—	0.60	—	0.21	4.16	
Lightweight aggregates including ex-	120	5.2	—	0.19	—		1.32	
panded shale, clay or slate; expanded	100	3.6	—	0.28	—		1.94	
slags; cinders; pumice; vermiculite;	80	2.5	—	0.40	—		2.77	
also cellular concretes	60	1.7	—	0.59	—		4.09	
	40	1.15	—	0.86	—		5.96	
	30	0.90	—	1.11	—		7.69	
	20	0.70		1.43			9.91	
Perlite, expanded.	40	0.93		1.08			7.48	
	30	0.71		1.41			9.77	
	20	0.50		2.00		0.32	13.86	
Sand and gravel or stone aggregate (oven dried).	140	9.0	—	0.11		0.22	0.76	
Sand and gravel or stone aggregate (not dried)	140	12.0		0.08			0.55	
Stucco.	116	5.0	—	0.20			1.39	
MASONRY UNITS								
Brick, common[i].	120	5.0	—	0.20	—	0.19	1.39	
Brick, face[i].	130	9.0	—	0.11	—		0.76	
Clay tile, hollow:								
1 cell deep . . . . 3 in.	—	—	1.25	—	0.80	0.21		0.14
1 cell deep . . . . 4 in.	—	—	0.90	—	1.11			0.20
2 cells deep. . . . . 6 in.	—	—	0.66	—	1.52			0.27
2 cells deep. . . . . 8 in.	—	—	0.54	—	1.85			0.33
2 cells deep. . . . . 10 in.	—	—	0.45	—	2.22			0.39
3 cells deep. . . . . 12 in.	—	—	0.40	—	2.50			0.44
Concrete blocks, three oval core:								
Sand and gravel aggregate . . . . 4 in.			1.40		0.71	0.22		0.13
. . . . 8 in.			0.90		1.11			0.20
. . . . 12 in.			0.78		1.28			0.23
Cinder aggregate . . . . 3 in.			1.16		0.86	0.21		0.15
. . . . 4 in.			0.90		1.11			0.20
. . . . 8 in.			0.58		1.72			0.30
. . . . 12 in.			0.53		1.89			0.33
Lightweight aggregate . . . . 3 in.			0.79		1.27	0.21		0.22
(expanded shale, clay, slate . . . . 4 in.			0.67		1.50			0.26
or slag; pumice). . . . . 8 in.			0.50		2.00			0.35
. . . . 12 in.			0.44		2.27			0.40

FIGURE 7-58 / *Resistance values (continued)*

Description	Density (lb/ft³)	Conductivity (k)	Conductance (C)	Resistance[b] (R) Per inch thickness (1/k)	Resistance[b] (R) For thickness listed (1/C)	Specific Heat, Btu/(lb) (deg F)	SI Unit Resistance[b] (R) (m·K)/W	SI Unit Resistance[b] (R) (m²·K)/W
Concrete blocks, rectangular core.*ʲ								
Sand and gravel aggregate								
2 core, 8 in. 36 lb.ᵏ*	—	—	0.96	—	1.04	0.22		0.18
Same with filled coresʲ*	—	—	0.52	—	1.93	0.22		0.34
Lightweight aggregate (expanded shale, clay, slate or slag, pumice):								
3 core, 6 in. 19 lb.ᵏ*	—	—	0.61	—	1.65	0.21		0.29
Same with filled coresⁱ*	—	—	0.33	—	2.99			0.53
2 core, 8 in. 24 lb.ᵏ*	—	—	0.46	—	2.18			0.38
Same with filled coresⁱ*	—	—	0.20	—	5.03			0.89
3 core, 12 in. 38 lb.ᵏ*	—	—	0.40	—	2.48			0.44
Same with filled coresⁱ*	—	—	0.17	—	5.82			1.02
Stone, lime or sand.	—	12.50	—	0.08	—	0.19	0.55	
Gypsum partition tile:								
3 × 12 × 30 in. solid	—	—	0.79	—	1.26	0.19		0.22
3 × 12 × 30 in. 4-cell	—	—	0.74	—	1.35			0.24
4 × 12 × 30 in. 3-cell	—	—	0.60	—	1.67			0.29
METALS								
(See Chapter 37, Table 3)								
PLASTERING MATERIALS								
Cement plaster, sand aggregate	116	5.0	—	0.20	—	0.20	1.39	
Sand aggregate ... 0.375 in.	—	—	13.3	—	0.08	0.20		0.01
Sand aggregate ... 0.75 in.	—	—	6.66	—	0.15	0.20		0.03
Gypsum plaster:								
Lightweight aggregate ... 0.5 in.	45	—	3.12	—	0.32			0.06
Lightweight aggregate ... 0.625 in.	45	—	2.67	—	0.39			0.07
Lightweight agg. on metal lath ... 0.75 in.	—	—	2.13	—	0.47			0.08
Perlite aggregate	45	1.5	—	0.67	—	0.32	4.64	
Sand aggregate	105	5.6	—	0.18	—	0.20	1.25	
Sand aggregate ... 0.5 in.	105	—	11.10	—	0.09			0.02
Sand aggregate ... 0.625 in.	105	—	9.10	—	0.11			0.02
Sand aggregate on metal lath ... 0.75 in.	—	—	7.70	—	0.13			0.02
Vermiculite aggregate	45	1.7	—	0.59	—		4.09	
ROOFING								
Asbestos-cement shingles	120	—	4.76	—	0.21	0.24		0.04
Asphalt roll roofing	70	—	6.50	—	0.15	0.36		0.03
Asphalt shingles	70	—	2.27	—	0.44	0.30		0.08
Built-up roofing ... 0.375 in.	70	—	3.00	—	0.33	0.35		0.06
Slate ... 0.5 in.	—	—	20.00	—	0.05	0.30		0.01
Wood shingles, plain and plastic film faced	—	—	1.06	—	0.94	0.31		0.17
SIDING MATERIALS (On Flat Surface)								
Shingles								
Asbestos-cement.	120	—	4.75	—	0.21			0.04
Wood, 16 in., 7.5 exposure.	—	—	1.15	—	0.87	0.31		0.15
Wood, double, 16-in., 12-in. exposure	—	—	0.84	—	1.19	0.28		0.21
Wood, plus insul. backer board, 0.3125 in.	—	—	0.71	—	1.40	0.31		0.25
Siding								
Asbestos-cement, 0.25 in., lapped.	—	—	4.76	—	0.21	0.24		0.04
Asphalt roll siding	—	—	6.50	—	0.15	0.35		0.03
Asphalt insulating siding (0.5 in. bed.)	—	—	0.69	—	1.46	0.35		0.26
Wood, drop, 1 × 8 in.	—	—	1.27	—	0.79	0.28		0.14
Wood, bevel, 0.5 × 8 in., lapped.	—	—	1.23	—	0.81	0.28		0.14
Wood, bevel, 0.75 × 10 in., lapped.	—	—	0.95	—	1.05	0.28		0.18
Wood, plywood, 0.375 in., lapped	—	—	1.59	—	0.59	0.29		0.10
Wood, medium density siding, 0.4375 in.	40	1.49	—	0.67	—	0.28	4.65	
Aluminum or Steelᵐ, over sheathing								
Hollow-backed.			1.61		0.61	0.29		0.11
Insulating-board backed nominal 0.375 in.			0.55		1.82	0.32		0.32
Insulating-board backed nominal 0.375 in., foil backed.			0.34		2.96			0.52
Architectural glass			10.00		0.10	0.20		0.02
WOODS								
Maple, oak, and similar hardwoods	45	1.10	—	0.91	—	0.30	6.31	
Fir, pine, and similar softwoods	32	0.80	—	1.25	—	0.33	8.66	
Fir, pine, and similar softwoods ... 0.75 in.	32	—	1.06	—	0.94	0.33		0.17
... 1.5 in.		—	0.53	—	1.89			0.33
... 2.5 in.		—	0.32	—	3.12			0.60
... 3.5 in.		—	0.23	—	4.35			0.75

FIGURE 7-58 / Resistance values (continued)

181

Position of Surface	Direction of Heat Flow	Surface *Emittance*					
		Non-reflective $\varepsilon = 0.90$		Reflective $\varepsilon = 0.20$		Reflective $\varepsilon = 0.05$	
		h_i	R	h_i	R	h_i	R
STILL AIR							
Horizontal	Upward	1.63	0.61	0.91	1.10	0.76	1.32
Sloping—45 deg	Upward	1.60	0.62	0.88	1.14	0.73	1.37
Vertical	Horizontal	1.46	0.68	0.74	1.35	0.59	1.70
Sloping—45 deg	Downward	1.32	0.76	0.60	1.67	0.45	2.22
Horizontal	Downward	1.08	0.92	0.37	2.70	0.22	4.55

Reprinted with permission from ASHRAE,
Fundamentals Handbook, 1977

FIGURE 7-59   /   *Inside air film*

Position of Surface	Direction of Heat Flow	Surface *Emittance*					
		Non-reflective $\varepsilon = 0.90$		Reflective $\varepsilon = 0.20$		Reflective $\varepsilon = 0.05$	
MOVING AIR (Any Position)		h_0	R	h_0	R	h_0	R
15-mph Wind (for winter)	Any	6.00	0.17				
7.5-mph Wind (for summer)	Any	4.00	0.25				

Reprinted with permission from ASHRAE,
Fundamentals Handbook, 1977

FIGURE 7-60   /   *Outside air film*

Thermal Resistances of Plane[a] Air Spaces[d,e,*]

All resistance values expressed in (hour)(square foot)(degree Fahrenheit temperature difference) per Btu

Values apply only to air spaces of uniform thickness bounded by plane, smooth, parallel surfaces with no leakage of air to or from the space. Thermal resistance values for multiple air spaces must be based on careful estimates of mean temperature differences for each air space.

See the Caution section, under Overall Coefficients and Their Practical Use.

Position of Air Space	Direction of Heat Flow	Mean Temp,[b] (F)	Temp Diff,[g] (deg F)	0.5-in. Air Space[d] Value of E[b,c] 0.03	0.05	0.2	0.5	0.82	0.75-in. Air Space[d] Value of E[b,c] 0.03	0.05	0.2	0.5	0.82
Horiz.	Up	90	10	2.13	2.03	1.51	0.99	0.73	2.34	2.22	1.61	1.04	0.75
		50	30	1.62	1.57	1.29	0.96	0.75	1.71	1.66	1.35	0.99	0.77
		50	10	2.13	2.05	1.60	1.11	0.84	2.30	2.21	1.70	1.16	0.87
		0	20	1.73	1.70	1.45	1.12	0.91	1.83	1.79	1.52	1.16	0.93
		0	10	2.10	2.04	1.70	1.27	1.00	2.23	2.16	1.78	1.31	1.02
		-50	20	1.69	1.66	1.49	1.23	1.04	1.77	1.74	1.55	1.27	1.07
		-50	10	2.04	2.00	1.75	1.40	1.16	2.16	2.11	1.84	1.46	1.20
45° Slope	Up	90	10	2.44	2.31	1.65	1.06	0.76	2.96	2.78	1.88	1.15	0.81
		50	30	2.06	1.98	1.56	1.10	0.83	1.99	1.92	1.52	1.08	0.82
		50	10	2.55	2.44	1.83	1.22	0.90	2.90	2.75	2.00	1.29	0.94
		0	20	2.20	2.14	1.76	1.30	1.02	2.13	2.07	1.72	1.28	1.00
		0	10	2.63	2.54	2.03	1.44	1.10	2.72	2.62	2.08	1.47	1.12
		-50	20	2.08	2.04	1.78	1.42	1.17	2.05	2.01	1.76	1.41	1.16
		-50	10	2.62	2.56	2.17	1.66	1.33	2.53	2.47	2.10	1.62	1.30
Vertical	Horiz.	90	10	2.47	2.34	1.67	1.06	0.77	3.50	3.24	2.08	1.22	0.84
		50	30	2.57	2.46	1.84	1.23	0.90	2.91	2.77	2.01	1.30	0.94
		50	10	2.66	2.54	1.88	1.24	0.91	3.70	3.46	2.35	1.43	1.01
		0	20	2.82	2.72	2.14	1.50	1.13	3.14	3.02	2.32	1.58	1.18
		0	10	2.93	2.82	2.20	1.53	1.15	3.77	3.59	2.64	1.73	1.26
		-50	20	2.90	2.82	2.35	1.76	1.39	2.90	2.83	2.36	1.77	1.39
		-50	10	3.20	3.10	2.54	1.87	1.46	3.72	3.60	2.87	2.04	1.56
45° Slope	Down	90	10	2.48	2.34	1.67	1.06	0.77	3.53	3.27	2.10	1.22	0.84
		50	30	2.64	2.52	1.87	1.24	0.91	3.43	3.23	2.24	1.39	0.99
		50	10	2.67	2.55	1.89	1.25	0.92	3.81	3.57	2.40	1.45	1.02
		0	20	2.91	2.80	2.19	1.52	1.15	3.75	3.57	2.63	1.72	1.26
		0	10	2.94	2.83	2.21	1.53	1.15	4.12	3.91	2.81	1.80	1.30
		-50	20	3.16	3.07	2.52	1.86	1.45	3.78	3.65	2.90	2.05	1.57
		-50	10	3.26	3.16	2.58	1.89	1.47	4.35	4.18	3.22	2.21	1.66
Horiz.	Down	90	10	2.48	2.34	1.67	1.06	0.77	3.55	3.29	2.10	1.22	0.85
		50	30	2.66	2.54	1.88	1.24	0.91	3.77	3.52	2.38	1.44	1.02
		50	10	2.67	2.55	1.89	1.25	0.92	3.84	3.59	2.41	1.45	1.02
		0	20	2.94	2.83	2.20	1.53	1.15	4.18	3.96	2.83	1.81	1.30
		0	10	2.96	2.85	2.22	1.53	1.16	4.25	4.02	2.87	1.82	1.31
		-50	20	3.25	3.15	2.58	1.89	1.47	4.60	4.41	3.36	2.28	1.69
		-50	10	3.28	3.18	2.60	1.90	1.47	4.71	4.51	3.42	2.30	1.71

FIGURE 7-61 / Air spaces

183

Thermal Resistances of Plane[a] Air Spaces[d,e]*

Position of Air Space	Direction of Heat Flow	Mean Temp,[b] (F)	Temp Diff,[b] (deg F)	1.5-in. Air Space[b,c] Value of E[d] 0.03	0.05	0.2	0.5	0.82	3.5-in. Air Space[d] Value of E[b,c] 0.03	0.05	0.2	0.5	0.82
Horiz	Up	90	10	2.55	2.41	1.71	1.08	0.77	2.84	2.66	1.83	1.13	0.80
		50	30	1.87	1.81	1.45	1.04	0.80	2.09	2.01	1.58	1.10	0.84
		50	10	2.50	2.40	1.81	1.21	0.89	2.80	2.66	1.95	1.28	0.93
		0	20	2.01	1.95	1.63	1.23	0.97	2.25	2.18	1.79	1.32	1.03
		0	10	2.43	2.35	1.90	1.38	1.06	2.71	2.62	2.07	1.47	1.12
		-50	20	1.94	1.91	1.68	1.36	1.13	2.19	2.14	1.86	1.47	1.20
		-50	10	2.37	2.31	1.99	1.55	1.26	2.65	2.58	2.18	1.67	1.33
45° Slope	Up	90	10	2.92	2.73	1.86	1.14	0.80	3.18	2.96	1.97	1.18	0.82
		50	30	2.14	2.06	1.61	1.12	0.84	2.26	2.17	1.67	1.15	0.86
		50	10	2.88	2.74	1.99	1.29	0.94	3.12	2.95	2.10	1.34	0.96
		0	20	2.30	2.23	1.82	1.34	1.04	2.42	2.35	1.90	1.38	1.06
		0	10	2.79	2.69	2.12	1.49	1.13	2.98	2.87	2.23	1.54	1.16
		-50	20	2.22	2.17	1.88	1.49	1.21	2.34	2.29	1.97	1.54	1.25
		-50	10	2.71	2.64	2.23	1.69	1.35	2.87	2.79	2.33	1.75	1.39
Vertical	Horiz.	90	10	3.99	3.66	2.25	1.27	0.87	3.69	3.40	2.15	1.24	0.85
		50	30	2.58	2.46	1.84	1.23	0.90	2.67	2.55	1.89	1.25	0.91
		50	10	3.79	3.55	2.39	1.45	1.02	3.63	3.40	2.32	1.42	1.01
		0	20	2.76	2.66	2.10	1.48	1.12	2.88	2.78	2.17	1.51	1.14
		0	10	3.51	3.35	2.51	1.67	1.23	3.49	3.33	2.50	1.67	1.23
		-50	20	2.64	2.58	2.18	1.66	1.33	2.82	2.75	2.30	1.73	1.37
		-50	10	3.31	3.21	2.62	1.91	1.48	3.40	3.30	2.67	1.94	1.50
45° Slope	Down	90	10	5.07	4.55	2.56	1.36	0.91	4.81	4.33	2.49	1.34	0.90
		50	30	3.58	3.36	2.31	1.42	1.00	3.51	3.30	2.28	1.40	1.00
		50	10	5.10	4.66	2.85	1.60	1.09	4.74	4.36	2.73	1.57	1.08
		0	20	3.85	3.66	2.68	1.74	1.27	3.81	3.63	2.66	1.74	1.27
		0	10	4.92	4.62	3.16	1.94	1.37	4.59	4.32	3.02	1.88	1.34
		-50	20	3.62	3.50	2.80	2.01	1.54	3.77	3.64	2.90	2.05	1.57
		-50	10	4.67	4.47	3.40	2.29	1.70	4.50	4.32	3.31	2.25	1.68
Horiz.	Down	90	10	6.09	5.35	2.79	1.43	0.94	10.07	8.19	3.41	1.57	1.00
		50	30	6.27	5.63	3.18	1.70	1.14	9.60	8.17	3.86	1.88	1.22
		50	10	6.61	5.90	3.27	1.73	1.15	11.15	9.27	4.09	1.93	1.24
		0	20	7.03	6.43	3.91	2.19	1.49	10.90	9.52	4.87	2.47	1.62
		0	10	7.31	6.66	4.00	2.22	1.51	11.97	10.32	5.08	2.52	1.64
		-50	20	7.73	7.20	4.77	2.85	1.99	11.64	10.49	6.02	3.25	2.18
		-50	10	8.09	7.52	4.91	2.89	2.01	12.98	11.56	6.36	3.34	2.22

[a] See Chapter 20, section or. Factors Affecting Heat Transfer across Air Spaces.

[b] Interpolation is permissible for other values of mean temperature, temperature differences, and effective emittance E. Interpolation and moderate extrapolation for air spaces greater than 3.5 in. are also permissible.

[c] Effective emittance of the space E is given by $1/E = 1/e_1 + 1/e_2 - 1$, where e_1 and e_2 are the emittances of the surfaces of the air space (See section B of Table 1.)

[d] Credit for an air space resistance value cannot be taken more than once and only for the boundary conditions established.

[e] Resistances of horizontal spaces with heat flow downward are substantially independent of temperature difference.

[f] Thermal resistance values were determined from the relation $R = 1/C$, where $C = h_c + Eh_r$, h_c is the conduction-convection coefficient, Eh_r is the radiation coefficient $\cong 0.00686\, E\,[(460 + t_m)/100]^3$, and t_m is the mean temperature of the air space. For interpretation from Table 2 to air space thicknesses less than 0.5 in. (as in insulating window glass), assume $h_c = 0.795\,(1 + 0.0016)$ and compute R-values from the above relations for an air space thickness of 0.2 in.

*Based on National Bureau of Standards data presented in Housing Research Paper No. 32, Housing and Home Finance Agency 1954, U. S. Government Printing Office, Washington, 20402.

Reprinted with permission from ASHRAE, Fundamentals Handbook, 1977

FIGURE 7-61 / Air spaces (continued)

Reflectivity and Emittance Values of Various Surfaces[c] and Effective Emittances of Air Spaces

Surface	Reflectivity in Percent	Average Emittance ε	Effective Emittance E of Air Space	
			One surface emittance ε; the other 0.90	Both surfaces emittances ε
Aluminum foil, bright	92 to 97	0.05	0.05	0.03
Aluminum sheet	80 to 95	0.12	0.12	0.06
Aluminum coated paper, polished	75 to 84	0.20	0.20	0.11
Steel, galvanized, bright. . .	70 to 80	0.25	0.24	0.15
Aluminum paint	30 to 70	0.50	0.47	0.35
Building materials: wood, paper, masonry, nonmetallic paints	5 to 15	0.90	0.82	0.82
Regular glass	5 to 15	0.84	0.77	0.72

Reprinted with permission from ASHRAE, Fundamentals Handbook, 1977

FIGURE 7-62   /   Surface values of reflectivity and emissivity

Coefficients of Transmission (U) of Frame Walls

These coefficients are expressed in Btu per (hour) (square foot) (degree Fahrenheit) difference in temperature between the air on the two sides), and are based on an outside wind velocity of 15 mph

Replace Air Space with 3.5-in. R-11 Blanket Insulation (New Item 4)

Construction	Resistance (R)			
	1		2	
	Between Framing	At Framing	Between Framing	At Framing
1. Outside surface (15 mph wind)	0.17	0.17	0.17	0.17
2. Siding, wood, 0.5 in.× 8 in. lapped (average)	0.81	0.81	0.81	0.81
3. Sheathing, 0.5-in. asphalt impregnated	1.32	1.32	1.32	1.32
4. Nonreflective air space, 3.5 in. (50 Fmean; 10 deg F temperature difference)	1.01	—	11.00	—
5. Nominal 2-in. × 4-in. wood stud	—	4.38	—	4.38
6. Gypsum wallboard, 0.5 in.	0.45	0.45	0.45	0.45
7. Inside surface (still air)	0.68	0.68	0.68	0.68
Total Thermal Resistance (R)	R_i=4.44	R_s=7.81	R_i=14.43	R_s=7.81

Construction No. 1: $U_i = 1/4.44 = 0.225$; $U_s = 1/7.81 = 0.128$. With 20% framing (typical of 2-in. × 4-in. studs @ 16-in. o.c.), $U_{av} = 0.8 (0.225) + 0.2 (0.128) = 0.206$ (See Eq 9)

Construction No. 2: $U_i = 1/14.43 = 0.069$; $U_s = 0.128$. With framing unchanged, $U_{av} = 0.8(0.069) + 0.2(0.128) = 0.081$

FIGURE 7-63   /   U values

Coefficients of Transmission *(U)* of Solid Masonry Walls

Coefficients are expressed in Btu per (hour) (square foot) (degree Fahrenheit difference in temperature between the air on the two sides), and are based on an outside wind velocity of 15 mph

Replace Furring Strips and Air Space with 1-in. Extruded Polystyrene (New Item 4)

Construction	1 Resistance *(R)* Between Furring	At Furring	2
1. Outside surface (15 mph wind)	0.17	0.17	0.17
2. Common brick, 8 in.	1.60	1.60	1.60
3. Nominal 1-in. ×3-in. vertical furring	—	0.94	—
4. Nonreflective air space, 0.75 in. (50 F mean; 10 deg F temperature difference)	1.01	—	5.00
5. Gypsum wallboard, 0.5 in.	0.45	0.45	0.45
6. Inside surface (still air)	0.68	0.68	0.68
Total Thermal Resistance (R)	$R_i = 3.91$	$R_s = 3.84$	$R_i = 7.90 = R_s$

Construction No. 1: $U_i = 1/3.91 = 0.256$; $U_s = 1/3.84 = 0.260$. With 20% framing (typical of 1-in. × 3-in. vertical furring on masonry @ 16-in. o.c.)
$U_{av} = 0.8 (0.256) + 0.2 (0.260) = 0.257$
Construction No. 2: $U_i = U_s = U_{av} = 1/7.90 = 0.127$

Coefficients of Transmission *(U)* of Frame Partitions or Interior Walls

Coefficients are expressed in Btu per (hour) (square foot) (degree Fahrenheit difference in temperature between the air on the two sides), and are based on still air (no wind) conditions on both sides

Replace Air Space with 3.5-in. R-11 Blanket Insulation (New Item 3)

Construction	1 Between Framing	At Framing	2 Between Framing	At Framing
1. Inside surface (still air)	0.68	0.68	0.68	0.68
2. Gypsum wallboard, 0.5 in.	0.45	0.45	0.45	0.45
3. Nonreflective air space, 3.5 in. (50 F mean; 10 deg F temperature difference)	1.01	—	11.00	—
4. Nominal 2-in. × 4-in. wood stud	—	4.38	—	4.38
5. Gypsum wallboard 0.5 in.	0.45	0.45	0.45	0.45
6. Inside surface (still air)	0.68	0.68	0.68	0.68
Total Thermal Resistance (R)	$R_i = 3.27$	$R_s = 6.64$	$R_i = 13.26$	$R_s = 6.64$

Construction No. 1: $U_i = 1/3.27 = 0.306$; $U_s = 1/6.64 = 0.151$. With 10% framing (typical of 2-in. × 4-in. studs @ 24-in. o.c.), $U_{av} = 0.9 (0.306) + 0.1 (0.151) = 0.290$
Construction No. 2: $U_i = 1/13.26 = 0.075$, $U_s = 1/6.64 = 0.151$. With framing unchanged, $U_{av} = 0.9(0.075) + 0.1(0.151) = 0.083$

Coefficients of Transmission *(U)* of Masonry Cavity Walls

Coefficients are expressed in Btu per (hour) (square foot) (degree Fahrenheit difference in temperature between the air on the two sides), and are based on an outside wind velocity of 15 mph

Replace Furring Strips and Gypsum Wallboard with 0.625-in. Plaster (Sand Aggregate) Applied Directly to Concrete Block–Fill 2.5-in. Air Space with Vermiculite Insulation (New Items 3 and 7.

Construction	1 Resistance *(R)* Between Furring	At Furring	2
1. Outside surface (15 mph wind)	0.17	0.17	0.17
2. Common brick, 8 in.	0.80	0.80	0.80
3. Nonreflective air space, 2.5 in. (30 F mean; 10 deg F temperature difference)	1.10*	1.10*	5.32**
4. Concrete block, stone aggregate, 4 in.	0.71	0.71	0.71
5. Nonreflective air space 0.75 in. (50 F mean; 10 deg F temperature difference)	1.01	—	—
6. Nominal 1-in. × 3-in. vertical furring	—	0.94	—
7. Gypsum wallboard, 0.5 in.	0.45	0.45	0.11
8. Inside surface (still air)	0.68	0.68	0.68
Total Thermal Resistance (R)	$R_i = 4.92$	$R_s = 4.85$	$R_i = R_s = 7.79$

Construction No. 1: $U_i = 1/4.92 = 0.203$; $U_s = 1/4.85 = 0.206$. With 20% framing (typical of 1-in. × 3-in. vertical furring on masonry @16-in. o.c.), $U_{av} = 0.8(0.203) + 0.2(0.206) = 0.204$
Construction No. 2: $U_i = U_s = U_{av} = 1.79 = 0.128$

FIGURE 7-63   /   U values (continued)

186

Coefficients of Transmission *(U)* of Masonry Partitions

Coefficients are expressed in Btu per (hour) (square foot) (degree Fahrenheit differencein temperature between the air on the two sides), and are based on still air (no wind) conditions on both sides

Replace Concrete Block with 4-in. Gypsum Tile (New Item 3) Construction	1	2
1. Inside surface (still air)	0.68	0.68
2. Plaster, lightweight aggregate, 0.625 in.	0.39	0.39
3. Concrete block, cinder aggregate, 4 in.	1.11	1.67
4. Plaster, lightweight aggregate, 0.625 in.	0.39	0.39
5. Inside surface (still air)	0.68	0.68
Total Thermal Resistance(R)	3.25	3.81

Construction No. 1: $U = 1/3.25 = 0.308$
Construction No. 2: $U = 1/3.81 = 0.262$

Coefficients of Transmission (U) of Frame Construction Ceilings and Floors

Coefficients are expressed in Btu per (hour) (square foot) (degree Fahrenheit difference between the air on the two sides), and are based on still air (no wind) on both sides

Assume Unheated Attic Space above Heated Room with Heat Flow Up—Remove Tile, Felt, Plywood, Sub-floor and Air Space—Replace with R-19 Blanket Insulation (New Item 4)

	1		2	
Heated Room Below Unheated Space	Resistance (R)			
Construction (Heat Flow Up)	Between Floor Joists	At Floor Joist	Between Floor Joists	At Floor Joists
1. Bottom surface (still air)	0.61	0.61	0.61	0.61
2. Metal lath and lightweight aggregate, plaster, 0.75 in.	0.47	0.47	0.47	0.47
3. Nominal 2-in. × 8-in. floor joist	—	9.06	—	9.06
4. Nonreflective airspace, 7.25-in.	0.93*	—	19.00	—
5. Wood subfloor, 0.75 in.	0.94	0.94	—	—
6. Plywood, 0.625 in.	0.78	0.78	—	—
7. Felt building membrane	0.06	0.06	—	—
8. Resilient tile	0.05	0.05	—	—
9. Top surface (still air)	0.61	0.61	0.61	0.61
Total Thermal Resistance (R)	$R_i = 4.45$	$R_s = 12.58$	$R_i = 20.69$	$R_s = 10.75$

Construction No. 1 $U_i = 1/4.45 = 0.225$; $U_s = 1/12.58 = 0.079$. With 10% framing (typical of 2-in. joists @ 16-in. o.c.), $U_{av} = 0.9 (0.225) + 0.1 (0.079) = 0.210$
Construction No. 2 $U_i = 1/20.69 = 0.048$; $U_s = 1/10.75 = 0.093$. With framing unchanged, $U_{av} = 0.9 (0.048) + 0.1 (0.093) = 0.053$

*Use largest air space (3.5 in.) value shown in Table 2.

Coefficients of Transmission *(U)* of Metal Construction Flat Roofs and Ceilings
(Winter Conditions, Upward Flow)

Coefficients are expressed in Btu per (hour) (square foot) (degree Fahrenheit difference in temperature between the air on the two sides), and are based on upon outside wind velocity of 15 mph

Replace Rigid Roof Deck Insulation ($C = 0.24$) and Sand Aggregate Plaster with Rigid Roof Deck Insulation, $C = 0.36$ and Lightweight Aggregate Plaster (New Items 2 and 6) Construction (Heat Flow Up)	1	2
1. Inside surface (still air)	0.61	0.61
2. Metal lath and sand aggregate plaster, 0.75 in	0.13	0.47
3. Structural beam	0.00*	0.00*
4. Nonreflective air space (50 F mean; 10 deg F temperature difference	0.93**	0.93**
5. Metal deck	0.00*	0.00*
6. Rigid roof deck insulation, $C = 0.24 (R = 1/c)$	4.17	2.78
7. Built-up roofing, 0.375 in.	0.33	0.33
8. Outside surface (15 mph wind)	0.17	0.17
Total Thermal Resistance (R)	6.34	5.29

Construction No. 1: $U = 1/6.34 = 0.158$
Construction No. 2: $U = 1/5.29 = 0.189$

*If structural beams and metal deck are to be considered, the technique shown in *Examples 1 and 2*, and Fig. 3 may be used to estimate total R. Full scale testing of a suitable portion of the construction is, however, preferable.
**Use largest air space (3.5 in.) value shown

FIGURE 7-63 / U values (continued)

187

Coefficients of Transmission (U) of Pitched Roofs [b]

Coefficients are expressed in Btu per (hour) (square foot) (degree Fahrenheit difference in temperature between the air on the two sides), and are based on an outside wind velocity of 15 mph for heat flow upward and 7.5 mph for heat flow downward

Find U_{av} for same Construction 2 with Heat Flow Down (Summer Conditions)

Construction 1 (Heat Flow Up) (Reflective Air Space)	1		2	
	Between Rafters	At Rafters	Between Rafters	At Rafters
1. Inside surface (still air)	0.62	0.62	0.76	0.76
2. Gypsum wallboard 0.5 in., foil backed	0.45	0.45	0.45	0.45
3. Nominal 2-in. × 4-in. ceiling rafter	—	4.38	—	4.38
4. 45 deg slope reflective air space, 3.5 in. (50 F mean, 30 deg F temperature difference)	2.17	—	4.33	—
5. Plywood sheathing, 0.625 in.	0.78	0.78	0.78	0.78
6. Felt building membrane	0.06	0.06	0.06	0.06
7. Asphalt shingle roofing	0.44	0.44	0.44	0.44
8. Outside surface (15 mph wind)	0.17	0.17	0.25**	0.25**
Total Thermal Resistance (R)	R_i=4.69	R_s=6.90	R_i=7.07	R_s=7.12

Construction No. 1: U_i = 1/4.69 = 0.213; U_s = 1/6.90 = 0.145. With 10% framing (typical of 2-in. rafters @16-in. o.c.), U_{av} = 0.9 (0.213) + 0.1 (0.145) = 0.206
Construction No. 2: U_i = 1/7.07 = 0.141; U_s = 1/7.12 = 0.140. With framing unchanged, U_{av} = 0.9 (0.141) + 0.1 (0.140) = 0.141

Find U_{av} for same Construction 2 with Heat Flow Down (Summer Conditions)

Construction 1 (Heat Flow Up) (Non-Reflective Air Space)	3		4	
	Between Rafters	At Rafters	Between Rafters	At Rafters
1. Inside surface (still air)	0.62	0.62	0.76	0.76
2. Gypsum wallboard, 0.5 in.	0.45	0.45	0.45	0.45
3. Nominal 2-in. × 4-in. ceiling rafter	—	4.38	—	4.38
4. 45 deg slope, nonreflective air space, 3.5 in. (50 F mean; 10 deg F temperature difference)	0.96	—	0.90*	—
5. Plywood sheathing, 0.625 in.	0.78	0.78	0.78	0.78
6. Felt building membrane	0.06	0.06	0.06	0.06
7. Asphalt shingle roofing	0.44	0.44	0.44	0.44
8. Outside surface (15-mph wind)	0.17	0.17	0.25**	0.25**
Total Thermal Resistance (R)	R_i=3.48	R_s=6.90	R_i=3.64	R_s=7.12

Construction No. 3: U_i = 1/3.48 = 0.287; U_s = 1/6.90 = 0.145. With 10% framing typical of 2-in. rafters @ 16-in. o.c., U_{av} = 0.9 (0.287) + 0.1 (0.145) = 0.273
Construction No. 4: U_i = 1/3.64 = 0.275; U_s = 1/7.12 = 0.140. With framing unchanged, U_{av} = 0.9 (0.275) + 0.1 (0.140) = 0.262

[b] Pitch of roof—45 deg.
* Air space value at 90 F mean, 10 F dif. temperature difference.
** 7.5-mph wind.

Coefficients of Transmission (U) of Masonry Walls

Coefficients are expressed in Btu per (hour) (square foot) (degree Fahrenheit difference in temperature between the air on the two sides), and are based on an outside wind velocity of 15 mph

Replace Cinder Aggregate Block with 6-in. Light-weight Aggregate Block with Cores Filled (New Item 4)

Construction	Resistance (R)			
	1		2	
	Between Furring	At Furring	Between Furring	At Furring
1. Outside surface (15 mph wind)	0.17	0.17	0.17	0.17
2. Face brick, 4 in.	0.44	0.44	0.44	0.44
3. Cement mortar, 0.5 in.	0.10	0.10	0.10	0.10
4. Concrete block, cinder aggregate, 8 in.	1.72	1.72	2.99	2.99
5. Reflective air space, 0.75 in. (50 F mean; 30 deg F temperature difference)	2.77	—	2.77	—
6. Nominal 1-in. × 3-in. vertical furring	—	0.94	—	0.94
7. Gypsum wallboard, 0.5 in., foil backed	0.45	0.45	0.45	0.45
8. Inside surface (still air)	0.68	0.68	0.68	0.68
Total Thermal Resistance (R)	R_i= 6.33	R_s= 4.50	R_i= 7.60	R_s= 5.77

Construction No. 1: U_i = 1/6.33 = 0.158; U_s = 1/4.50 = 0.222. With 20% framing (typical of 1-in. × 3-in. vertical furring on masonry @ 16-in. o.c.), U_{av} = 0.8 (0.158) + 0.2 (0.222) = 0.171
Construction No. 2: U_i = 1/7.60 = 0.132. U_s = 1/5.77 = 0.173. With framing unchanged, U_{av} = 0.8(0.132) + 0.2(0.173) = 1.40

FIGURE 7-63 / U values (continued)

Coefficients of Transmission (*U*) of Windows, Skylights, and Light Transmitting Partitions

These values are for heat transfer from air to air, Btu/(hr · ft² · F).

PART A—VERTICAL PANELS (EXTERIOR WINDOWS, SLIDING PATIO DOORS, AND PARTITIONS)— FLAT GLASS, GLASS BLOCK, AND PLASTIC SHEET

Description	Exterior[a] Winter	Summer	Interior
Flat Glass[b]			
single glass	1.10	1.04	0.73
insulating glass—double[c]			
0.1875-in. air space[d]	0.62	0.65	0.51
0.25-in. air space[d]	0.58	0.61	0.49
0.5-in. air space[e]	0.49	0.56	0.46
0.5-in. air space, low emittance coating[f]			
$e = 0.20$	0.32	0.38	0.32
$e = 0.40$	0.38	0.45	0.38
$e = 0.60$	0.43	0.51	0.42
insulating glass—triple[c]			
0.25-in. air spaces[d]	0.39	0.44	0.38
0.5-in. air spaces[g]	0.31	0.39	0.30
storm windows			
1-in. to 4-in. air space[d]	0.50	0.50	0.44
Plastic Sheet			
single glazed			
0.125-in. thick	1.06	0.98	—
0.25-in. thick	0.96	0.89	—
0.5-in. thick	0.81	0.76	—
insulating unit—double[c]			
0.25-in. air space[d]	0.55	0.56	—
0.5-in. air space[c]	0.43	0.45	—
Glass Block[h]			
6 × 6 × 4 in. thick	0.60	0.57	0.46
8 × 8 × 4 in. thick	0.56	0.54	0.44
—with cavity divider	0.48	0.46	0.38
12 × 12 × 4 in. thick	0.52	0.50	0.41
—with cavity divider	0.44	0.42	0.36
12 × 12 × 2 in. thick	0.60	0.57	0.46

PART B—HORIZONTAL PANELS (SKYLIGHTS)— FLAT GLASS, GLASS BLOCK, AND PLASTIC DOMES

Description	Exterior[a] Winter[i]	Summer[j]	Interior[f]
Flat Glass[e]			
single glass	1.23	0.83	0.96
insulating glass—double[c]			
0.1875-in. air space[d]	0.70	0.57	0.62
0.25-in. air space[d]	0.65	0.54	0.59
0.5-in. air space[c]	0.59	0.49	0.56
0.5-in. air space, low emittance coating[f]			
$e = 0.20$	0.48	0.36	0.39
$e = 0.40$	0.52	0.42	0.45
$e = 0.60$	0.56	0.46	0.50
Glass Block[h]			
11 × 11 × 3 in. thick with cavity divider	0.53	0.35	0.44
12 × 12 × 4 in. thick with cavity divider	0.51	0.34	0.42
Plastic Domes[k]			
single-walled	1.15	0.80	—
double-walled	0.70	0.46	—

PART C—ADJUSTMENT FACTORS FOR VARIOUS WINDOW AND SLIDING PATIO DOOR TYPES (MULTIPLY *U* VALUES IN PARTS A AND B BY THESE FACTORS)

Description	Single Glass	Double or Triple Glass	Storm Windows
Windows			
All Glass[l]	1.00	1.00	1.00
Wood Sash—80% Glass	0.90	0.95	0.90
Wood Sash—60% Glass	0.80	0.85	0.80
Metal Sash—80% Glass	1.00	1.20[m]	1.20[m]
Sliding Patio Doors			
Wood Frame	0.95	1.00	—
Metal Frame	1.00	1.10[m]	—

[a] See Part C for adjustment for various window and sliding patio door types.
[b] Emittance of uncooled glass surface = 0.84.
[c] Double and triple refer to the number of lights of glass.
[d] 0.125-in. glass.
[e] 0.25-in. glass.
[f] Coating on either glass surface facing air space; all other glass surfaces uncoated.
[g] Window design: 0.25-in. glass—0.125-in. glass—0.25-in. glass.
[h] Dimensions are nominal.
[i] For heat flow up.
[j] For heat flow down.
[k] Based on area of opening, not total surface area.
[l] Refers to windows with negligible opaque area.
[m] Values will be less than these when metal sash and frame incorporate thermal breaks. In some thermal break designs, *U*-values will be equal to or less than those for the glass. Window manufacturers should be consulted for specific data.

Reprinted with permission from ASHRAE, Fundamentals Handbook, 1977

FIGURE 7-63 / U values (continued)

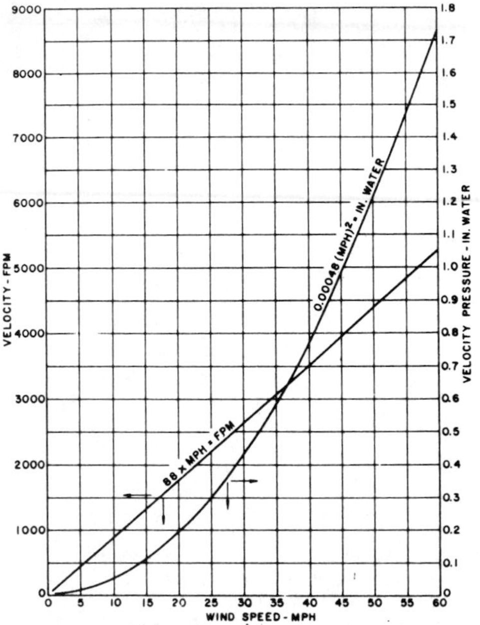

Wind vs Velocity Pressure and Velocity in FPM

Reprinted with permission from ASHRAE, Fundamentals Handbook, 1977

FIGURE 7-64 / Infiltration

Infiltration Through Double-Hung Wood Windows
Expressed in cubic feet per (hour) (foot of crack)[d]

Type of Window	Pressure Difference (Inches of Water)				
	0.10	0.20	0.30	0.40	0.50
A. Wood Double-Hung Window (Locked) (Leakage expressed as cubic feet per hour per foot of sash crack; only leakage around sash and through frame given)	25	50	25	100	125
1. Nonweatherstripped, loose fit[a]	77[d]	122[d]	150[d]	194[d]	225[d]
2. Nonweatherstripped, average fit[b]	27[d]	43[d]	57[d]	69[d]	80[d]
3. Weatherstripped, loose fit	28[d]	44[d]	58[d]	70[d]	81[d]
4. Weatherstripped, average fit	14[d]	23[d]	30[d]	36[d]	42[d]
B. Frame-Wall Leakage[c] (Leakage is that passing between the frame of a wood double-hung window and the wall)					
1. Around frame in masonry wall, not caulked	17[d]	26[d]	34[d]	41[d]	48[d]
2. Around frame in masonry wall, caulked	3[d]	5[d]	6[d]	7[d]	8[d]
3. Around frame in wood frame wall	13[d]	21[d]	29[d]	35[d]	42[d]

[a] A 0.094-in. crack and clearance represent a poorly fitted window, much poorer than average.
[b] The fit of the average double-hung wood window was determined as 0.0625-in. crack and 0.047-in. clearance by measurements on approximately 600 windows under heating season conditions.
[c] The values given for frame leakage are per foot of sash perimeter, as determined for double-hung wood windows. Some of the frame leakage in masonry walls originates in the brick wall itself, and cannot be prevented by caulking. For the additional reason that caulking is not done perfectly and deteriorates with time, it is considered advisable to choose the masonry frame leakage values for caulked frames as the average determined by the caulked and non-caulked tests.
[d] Multiply by 0.0258 for l/s per metre of crack.

Reprinted with permission from ASHRAE, Fundamentals Handbook, 1977

Heat Loss of Concrete Floors at or Near Grade Level per Foot of Exposed Edge

Outdoor Design Temperature, F	Heat Loss per Foot of Exposed Edge, Btuh	
	Recommended 2-in. Edge Insulation	1-in. Edge Insulation
−20 to −30	50	55
−10 to −20	45	50
0 to −10	40	45

Outdoor Design Temperature, F	1-in. Edge Insulation	No Edge Insulation[a]
−20 to −30	60	75
−10 to −20	55	65
0 to −10	50	60

[a]This construction not recommended; shown for comparison only.

FIGURE 7-65 / Slab edge losses

Floor Heat Loss to be Used When Warm Air Perimeter Heating Ducts Are Embedded in Slabs[a]
Btuh per (linear foot of heated edge)

Outdoor Design Temperature, F	Edge Insulation		
	1-in. Vertical Extending Down 18 in. Below Floor Surface	1-in. L-Type Extending at Least 12 in. Deep and 12 in. Under	2-in. L-Type Extending at Least 12 in. Down and 12 in. Under
−20	105	100	85
−10	95	90	75
0	85	80	65
10	75	70	55
20	62	57	45

[a] Factors include loss downward through inner area of slab.

Reprinted with permission from ASHRAE, Fundamentals Handbook, 1977

190

State & City	Winter Dry-Bulb Temp¹ (F)	Summer Dry-Bulb Temp¹ (F)	North Latitude (0)	Daily Range
ALABAMA				
Alexander City	20	95	35	M
Anniston	15	95	35	M
Auburn	25	95	30	M
Birmingham	20	95	35	M
Decatur	15	95	35	M
Dothan	25	95	30	M
Florence	15	95	35	M
Gadsden	20	95	35	M
Huntsville	15	95	35	M
Mobile ★ {AP	25	95	30	M
{CO	30	95	30	M
Montgomery	25	95	30	M
Selma	25	95	30	M
Talladega	15	95	35	M
Tuscaloosa	20	95	35	M
ALASKA				
Anchorage	−20	70	60	M
Barrow	−45	55	70	L
Fairbanks	−50	80	65	M
Juneau	−5	70	60	M
Kodiak	5	65	55	L
Nome	−30	60	65	L
ARIZONA				
Douglas	20	100	30	H
Flagstaff	5	80	35	H
Fort Huachuca	25	95	30	H
Kingman	25	100	35	H
Nogales	20	100	30	H
Phoenix	30	105	35	H
Prescott	15	95	35	H
Tucson	30	100	35	H
Winslow	10	95	35	H
Yuma	40	110	30	H
ARKANSAS				
Blytheville	15	95	35	M
Camden	20	95	35	M
El Dorado	20	95	35	M
Fayetteville	10	95	35	M
Fort Smith	15	100	35	M
Hot Springs	20	95	35	M
Jonesboro	15	95	35	M
Little Rock	20	95	35	M
Pine Bluff	20	95	35	M
Texarkana	25	95	35	M
CALIFORNIA				
Bakersfield	30	100	35	H
Barstow	25	100	35	H
Blythe	35	110	35	H
Burbank	35	95	35	M
Chico	30	100	40	H
Concord	35	90	40	H
Covina	35	95	35	H
Crescent City	35	70	40	M
Downey	35	90	35	M
El Cajon	30	95	30	H
El Centro	35	110	35	H
Escondido	35	90	35	H
Eureka Arcata	35	65	40	L
Fairfield	30	95	40	H
Fresno	30	100	35	H
Laguna Beach	35	80	35	M
Livermore	30	95	35	M
Lompoc	35	80	35	M
Long Beach	35	85	35	M
Los Angeles ★ {AP	40	85	35	M
{CO	40	90	35	M
Merced	30	100	35	H
Modesto	35	100	35	H
Monterey	35	80	35	M
Napa	30	90	40	H
Needles	35	110	35	H
Oakland	35	80	35	M
Oceanside	40	80	35	L
Ontario	30	95	35	H
Oxnard	35	80	35	M
Palmdale	25	100	35	H
Palm Springs	35	110	35	H
Pasadena	35	95	35	H
Petaluma	30	90	40	H
Pomona	30	95	35	H
Redding	35	100	40	H
Redlands	35	95	35	H
Richmond	35	80	40	M
Riverside	30	95	35	H
Sacramento	30	95	40	H
Salinas	35	85	35	M
San Bernardino	30	100	35	H
San Diego	40	85	30	L
San Fernando	35	95	35	H
San Francisco ★ {AP	35	80	35	M
{CO	40	75	40	L

State & City	Winter Dry-Bulb Temp¹ (F)	Summer Dry-Bulb Temp¹ (F)	North Latitude (0)	Daily Range
CALIFORNIA Cont.				
San Jose	35	90	35	H
San Luis Obispo	35	85	35	H
Santa Ana	35	90	35	H
Santa Barbara	35	85	35	M
Santa Cruz	30	85	35	H
Santa Maria	30	80	35	M
Santa Monica	45	75	35	M
Santa Paula	35	90	35	H
Santa Rosa	30	95	40	H
Stockton	30	100	40	H
Ukiah	30	95	40	H
Visalia	35	100	35	H
Yreka	15	95	40	H
Yuba City	30	100	40	H
COLORADO				
Alamosa	−15	80	35	H
Boulder	5	90	40	H
Colorado Springs	0	90	40	H
Denver	0	90	40	H
Durango	0	85	35	H
Fort Collins	−5	90	40	H
Grand Junction	10	95	40	H
Greeley	−5	90	40	H
La Junta	−5	95	40	H
Leadville	−5	75	40	H
Pueblo	−5	95	40	H
Sterling	−5	95	40	H
Trinidad	5	90	35	H
CONNECTICUT				
Bridgeport	5	90	40	M
Hartford	5	90	40	M
New Haven	5	85	40	M
New London	5	85	40	M
Norwalk	0	90	40	M
Norwich	0	85	40	M
Waterbury	0	90	40	M
Windsor Locks	0	90	40	M
DELAWARE				
Dover	15	90	40	M
Wilmington	15	90	40	M
DISTRICT OF COLUMBIA				
Washington	15	90	40	M
FLORIDA				
Belle Glade	35	90	25	M
Cape Kennedy	35	90	30	M
Daytona Beach	35	90	30	M
Fort Lauderdale	45	90	25	M
Fort Myers	40	90	25	M
Fort Pierce	40	90	25	M
Gainesville	30	95	30	M
Jacksonville	25	95	30	M
Key West	55	90	25	L
Lakeland	35	95	30	M
Miami	40	90	25	M
Miami Beach	45	90	25	M
Ocala	30	95	30	M
Orlando	35	95	30	M
Panama City	30	90	30	L
Pensacola	25	90	30	M
St. Augustine	30	90	30	M
St. Petersburg	35	90	30	M
Sanford	30	95	30	M
Sarasota	35	90	25	M
Tallahassee	25	95	30	M
Tampa	35	90	30	M
GEORGIA				
Albany	30	95	30	M
Americus	25	95	30	M
Athens	20	95	35	M
Atlanta	20	90	35	M
Augusta	20	95	35	M
Brunswick	25	95	30	M
Columbus	25	95	30	M
Dalton	15	95	35	M
Dublin	25	95	30	M
Gainesville	20	90	35	M
Griffin	20	95	35	M
La Grange	20	95	35	M
Macon	25	95	35	M
Marietta	20	95	35	M
Moultrie	30	95	30	M
Rome	20	95	35	M
Savannah	25	95	30	M
Valdosta	30	95	30	M
Waycross	25	95	30	M
HAWAII				
Hilo	55	85	20	M
Honolulu	60	85	20	L

State & City	Winter Dry-Bulb Temp¹ (F)	Summer Dry-Bulb Temp¹ (F)	North Latitude (0)	Daily Range
HAWAII Cont.				
Kaneoke	60	85	20	L
Wakiawa	60	85	20	L
IDAHO				
Boise	10	95	45	H
Burley	5	95	40	H
Coeur d'Alene	5	90	50	H
Idaho Falls	−10	90	45	H
Lewiston	10	95	45	H
Moscow	0	90	45	H
Mountain Home	5	95	45	H
Pocatello	−5	90	45	H
Twin Falls	5	95	40	H
ILLINOIS				
Aurora	−5	90	40	M
Belleville	10	95	40	M
Bloomington	0	95	40	M
Carbondale	10	95	40	M
Champaign/Urbana	0	95	40	M
Chicago	0	90	40	M
Danville	0	95	40	M
Decatur	0	95	40	M
Dixon	−5	90	40	M
Elgin	−5	90	40	M
Freeport	−10	90	40	M
Galesburg	0	90	40	M
Greenville	5	95	40	M
Joliet	−5	90	40	M
Kankakee	0	90	40	M
LaSalle/Peru	0	95	40	M
Macomb	0	95	40	M
Moline	−5	95	40	M
Mt. Vernon	10	95	40	M
Peoria	0	90	40	M
Quincy	0	95	40	M
Rantoul	0	90	40	M
Rockford	−5	90	40	M
Springfield	0	90	40	M
Waukegan	−5	90	40	M
INDIANA				
Anderson	5	90	40	M
Bedford	5	95	40	M
Bloomington	5	90	40	M
Columbus	5	90	40	M
Crawfordsville	0	95	40	M
Evansville	10	95	40	M
Fort Wayne	5	90	40	M
Goshen	0	90	40	M
Hobart	0	90	40	M
Huntington	0	90	40	M
Indianapolis	0	90	40	M
Jeffersonville	10	95	40	M
Kokomo	0	90	40	M
Lafayette	0	90	40	M
La Porte	0	90	40	M
Marion	0	90	40	M
Muncie	0	90	40	M
Peru	0	90	40	M
Richmond	0	90	40	M
Shelbyville	5	90	40	M
South Bend	0	90	40	M
Terre Haute	5	95	40	M
Valparaiso	−5	90	40	M
Vincennes	5	95	40	M
IOWA				
Ames	−10	90	40	M
Burlington	0	90	40	M
Cedar Rapids	−5	90	40	M
Clinton	−5	90	40	M
Council Bluffs	−5	95	40	M
Des Moines	−5	90	40	M
Dubuque	−10	90	40	M
Fort Dodge	−10	90	40	M
Iowa City	−5	90	40	M
Keokuk	0	95	40	M
Marshalltown	−10	90	40	M
Mason City	−10	90	45	M
Newton	−5	95	40	M
Ottumwa	−5	95	40	M
Sioux City	−10	95	40	M
Waterloo	−10	90	40	M
KANSAS				
Atchison	0	95	40	M
Chanute	5	95	35	M
Dodge City	5	95	40	M
El Dorado	5	100	40	M
Emporia	5	95	40	M
Garden City	0	100	40	H
Goodland	0	95	40	H
Great Bend	5	100	40	H
Hutchinson	5	100	40	H
Liberal	5	100	35	H

★ AP - Airport
CO - City Office
¹ Temperatures are rounded off to permit use of precalculated HTM tables.

FIGURE 7-66 / *Outside design temperatures*

State & City	Winter Dry-Bulb Temp[1] (F)	Summer Dry-Bulb Temp[1] (F)	North Latitude[1] (0)	Daily Range
KANSAS Cont.				
Manhattan	0	100	40	M
Parsons	5	95	35	M
Russell	0	100	40	H
Salina	5	100	40	H
Topeka	5	95	40	M
Wichita	5	100	35	M
KENTUCKY				
Ashland	10	90	40	M
Bowling Green	10	95	35	M
Corbin	5	90	35	M
Covington	5	90	40	M
Hopkinsville	10	95	35	M
Lexington	10	90	40	M
Louisville	10	95	40	M
Madisonville	10	95	35	M
Owensboro	10	95	40	M
Paducah	10	95	35	M
LOUISIANA				
Alexandria	25	95	30	M
Baton Rouge	30	95	30	M
Bogalusa	25	95	30	M
Houma	25	90	30	M
Lafayette	25	95	30	M
Lake Charles	30	95	30	M
Minden	25	95	30	M
Monroe	25	95	30	M
Natchitoches	25	95	30	M
New Orleans	35	95	30	M
Shreveport	25	95	30	M
MAINE				
Augusta	−5	85	45	M
Bangor	−5	85	45	M
Caribou	−15	80	45	M
Lewiston	−5	85	45	M
Millinocket	−15	85	45	M
Portland	0	85	45	M
Waterville	−5	85	45	M
MARYLAND				
Baltimore ★ AP	15	90	40	M
Baltimore ★ CO	20	90	40	M
Cumberland	5	90	40	M
Frederick	10	90	40	M
Hagerstown	10	90	40	M
Salisbury	15	90	40	M
MASSACHUSETTS				
Boston	10	90	40	M
Clinton	0	85	40	M
Fall River	5	85	40	M
Framingham	0	85	40	M
Gloucester	5	85	40	M
Greenfield	5	85	40	M
Lawrence	0	90	40	M
Lowell	0	90	40	M
New Bedford	10	85	40	M
Pittsfield	−5	85	40	M
Springfield	0	90	40	M
Taunton	0	85	40	M
Worcester	0	85	40	M
MICHIGAN				
Adrian	0	90	40	M
Alpena	−5	85	45	H
Battle Creek	5	90	40	M
Benton Harbor	5	90	40	M
Detroit	5	90	40	M
Escanaba	−5	80	45	M
Flint	0	85	45	M
Grand Rapids	5	90	45	M
Holland	5	90	40	M
Jackson	0	90	40	M
Kalamazoo	5	90	40	M
Lansing	5	85	45	M
Marquette	−5	85	45	M
Mt. Pleasant	5	85	45	M
Muskegon	5	85	45	M
Pontiac	0	90	40	M
Port Huron	0	90	45	M
Saginaw	0	85	45	M
Sault Ste. Marie	−10	80	45	M
Traverse City	0	85	45	M
Ypsilanti	5	90	40	M
MINNESOTA				
Albert Lea	−10	90	45	M
Alexandria	−15	90	45	M
Bemidji	−30	85	45	M
Brainerd	−20	85	45	M
Duluth	−15	80	45	M
Faribault	−15	90	45	M
Fergus Falls	−20	90	45	M

State & City	Winter Dry-Bulb Temp[1] (F)	Summer Dry-Bulb Temp[1] (F)	North Latitude[1] (0)	Daily Range
MINNESOTA Cont.				
International Falls	−25	80	50	H
Mankato	−15	90	45	M
Minneapolis/ St. Paul	−10	90	45	M
Rochester	−15	90	45	M
St. Cloud	−20	90	45	M
Virginia	−25	85	45	M
Willmar	−15	90	45	M
Winona	−10	90	45	M
MISSISSIPPI				
Biloxi	30	90	30	M
Clarksdale	20	95	35	M
Columbus	15	95	35	M
Greenville	20	95	35	M
Greenwood	20	95	35	M
Hattiesburg	25	95	30	M
Jackson	20	95	30	M
Laurel	25	95	30	M
McComb	25	95	30	M
Meridian	20	95	30	M
Natchez	25	95	30	M
Tupelo	20	95	35	M
Vicksburg	25	95	30	M
MISSOURI				
Cape Girardeau	10	95	35	M
Columbia	5	95	40	M
Farmington	5	95	40	M
Hannibal	0	95	40	M
Jefferson City	5	95	40	M
Joplin	10	95	35	M
Kansas City	5	95	40	M
Kirksville	5	95	40	M
Mexico	0	95	40	M
Moberly	5	95	40	M
Poplar Bluff	10	95	35	M
Rolla	5	95	40	M
St. Joseph	0	95	40	M
St. Louis ★ AP	5	95	40	M
St. Louis ★ CO	10	95	40	M
Sedalia	5	95	40	M
Sikeston	10	95	35	M
Springfield	10	95	35	M
MONTANA				
Billings	−10	90	45	H
Bozeman	−15	85	45	H
Butte	−20	85	45	H
Cut Bank	−20	85	50	H
Glasgow	−20	90	50	H
Glendive	−20	95	45	H
Great Falls	−20	90	45	H
Havre	−15	85	50	H
Helena	−15	85	45	H
Kalispell	−5	85	50	H
Lewistown	−15	85	45	H
Livingston	−15	90	45	H
Miles City	−15	95	45	H
Missoula	−5	90	45	H
NEBRASKA				
Beatrice	0	95	40	M
Chadron	−10	95	45	H
Columbus	−5	95	40	M
Fremont	−5	95	40	M
Grand Island	−5	95	40	H
Hastings	0	95	40	H
Kearney	−5	95	40	H
Lincoln	0	95	40	M
McCook	0	95	40	H
Norfolk	−10	95	40	H
North Platte	−5	95	40	H
Omaha	−5	95	40	M
Scottsbluff	−5	95	40	H
Sidney	−5	90	40	H
NEVADA				
Carson City	5	90	40	H
Elko	−10	90	40	H
Ely	−5	90	40	H
Las Vegas	25	105	35	H
Lovelock	10	95	40	H
Reno ★ AP	5	90	40	H
Reno ★ CO	15	90	40	H
Tonopah	10	90	40	H
Winnemucca	5	95	40	H
NEW HAMPSHIRE				
Berlin	−15	85	45	M
Claremont	−10	85	45	M
Concord	−10	90	45	H
Keene	−10	90	45	M
Laconia	−10	85	45	M
Manchester	0	90	45	M
Portsmouth	0	85	45	M

State & City	Winter Dry-Bulb Temp[1] (F)	Summer Dry-Bulb Temp[1] (F)	North Latitude[1] (0)	Daily Range
NEW JERSEY				
Atlantic City	15	90	40	M
Long Branch	10	90	40	M
Newark	15	90	40	M
New Brunswick	10	90	40	M
Paterson	10	90	40	M
Phillipsburg	10	90	40	M
Trenton	15	90	40	M
Vineland	15	90	40	M
NEW MEXICO				
Alamagordo	20	100	35	H
Albuquerque	15	95	35	H
Artesia	15	100	35	H
Carlsbad	20	100	30	H
Clovis	15	95	35	H
Farmington	5	90	35	H
Gallup	−5	90	35	H
Grants	−5	90	35	H
Hobbs	15	100	30	H
Las Cruces	20	100	30	H
Los Alamos	5	85	35	H
Raton	0	90	35	H
Roswell	15	100	35	H
Santa Fe	10	90	35	H
Silver City	15	95	30	H
Socorro	15	95	35	H
Tucumcari	10	95	35	H
NEW YORK				
Albany ★ AP	0	90	45	M
Albany ★ CO	5	90	45	M
Auburn	0	85	45	M
Batavia	0	85	45	M
Binghampton	0	85	40	M
Buffalo	5	85	45	M
Cortland	−5	90	40	M
Dunkirk	5	85	40	M
Elmira	5	90	40	M
Geneva	0	90	45	M
Glens Falls	−10	85	45	M
Gloversville	−5	85	45	M
Hornell	−5	85	40	M
Ithaca	0	90	40	M
Jamestown	5	85	40	M
Kingston	0	90	40	M
Lockport	5	85	45	M
Massena	−15	85	45	M
Newburgh	5	90	40	M
New York City (Kennedy) CO	15	90	40	M
New York City (LaGuardia) AP	15	90	40	M
Niagara Falls	5	85	45	M
Olean	−5	85	40	M
Oneonta	−5	85	40	M
Oswego	5	85	45	M
Plattsburgh	−10	85	45	M
Poughkeepsie	0	90	40	M
Rochester	5	90	45	M
Rome	−5	85	45	M
Schenectady	−5	85	45	M
Syracuse	0	85	34	M
Utica	−5	85	40	M
Watertown	−10	85	45	M
NORTH CAROLINA				
Asheville	15	90	35	M
Charlotte	20	95	35	M
Durham	15	90	35	M
Elizabeth City	20	90	35	M
Fayetteville	20	95	35	M
Goldsboro	20	90	35	M
Greensboro	15	90	35	M
Greenville	20	90	35	M
Henderson	15	90	35	M
Hickory	15	90	35	M
Jacksonville	20	90	35	M
Lumberton	20	95	35	M
New Bern	20	90	35	M
Raleigh	20	90	35	M
Rocky Mount	20	95	35	M
Wilmington	25	90	35	M
Winston-Salem	15	90	35	M
NORTH DAKOTA				
Bismarck	−20	90	45	H
Devil's Lake	−20	90	50	M
Dickinson	−20	95	45	M
Fargo	−20	90	45	M
Grand Forks	−25	85	50	M
Jamestown	−20	90	45	H
Minot	−20	90	50	M
Williston	−20	90	50	M
OHIO				
Akron	5	85	40	M
Ashtabula	5	85	40	M

★ AP - Airport
CO - City Office
[1]Temperatures are rounded off to permit use of precalculated HTM tables.

FIGURE 7-66 / Outside design temperatures (continued)

State & City	Winter Dry-Bulb Temp (F)	Summer Dry-Bulb Temp (F)	North Latitude (0)	Daily Range
OHIO Cont.				
Athens	5	90	40	M
Bowling Green	0	90	40	M
Cambridge	0	90	40	M
Chillicothe	5	90	40	M
Cincinnati	10	90	40	M
Cleveland	5	90	40	M
Columbus	5	90	40	M
Dayton	5	90	40	M
Defiance	0	90	40	M
Findlay	0	90	40	M
Fremont	0	90	40	M
Hamilton	5	90	40	M
Lancaster	5	90	40	M
Lima	0	90	40	M
Mansfield	0	90	40	M
Marion	5	90	40	M
Middletown	5	90	40	M
Newark	0	90	40	M
Norwalk	0	90	40	M
Portsmouth	5	90	40	M
Sandusky	5	90	40	M
Springfield	5	90	40	M
Steubenville	5	90	40	M
Toledo	5	90	40	M
Warren	0	90	40	M
Wooster	0	90	10	M
Youngstown	5	85	40	M
Zanesville	0	90	40	M
OKLAHOMA				
Ada	15	100	35	M
Altus	15	100	35	M
Ardmore	15	100	35	M
Bartlesville	5	100	35	M
Chickasha	15	100	35	M
Enid	10	100	35	M
Lawton	15	100	35	M
McAlester	15	100	35	M
Muskogee	10	100	35	M
Norman	15	100	35	M
Oklahoma City	15	95	35	M
Ponca City	10	100	35	M
Seminole	15	100	35	M
Stillwater	15	100	35	M
Tulsa	15	100	35	M
Woodward	5	100	35	H
OREGON				
Albany	25	90	45	H
Astoria	30	75	45	M
Baker	0	90	45	H
Bend	0	85	45	H
Corvallis	25	90	45	H
Eugene	25	90	45	H
Grants Pass	25	90	40	H
Klamath Falls	5	85	40	H
Medford	20	95	40	H
Pendleton	10	95	45	H
Portland ★ (AP)	20	85	45	M
Portland ★ (CO)	25	90	45	H
Roseburg	25	90	45	H
Salem	25	90	45	H
The Dalles	15	90	45	H
PENNSYLVANIA				
Allentown	5	90	40	M
Altoona	5	85	40	M
Butler	0	90	40	M
Chambersburg	5	90	40	M
Erie	10	85	40	M
Harrisburg	10	90	40	M
Johnstown	5	85	40	M
Lancaster	5	90	40	M
Meadville	0	85	40	M
New Castle	0	90	40	M
Philadelphia	15	90	40	M
Pittsburgh ★ (AP)	5	85	40	M
Pittsburgh ★ (CO)	10	90	40	M
Reading	5	90	40	M
Scranton				
Wilkes-Barre	5	85	40	M
State College	5	85	40	M
Sunbury	5	90	40	M
Uniontown	5	90	40	M
Warren	0	85	40	M
West Chester	10	90	40	M
Williamsport	5	90	40	M
York	5	90	40	M
RHODE ISLAND				
Newport	10	85	40	M
Providence	10	85	40	M
SOUTH CAROLINA				
Anderson	20	95	35	M

State & City	Winter Dry-Bulb Temp (F)	Summer Dry-Bulb Temp (F)	North Latitude (0)	Daily Range
SOUTH CAROLINA Cont.				
Charleston ★ (AP)	25	90	35	M
Charleston ★ (CO)	30	95	35	L
Columbia	20	95	35	M
Florence	25	95	35	M
Georgetown	25	90	35	M
Greenville	20	95	35	M
Greenwood	20	95	35	M
Orangeburg	25	95	35	M
Rock Hill	20	95	35	M
Spartanburg	20	95	35	M
Sumter	25	95	35	M
SOUTH DAKOTA				
Aberdeen	-20	90	45	H
Brookings	-15	90	45	H
Huron	-15	95	45	H
Mitchell	-15	95	45	H
Pierre	-10	95	45	H
Rapid City	-10	95	45	H
Sioux Falls	-10	95	45	H
Watertown	-20	90	45	H
Yankton	-10	95	45	M
TENNESSEE				
Athens	15	95	35	M
Bristol	15	90	35	M
Chattanooga	15	95	35	M
Clarksville	15	95	35	M
Columbia	15	95	35	M
Dyersburg	15	95	35	M
Greenville	10	90	35	M
Jackson	15	95	35	M
Knoxville	15	90	35	M
Memphis	20	95	35	M
Murfreesboro	15	95	35	M
Nashville	15	95	35	M
Tullahoma	15	95	35	M
TEXAS				
Abilene	20	100	30	M
Alice	30	100	25	M
Amarillo	10	95	35	H
Austin	25	100	30	M
Bay City	30	95	30	M
Beaumont	25	95	30	M
Beeville	30	95	30	M
Big Spring	20	100	30	H
Brownsville	40	90	25	M
Brownwood	25	100	30	M
Bryan	30	100	30	M
Corpus Christi	35	95	30	M
Crosicana	25	100	30	M
Dallas	20	100	35	M
Del Rio	30	100	30	M
Denton	20	100	35	M
Eagle Pass	30	105	30	M
El Paso	25	100	30	H
Fort Worth	20	100	35	M
Galveston	35	90	30	L
Greenville	20	100	35	M
Harlingen	35	95	25	M
Houston	30	95	30	M
Huntsville	25	100	30	M
Killeen	25	100	30	M
Lamesa	15	100	35	H
Laredo	35	100	25	M
Longview	25	100	30	M
Lubbock	15	95	35	H
Lufkin	25	95	30	M
McAllen	35	100	25	M
Midland	20	100	30	H
Mineral Wells	20	100	35	M
Palestine	25	95	36	M
Pampa	10	100	35	H
Pecos	15	100	30	H
Plainview	10	100	35	H
Port Arthur	30	90	30	M
San Angelo	25	100	30	M
San Antonio	30	95	30	M
Sherman	20	100	35	M
Snyder	15	100	30	M
Temple	25	100	30	M
Tyler	20	95	30	M
Vernon	15	100	35	M
Victoria	30	95	30	M
Waco	25	100	30	M
Wichita Falls	15	100	35	M.
UTAH				
Cedar City	5	90	35	H
Logan	5	90	40	H
Moab	15	100	40	H
Ogden	10	90	40	H
Price	5	90	40	H
Provo	5	95	40	H
Richfield	0	90	40	H

State & City	Winter Dry-Bulb Temp (F)	Summer Dry-Bulb Temp (F)	North Latitude (0)	Daily Range
UTAH Cont.				
St. George	25	100	35	H
Salt Lake City	5	95	40	H
Vernal	-10	90	40	H
VERMONT				
Barre	-15	85	45	M
Burlington	-10	85	45	M
Rutland	-10	85	45	M
VIRGINIA				
Charlottesville	15	90	40	M
Danville	15	90	35	M
Fredericksburg	10	90	40	M
Harrisonburg	5	90	40	M
Lynchburg	15	90	35	M
Norfolk	20	95	35	M
Petersburg	15	95	35	M
Richmond	15	95	35	M
Roanoke	15	90	35	M
Staunton	10	90	40	M
Winchester	10	90	40	M
WASHINGTON				
Aberdeen	20	80	46	M
Bellingham	15	75	50	M
Bremerton	25	80	45	M
Ellensburg	5	90	45	H
Everett	20	80	50	M
Kennewick	15	95	45	H
Longview	20	85	45	M
Moses Lake	-5	95	45	H
Olympia	25	85	45	H
Port Angeles	25	75	50	M
Seattle ★ (CO)	20	80	45	M
(Boeing Field) (AP)	15	80	45	M
(Seattle-Tacoma)	10	80	45	M
Spokane	0	90	45	H
Tacoma	20	80	45	M
Walla Walla	15	95	45	H
Wenatchee	5	90	45	H
Yakima	10	90	45	H
WEST VIRGINIA				
Beckley	5	90	40	M
Bluefield	10	85	35	M
Charleston	10	90	40	M
Clarksburg	5	90	40	M
Elkins	5	85	40	M
Huntington	10	95	40	M
Martinsburg	10	95	40	M
Morgantown	5	90	40	M
Parkersburg	10	90	40	M
Wheeling	5	90	40	M
WISCONSIN				
Appleton	-10	85	45	M
Ashland	-20	85	45	M
Beloit	-5	90	40	M
Eau Claire	-15	90	45	M
Fond du Lac	-10	85	45	M
Green Bay	-10	85	45	M
La Crosse	-10	90	45	M
Madison	-5	90	45	M
Manitowoc	-5	85	45	M
Marinette	-5	85	45	M
Milwaukee	-5	85	45	M
Racine	0	90	45	M
Sheboygan	0	85	45	M
Stevens Point	-15	85	45	M
Waukesha	-5	90	45	M
Wausau	-15	85	45	M
WYOMING				
Casper	-5	90	45	H
Cheyenne	-5	85	40	H
Cody	-10	85	45	H
Evanston	-10	80	40	H
Lander	-15	90	45	H
Laramie	-5	80	40	H
Newcastle	-5	90	45	H
Rawlins	-15	85	40	H
Rock Springs	-5	85	40	H
Sheridan	-10	90	45	H
Torrington	-10	90	40	H

★ AP - Airport
CO - City Office
Temperatures are rounded off to permit use of precalculated HTM tables

FIGURE 7-66   /   Outside design temperatures (continued)

Average Yearly Degree-Days for Cities in the United States (Base 65 F)

State	Station	Avg. Winter Temp[d]	Yearly Total	State	Station	Avg. Winter Temp[d]	Yearly Total
Ala.	Birmingham .... A	54.2	2551	Fla.	Miami Beach C	72.5	141
	Huntsville .... A	51.3	3070	(Cont'd)	Orlando........................... A	65.7	766
	Mobile............................ A	59.9	1560		Pensacola .... A	60.4	1463
	Montgomery .... A	55.4	2291				
					Tallahassee .... A	60.1	1485
Alaska	Anchorage .... A	23.0	10864		Tampa............................ A	66.4	683
	Fairbanks .... A	6.7	14279		West Palm Beach.............. A	68.4	253
	Juneau .... A	32.1	9075				
	Nome .... A	13.1	14171	Ga.	Athens .... A	51.8	2929
					Atlanta........................... A	51.7	2961
Ariz.	Flagstaff .... A	35.6	7152		Augusta .... A	54.5	2397
	Phoenix.......................... A	58.5	1765		Columbus .... A	54.8	2383
	Tucson .... A	58.1	1800		Macon............................ A	56.2	2136
	Winslow .... A	43.0	4782		Rome .... A	49.9	3326
	Yuma .... A	64.2	974		Savannah .... A	57.8	1819
					Thomasville C	60.0	1529
Ark.	Fort Smith .... A	50.3	3292				
	Little Rock .... A	50.5	3219	Hawaii	Lihue .... A	72.7	0
	Texarkana .... A	54.2	2533		Honolulu......................... A	74.2	0
					Hilo .... A	71.9	0
Calif.	Bakersfield .... A	55.4	2122				
	Bishop .... A	46.0	4275	Idaho	Boise .... A	39.7	5809
	Blue Canyon .... A	42.2	5596		Lewiston .... A	41.0	5542
	Burbank .... A	58.6	1646		Pocatello .... A	34.8	7033
	Eureka C	49.9	4643				
				Ill.	Cairo C	47.9	3821
	Fresno .... A	53.3	2611		Chicago (O'Hare)............... A	35.8	6639
	Long Beach .... A	57.8	1803		Chicago (Midway) .... A	37.5	6155
	Los Angeles .... A	57.4	2061		Chicago........................... C	38.9	5882
	Los Angeles C	60.3	1349		Moline .... A	36.4	6408
	Mt. Shasta C	41.2	5722		Peoria .... A	38.1	6025
					Rockford.......................... A	34.8	6830
	Oakland .... A	53.5	2870		Springfield .... A	40.6	5429
	Red Bluff .... A	53.8	2515				
	Sacramento .... A	53.9	2502	Ind.	Evansville .... A	45.0	4435
	Sacramento C	54.4	2419		Fort Wayne .... A	37.3	6205
	Sandberg C	46.8	4209		Indianapolis .... A	39.6	5699
					South Bend .... A	36.6	6439
	San Diego....................... A	59.5	1458				
	San Francisco .... A	53.4	3015	Iowa	Burlington .... A	37.6	6114
	San Francisco C	55.1	3001		Des Moines .... A	35.5	6588
	Santa Maria .... A	54.3	2967		Dubuque.......................... A	32.7	7376
					Sioux City....................... A	34.0	6951
.Colo.	Alamosa .... A	29.7	8529		Waterloo .... A	32.6	7320
	Colorado Springs .... A	37.3	6423				
	Denver .... A	37.6	6283	Kans.	Concordia .... A	40.4	5479
	Denver C	40.8	5524		Dodge City .... A	42.5	4986
	Grand Junction .... A	39.3	5641		Goodland .... A	37.8	6141
	Pueblo............................ A	40.4	5462		Topeka .... A	41.7	5182
					Wichita .... A	44.2	4620
Conn.	Bridgeport .... A	39.9	5617				
	Hartford .... A	37.3	6235	Ky.	Covington .... A	41.4	5265
	New Haven .... A	39.0	5897		Lexington .... A	43.8	4683
					Louisville .... A	44.0	4660
Del.	Wilmington...................... A	42.5	4930				
				La.	Alexandria .... A	57.5	1921
D.C.	Washington .... A	45.7	4224		Baton Rouge .... A	59.8	1560
					Lake Charles .... A	60.5	1459
Fla.	Apalachicola C	61.2	1308		New Orleans..................... A	61.0	1385
	Daytona Beach .... A	64.5	879		New Orleans..................... C	61.8	1254
	Fort Myers .... A	68.6	442		Shreveport .... A	56.2	2184
	Jacksonville .... A	61.9	1239				
				Me.	Caribou........................... A	24.4	9767
	Key West .... A	73.1	108		Portland .... A	33.0	7511
	Lakeland C	66.7	661				
	Miami .... A	71.1	214	Md.	Baltimore .... A	43.7	4654

[a] Data for United States cities from a publication of the United States Weather Bureau, *Monthly Normals of Temperature, Precipitation and Heating Degree Days*, 1962, are for the period 1931 to 1960 inclusive. These data also include information from the 1963 revisions to this publication, where available.
[b] Data for airport stations, A, and city stations, C, are both given where available.
[c] Data for Canadian cities were computed by the Climatology Division, Department of Transport from normal monthly mean temperatures, and the monthly values of heating degree days data were obtained using the National Research Council computer and a method devised by H. C. S. Thom of the United States Weather Bureau. The heating degree days are based on the period from 1931 to 1960.
[d] For period October to April, inclusive.

FIGURE 7-67 / Degree days

State	Station	Avg. Winter Temp^d	Yearly Total
	Baltimore C	46.2	4111
	Frederich .... A	42.0	5087
Mass.	Boston..................... A	40.0	5634
	Nantucket................ A	40.2	5891
	Pittsfield................. A	32.6	7578
	Worcester .... A	34.7	6969
Mich.	Alpena .... A	29.7	8506
	Detroit (City) .... A	37.2	6232
	Detroit (Wayne) ...... A	37.1	6293
	Detroit (Willow Run) ...... A	37.2	6258
	Escanaba C	29.6	8481
	Flint .... A	33.1	7377
	Grand Rapids.......... A	34.9	6894
	Lansing .... A	34.8	6909
	Marquette C	30.2	8393
	Muskegon .... A	36.0	6696
	Sault Ste. Marie ...... A	27.7	9048
Minn.	Duluth .... A	23.4	10000
	Minneapolis .... A	28.3	8382
	Rochester .... A	28.8	8295
Miss.	Jackson .... A	55.7	2239
	Meridian .... A	55.4	2289
	Vicksburg C	56.9	2041
Mo.	Columbia .... A	42.3	5046
	Kansas City .... A	43.9	4711
	St. Joseph .... A	40.3	5484
	St. Louis .... A	43.1	4900
	St. Louis C	44.8	4484
	Springfield............. A	44.5	4900
Mont.	Billings .... A	34.5	7049
	Glasgow .... A	26.4	8996
	Great Falls .... A	32.8	7750
	Havre .... A	28.1	8700
	Havre C	29.8	8182
	Helena .... A	31.1	8129
	Kalispell .... A	31.4	8191
	Miles City.............. A	31.2	7723
	Missoula .... A	31.5	8125
Neb.	Grand Island .... A	36.0	6530
	Lincoln C	38.8	5864
	Norfolk .... A	34.0	6979
	North Platte .... A	35.5	6684
	Omaha .... A	35.6	6612
	Scottsbluff .... A	35.9	6673
	Valentine .... A	32.6	7425
Nev.	Elko .... A	34.0	7433
	Ely .... A	33.1	7733
	Las Vegas .... A	53.5	2709
	Reno .... A	39.3	6332
	Winnemucca .... A	36.7	6761
N.H.	Concord .... A	33.0	7383
	Mt. Washington Obsv.............	15.2	13817
N.J.	Atlantic City .... A	43.2	4812
	Newark .... A	42.8	4589
	Trenton C	42.4	4980
N. M.	Albuquerque .... A	45.0	4348
	Clayton .... A	42.0	5158
	Raton .... A	38.1	6228
	Roswell .... A	47.5	3793
	Silver City .... A	48.0	3705
N.Y.	Albany .... A	34.6	6875
	Albany C	37.2	6201
	Binghamton .... A	33.9	7286
	Binghamton C	36.6	6451
	Buffalo .... A	34.5	7062
	New York (Cent. Park)..... C	42.8	4871
	New York (La Guardia) ...... A	43.1	4811

State	Station	Avg. Winter Temp^d	Yearly Total
	New York (Kennedy) ...... A	41.4	5219
	Rochester .... A	35.4	6748
	Schenectady C	35.4	6650
	Syracuse .... A	35.2	6756
N. C.	Asheville C	46.7	4042
	Cape Hatteras	53.3	2612
	Charlotte................ A	50.4	3191
	Greensboro .... A	47.5	3805
	Raleigh .... A	49.4	3393
	Wilmington............ A	54.6	2347
	Winston-Salem .... A	48.4	3595
N. D.	Bismarck................ A	26.6	8851
	Devils Lake C	22.4	9901
	Fargo .... A	24.8	9226
	Williston................ A	25.2	9243
Ohio	Akron-Canton .... A	38.1	6037
	Cincinnati C	45.1	4410
	Cleveland .... A	37.2	6351
	Columbus .... A	39.7	5660
	Columbus C	41.5	5211
	Dayton .... A	39.8	5622
	Mansfield .... A	36.9	6403
	Sandusky C	39.1	5796
	Toledo.................... A	36.4	6494
	Youngstown .... A	36.8	6417
Okla.	Oklahoma City........ A	48.3	3725
	Tulsa .... A	47.7	3860
Ore.	Astoria .... A	45.6	5186
	Burns C	35.9	6957
	Eugene .... A	45.6	4726
	Meacham .... A	34.2	7874
	Medford .... A	43.2	5008
	Pendleton .... A	42.6	5127
	Portland .... A	45.6	4635
	Portland C	47.4	4109
	Roseburg................ A	46.3	4491
	Salem .... A	45.4	4754
Pa.	Allentown .... A	38.9	5810
	Erie .... A	36.8	6451
	Harrisburg .... A	41.2	5251
	Philadelphia .... A	41.8	5144
	Philadelphia C	44.5	4486
	Pittsburgh............... A	38.4	5987
	Pittsburgh............... C	42.2	5053
	Reading.................. C	42.4	4945
	Scranton .... A	37.2	6254
	Williamsport .... A	38.5	5934
R. I.	Block Island .... A	40.1	5804
	Providence .... A	38.8	5954
S. C.	Charleston .... A	56.4	2033
	Charleston C	57.9	1794
	Columbia .... A	54.0	2484
	Florence .... A	54.5	2387
	Greenville-Spartanburg ... A	51.6	2980
S. D.	Huron .... A	28.8	8223
	Rapid City .... A	33.4	7345
	Sioux Falls .... A	30.6	7839
Tenn.	Bristol .... A	46.2	4143
	Chattanooga .... A	50.3	3254
	Knoxville .... A	49.2	3494
	Memphis .... A	50.5	3232
	Memphis C	51.6	3015
	Nashville .... A	48.9	3578
	Oak Ridge C	47.7	3817
Tex.	Abilene .... A	53.9	2624
	Amarillo .... A	47.0	3985
	Austin .... A	59.1	1711
	Brownsville .... A	67.7	600

FIGURE 7-67 / Degree days (continued)

195

State	Station	Avg. Winter Temp	Yearly Total	State	Station	Avg. Winter Temp	Yearly Total
	Corpus Christi .... A	64.6	914		Lynchburg .... A	46.0	4166
	Dallas .... A	55.3	2363		Norfolk................................ A	49.2	3421
	El Paso .... A	52.9	2700		Richmond............................ A	47.3	3865
					Roanoke .... A	46.1	4150
	Fort Worth........................... A	55.1	2405				
	Galveston .... A	62.2	1274	Wash.	Olympia .... A	44.2	5236
	Galveston C	62.0	1235		Seattle-Tacoma...................... A	44.2	5145
	Houston .... A	61.0	1396		Seattle................................ C	46.9	4424
	Houston C	62.0	1278		Spokane .... A	36.5	6655
	Laredo .... A	66.0	797		Walla Walla C	43.8	4805
	Lubbock .... A	48.8	3578		Yakima .... A	39.1	5941
	Midland .... A	53.8	2591	W. Va.	Charleston .... A	44.8	4476
	Port Arthur .... A	60.5	1447		Elkins .... A	40.1	5675
	San Angelo .... A	56.0	2255		Huntington .... A	45.0	4446
	San Antonio .... A	60.1	1546		Parkersburg C	43.5	4754
	Victoria............................... A	62.7	1173				
	Waco.................................. A	57.2	2030	Wisc.	Green Bay .... A	30.3	8029
	Wichita Falls .... A	53.0	2832		La Crosse .... A	31.5	7589
					Madison .... A	30.9	7863
Utah	Milford .... A	36.5	6497		Milwaukee .... A	32.6	7635
	Salt Lake City .... A	38.4	6052				
	Wendover .... A	39.1	5778	Wyo.	Casper................................ A	33.4	7410
					Cheyenne .... A	34.2	7381
Vt.	Burlington .... A	29.4	8269		Lander .... A	31.4	7870
					Sheridan .... A	32.5	7680
Va.	Cape Henry C	50.0	3279				

Reprinted with permission from ASHRAE, Fundamentals Handbook, 1977

FIGURE 7-67   /   Degree days (continued)

Questions

7-1. Describe the factors used in calculating heat loss.

7-2. What are the relationships of *R, C, k,* and *U* values?

7-3. How is the outside design temperature determined?

7-4. What is meant by *infiltration heat loss,* where does it occur, and how is it calculated?

7-5. Why must the designer check the architect's specifications and drawings?

7-6. What is meant by the term *degree days,* and how will it affect the amount of fuel used per year?

7-7. List some of the ways in which the heat loss of a building can be controlled.

7-8. Why is limiting of window areas important in keeping the heat loss low?

Design Exercises:

7-9. The *U* value of an uninsulated wall is 0.29 and of the same wall insulated, 0.08. What is the resistance value of the insulation?

7-10. Using resistance values, what is the *U* value of the wall construction shown in Fig. E7-10?

7-11. What would be the *U* value for the wall used in Exercise 7-10 if 3-in. batt insulation is installed in the studs?

7-12. Using resistance values, what is the *U* value of the wall construction shown in Fig. E7-12?

7-13. What would be the *U* value for the wall used in Exercise 7-12 if 1-in. urethanc and ⅜-in. gypsum board were glued to the inside of the wall?

7-14. Using resistance values, what is the *U* value of the wall construction shown in Fig. E7-14?

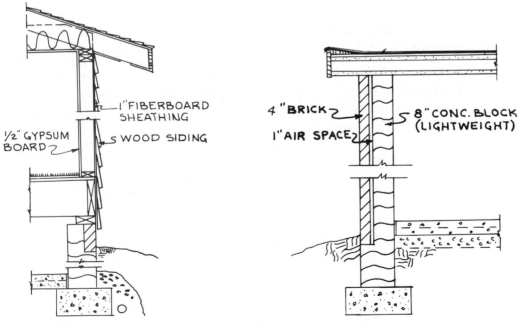

FIGURE E7-10   *FIGURE E7-12*

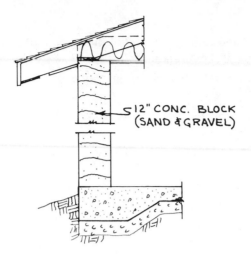

12" CONC. BLOCK
(SAND & GRAVEL)

FIGURE E7-14

7-15. What factors must be considered when determining heat gain in buildings?

7-16. Define *sensible* and *latent heat.*

7-17. How does the orientation of the windows in the building affect the heat gain?

7-18. Why must the number of occupants and the type of activity be considered in a heat gain calculation?

7-19. What factors does a heat transfer multiplier take into account?

7-20. How is infiltration calculated for heat gain, and how does this compare with infiltration calculations in heat loss?

Chapter 8
Heating and Air-Conditioning Systems

8-1   Types of Systems

The selection of a heating system and the possible inclusion of air conditioning will depend on local climate conditions, degree of comfort desired, client's budget and fuel costs. An increasing number of clients want a system which incorporates total year-round air conditioning.

There are three basic methods of delivering heat to a space: forced air, hot water, and radiant electric. Of these three, only one, forced air, is used for central air conditioning in residences.

In *forced air systems,* the air is heated or cooled in a central unit and then delivered to the room through supply ducts. Air is returned to the central unit for treatment (to heat, cool, add humidity, or purify) and then recirculated through the rooms. (Chapter 9 contains a complete discussion and description of forced air systems for heating and cooling.)

Hot water heating systems heat the water in a central unit and pass it through pipes to a heating device in the room. As the water goes through the pipes and devices, it cools, and then it goes back through the central unit to be reheated.

Cooling with water follows the same principle. Hot water heating is discussed in Chapter 10.

Radiant electric heat delivers the heat by electricity running through a cable, and the resistance produced gives off the heat. The radiant heating devices are actually in the room and may be ceiling, floor, or baseboard units. There is a complete discussion on radiant electric systems in Chapter 11.

In addition, *infrared heaters* use a lamp (bulb) which transfers heat by radiation to any people or objects which its heat rays come in contact with. It is effectively used when it is necessary to warm people, yet the surrounding air need not be heated or, perhaps, cannot be effectively heated. They are commonly used in bathrooms where for a short period of time (such as when a person steps out of a hot shower in the winter) extra heat is needed for the person to feel comfortable. Other locations include covered walkways and entries to commercial and industrial buildings.

Water may be delivered either hot or chilled, and chilled water systems are used for air conditioning in many larger projects. *Chilled water systems* cool the water at a central point, in a condenser, and then distribute chilled water throughout the building—either to convectors in the space or through pipes embedded in the floor or ceiling.

8-2   Heating System Combinations

It is not unusual for industrial and commercial buildings to use different types of systems to heat and cool different areas of a building. The systems may vary in use of hot water heat, with finned tube units being used in offices and convector units being used in storage or warehouse areas. Similarly, completely different systems may be used, with radiant hot water heat in the floor of an office area and electric unit heaters in the warehouse or storage areas. Any combination may be used, and the selection may vary, depending on the type of heat required, the type of fuels available, and to a great extent, how much heat is required, how often it is required, and what method of supplying the heat will provide the best results in the designer's opinion.

Residential designs may use combinations of systems such as hot water for heat and forced air for cooling, hot water or forced air heat with electric supplements (particularly in bathrooms or kitchens), and finned tube units with supplemental hot water unit heaters in areas such as a kitchen or basement.

As mentioned previously, chilled water may be used to provide cooling in a building by running it through the same pipes used for hot water heating. This means that once the system is changed over from one function to the other—say, from heating to cooling as summer approaches—it is not easily reversed if cold weather comes for several days. This type of system has little flexibility in that it provides either heating or cooling and cannot provide both at one time.

However, different uses, activities, type of exterior wall construction, and location in the building (especially larger buildings) may make it desirable to have heating in some spaces while cooling is required in others. This may be accomplished by putting in separate pipes for hot and chilled water. In this manner, areas which require cooling can get chilled water while those requiring heat can get hot water. Of course, there is the extra cost of piping and controls to regulate the flow of the water to the desired location.

The actual design of any particular system will involve the size of the building, amount of insulation, doors, windows, climate in the area, and fuel to be used.

8-3   Fuels

The most commonly used sources of building heat are the sun, electricity, gas, oil, and coal. Use of the sun as an energy source is discussed in Chapter 12. The decision on which of the other four fuels to use is based on availability and cost of operation. In this section, we will review the advantages and disadvantages of each fuel and the method used to determine the cost of operation.

Electricity

Electricity is used as a fuel for a variety of heating systems, including baseboard radiant heat and electric coils in the ceiling and/or walls (refer to Chapter 11). In addition, there are electric furnaces for forced hot air systems, and it is used with heat pumps both to operate the system and to provide supplemental electric resistance heat for the system. Electricity has as its advantage its simplicity. It requires no chimney to remove toxic gases, and when baseboard strips and ceiling and wall coils are used, the system has individual room controls, providing a high degree of flexibility and comfort. Electric systems cost significantly less to install than other systems (including electric furnaces for forced hot air), and all electric systems (except heat pumps) require much less upkeep and maintenance than those using the other fuels.

The primary disadvantage of electric heat is its yearly cost of operation when compared with those of other fuels. Electricity rates vary tremendously throughout the country, and the rates are continuing to climb. It is necessary to determine the rates in the geographical area of construction to do a cost analysis. Electric heat is quite popular, and generally most economical, in the southern regions since winter is shorter and heat bills are generally lower. It is also used extensively in apartments, offices, and similar buildings where the developer is primarily interested in building the units as inexpensively as possible and where the cost of heating is usually paid by the person renting the space. Its minimal need for maintenance and repairs is also a factor in such construction. Builders of some homes, especially those which they may want to be able to sell at the lowest price, may use electric baseboard heat.

Gas

Gas, also a popular fuel for heating, is used to heat the water in hot water systems and the air in forced air systems. Gas fuels available include natural gas, which is piped to the residence or building, and propane gas, which is delivered in pressurized cylinders in trucks and tanks and stored in tanks at or near the building. Since natural gas is simply available as needed, with no storage or individual delivery required, it is considered simpler to use. However, it is not available in many areas, and the more suburban the area, the less likely it is that natural gas will be available. So the designer must first determine if natural gas is available. Secondly, at the present time, there is a shortage of natural gas. While this shortage may be alleviated in the future, many areas do not permit any new natural gas customers. In periods of shortages, the residential customer can be reasonably assured that he will have sufficient natural gas for his use, but industrial and commercial customers cannot be so assured. Since 1975, hundreds of businesses have been faced with the option of converting to another fuel or closing, and many did close for the winter months. While the reasons for such shortages may be debated as to whether they are real or contrived—caused by government, industry, or both—the designer is concerned with one thing: Is it available, and will it continue to be available, or not?

The primary advantages of natural gas have been its relatively low cost and its simple and clean burning which reduces the maintenance required on the heating unit. As with all of the fuels, as costs go up in the future, it is difficult to say which will be the most economical.

Propane gas is equally as clean as natural gas, and its availability is not limited to areas where supply pipes have been installed. To date the cost of propane gas has generally been higher than that of natural gas.

Oil

Oil is one of the most popular fuels, and it is used extensively in the Northeast. The primary reason for its use has been its availability and historic low cost. It does require delivery by trucks to storage tanks located in or near the building, and the heating unit will generally require more maintenance than a gas heating unit. The selection of oil as a heating fuel has diminished somewhat since the oil embargo in the early 1970's. In addition, the cost of this fuel has risen dramatically since that time. Costs of other fuels have also risen, but it is the fear of not having oil if another embargo is imposed that is one of the most important concerns.

Oil is available in various weights (Fig. 8-1) with various heating values and at different costs. Generally, the lower the number, the more refined it is and the higher the cost. Number 2 oil is commonly used in residences while numbers 4, 5, and 6 are commonly used in commercial and industrial projects.

Commercial standard number	Weight (lb./gal.)	Btu per gallon	Btu average
1	6.675-7.076	132,900 138,800	136,000
2	6.870-7.481	135,800-144,300	140,000
4	7.529-8.212	145,000-153,000	149,000
5	7.627-8.328	146,200-154,600	150,000
6	7.909-8.448	149,700-156,000	154,000

FIGURE 8-1   /   Fuel characteristics

Coal

Coal is rarely used for residential heating in new construction, and its use in industrial and commercial construction fluctuates. Its primary advantage is that it is available and there are ample supplies so that a shortage seems unlikely at this time. Generally, its cost is competitive with those of other fuels. Its disadvantages lie in the amount of space required for storage and the fact that it does not burn as completely as oil or gas, thus producing more pollution. Government regulations for clean air have also limited the use of some more polluting coals for industrial purposes.

Coal's decreased use for heating residences is due to the handling required in delivery and the inconvenience of having a coal bin as part of a basement. Also, originally the coal had to be shoveled into the furnace by the occupant of the house, which is sufficient reason to change to oil, gas, or electricity. Now, coal heating units are fed by automatic stokers which require no hand shoveling.

Since coal is used so little as a residential and commercial heating fuel, it will not be considered further.

8-4   Cooling Principles

While the principle of providing heat to a source (water or air) which is then used to heat the space is easily understood, the principles of providing cooling should be discussed. The fundamental principles on which the cooling process is based are derived from physics:

1.   As a gas is compressed, it will liquefy at a given point, and as it liquefies, it will *release* a large amount of latent *heat* from within the gas/liquid.

2.   As the pressure on the liquid is lowered, it vaporizes back to a gas, and as it boils through the vaporizing process, it *absorbs* a large amount of latent heat into the liquid/gas.

The refrigerant medium in the cooling system is cycled through three components (Fig. 8-2):

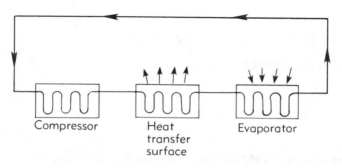

Compressor   Heat   Evaporator
                    transfer
                    surface

FIGURE 8-2 / *Refrigerant cycle*

1.   A *compressor* which will compress the refrigerant, causing it to liquefy.

2.   A heat transfer surface which will distribute the *heat released* to a surrounding medium such as water or air. This heat transfer surface is called a *condenser.*

3.   A second heat transfer surface which will *extract heat* from the surrounding medium, such as water or air, as it is *absorbed* into the refrigerant. This heat transfer surface is called an *evaporator.*

The refrigerant is run continuously through the cycle while the system is in operation:

1.   The refrigerant is compressed to a liquid in the compressor, generally located in or near the condenser.

2.   The liquid passes through the condenser which allows the latent heat to be released. The condenser is often located on the exterior of the building. For most residences and small commercial projects, it is located on the ground; however, it may be located on the roof, often the case on larger projects. The heat is released through the condenser to a surrounding medium. This sur-

rounding medium is the outside air for most installations, but water, such as a pond, can be used. In the typical installation, the condenser unit has a fan which pushes the air past the refrigerant to take as much heat away from it as possible.

3. The refrigerant then passes out of the condenser to the second heat transfer surface (the evaporator) which will extract heat from the surrounding medium. So, as the liquid vaporizes to a gas, it draws heat out of the surrounding medium as it passes through the evaporator. The surrounding medium may be air or water. In a forced air system, air would be the medium, and this drawing of heat from the air and into the refrigerant causes the air to cool. As the air is forced back through the system, it is cool air. When water is used as the medium, the heat is drawn from the water, making it cool or chilled; the water is then circulated through the system to cool the space.

These basic principles apply for all types of cooling systems. Some equipment, such as a room air conditioner, may be designed to combine all the components in one unit (Fig. 8-3), or they may be separate pieces of equipment. These principles are also the basic principles of heat pump operation (Sec. 12-8).

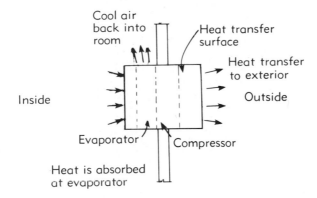

FIGURE 8-3 / Single unit cooling

Questions

8-1. What three basic methods are used to deliver heat to a space?

8-2. Why might combinations of systems be used in a building?

8-3. What type of system is most commonly used for residential cooling?

8-4. When might a chilled water system be used?

8-5. Describe the advantages and disadvantages of electricity as a fuel.

8-6. Why is electric heat often used in projects such as apartments?

8-7. List the fuels most commonly used for heating in a residence.

8-8. What are the two fundamental principles on which the cooling process is based?

8-9. Describe the three components used in the refrigeration process.

8-10. What types of surrounding mediums are generally used to take the heat from the refrigerant?

Chapter 9

Forced Air Systems and Design

9-1   Forced Air Systems

A motor-driven fan is used to circulate filtered, heated or cooled air from a central heating or air conditioning unit through supply ducts to each of the rooms. As the air is delivered through the ducts and into the room through the supply outlet, new air from the space (room) is being returned through return grilles, into ducts, and back through the central unit to be heated or cooled and sent back to the space. The ducts may be circular or rectangular, and their size depends on the amount of treated air which must flow through them to maintain the desired temperature of the room. A variety of duct systems, or basic designs, may be used; several of the most common are shown in Fig. 9-1.

Forced air systems are economical and generally easy to install. Filters are put in the system to reduce the amount of dust in the air. The unit may be located wherever convenient in the building including the basement, crawl space, attic, utility room, or garage; in larger buildings it is sometimes located on the roof or in the structural systems.

Humidifiers (discussed in Sec. 6-5) are recommended for use in most heating systems. They provide extra comfort at a minimal cost, making them a good investment. The humidifier will fit right into the duct system as it is being installed.

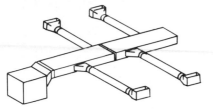

Extended plenum supply

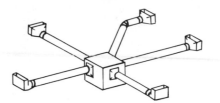

Individual supply system

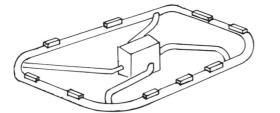

Perimeter-loop system

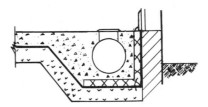

FIGURE 9-1   /   *Typical heating duct systems*

9-2   Ducts and Fittings

The ductwork is used to take the forced treated air from the furnace to the supply outlet, and the return register takes air back to the unit.

The most commonly used materials for ducts are galvanized iron and aluminum. Both materials are relatively lightweight and easily shaped to whatever size duct is required, either round or rectangular. Minimum metal thicknesses required of these materials vary according to the size of the duct required and are shown in Fig. 9-2. These ducts may have to be insulated as discussed in Sec. 9-3.

Another very popular ductwork material is glass fiber, molded duct board. These ducts are available in a large variety of sizes, both round and rectangular. Its principal advantage is that for installations which need insulating (Sec. 9-3), it is less expensive and installed in one operation, as opposed to metal ducts which are installed in one operation and insulated in a second operation. The round fiber ducts are compatible with standard round metal ducts and may be used as part of a system which also uses metal ducts. The round fiber duct makes use of metal fittings to connect, reduce, and make elbows as shown in Fig. 9-3. Another advantage of this type of duct is its excellent acoustic properties to ensure a quiet system. Fiber duct is also sometimes used for the section of ductwork connecting the main trunk supply and the return lines to the furnace (Fig. 9-4).

| Round Ducts Diameter, In. | Minimum Thickness | | Minimum Weight of Tinplate |
	Galv. Iron, U.S. Gage	Aluminum, B&S Gage	
Less than 14	30	26	
14 or more	28	24	IX (135 lb)

| Rectangular Ducts Width, In. | Minimum Thickness | | Minimum Weight of Tinplate |
	Galv. Iron, U.S. Gage	Aluminum, B&S Gage	
Ducts Enclosed in Partitions			
14 or less	30	26	
Over 14	28	24	IX (135 lb)
Ducts Not Enclosed in Partitions			
Less than 14	28	24	—
14 or more	26	23	—

Note: The table is in accordance with Standard 90B of the National Board of Fire Underwriters.' Industry practice is to use heavier gage metals where maximum duct widths exceed 24 in. (see also NBFU No. 90A).'

Reprinted with permission from ASHRAE, Systems Handbook, 1976

FIGURE 9-2 / Metal duct thicknesses

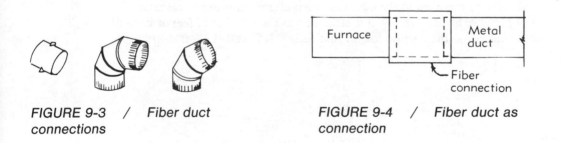

FIGURE 9-3 / Fiber duct connections

FIGURE 9-4 / Fiber duct as connection

Where the ducts will be in and under a concrete slab, an asbestos–cement round duct is most commonly used. Ducts placed below a slab must be made from a material which is not subject to moisture transmission or corrosion by concrete, will not float as the concrete is poured, and is noncombustible. The asbestos–cement duct is available with inside diameters from 4 to 36 in. The ducts are joined with an impermeable rubber sleeve and two stainless steel straps (Fig. 9-5). The tees, wyes, elbows, reducers, and end caps are also made of asbestos–cement. This type of duct material is much more expensive than the fiber glass or metal and is rarely used except, for example, for installations in or under a concrete slab.

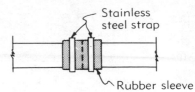

FIGURE 9-5   /   Asbestos–cement duct
connection

Oftentimes the ducts are made an integral part of the construction of the building, especially the returns. In large buildings (hospitals, nursing homes, office buildings) the ceiling area over a corridor is sometimes used as an air return (also called an *air plenum*). A typical section through a corridor with an air plenum above it is shown in Fig. 9-6. The ceiling used should be tight fitting so that the air will not "leak" out of the space. Quite often gypsum board is used. The spaces between joists may also be used for air returns, with the bottom usually formed from sheet metal nailed to the bottom of the joists (Fig. 9-7). If the joist runs through cold spaces, it may be desirable to insulate the underside of the return. Also, the designer must check to be certain that the joists run in the direction in which the return air must run.

A wide variety of fittings may be used to make all of the reductions, branch take-offs, turns, and bends required in many duct systems. Ideally, the best system layout has the fewest and simplest duct fittings since fittings restrict the flow of the forced air and increase the friction in the system. The friction of the various fittings used must be included in the duct size calculations. In order to calculate the amount of pressure lost in a fitting, it is estimated as the number of feet of straight run that would equal the friction loss in that fitting. It is called *equivalent length*.

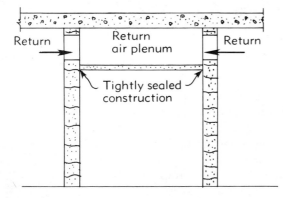

FIGURE 9-6   /   Return air plenum

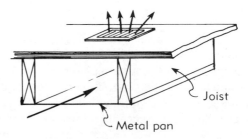

FIGURE 9-7   /   Joists as
ducts

Example

The friction loss of boot fitting A (which is the piece used to connect the branch duct to the supply register) is listed in Fig. 9-29 as A-30. This means that the friction loss in the boot fitting is the equivalent length of 30 ft of straight duct.

During the duct design, it will be necessary to make preliminary selections of fittings so that the duct design will be as accurate as possible. Fittings and their equivalent lengths are given in Fig. 9-29.

Supply ducts should be equipped with an adjustable locking-type damper (Fig. 9-8) so that the air volume can be controlled. The damper should be located in an accessible spot in the branch duct as far from the supply outlet as possible. This allows a measure of control over the flow of the air and also allows a branch to be shut off when desired.

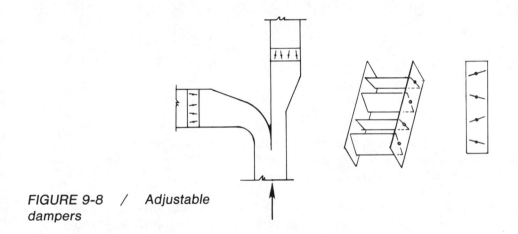

FIGURE 9-8 / Adjustable dampers

Splitter dampers (Fig. 9-9) are used to direct part of the air into the branch where it is taken off the trunk. They do not give precise volume control.

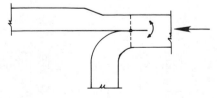

FIGURE 9-9 / Splitter damper

Squeeze dampers (Fig. 9-10) are placed in a duct to provide a means to control the air volume in the duct.

FIGURE 9-10 / Squeeze dampers
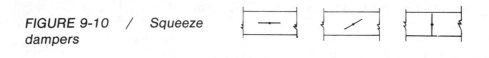

Turning vanes may be used to direct the flow of air smoothly around a corner or a bend, as shown in Fig. 9-11.

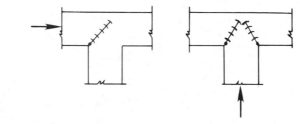

FIGURE 9-11 / Turning vanes

The entire system should be checked to be certain that proper attention has been given to the elimination of as much noise as possible from the system. The following suggestions will help keep noise to a minimum.

1. The furnace and metal ducts should be connected with a flexible fire-resistant fabric. In this manner, any noises or vibrations will not be transmitted directly through the system (Fig. 9-12).
2. All electrical conduits and pipes should have flexible connections to the furnace.
3. Do not locate the return air immediately adjacent to the furnace.
4. Do not install a fan directly below the return air grille.

FIGURE 9-12 / Boiler–duct connection
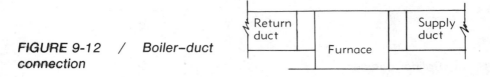

9-3 Duct Insulation

Ducts located in heated spaces do not need to be insulated. But ducts which run through enclosed, unheated spaces or in spaces which are exposed to outdoor temperatures should be insulated. While glass fiber ducts are made of an insulating material (the glass fiber), sheet metal ducts must be wrapped in an insulation. For supply ducts located in enclosed, unheated spaces, 1 in. of insulation is recommended; for supply ducts located in a space which is exposed to outdoor temperatures, 2 in. of insulation are recommended. For return ducts not located in a heated space, use 1 in. of insulation.

The most commonly used insulation on residential and small commercial buildings is fiberglass with a facing of reinforced aluminum foil vapor-barrier which goes to the outside. In large buildings, the ducts may be sprayed with an insulating/fire-resistant coating.

9-4 Supply and Return Locations

This information on the location of supply and return ducts is for installations where only heating will be supplied or in areas where heat is required much of the time while any cooling requirements are small. (For example, in an upstate New York residence, heat will probably be required regularly for about six to seven months, October 15–May 15, and air conditioning intermittently for two months.)

The supply registers should be located in the floor, 4 in. out from the baseboard, or be very low in an exterior wall (Fig. 9-13) and near or under windows, in exterior walls, and near exterior doors. In effect, put the heat supplying registers as close as possible to the spots where the most heat is lost. These registers should

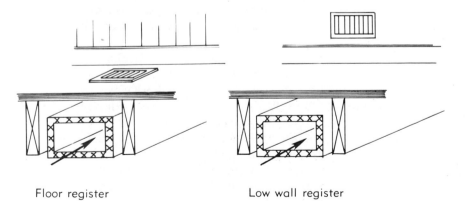

Floor register   Low wall register

FIGURE 9-13   /   Register location

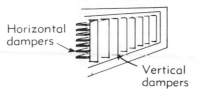

Horizontal dampers

Vertical dampers

FIGURE 9-14   /   Register dampers

have both vertical and horizontal dampers (Fig. 9-14) so that the air will be directed downward at the floor by the horizontal dampers and diffused to the sides by the vertical dampers.

Returns are often located on interior walls, in hallways, and in exposed corners. A low baseboard location is required for a return on the floor, and a centrally located return, perhaps one for a small residence and two for a large one, provides satisfactory results. If there is only one central return, it is important to put it in a location where it will be able to draw return air from as much of the building as possible. This is why they are frequently located in hallways. More expensive, individual room exhausts may be used if the designer feels that the layout of rooms may cause an uneven return of air or that the air flow from the rooms to the return (under doorways or through adjoining rooms) may cause a problem. For example, if there is a central return in the hallway and the door to a bedroom is closed all night, it will be very difficult for air to flow from the room to the return, unless the bottom of the door is trimmed (undercut) up about an inch or so. Unless air is drawn from the room as the supply keeps bringing air into the room, a slight pressure is built up in the room, reducing the amount of warm air coming through the supply outlets, and the room will tend to be cool. The same situation will occur in any other room closed off from the return. If the designer is aware that such a problem may exist, the solution would be to put a separate return in the room.

The returns are covered with grilles which are put over the opening primarily to "cover it up" so there won't be a big hole in the wall. There are no movable dampers. The type of grille used will determine the required grille size (in conjunction with the cfm required for the system). This is because air can only flow through the openings in the grille (called the *face openings*) and not through the material. Therefore, the percentage of face opening for the grille used must be determined from the manufacturer's specifications. The register must be proportionally larger than the return duct, based on the percentage of face opening of the grille required. For example, if a grille with 50% face opening is used on a 20-in. × 14-in. duct carrying 1,400 cfm, it will be necessary to have a grille twice as large as the duct branch (or trunk).

9-5 Furnace Location

Furnaces for forced air systems are available in various designs so that they may be located in the basement, crawl space, attic, or first floor of the building. In addition, each is usually classified in terms of the direction in which the air is delivered. The three basic types are *upflow, counter flow,* and *horizontal,* and there are several variations depending on the actual installation (Fig. 9-15).

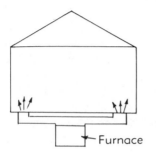

Lowboy (upflow)

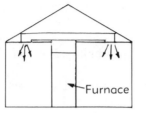

Highboy (upflow)

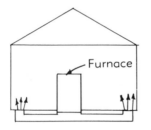

Counterflow

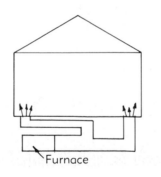

Horizontal

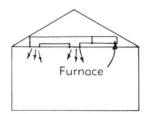

Horizontal

FIGURE 9-15 / Boiler locations

A lowboy-style (upflow) furnace (Fig. 9-15) is installed in the basement of a building, and the air is delivered to the building through ducts from the top of the boiler.

The highboy (upflow) furnace (Fig 9-15) is used primarily in single-level homes when the ducts are placed in the attic. This may be because of the slab on grade construction or because there is limited crawl space. The furnace may be located in a closet or recessed area in the wall. The air enters the furnace through a low side entry or through the bottom, and it leaves through the top.

The counterflow (downflow) furnace (Fig. 9-15) is used primarily where it is preferable to have the furnace in the building, on the first floor, and not in a crawl space. The air enters the furnace at the top, and it leaves through the bottom. It is usually used with crawl spaces and slabs on grade. While it may be used in a building with a basement, such buildings usually have the furnace located in the basement.

The horizontal furnace (Fig. 9-15) is used primarily in homes with crawl spaces or concrete slab floors (i.e., no basement). The furnace may be set off the ground in the crawl space, placed in the attic, or suspended from posts in an attic or utility room. The air enters the furnace at one end, and it leaves through the opposite end.

Combinations of systems are often used in larger homes and in many industrial, commercial, or institutional buildings. In a two-story home it may be desirable to heat the first floor with an upflow furnace in the basement and the second floor with a horizontal furnace in the attic.

9-6   Duct Design (Heating Only)

Step-by-Step Approach

1. Determine the heat loss of each individual room and list them.

2. Next, determine the location and number of supply outlets (in this case, located on outside walls under windows; read Sec. 9-4 for a complete discussion) and return air intakes. Sketch the proposed locations on the floor plan. As a general rule, in residential design, no one supply outlet should supply more than 8,000 Btuh.

3. Note on the sketch the types of fittings which will be used and the actual length of each duct. The fittings may be selected from Fig. 9-29, which also gives the equivalent length for each type of fitting.

4. Bonnet temperature.
    a. If a tentative furnace size has been selected and the manufactuer's speci-

fications give the *bonnet temperature,* note it on the worksheet and proceed to step 5. If not, proceed to step 4b.

b. Many times the bonnet temperature is not specific, or perhaps the actual
furnace has not been selected at this point. In this case, the bonnet temperature required must be determined. This is done by first listing the
shortest *actual* (not equivalent) length from the bonnet to the supply outlet and then the longest actual length from the bonnet to the supply outlet. These lengths must include any vertical riser ducts which may be in
the run.

Next, the bonnet temperature is found by referring to the appropriate table,
based on the building heat loss:

Fig. 9-23: Heat loss up to 150,000 Btuh
Fig. 9-24: Heat loss from 150,000 to 300,000 Btuh
Fig. 9-25: Heat loss from 300,000 to 450,000 Btuh
Fig. 9-26: Heat loss over 450,000 Btuh

Referring to the table selected, find the shortest linear distance from bonnet
to outlet across the top of the table. Follow the distance column downward
to the number just above the lowest heavy horizontal line. Now move
directly to the left and read the bonnet temperature.

Now find the longest linear distance from the bonnet to outlet across the top
of the table. Follow the distance column downward to the number just *below*
the first heavy horizontal line. Move horizontally to the left and read the
bonnet temperature. The design bonnet temperature selected may be any
value between the two limits determined in this step. It should be noted that
the lower the bonnet temperature is, the larger the duct sizes will have to
be.

5. Next, determine the air volume (in cubic feet per minute, cfm) which will be
delivered through each supply outlet. Using the appropriate table for the
heat loss of the building (described in step 4b) and the bonnet temperature,
it will be possible to determine the cfm required for each 1,000 Btuh required. In each of the tables, the upper number is the air temperature at the
bonnet or register, and the lower value is the cfm required for each 1,000
Btuh. List the cfm required per 1,000 Btuh for each length of run from bonnet to supply.

6. Calculate the Btuh for each outlet by dividing the number of outlets in each
room into the heat loss of the room.

7. Calculate the cfm required from each of the supply outlets by multiplying
the cfm per 1,000 Btuh (found in step 5) times the Btuh for each outlet
(found in step 6).

8. Next, the supply outlet size and its pressure loss are selected from the manufacturer's engineering data. A typical example of the manufacturer's data is shown in Fig. 9-27. Typically, the pressure loss will range from 0.01 to 0.02 in., and many designers simply allow 0.02 in.

9. Bonnet pressure.
    a. The bonnet pressure is selected next. The approximate bonnet pressure required for a trunk (main duct) to carry the maximum volume of air (cfm) is found in Fig. 9-28.
    b. If a furnace has been selected, the rated capacity of the unit must be checked. Most residential units are designed for a pressure of 0.20 in., although units will handle greater pressures.

10. The available bonnet pressure is divided proportionally by length between the supply and return runs. In perimeter heating (Fig. 9-1), the supply runs are longer than the returns, and a 0.20-in. pressure might be divided with 0.12 in. on the supply and 0.08 in. on the return. For other systems the sketch plan layout shows the approximate proportion of supply to return runs.

    Note: If later during the design the proportion selected does not provide satisfactory results, it can be reapportioned between supply and return.

11. Next, the actual pressure which is available for duct loss is obtained by subtracting the supply outlet loss (step 8) from the total pressure available for supply runs.

12. In order to make a workable table of duct sizes, the pressure drop for duct loss must be calculated as the pressure drop per *100 ft* of the duct. Since the various supply runs are all different lengths, it is necessary to find the allowable *pressure drop per 100 ft* based on the *allowable duct loss* and the *total equivalent length* of the supply run. This allowable pressure drop may be taken from the table in Fig. 9-33, or it may be calculated by using the equation:

$$\text{Allowable pressure drop per 100 ft} = \frac{\text{Allowable duct loss} \times 100}{\text{Total equivalent length}}$$

13. The branch duct sizes may be determined by using the table in Fig. 9-34. This table gives the size of the round duct based on the cfm required and the allowable pressure drop per 100 ft (step 12). The size of the round duct may be converted to an equivalent rectangular duct size which will handle the required cfm within the allowable pressure drop.

14. The round duct sizes selected in step 13 may be changed to equivalent rectangular duct sizes, carrying the same cfm required while maintaining the allowable pressure drops. Using the table in Fig. 9-35, find the round duct (pipe) diameter along the left; reading to the right, a variety of rectangular sizes which may be used are listed. An air duct calculator may also be used.

15. Add the air volumes of all of the branch supply runs from each trunk duct. When there is more than one, keep the totals for each trunk duct separate.

16. For best air flow distribution through the ducts, it is important that the friction losses per 100 ft be approximately equal in both trunk ducts.

    Using the table in Fig. 9-34, select the trunk sizes required. When there is more than one trunk duct, size each separately using the required air volume (cfm) and the allowable duct friction (step 12).

17. Review the supply trunk duct to determine if it is desirable to reduce the size of the duct as each duct leaves the trunk. Generally, such a reduction is suggested so that the velocity of air through the duct will not drop too low. Using the remaining air volume in the trunk duct, after each branch, and the allowable pressure drop per 100 ft of duct (step 10), select the reduced trunk sizes from Fig. 9-34.

18. Next, the design turns to the return ducts. The first step is to select an allowable return air pressure drop. This was previously decided (step 10), but it is reviewed at this point as the designer reviews the supply trunk and branch duct sizes to see if he might want to increase the duct sizes (reducing the allowable air pressure drop) or perhaps to reduce the duct sizes (increasing the allowable air pressure drop for the supply runs). Remember that a change in allowable air pressure drop for the supply will affect the allowable air pressure drop for the return runs (step 10).

19. The return trunk duct size is determined by the air volume it must handle and the allowable pressure drop. This allowable pressure drop must be converted to allowable pressure drop *per 100 ft* just as was done for the supply runs. Using the air volume and the allowable pressure drop per 100 ft, the round return duct size may be selected from Fig. 9-34.

    If the return trunk sizes are too large, they may be reduced in size by:

    a. Reapportioning the pressure drop available so there is less drop allowed for the supply runs and more pressure allowed for the return runs. This may require a revision of supply branch and trunk duct sizes.

    b. Checking to see if the return air grille can be located closer to the furnace, which would reduce the actual length of duct. This increases the allowable pressure drop per 100 ft, resulting in a smaller duct size.

20. The size of the blower on the furnace is determined from the total air volume (the total cfm to be delivered) and the total static pressure requirements.

The total static pressure of a furnace–blower combination unit is the total of the actual pressure drops in the supply and return ducts. Most residential and small commercial buildings have furnace–blower combination units.

When the blowers are selected separately from the furnace, the total static pressure is the sum of the actual pressure losses in the supply and return ducts, the filter loss, the casing loss, and losses through any devices which are put on the system, such as air washers and purifiers.

21. The capacity of the furnace to be selected is found next. The first step is to determine the Btuh requirements of all supply outlets.

22. Determine the required bonnet capacity of the furnace in Btuh or MBH (thousands of Btuh).

    When all the ductwork for a building will be located within heated spaces (spaces in which heat loss is calculated), the required bonnet capacity will be the same as the calculated heat loss plus any allowance for "pickup load" in step 23.

    When the furnace and ductwork will not be located in spaces included in the heat loss, the required bonnet capacity can be determined by the use of the formula:

$$\text{Btuh} = \text{cfm} \times \text{Unit temperature rise} \times 1.08$$

23. Add any allowance which is required for pickup load.

    Typically, the designer allows about 20% for the heat loss in the ductwork and an additional 15 to 20% as a pickup allowance. This pickup allowance allows for the rapid temperature change occasionally required. For example a store may have the temperature set for 60 °F at night and then raised to 70 °F in the daytime. It requires extra boiler or furnace heating capacity to provide this heating pickup.

9-7   Air Conditioning Equipment

The forced air heating and cooling system may obtain its heat from a furnace, just as is used in forced air systems which supply only heat, with an added-on package of cooling coils placed next to the furnace bonnet and a condenser located outside the building (Fig. 9-16). The other unit which is becoming increasingly popular is the heat pump (Sec. 12-8) which produces both warm and cool air. Use of a heat pump means a furnace is not necessary.

In this section, the furnace with a separate cooling unit (commonly called an air conditioner) will be discussed. The size of the cooling unit is rated according to its cooling capacity in Btuh, often referred to as "tons." One ton is equal to 12,000

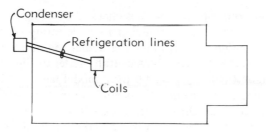

FIGURE 9-16 / Split system

Btuh (so, a 3-ton unit would have a capacity of 36,000 Btuh). The rating of the unit selected should be adequate to provide cooling Btuh equal to, or slightly more than, what the heat gain calculations call for. The wide range of sizes commonly available allows for the selection of a unit with the rated cooling capacity close to the required cooling calculated. Selection of a much larger unit will result in less efficient operation, and thus higher costs (due to the inefficiency of the on–off cycles, the time it takes to begin to cool and the warming of the system as it is off, only to be cooled again as it is turned back on). But if a unit is too small, it may not be able to provide sufficient cool air. This becomes especially critical if any of the design assumptions (such as the amount of moisture, insulation, or the size or type of glass used) vary, and the designer is not aware of the change. Also, the "tightness" of the construction (how well it is built) is assumed by the designer to be average. If it is not, there may be more heat gain than was calculated.

The unit selected for use should also be checked for its energy efficiency. Most manufacturers have more than one type of unit available. It is important to get the most efficient model available. The tables in Fig. 9-17 give the manufacturer's specifications for "standard" and "high-efficiency" models.

Cooling capacity (Btuh)	Watts	EER (Btuh per watt)
24,000	2750	8.9
29,000	3100	9.4
36,000	4050	9.0
42,000	5000	8.4

Highest efficiency

Cooling capacity (Btuh)	Watts	EER (Btuh per watt)
24,000	3800	6.3
30,000	4600	6.3
36,000	5800	6.2
42,000	7100	5.9

Standard

FIGURE 9-17 / Energy efficiency ratios

The efficiency of the models is checked by comparing the EER (energy efficiency ratio) listed for each model. This EER rating is obtained by dividing the total Btuh of the unit by its watts; the higher the number, the more efficient the unit. Note that the standard 24,000-Btuh model in Fig. 9-17 has an EER of 6.3, while the highest-efficiency 24,000-Btuh model has an EER of 8.9. This indicates that the highest-efficiency model is slightly more than 40% more efficient than the standard model. Thus, the fuel bill for cooling will be about 40% less when using the highest-efficiency model, compared to the standard. High-efficiency units typically cost 50% more than the standard, but in terms of dollars, it may only be $200 to $300. The EER ratings shown are typical, but each manufacturer must be checked since they will vary.

9-8   Duct Design, Air Conditioning (Heating *and* Cooling)

Step-by-Step Approach

1. Determine the heat loss and heat gain of each individual room, and tabulate them.

2. The cooling unit size is selected based on the heat gain calculated. The unit selected should be as close as possible to the heat gain which was calculated.

    When the heat gain calculations are more than the capacity of an available unit, yet going to the next available unit would provide far too much capacity, the designer may want to review his calculations and suggest changes (perhaps in insulation, type of glass, or sunshields) that will reduce the load.

3. Next, determine the location and number of supply outlets and return air intakes. The layout should allow a heat loss of no more than 8,000 Btuh per outlet, and a heat gain of no more than 4,000 Btuh per outlet.

    Extra outlets may be desirable in some rooms to provide the best air distribution. This is particularly true in large rooms.

4. Note on the sketch the types of fittings which will be used and the actual length of each run from the furnace to the outlet. The fittings are the same as those used for heating and are included at the end of this chapter. Fittings may be selected from Fig. 9-29, and the equivalent lengths are given for

each type of fitting shown in the illustrations. Note the equivalent length of each fitting on the sketch.

5. Determine the total equivalent length of each run from bonnet to outlet by adding the actual length and the equivalent length of each fitting in the run, and tabulate the totals.

6. Determine the air volume (cfm) required per MBH (1,000 Btuh) for each run from the table in Fig. 9-30. This table uses the duct length and daily temperature range to determine the cfm per MBH.

7. Determine the total air volume (cfm) required by adding up the cfm for each branch from step 6.

8. Determine the most desirable bonnet temperature for each of the branches by using the actual length of duct (step 4), the air volume (cfm) for cooling (step 6), the *heat loss* in MBH (step 1), and the table in Fig. 9-31. Repeat this process of selecting design bonnet temperatures for each of the branches, and tabulate the information.

9. Determine the average design bonnet temperature for the system. First, multiply the cooling cfm times the bonnet temperature for each run, and tabulate the information. Then add the values of cfm × bonnet temperature for each branch, and divide by the total cooling cfm required.

10. Select a design bonnet system temperature for the system based on the average found in step 9.

    Bonnet temperatures should not exceed 170°F unless the manufacturer allows higher temperatures. The final selection of a bonnet temperature is often governed by branches serving the living spaces of the residence.

    Branches which have a design bonnet temperature (step 8) *higher* than the bonnet temperature selected will compensate by requiring more air for heating than for cooling. This may require a larger duct and more cfm which will have to be dampered during the cooling season.

    Branches which have a design bonnet temperature *lower* than the bonnet temperature selected will compensate by requiring more air for cooling than for heating.

11. The heating cfm for each supply outlet is found using the bonnet temperature selected (step 10), the heat loss in MBH (step 1), the actual length of the branch (step 5), and the table in Fig. 9-31.

12. The bonnet pressure is selected next. The approximate bonnet pressure required for a trunk (main duct) to carry the maximum volume of air (either heating or cooling cfm, whichever is larger) is found in Fig. 9-32.

13. Next, the supply outlet size and its pressure loss are selected from the manufacturer's engineering data. A typical example of a manufacturer's data is shown in Fig. 9-27. The exact pressure loss will depend on variables such as

the duct velocity and the angles at which the register blades are set. Typically, the pressure loss will range from 0.01 to 0.02 in.; many designers assume a 0.02-in. loss and make a final selection later.

14. The available bonnet pressure is divided between the supply and the return runs. It should be divided in proportion to the amount of supply and return runs on the project. A review of the sketch plan layout shows the approximate proportions of supply to return runs.

> *Note:* If later during the design the proportion selected does not provide satisfactory results, the available bonnet pressure can be reapportioned between supply and return.

15. Determine the pressure available for duct loss by subtracting the supply outlet loss (step 13) from the total pressure available for supply runs (step 14).

16. In order to make a workable table of duct sizes, the pressure drop for duct loss must be calculated as the pressure drop *per 100 ft* of duct.
    Since the various supply runs are all of different lengths, it is necessary to find the *allowable pressure drop per 100 ft* based on the *allowable duct loss* and the *total equivalent length* of the supply run. This allowable pressure drop may be taken from the table in Fig. 9-33, or it may be calculated by using the equation:

$$\text{Allowable pressure drop per 100 ft} = \frac{\text{Allowable duct loss} \times 100}{\text{Total equivalent length}}$$

17. The branch duct sizes may be determined by using Fig. 9-34. This table gives the size of round ducts based on the larger cfm required (either heating or cooling) and the allowable pressure drop per 100 ft (step 16). The size of the round duct may be converted to an equivalent rectangular duct size which will handle the required cfm within the allowable pressure drop.

18. Round duct sizes selected in step 17 may be changed to equivalent rectangular duct sizes, carrying the same cfm required while maintaining the allowable pressure drops, by using the table in Fig. 9-35.

19. Add the air volume of all of the branch supply runs from each trunk duct. When there is more than one trunk duct, keep the totals for each trunk duct separate.

20. For best air flow distribution through the ducts, it is important that the friction losses per 100 ft be approximately equal in both trunk ducts.

Using the table in Fig. 9-34, select the trunk sizes required. When there is more than one trunk duct, size each separately using the required air volume (cfm) and the allowable duct friction (step 15).

21. Review the supply trunk duct to determine if it is desirable to reduce its size as each branch duct leaves the trunk. Generally, such a reduction is suggested so that the velocity of air through the duct will not drop too low. Using the remaining air volume in the trunk duct, after each branch and the allowable pressure drop per 100 ft of duct (step 12), select the reduced trunk sizes from Figs. 9-34 and 9-35.

22. Next, the design turns to the return ducts. The first step is to select an allowable return air pressure drop. This was previously decided (step 14), but it is reviewed at this point as the designer reviews the supply trunk and branch duct sizes to see if he might want to increase the duct sizes (reducing the allowable air pressure drop) or perhaps to reduce the duct sizes (increasing the allowable air pressure drop for the supply runs). Remember that a change in allowable air pressure drop for the supply will affect the allowable air pressure drop for the return runs (step 14).

23. The return trunk duct size is determined by the air volume it must handle and the allowable pressure drop. This allowable pressure drop must be converted to allowable pressure drop *per 100 ft,* just as was done for the supply runs. Using the air volume and the allowable pressure drop per 100 ft, the round return duct size may be selected from Fig. 9-34. The rectangular duct of equivalent size may be found in Fig. 9-35.

24. The size of the blower on the furnace is determined by the total air volume (the total cfm to be delivered) and the total static pressure requirements.

The total static pressure for furnace–blower combination units is the total of the actual pressure drops in the supply and return ducts. Most residential and small commercial buildings have furnace–blower combination units.

When the blowers are selected separately from the furnace, the total static pressure is the sum of the actual pressure losses in the supply and return ducts, filter loss, casing loss, and losses through any devices which are put on the system, such as air washers and purifiers.

25. The capacity of the furnace to be selected is found next. The first step is to determine the Btuh requirements of all supply outlets.

26. Determine the required bonnet capacity of the furnace in Btuh or MBH.

When all the ductwork for a building will be located within heated spaces (spaces on which heat losses are calculated), the required bonnet capacity will be the same as the calculated heat loss plus any allowance for "pickup load."

When the furnace and ductwork will not be located in spaces included in the heat loss, the required bonnet capacity can be determined by the use of the formula:

$$Btuh = cfm \times Unit\ temperature\ rise \times 1.08$$

When the calculations show that the cfm required is not balanced for cooling and heating, two blowers may be required, one for the cooling and one for the heating. An alternate solution is to have bypass ducts around the furnace so that only the volume of air required will be heated.

When it is desirable to have one blower for both the heating and the cooling cycles, the system is designed by first determining the cooling cfm, using the cooling cfm to determine the required bonnet temperature, and then using the bonnet temperature less 65 °F times the cooling cfm to determine furnace capacity.

27.   Add any allowance which is required for pickup load (Sec. 9-6).

Room	Heat gain (Btuh)	Heat loss (Btuh)	Actual length (ft.)	Cooling (cfm per Mbh)	Cooling (cfm)	Bonnet temp. (F)	Cooling (cfm) × Bonnet temp. (F)	Heating (cfm)	Supply outlet size (in.)	Supply outlet pressure loss	Pressure available for duct loss	Equivalent length (ft.)	Loss per 100'	Round duct size (in.)	Rectangular duct size (in.)
BEDROOM 1	2,887	4,283	36	34	98	120	11,760	92	12×6	0.02	0.05	116	0.043	7.0	11×4
BEDROOM 2	1,492	2,310	26	33	49	120	5,880	47	10×6	0.02	0.05	131	0.038	5.5	10×3¼
LIVING	3,571	4,108	33	34	121	110	13,310	86	12×6	0.02	005	138	0.036	8.0	11×5
LIVING	3,571	4,108	55	37	132	110	14,520	93	12×6	0.02	0.05	135	0.037	8.5	10×6
KITCHEN	4,685	3,752	46	36	167	110	18,370	84	12×6	0.02	0.05	126	0.040	9.0	12×6
DINING	2,175	3,047	27	33	72	120	8,640	62	10×6	0.02	0.05	132	0.038	6.5	9×4
ENTRY	1,038	1,682	16	32	33	120	3,960	22	10×6	0.02	0.05	131	0.038	5.0	8×3¼
HALL	1,037	1,682	10	31	32	120	3,840	21	10×6	0.02	005	90	0.055	5.0	8×3¼
BEDROOM 3	2,188	3,008	30	39	85	110	9,350	62	12×6	0.02	005	135	0.037	7.0	11×4
BATH	697	960	25	33	23	110	2,530	23	10×6	0.02	005	115	0043	4.5	6×3
TOTALS	23,447	28,940			812		92,160	592							

BONNET TEMP = $\frac{92,160}{812}$ = 113.5° (USE 120°F)

DUCT PRESSURE AVAILABLE
        BEDROOM BRANCH 0.036 PSI PER 100'
        LIVING BRANCH 0.037 PSI PER 100'

FIGURE 9-18   /   Typical tabulated duct sizes

Duct	Cfm	Loss per 100'	Round duct size (in.)	Rectangular duct size (in.)
MAIN BRANCH	812	0.036	16.0	30 × 8
BEDROOM BRANCH	255	0.037	10.5	12 × 8
LIVING BRANCH	557	0.036	14.0	22 × 8

FIGURE 9-19   /   *Typical tabulated main trunk ducts*

Duct		Cfm	Loss per 100'	Round duct size (in.)	Rectangular duct size (in.)	
MAIN TRUNK	A-B	812	0.036	16.0	30 × 8	
BEDROOM						
	B-C	255	0.037	10.5	12 × 8	
	C-D	206	0.037	9.5	9 × 8	
	D-E	121	0.043	7.5	8 × 6	← REDUCE DUCT SIZE HERE
	E-F	98	0.043	7.0	7 × 6	
LIVING						
	B-G	557	0.036	14.0	22 × 8	
	G-H	525	0.036	13.5	20 × 8	
	H-I	492	0.036	13.5	20 × 8	
	I-J	420	0.036	12.5	17 × 8	
	J-K	299	0.037	11.0	13 × 8	← REDUCE DUCT SIZE HERE
	K-L	132	0.037	8.5	8 × 8	

FIGURE 9-20   /   *Typical reduced trunk sizes*

Duct	Cfm	Actual length	Equivalent length	Total equivalent length	Loss per 100'	Round duct size (in.)	Rectangular duct size (in.)
RETURN	812	12	70	82	0.036	16.0	45 × 6 36 × 7 30 × 8 25 × 9

FIGURE 9-21 / Typical return duct sizes

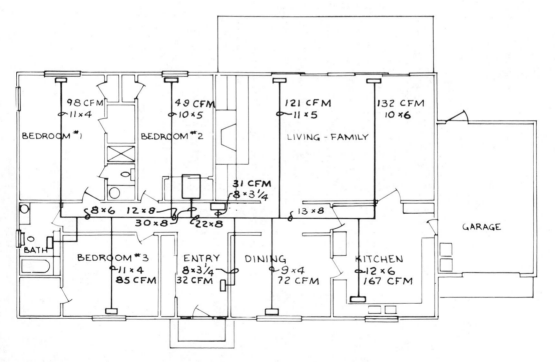

FIGURE 9-22 / Typical duct layout

Design Bonnet Temperature, Register Temperature, and Volume in CFM per 1000 Btuh[a,8]

Temp At Bonnet, F	Linear Distance From Bonnet To Outlet, Ft																							
	10	20	30	40	50	60	70	80	90	100	110	120	130	140	150	160	170	180	190	200	210	220	230	240
110	108	107	105	104	103	101	100	99	98	97	96	95	94	93	92	91	90	89	89	88	87	87	86	85
23.2	24.1	25.1	26.2	27.2	28.4	29.5	30.7	31.9	33.3	34.7	36.0	37.5	39.1	40.6	42.5	44.1	45.9	47.7	49.8	52.0	53.8	56.1	58.6	60.9
120	118	116	114	113	111	109	108	106	105	103	102	101	100	99	97	96	95	94	93	92	92	91	90	89
18.5	19.2	20.1	20.9	21.7	22.7	23.6	24.6	25.6	26.6	27.7	28.8	30.0	31.3	32.5	33.9	35.2	36.7	38.2	39.7	41.5	43.0	44.9	46.8	48.7
130	128	125	123	121	119	117	115	113	112	110	109	107	106	104	103	102	100	99	98	97	96	95	94	93
15.4	16.0	16.7	17.4	18.1	18.9	19.6	20.5	21.3	22.2	23.1	24.1	25.0	26.1	27.2	28.2	29.4	30.7	31.9	33.2	34.6	36.0	37.5	38.9	40.6
140	137	135	132	130	127	125	123	121	118	117	115	113	111	110	108	107	105	104	103	101	100	99	98	97
13.2	13.8	14.4	14.9	15.5	16.2	16.8	17.5	18.3	19.0	19.8	20.6	21.4	22.4	23.3	24.2	25.2	26.2	27.3	28.4	29.7	30.9	32.2	33.4	34.8
150	147	144	141	138	135	133	130	128	126	123	121	119	117	116	114	112	110	109	107	106	104	103	102	100
11.6	12.0	12.5	13.1	13.6	14.2	14.7	15.4	16.0	16.7	17.3	18.0	18.7	19.5	20.4	21.2	22.0	23.0	23.9	24.9	25.9	27.0	28.1	29.2	30.5
160	156	153	150	147	144	141	138	135	133	130	128	126	123	121	119	117	115	114	112	110	109	107	106	104
10.3	10.7	11.2	11.6	12.1	12.6	13.1	13.6	14.2	14.8	15.4	16.0	16.7	17.4	18.1	18.9	19.6	20.4	21.2	22.1	23.1	24.0	25.0	26.0	27.1
170	166	162	159	155	152	149	145	142	140	137	134	132	129	127	125	123	120	118	117	115	113	111	110	108
9.3	9.6	10.0	10.5	10.9	11.3	11.8	12.3	12.8	13.3	13.9	14.4	15.0	15.6	16.3	17.0	17.6	18.4	19.1	19.9	20.8	21.6	22.5	23.4	24.4
180	176	171	167	164	160	156	153	150	146	144	141	138	135	133	130	128	125	123	121	119	117	115	114	112
8.4	8.8	9.1	9.5	9.9	10.3	10.7	11.2	11.6	12.1	12.6	13.1	13.6	14.2	14.8	15.4	16.0	16.7	17.4	18.1	18.9	19.6	20.4	21.2	22.2
190	185	181	176	172	168	164	160	157	153	150	147	144	141	138	136	133	131	128	126	124	122	119	118	116
7.7	8.0	8.4	8.7	9.1	9.4	9.8	10.2	10.7	11.1	11.5	12.0	12.5	13.0	13.6	14.1	14.7	15.3	15.9	16.6	17.3	18.0	18.7	19.5	20.3
200	195	190	185	181	176	172	168	164	160	157	153	150	147	144	141	138	136	133	130	128	126	124	122	119
7.1	7.4	7.7	8.0	8.4	8.7	9.1	9.4	9.8	10.2	10.7	11.1	11.5	12.0	12.5	13.0	13.6	14.1	14.7	15.3	16.0	16.6	17.3	18.0	18.7

[a] For a building having a heat loss up to 150,000 Btuh.

Reprinted with permission from ASHRAE, Systems Handbook, 1976

FIGURE 9-23 / Bonnet temperatures—up to 150,000 Btuh

Design Bonnet Temperature, Register Temperature, and Volume in CFM per 1000 Btuh[a,8]

Temp At Bonnet, F	Linear Distance From Bonnet To Outlet, Ft																							
	10	20	30	40	50	60	70	80	90	100	110	120	130	140	150	160	170	180	190	200	210	220	230	240
100	99	98	98	97	96	95	95	94	93	93	92	92	91	90	90	89	89	88	88	87	87	86	86	85
30.9	31.7	32.6	33.6	34.6	35.5	36.5	37.5	38.6	39.7	40.8	41.9	43.1	44.3	45.6	47.0	48.2	49.5	50.9	52.3	53.8	55.4	57.2	58.6	60.1
110	109	108	107	106	105	104	103	102	101	100	99	99	98	97	96	95	94	94	93	92	92	91	91	90
23.2	23.8	24.5	25.2	25.9	26.6	27.4	28.1	28.9	29.8	30.7	31.5	32.4	33.3	34.3	35.2	36.2	37.2	38.3	39.2	40.4	41.7	42.9	44.1	45.2
120	119	117	116	115	114	112	111	110	109	108	107	106	105	104	103	102	101	100	100	99	98	97	96	96
18.5	19.1	19.6	20.1	20.7	21.3	21.9	22.5	23.2	23.8	24.5	25.2	25.9	26.6	27.4	28.1	28.9	29.7	30.6	31.4	32.4	33.3	34.2	35.2	36.2
130	128	127	125	124	122	121	119	118	117	115	114	113	112	110	108	107	106	105	104	103	103	102	101	101
15.4	15.9	16.3	16.8	17.3	17.8	18.2	18.7	19.3	19.8	20.4	21.0	21.6	22.2	22.8	23.4	24.2	24.8	25.5	26.2	27.0	27.7	28.5	29.3	30.2
140	138	136	134	133	131	129	128	126	125	123	122	120	119	117	116	115	114	112	111	110	109	108	107	106
13.2	13.6	14.0	14.4	14.8	15.2	15.6	16.1	16.5	17.0	17.5	18.0	18.5	19.0	19.6	20.1	20.7	21.2	21.8	22.5	23.2	23.8	24.4	25.2	25.9
150	148	146	144	142	140	138	136	134	132	130	129	127	126	124	123	121	120	118	117	116	115	113	112	110
11.6	11.9	12.2	12.6	13.0	13.3	13.7	14.1	14.5	14.9	15.3	15.7	16.2	16.7	17.1	17.6	18.1	18.6	19.1	19.7	20.2	20.8	21.4	22.0	22.6
160	158	155	153	151	148	146	144	142	140	138	136	134	133	131	129	128	126	125	123	122	120	119	117	116
10.3	10.6	10.9	11.2	11.5	11.8	12.2	12.5	12.9	13.2	13.6	14.0	14.4	14.8	15.2	15.6	16.1	16.5	17.0	17.5	18.0	18.5	19.0	19.6	20.1
170	167	165	162	159	157	155	152	150	148	146	144	142	140	138	136	134	132	131	130	127	126	124	123	121
9.3	9.5	9.8	10.1	10.4	10.7	10.9	11.3	11.6	11.9	12.2	12.6	13.0	13.3	13.7	14.1	14.5	14.9	15.3	15.7	16.2	16.7	17.1	17.6	18.1
180	177	174	171	168	166	163	161	158	156	153	151	149	147	144	142	140	139	137	135	133	131	130	128	126
8.4	8.7	8.9	9.2	9.4	9.7	9.9	10.2	10.5	10.8	11.1	11.4	11.8	12.1	12.4	12.8	13.2	13.5	13.9	14.3	14.7	15.1	15.6	16.0	16.4
190	187	184	180	177	174	172	169	166	163	161	158	156	153	151	149	147	145	143	141	139	137	135	133	131
7.7	7.9	8.2	8.4	8.6	8.9	9.1	9.4	9.6	9.9	10.2	10.5	10.8	11.1	11.4	11.7	12.1	12.4	12.8	13.1	13.5	13.9	14.3	14.7	15.1
200	196	193	190	186	183	180	177	174	171	168	166	163	160	158	156	153	151	149	147	144	142	140	138	137
7.1	7.3	7.5	7.7	8.0	8.2	8.4	8.7	8.9	9.2	9.4	9.7	10.0	10.2	10.5	10.8	11.1	11.4	11.8	12.1	12.4	12.8	13.2	13.5	13.9

[a] For a building having a heat loss between 150,000 And 300,000 Btuh.

Reprinted with permission from ASHRAE, Systems Handbook, 1976

FIGURE 9-24 / Bonnet temperatures—150,000 to 300,000 Btuh

Design Bonnet Temperature, Register Temperature, and Volume in CFM per 1000 Btuh[a,8]

Temp At Bonnet, F	Linear Distance From Bonnet To Outlet, Ft																							
	10	20	30	40	50	60	70	80	90	100	110	120	130	140	150	160	170	180	190	200	210	220	230	240
100 / 30.9	99 / 31.5	99 / 32.2	98 / 32.8	98 / 33.6	97 / 34.2	97 / 34.9	96 / 35.6	96 / 36.3	95 / 37.2	95 / 37.8	94 / 38.7	94 / 39.4	93 / 40.3	93 / 41.2	92 / 41.9	92 / 42.9	91 / 43.7	91 / 44.5	90 / 45.6	90 / 46.5	90 / 47.5	89 / 48.5	89 / 49.5	88 / 50.6
110 / 23.2	109 / 23.6	108 / 24.1	108 / 24.6	107 / 25.2	106 / 25.7	105 / 26.2	105 / 26.8	104 / 27.2	103 / 27.9	103 / 28.4	102 / 29.0	101 / 29.6	101 / 30.3	100 / 30.9	100 / 31.5	99 / 32.2	99 / 32.8	98 / 33.4	97 / 34.2	97 / 34.8	96 / 35.6	96 / 36.3	95 / 37.2	94 / 38.0
120 / 18.5	119 / 18.9	118 / 19.3	117 / 19.7	116 / 20.1	115 / 20.5	114 / 21.0	113 / 21.4	113 / 21.8	112 / 22.3	111 / 22.7	110 / 23.2	109 / 23.7	108 / 24.2	108 / 24.7	107 / 25.2	106 / 25.7	105 / 26.2	105 / 26.8	104 / 27.3	103 / 27.9	103 / 28.5	102 / 29.0	101 / 29.7	101 / 30.3
130 / 15.4	129 / 15.8	128 / 16.1	126 / 16.4	125 / 16.7	124 / 17.1	123 / 17.5	122 / 17.8	121 / 18.2	120 / 18.6	119 / 18.9	118 / 19.3	117 / 19.7	116 / 20.1	115 / 20.6	114 / 21.0	113 / 21.4	112 / 21.8	112 / 22.3	111 / 22.8	110 / 23.3	109 / 23.8	108 / 24.2	107 / 24.8	107 / 25.2
140 / 13.2	139 / 13.5	137 / 13.8	136 / 14.1	135 / 14.4	133 / 14.7	132 / 15.0	131 / 15.3	129 / 15.6	128 / 15.9	127 / 16.2	126 / 16.6	125 / 16.9	124 / 17.3	123 / 17.6	122 / 18.0	120 / 18.4	119 / 18.7	118 / 19.1	118 / 19.5	117 / 19.9	115 / 20.4	115 / 20.8	114 / 21.2	113 / 21.6
150 / 11.6	148 / 11.8	147 / 12.1	145 / 12.3	144 / 12.6	142 / 12.8	141 / 13.1	139 / 13.4	138 / 13.6	137 / 13.9	135 / 14.2	134 / 14.5	133 / 14.8	131 / 15.1	130 / 15.4	129 / 15.7	128 / 16.1	127 / 16.4	125 / 16.7	124 / 17.1	123 / 17.4	122 / 17.8	121 / 18.2	120 / 18.6	119 / 18.9
160 / 10.3	158 / 10.5	156 / 10.7	155 / 10.9	153 / 11.2	151 / 11.4	150 / 11.6	148 / 11.9	146 / 12.1	145 / 12.4	143 / 12.6	142 / 12.9	140 / 13.2	139 / 13.4	138 / 13.7	136 / 14.0	135 / 14.3	134 / 14.6	132 / 14.9	131 / 15.2	130 / 15.5	128 / 15.9	127 / 16.2	126 / 16.5	125 / 16.8
170 / 9.3	168 / 9.5	166 / 9.6	164 / 9.9	162 / 10.1	160 / 10.3	158 / 10.5	157 / 10.7	155 / 10.9	153 / 11.1	152 / 11.4	150 / 11.4	148 / 11.8	147 / 12.1	145 / 12.3	144 / 12.6	142 / 12.9	141 / 13.1	139 / 13.4	138 / 13.7	136 / 13.9	135 / 14.3	134 / 14.5	132 / 14.9	131 / 15.2
180 / 8.4	178 / 8.6	176 / 8.8	173 / 9.0	171 / 9.1	169 / 9.3	167 / 9.5	165 / 9.7	163 / 9.9	161 / 10.1	160 / 10.3	158 / 10.5	156 / 10.8	154 / 11.0	153 / 11.2	151 / 11.4	149 / 11.7	148 / 11.9	146 / 12.2	145 / 12.4	143 / 12.7	141 / 13.0	140 / 13.2	139 / 13.5	138 / 13.8
190 / 7.7	188 / 7.9	185 / 8.0	183 / 8.2	181 / 8.4	178 / 8.6	176 / 8.7	174 / 8.9	172 / 9.1	170 / 9.3	168 / 9.5	166 / 9.7	164 / 9.9	162 / 10.1	160 / 10.3	158 / 10.5	156 / 10.7	155 / 10.9	153 / 11.2	151 / 11.4	150 / 11.6	148 / 11.9	146 / 12.1	145 / 12.4	143 / 12.6
200 / 7.1	197 / 7.3	195 / 7.4	192 / 7.6	188 / 7.7	187 / 7.9	185 / 8.1	183 / 8.2	180 / 8.4	178 / 8.6	176 / 8.7	174 / 8.9	172 / 9.1	170 / 9.3	168 / 9.5	166 / 9.7	164 / 9.9	162 / 10.1	160 / 10.5	158 / 10.5	156 / 10.7	154 / 11.0	153 / 11.2	151 / 11.4	149 / 11.7

[a] For a building having a heat loss from 300,000 To 450,000 Btuh.

Reprinted with permission from ASHRAE, Systems Handbook, 1976

FIGURE 9-25 / Bonnet temperatures—300,000 to 450,000 Btuh

Design Bonnet Temperature, Register Temperature, and Volume in CFM per 1000 Btuh[a,8]

Temp At Bonnet, F	Linear Distance From Bonnet To Outlet, Ft																							
	10	20	30	40	50	60	70	80	90	100	110	120	130	140	150	160	170	180	190	200	210	220	230	240
100 / 30.9	100 / 31.4	99 / 31.8	99 / 32.4	98 / 32.8	98 / 33.3	97 / 33.9	97 / 34.4	97 / 34.9	96 / 35.6	96 / 36.0	95 / 36.7	95 / 37.2	95 / 37.8	94 / 38.4	94 / 39.1	93 / 39.7	93 / 40.3	93 / 41.0	92 / 41.5	92 / 42.3	92 / 42.9	91 / 43.7	91 / 44.3	91 / 45.0
110 / 23.2	109 / 23.5	109 / 23.9	108 / 24.2	107 / 24.6	106 / 25.0	106 / 25.4	105 / 25.9	105 / 26.2	104 / 26.7	103 / 27.1	103 / 27.6	102 / 27.9	102 / 28.4	102 / 28.8	101 / 29.3	101 / 29.8	101 / 30.3	101 / 30.7	100 / 31.2	99 / 31.7	99 / 32.2	98 / 32.7	98 / 33.2	97 / 33.8
120 / 18.5	119 / 18.8	119 / 19.1	118 / 19.4	117 / 19.7	116 / 20.0	116 / 20.4	115 / 20.7	114 / 21.0	113 / 21.3	113 / 21.6	112 / 22.0	112 / 22.3	111 / 22.7	110 / 23.0	110 / 23.4	109 / 23.8	108 / 24.2	108 / 24.6	107 / 25.0	107 / 25.4	106 / 25.7	105 / 26.2	105 / 26.5	104 / 27.0
130 / 15.4	129 / 15.7	128 / 15.9	127 / 16.2	126 / 16.4	126 / 16.7	125 / 17.0	124 / 17.2	123 / 17.5	122 / 17.8	121 / 18.1	121 / 18.6	120 / 18.9	119 / 19.2	118 / 19.5	117 / 20.1	117 / 20.5	116 / 20.8	115 / 21.1	115 / 21.5	114 / 21.8	113 / 22.2	113 / 22.2	112 / 22.2	111 / 22.5
140 / 13.2	139 / 12.4	138 / 13.7	137 / 13.9	136 / 14.1	135 / 14.3	134 / 14.5	133 / 14.8	132 / 15.0	131 / 15.2	130 / 15.5	129 / 15.7	128 / 16.0	127 / 16.2	126 / 16.5	125 / 16.7	125 / 17.0	124 / 17.3	123 / 17.5	122 / 17.8	121 / 18.1	120 / 18.4	120 / 18.7	119 / 19.0	119 / 19.3
150 / 11.6	149 / 11.8	148 / 11.9	146 / 12.1	145 / 12.3	144 / 12.5	143 / 12.7	142 / 12.9	141 / 13.1	139 / 13.3	138 / 13.5	137 / 13.8	136 / 14.0	135 / 14.2	134 / 14.4	133 / 14.7	132 / 14.9	131 / 15.1	130 / 15.4	129 / 15.6	128 / 15.9	128 / 16.1	127 / 16.4	126 / 16.6	125 / 16.9
160 / 10.3	159 / 10.5	157 / 10.6	156 / 10.8	155 / 11.0	153 / 11.1	152 / 11.3	151 / 11.5	149 / 11.7	148 / 11.9	147 / 12.0	146 / 12.2	145 / 12.4	143 / 12.6	142 / 12.8	141 / 13.0	140 / 13.2	139 / 13.4	138 / 13.6	137 / 13.9	136 / 14.1	135 / 14.3	134 / 14.5	133 / 14.8	132 / 15.0
170 / 9.3	168 / 9.4	167 / 9.6	165 / 9.7	164 / 9.9	163 / 10.0	161 / 10.2	160 / 10.3	158 / 10.5	157 / 10.7	156 / 10.8	154 / 11.0	153 / 11.2	152 / 11.4	150 / 11.5	149 / 11.7	148 / 11.9	147 / 12.1	145 / 12.3	144 / 12.5	143 / 12.7	142 / 12.9	141 / 13.1	140 / 13.3	139 / 13.5
180 / 8.4	178 / 8.6	177 / 8.7	175 / 8.8	173 / 9.0	172 / 9.1	170 / 9.3	169 / 9.4	167 / 9.5	166 / 9.7	164 / 9.8	163 / 10.0	161 / 10.2	160 / 10.3	158 / 10.5	157 / 10.7	156 / 10.8	154 / 11.0	153 / 11.2	152 / 11.3	150 / 11.5	149 / 11.7	148 / 11.9	147 / 12.1	146 / 12.3
190 / 7.7	188 / 7.8	186 / 8.0	185 / 8.1	183 / 8.2	181 / 8.3	179 / 8.5	178 / 8.6	176 / 8.8	174 / 8.9	173 / 9.0	171 / 9.2	170 / 9.3	168 / 9.5	166 / 9.6	165 / 9.8	163 / 9.9	162 / 10.1	161 / 10.2	159 / 10.4	158 / 10.6	156 / 10.7	155 / 10.9	154 / 11.1	152 / 11.3
200 / 7.1	198 / 7.2	196 / 7.3	194 / 7.5	192 / 7.6	190 / 7.8	188 / 7.9	187 / 8.1	185 / 8.2	183 / 8.3	181 / 8.5	179 / 8.6	178 / 8.7	176 / 8.9	174 / 9.0	173 / 9.2	171 / 9.3	170 / 9.4	168 / 9.6	167 / 9.8	165 / 9.9	164 / 10.1	162 / 10.2	161 / 10.2	159 / 10.4

[a] For a building having a heat loss greater than 450,000 Btuh.

Reprinted with permission from ASHRAE, Systems Handbook, 1976

FIGURE 9-26 / Bonnet temperature, more than 450,000 Btuh

LISTED WIDTH															
6	8	10	12	14	16	18	20	22	24	26	28	30	32	34	36
6	4														
	8	6	5		4										
		10	8		6		5		4						
			12	10		8			6		5				4

V = Duct Vel.	300			400			500			600		
Blade Set °	0	22½	45	0	22½	45	0	22½	45	0	22½	45
P_t	.01	.012	.027	.014	.021	.050	.023	.034	.082	.034	.051	.120
CFM	75			100			125			150		
T PWL-NC	8	L		10	L		13	L		16	L	
CFM	130			180			220			260		
T PWL-NC	9	L		13	L		17	L		20	L	
CFM	210			280			350			400		
T PWL-NC	13	L		17	L		21	L		24	28	
CFM	300			400			500			600		
T PWL-NC	15	L		20	L		25	26		29	32	

SYMBOLS:

V = Duct velocity in fpm.
CFM = Quantity of air in cubic ft./min.
NC = Noise criteria (8 db room attenuation).
D = Drop in feet.
P_t = Total pressure inches H_2O
T = Throw in Feet
PWL-NC INDEX = A single number which expresses the PWL (sound power level) in relation to NC (noise criteria) curves.

FIGURE 9-27 / Supply outlet data

CFM	Type A	Type B	Type C
1000	0.10	0.15	0.20
1500	.12	.17	.22
2000	.13	.18	.24
2500	.14	.20	.27
3000	.16	.22	.29
3500	.17	.24	.31
4000	.18	.26	.33
4500	0.20	0.28	0.36
5000	.21	.29	.38
5500	.22	.31	.40
6000	.24	.33	.42
6500	.25	.34	.45
7000	.27	.36	.47
7500	.28	.38	.49
8000	0.29	0.39	0.51
8500	.30	.41	.53
9000	.32	.43	.56
9500	.34	.45	.58
10,000	.34	.47	.60
10,500	.37	.48	.60
11,000	.39	.50	.60
11,500	0.40	0.50	0.60
12,000	.40	.50	.60
12,500	.40	.50	.60
13,000	.40	.50	.60
14,000	.40	.50	.60

CFM = Maximum cfm in any one duct.
Type A = Systems for quiet operation in residences, churches, concert halls, broadcasting studios, funeral homes, etc.
Type B = Systems for schools, theaters, public buildings, etc.
Type C = Systems for industrial buildings.

FIGURE 9-28 / Suggested bonnet and return pressures

231

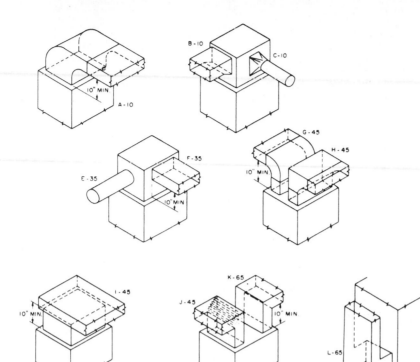

Equivalent of Supply and Return Air Plenum Fittings[8]

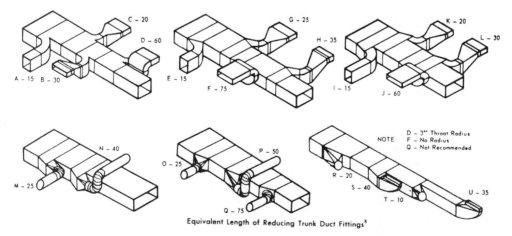

Equivalent Length of Reducing Trunk Duct Fittings[8]

FIGURE 9-29 / Equivalent fittings

232

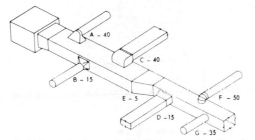

12.7

a Add 25 equivalent feet to each of the 3 fittings nearest the unit in each trunk duct after a reduction.

Equivalent Length of Extended Plenum Fittings[a,8]

a Add 25 equivalent feet to each of the 3 fittings nearest the unit in each trunk duct.

Equivalent Length of Round Trunk Duct Fittings[a,8]

A – 30

B – 35

C – 60

D – 55

E – 70

F – 45

G – 30

H – 50

I – 5

J – 15

K – 30

L – 30

M – 5

N – 15

O – 15

P – 5

a These values may also be used for floor diffuser boxes.

Equivalent Length of Boot Fittings[a,8]

A – 5

B – 10

C – 25

D – 5

E – 10

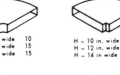

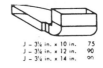

F – 5

G – 10 in. wide 10
G – 12 in. wide 15
G – 14 in. wide 15

H – 10 in. wide 40
H – 12 in. wide 55
H – 14 in wide 55

I – 3¼ in. x 10 in. 60
I – 3¼ in. x 12 in. 75
I – 3¼ in. x 14 in. 75

J – 3¼ in. x 10 in. 75
J – 3¼ in. x 12 in. 90
J – 3¼ in. x 14 in. 90

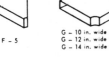

K – 125

L – 35

M – 10

N – 95

FIGURE 9-29 / *Equivalent fittings (continued)*

233

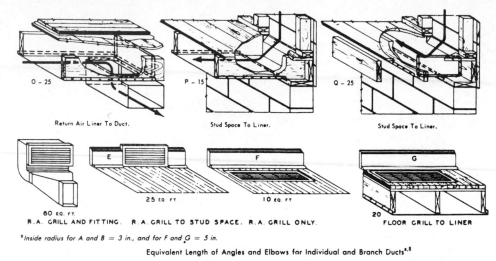

O – 25   Return Air Liner To Duct.

P – 15   Stud Space To Liner.

Q – 25   Stud Space To Liner.

60 SQ. FT.   E   25 SQ. FT.   F   10 SQ. FT.   G

R.A. GRILL AND FITTING.   R.A. GRILL TO STUD SPACE.   R.A. GRILL ONLY.

20   FLOOR GRILL TO LINER

[a]Inside radius for A and B = 3 in., and for F and G = 5 in.

Equivalent Length of Angles and Elbows for Individual and Branch Ducts[a,8]

Reprinted with permission from ASHRAE, Systems Handbook, 1976

FIGURE 9-29 / Equivalent fittings (continued)

CFM per 1000 Btuh (MBh) for Total Heat Gain[a, 8]

Duct Length Bonnet to Reg.	Daily Temperature Range[*]		
	Low	Medium	High
0	25	30	35
5	25	30	36
10	26	31	36
15	27	32	37
20	27	32	38
25	28	33	39
30	28	34	39
35	29	34	40
40	29	35	41
45	30	36	42
50	31	36	43
55	31	37	43
60	32	38	44
65	32	39	45
70	33	40	46
75	34	40	47
80	34	41	48
85	35	42	49
90	36	43	50
95	37	44	51
100	37	45	52

[*]Based on:
  Low = 300 CFM per ton
  Medium = 360 CFM per ton
  High = 420 CFM per ton

[a]Calculated from Chapter 22 of the 1972 HANDBOOK OF FUNDAMENTALS. The values in this table are based on total heat gain. If the distribution system is to be based on sensible load only, multiply these values by 1.3.

Reprinted with permission from ASHRAE, Systems Handbook, 1976

FIGURE 9-30 / Cooling cfm per 1000 Btuh (MBh)

Heating Capacity, MBh										Require Air Volume for Cooling, Cfm										
Design Bonnet Temperature, F										Duct Length, Ft										
110	120	130	140	150	160	170	180	190	200	0	10	20	30	40	50	60	70	80	90	100
0.9	1.1	1.3	1.5	1.7	1.9	2.2	2.4	2.6	2.8	20	21	22	23	24	24	25	26	28	29	30
1.1	1.4	1.6	1.9	2.2	2.4	2.7	3.0	3.3	3.5	25	26	27	28	29	30	32	33	35	36	38
1.3	1.6	2.0	2.3	2.6	2.9	3.2	3.6	3.9	4.2	30	31	32	34	35	37	38	40	42	43	45
1.5	1.9	2.3	2.7	3.0	3.4	3.8	4.2	4.6	4.9	35	36	38	39	41	43	45	46	48	50	53
1.7	2.2	2.6	3.0	3.4	3.8	4.3	4.8	5.2	5.6	40	42	43	45	47	49	41	53	55	58	60
1.9	2.4	2.9	3.4	3.9	4.4	4.8	5.4	5.9	6.3	45	47	49	51	53	55	57	60	62	65	68
2.2	2.7	3.3	3.8	4.3	4.9	5.4	6.0	6.5	7.1	50	52	54	56	59	61	64	66	69	72	75
2.4	3.0	3.6	4.2	4.7	5.3	5.9	6.5	7.2	7.8	55	57	60	62	65	67	70	73	76	79	83
2.6	3.2	3.9	4.6	5.2	5.8	6.5	7.1	7.8	8.5	60	62	65	68	71	73	76	80	83	87	90
2.8	3.5	4.2	4.9	5.6	6.3	7.0	7.7	8.5	9.2	65	68	70	73	76	79	83	86	90	94	98
3.0	3.8	4.6	5.3	6.0	6.8	7.5	8.3	9.1	9.9	70	73	76	79	82	85	89	93	97	101	105
3.2	4.1	4.9	5.7	6.5	7.3	8.1	8.9	9.8	10.6	75	78	81	85	88	91	95	99	104	108	113
3.4	4.3	5.2	6.1	6.9	7.8	8.6	9.5	10.4	11.3	80	83	87	90	94	98	102	106	111	116	120
3.7	4.6	5.5	6.4	7.3	8.3	9.1	10.1	11.1	12.0	85	88	92	96	100	104	108	113	118	123	128
3.9	4.9	5.9	6.8	7.7	8.7	9.7	10.7	11.7	12.7	90	94	97	101	106	110	114	119	125	130	135
4.1	5.1	6.2	7.2	8.2	9.2	10.2	11.3	12.4	13.4	95	99	103	107	112	116	121	126	132	137	143
4.3	5.4	6.5	7.6	8.6	9.7	10.8	11.9	13.0	14.1	100	104	108	113	118	122	127	133	139	144	150
4.5	5.7	6.8	8.0	9.1	10.2	11.3	12.5	13.7	14.8	105	109	114	118	124	128	134	139	145	152	158
4.7	6.0	7.2	8.3	9.5	10.7	11.8	13.1	14.3	15.5	110	114	119	124	129	134	140	146	152	159	165
5.0	6.2	7.5	8.7	9.9	11.2	12.4	13.7	15.0	16.2	115	120	125	130	135	140	146	152	159	166	173
5.2	6.5	7.8	9.1	10.4	11.7	12.9	14.3	15.6	16.9	120	125	130	135	141	146	153	159	166	173	180
5.4	6.8	8.1	9.5	10.8	12.1	13.5	14.9	16.3	17.6	125	130	136	141	147	152	159	166	173	180	188
5.6	7.0	8.5	9.9	11.2	12.6	14.0	15.5	16.9	18.3	130	135	141	147	153	159	165	172	180	188	195
5.8	7.3	8.8	10.2	11.6	13.1	14.5	16.1	17.6	19.0	135	140	146	152	159	165	172	179	187	195	203
6.0	7.6	9.1	10.6	12.1	13.6	15.1	16.7	18.2	19.7	140	146	152	158	165	171	178	186	194	202	210
6.3	7.9	9.4	11.0	12.5	14.1	15.6	17.3	18.9	20.4	145	151	157	164	170	177	184	192	201	209	218
6.5	8.1	9.8	11.4	12.9	14.6	16.1	17.9	19.5	21.2	150	156	163	169	176	183	191	199	208	216	225
6.7	8.4	10.1	11.8	13.4	15.1	16.7	18.4	20.2	21.9	155	161	168	175	182	189	197	205	215	224	233
6.9	8.7	10.4	12.1	13.8	15.5	17.2	19.0	20.8	22.6	160	166	174	180	188	195	203	212	222	231	240
7.1	8.9	10.7	12.5	14.2	16.0	17.8	19.6	21.5	23.3	165	171	179	186	194	201	210	219	228	238	248
7.3	9.2	11.0	12.9	14.7	16.5	18.3	20.2	22.1	24.0	170	177	184	192	200	207	216	225	235	245	255
7.6	9.5	11.4	13.3	15.1	17.0	18.8	20.8	22.8	24.7	175	182	190	198	206	214	222	232	242	253	263
7.8	9.7	11.7	13.6	15.5	17.5	19.4	21.4	23.4	25.4	180	187	195	203	212	220	229	239	249	260	270
8.0	10.0	12.0	14.0	15.9	18.0	19.9	22.0	24.1	26.1	185	192	201	209	217	226	235	245	256	267	278
8.2	10.3	12.4	14.4	16.4	18.4	20.4	22.6	24.7	26.8	190	198	206	215	223	232	241	252	263	274	285
8.4	10.5	12.7	14.8	16.8	18.9	21.0	23.2	25.4	27.5	195	203	211	220	229	238	248	259	270	282	293
8.6	10.8	13.0	15.2	17.2	19.4	21.5	23.8	26.0	28.2	200	208	217	226	235	244	254	265	277	289	300
8.8	11.1	13.3	15.5	17.7	19.9	22.1	24.4	26.7	28.9	205	213	222	231	241	250	261	272	284	296	308
9.1	11.4	13.7	15.9	18.1	20.4	22.6	25.0	27.3	29.6	210	218	228	237	247	256	267	278	291	303	315
9.3	11.6	14.0	16.3	18.5	20.9	23.1	25.6	28.0	30.3	215	224	233	243	253	262	273	285	298	310	323
9.5	11.9	14.3	16.7	19.0	21.4	23.7	26.2	28.6	31.0	220	229	238	248	259	268	280	292	305	318	330
9.7	12.2	14.6	17.1	19.4	21.8	24.2	26.8	29.3	31.7	225	234	244	254	264	275	286	298	312	325	338
9.9	12.4	15.0	17.4	19.8	22.3	24.7	27.4	29.9	32.4	230	239	249	260	270	281	292	305	319	332	345
10.1	12.7	15.3	17.8	20.3	22.8	25.3	28.0	30.6	33.1	235	244	255	265	276	287	299	312	325	339	353
10.4	13.0	15.6	18.2	20.7	23.3	25.8	28.6	31.2	33.8	240	250	260	271	282	293	305	318	332	347	360
10.6	13.3	15.9	18.6	21.1	23.8	26.4	29.2	31.9	34.5	245	255	266	277	288	299	311	325	339	354	368
10.8	13.5	16.3	19.0	21.6	24.3	26.9	29.8	32.5	35.3	250	260	271	282	294	305	318	332	346	361	375
11.0	13.8	16.6	19.3	22.0	24.8	27.4	30.3	33.2	36.0	255	265	276	288	300	311	324	338	353	368	383
11.2	14.1	16.9	19.7	22.4	25.2	28.0	30.9	33.8	36.7	260	270	282	294	306	317	330	345	360	375	390
11.4	14.3	17.2	20.1	22.8	25.7	28.5	31.5	34.5	37.4	265	276	287	299	311	323	337	351	367	383	398
11.6	14.6	17.6	20.5	23.3	26.2	29.1	32.1	35.1	38.1	270	281	293	305	317	329	343	358	374	390	405
11.9	14.9	17.9	20.8	23.7	26.7	29.6	32.7	35.8	38.8	275	286	298	310	323	336	350	365	381	397	413
12.1	15.1	18.2	21.2	24.1	27.2	30.1	33.3	36.4	39.5	280	291	304	316	329	342	356	371	388	404	420
12.3	15.4	18.5	21.6	24.6	27.7	30.7	33.9	37.1	40.2	285	296	309	322	335	348	362	378	395	412	428
12.5	15.7	18.9	22.0	25.0	28.2	31.2	34.5	37.7	40.9	290	302	314	327	341	354	369	385	402	419	435
12.7	16.0	19.2	22.4	25.4	28.6	31.7	35.1	38.4	41.6	295	307	320	333	347	360	375	391	409	426	443
12.9	16.2	19.5	22.7	25.9	29.1	32.3	35.7	39.0	42.3	300	312	325	339	353	366	381	398	416	433	450

Reprinted with permission from ASHRAE, Systems Handbook, 1976

FIGURE 9-31 / Bonnet temperature selection table.

CFM	Type A	Type B	Type C
1000	0.10	0.15	0.20
1500	.12	.17	.22
2000	.13	.18	.24
2500	.14	.20	.27
3000	.16	.22	.29
3500	.17	.24	.31
4000	.18	.26	.33
4500	0.20	0.28	0.36
5000	.21	.29	.38
5500	.22	.31	.40
6000	.24	.33	.42
6500	.25	.34	.45
7000	.27	.36	.47
7500	.28	.38	.49
8000	0.29	0.39	0.51
8500	.30	.41	.53
9000	.32	.43	.56
9500	.34	.45	.58
10,000	.34	.47	.60
10,500	.37	.48	.60
11,000	.39	.50	.60
11,500	0.40	0.50	0.60
12,000	.40	.50	.60
12,500	.40	.50	.60
13,000	.40	.50	.60
14,000	.40	.50	.60

CFM = Maximum cfm in any one duct.
Type A = Systems for quiet operation in residences, churches, concert
halls, broadcasting studios, funeral homes, etc.
Type B = Systems for schools, theaters, public buildings, etc.
Type C = Systems for industrial buildings.

FIGURE 9-32 / Suggested bonnet and return pressures (inches of water)

Reprinted with permission from ASHRAE, Systems Handbook, 1976

Equivalent Length of Duct (Ft)	Total Pressure Drop in Duct (In. of Water)																
	0.04	0.05	0.06	0.07	0.08	0.09	0.10	0.11	0.12	0.13	0.14	0.15	0.16	0.17	0.18	0.19	0.20
35–44	0.10	0.13	0.15	0.18	0.20	0.23	0.25	0.28	0.30	0.33	0.35	0.38	0.40	0.43	0.45	0.48	0.50
45–54	.08	.10	.12	.14	.16	.18	.20	.22	.24	.26	.28	.30	.32	.34	.36	.38	.40
55–64	.07	.08	.10	.12	.13	.15	.17	.18	.20	.22	.23	.25	.27	.28	.30	.32	.33
65–74	.06	.07	.09	.10	.11	.13	.14	.16	.17	.19	.20	.21	.23	.24	.26	.28	.29
75–84	0.05	0.06	0.08	0.09	0.10	0.11	0.13	0.14	0.15	0.16	0.18	0.19	0.20	0.21	0.23	0.24	0.25
85–94	.05	.06	.07	.08	.09	.10	.11	.12	.13	.14	.16	.17	18	.19	.20	.21	.22
95–104	.04	.05	.06	.07	.08	.09	.10	.11	.12	.13	.14	.15	.16	.17	.18	.19	.20
105–114	.04	.05	.05	.06	.07	.08	.09	.10	.11	.12	.13	.14	.15	.15	.16	.17	.18
115–129	0.03	0.04	0.05	0.06	0.07	0.08	0.08	0.09	0.10	0.11	0.12	0.12	0.13	0.14	0.15	0.16	0.17
130–149	.03	.04	.04	.05	.06	.07	.07	.08	.09	.09	.10	.11	.11	.12	.13	.14	.14
150–169	.03	.03	.04	.04	.05	.06	.06	.07	.08	.08	.09	.09	.10	.11	.11	.12	.13
170–189	.02	.03	.03	.04	.04	.05	.06	.06	.07	.07	.08	.08	.09	.09	.10	.11	.11
190–214	0.02	0.03	0.03	0.04	0.04	0.05	0.05	0.06	0.06	0.07	0.07	0.08	0.08	0.09	0.09	0.10	0.10
215–239	.02	.02	.03	.03	.04	.04	.05	.05	.05	.06	.06	.07	.07	.08	.08	.09	.09
240–264	.02	.02	.02	.03	.03	.04	.04	.04	.05	.05	.06	.06	.06	.07	.07	.08	.08
265–289	.01	.02	.02	.03	.03	.03	.04	.04	.04	.05	.05	.05	.06	.06	.07	.07	.07
290–324	0.01	0.02	0.02	0.03	0.03	0.03	0.03	0.04	0.04	0.04	0.05	0.05	0.05	0.06	0.06	0.06	0.07
325–374	.01	.02	.02	.02	.02	.03	.03	.03	.03	.04	.04	.04	.05	.05	.05	.05	.06
375–424	.01	.01	.02	.02	.02	.02	.02	.03	.03	.03	.03	.04	.04	.04	.05	.05	.05
425–474	.01	.01	.01	.02	.02	.02	.03	.03	.03	.03	.03	.03	.04	.04	.04	.04	.05
475–524	0.01	0.01	0.01	0.02	0.02	0.02	0.02	0.02	0.02	0.03	0.03	0.03	0.03	0.03	0.04	0.04	0.04
525–574	.01	.01	.01	.01	.02	.02	.02	.02	.02	.02	.03	.03	.03	.03	.03	.03	.04
575–625	.01	.01	.01	.01	.01	.02	.02	.02	.02	.02	.02	.02	.03	.03	.03	.03	.03

Equivalent Length of Duct (Ft)	Total Pressure Drop in Duct (In. of Water)																
	0.21	0.22	0.23	0.24	0.25	0.26	0.27	0.28	0.29	0.30	0.32	0.34	0.36	0.38	0.40	0.45	0.50
35–44	0.53	0.55	0.58	0.60	0.63	0.65	0.68	0.70	0.73	0.75	0.80	0.85	0.90	0.95	1.00	1.13	1.25
45–54	.42	.44	.46	.48	.50	.52	.54	.56	.58	.60	.64	.68	.72	.76	.80	.90	1.00
55–64	.35	.37	.39	.40	.42	.43	.45	.47	.48	.50	.53	.57	.60	.64	.67	.75	.83
65–74	.30	.32	.33	.34	.36	.37	.39	.40	.42	.43	.46	.49	.52	.54	.57	.64	.72
75–84	0.26	0.28	0.29	0.30	0.31	0.33	0.34	0.35	0.36	0.38	0.40	0.43	0.45	0.48	0.50	0.56	0.63
85–94	.23	.25	.26	.27	.28	.29	.30	.31	.32	.33	.36	.38	.40	.42	.45	.50	.56
95–104	.21	.22	.23	.24	.25	.26	.27	.28	.29	.30	.32	.36	.36	.38	.40	.45	.50
105–114	.19	.20	.21	.22	.23	.24	.25	.26	.27	.28	.29	.31	.33	.35	.37	.41	.46
115–129	0.18	0.18	0.19	0.20	0.21	0.22	0.23	0.23	0.24	0.25	0.27	0.28	0.30	0.32	0.33	0.38	0.47
130–149	.15	.16	.16	.17	.18	.19	.19	.20	.21	.21	.23	.24	.26	.27	.29	.32	.36
150–169	.13	.14	.14	.15	.16	.16	.17	.18	.18	.19	.20	.21	23	.24	.25	.28	.31
170–189	.12	.12	.13	.13	.14	.15	.15	.16	.16	.17	.18	.19	.20	.21	.22	.25	.28
190–214	0.11	0.11	0.12	0.12	0.13	0.13	0.14	0.14	0.15	0.15	0.16	0.17	0.18	0.19	0.20	0.23	0.25
215–239	.09	.10	.10	.11	.11	.12	.12	.13	.13	.13	.14	.15	.16	.17	.18	.20	.22
240–264	.08	.09	.09	.10	.10	.10	.11	.11	.12	.12	.13	.14	.15	.15	.16	.18	.20
265–289	.08	.08	.08	.08	.09	.09	.10	.10	.10	.11	.11	.12	.12	.13	.14	.15	.18
290–324	0.07	0.07	0.08	0.08	0.08	0.09	0.09	0.09	0.10	0.10	0.11	0.11	0.12	0.13	0.13	0.15	0.17
325–374	.06	.06	.07	.07	.07	.08	.08	.08	.09	.09	.09	.10	.10	.11	.11	.13	.14
375–424	.05	.06	.06	.06	.06	.07	.07	.07	.08	.08	.08	.09	.09	.09	.10	.11	.13
425–474	.05	.05	.05	.05	.06	.06	.06	.06	.07	.07	.07	.08	.08	.09	.09	.10	.11
475–524	0.04	0.04	0.05	0.05	0.05	0.05	0.05	0.06	0.06	0.06	0.06	0.07	0.07	0.08	0.08	0.09	0.10
525–574	.04	.04	.04	.04	.05	.05	.05	.05	.05	.05	.06	.06	.07	.07	.07	.08	.09
575–625	.04	.04	.04	.04	.04	.04	.05	.05	.05	.05	.05	.06	.06	.06	.07	.08	.08

FIGURE 9-33 / Pressure loss per 100 ft of duct length

500 750

Round Duct Size	0.02	0.03	0.04	0.05	0.06	0.07	0.08	0.09	0.10	0.11	0.12	0.13	0.14	0.15	0.16	0.18	0.20	0.25	0.30	0.35	0.40	0.45	0.50	Vel., fpm
	PRESSURE DROP (IN. OF WATER) PER 100 FEET OF DUCT																							
3.0				10	11	12	13	14	15	16	17	18	19	19	20	21	23	26	29	32	35	38	40	
3.5	10	13	15	17	19	21	22	24	25	27	28	29	31	32	33	35	37	42	47	51	55	59	63	
4.0	[illegible]	19	22	25	28	31	33	36	38	40	42	44	46	48	49	52	55	63	70	76	82	88	93	1000
4.5	21	26	31	35	39	42	46	49	52	54	57	60	63	65	68	72	76	87	97	106	115	122	129	
5.0	26	33	39	44	49	54	58	62	66	70	74	78	81	84	88	94	100	114	126	138	149	160	169	
5.5	34	48	50	57	64	70	75	81	86	90	96	100	104	108	112	120	126	144	160	175	190	203	215	
6.0	41	53	62	71	79	86	93	99	105	111	117	123	128	133	138	148	156	177	197	215	232	248	263	
6.5	54	68	80	90	100	109	118	125	131	140	146	153	160	165	171	182	194	220	242	264	285	302	324	
7.0	65	82	97	110	121	132	142	152	160	170	178	186	192	200	209	221	233	263	291	316	342	365	385	
7.5	80	101	117	132	147	159	170	180	192	200	213	222	230	240	248	264	280	315	352	380	406	435	460	1500
8.0	98	118	138	156	172	188	200	215	230	240	250	262	272	282	292	310	330	370	410	442	495	510	535	
8.5	114	142	166	187	207	225	242	258	273	287	301	315	328	341	353	376	398	450	497	540	581	624	452	
,9.0	133	166	194	218	241	263	282	301	322	336	352	367	382	397	412	440	465	526	581	633	680	723	765	
9.5	153	191	223	252	278	303	325	347	368	387	406	425	442	460	475	507	538	608	670	728	685	837	886	
10.0	177	220	257	292	321	350	376	402	427	450	471	491	511	530	549	586	618	700	773	840	903	962	1015	
10.5	201	252	293	331	364	396	426	455	482	507	531	555	578	600	621	662	702	791	875	950	1020	1085	1150	
11.0	228	284	332	375	413	450	482	514	544	573	600	628	654	680	703	748	793	893	988	1070	1155	1230	1305	
11.5	258	322	375	423	468	508	546	582	617	648	681	711	741	768	798	849	898	1015	1120	1218	1310	1393	1475	
12.0	291	361	422	475	525	572	612	652	692	729	765	798	830	862	892	950	1007	1135	1252	1360	1463	1560	1554	2000
12.5	321	400	467	527	581	632	678	724	767	807	846	883	919	954	988	1056	1118	1260	1390	1513	1628	1738	1836	
13.0	355	442	517	583	543	698	751	792	847	893	937	979	1020	1058	1096	1170	1232	1396	1540	1672	1800	1918	2020	
13.5	392	488	570	642	708	770	827	882	932	982	1030	1075	1122	1164	1205	1285	1360	1535	1692	1842	1976	2108	2235	
14.0	432	537	627	707	781	848	911	971	1026	1078	1130	1180	1230	1277	1322	1408	1497	1683	1858	2020	2172	2315	2450	
14.5	476	591	688	777	857	928	998	1063	1128	1185	1245	1300	1350	1400	1450	1545	1638	1643	2035	2205	2365	2520	2663	
15.0	521	648	766	852	938	1022	1092	1155	1285	1298	1359	1422	1476	1528	1587	1687	1788	2007	2210	2405	2585	2745	2910	2500
15.5	572	709	827	930	1025	1112	1190	1268	1343	1416	1485	1548	1610	1669	1726	1839	1943	2191	2407	2610	2800	2985		
16.0	627	777	903	1015	1120	1215	1302	1385	1465	1540	1613	1683	1750	1815	1877	1997	2108	2375	2612	2840	3045	3230		
16.5	681	842	978	1100	1213	1313	1408	1500	1585	1665	1745	1823	1893	1960	2023	2155	2277	2558	2815	3045	3270	3480		
17.0	738	911	1012	1192	1312	1495	1527	1625	1722	1808	1892	1972	2050	2127	2200	1338	2465	2778	3050	3310	3550	3790		
17.5	800	987	1144	1237	1415	1530	1543	1750	1850	1945	2035	2123	2208	2285	2365	2512	2660	2990	3290	3560	3820			
18.0	862	1065	1235	1385	1525	1650	1772	1885	1995	2100	2200	2295	2385	2470	2555	2720	2875	3230	3560	3865	4140			
18.5	922	1140	1325	1490	1640	1775	1900	2023	2140	2250	2355	2450	2550	2640	2735	2910	3035	3460	3790	4110	4400			
19.0	985	1223	1415	1590	1750	1890	2025	2160	2280	2400	2510	2618	2723	2815	2915	3105	3275	3680	4040	4385	4710			
19.5	1062	1308	1513	1705	1872	2025	2175	2310	2445	2570	2690	2860	2910	3015	3120	3320	3510	3920	4315	4700				
20.0	1125	1390	1610	1810	1990	2155	2310	2460	2600	2735	2860	2985	3100	3210	3320	3535	3740	4200	4620	5000				
20.5	1192	1475	1717	1925	2122	2300	2455	2650	2775	2915	3050	3190	3310	3430	3550	3780	4000	4500	4950	5365				
21.0	1262	1565	1825	2055	2260	2455	2630	2800	2960	3115	2160	3400	3540	3670	3800	4040	4280	4815	5290	5735				
21.5	1350	1673	1950	2192	2415	2615	2810	2990	3160	3325	3485	3635	3780	3820	4050	4320	4560	5130	5645	5100				
22.0	1435	1780	2075	2330	2565	2780	2985	3180	3360	3535	3705	3870	4025	4165	4310	4580	4850	5450	6000					
22.5	1527	1890	2210	2485	2735	2960	3180	3380	3580	3765	3940	4115	4280	4440	4590	4885	5160	5815	6400					
23.0	1635	2023	2355	2645	2920	3155	3385	3610	3820	4010	4200	4390	4550	4720	4900	4210	4410	6190	6830					
23.5	1740	2160	2510	2830	3115	3375	3620	3855	4075	4290	4495	4680	4860	5035	5210	5540	5855	6585	7260					
24.0	1855	2300	2675	3000	3310	3575	3840	4085	4320	4535	4750	4950	5150	5335	5520	5885	6210	6980	7675					
24.5	1950	2415	2810	3160	3480	3775	4040	4300	4550	4780	5000	4220	5430	5650	5835	6200	6540	7330	8070					
25.0	2040	2525	2940	3315	3640	3950	4240	4510	4760	5010	5245	5480	5700	5900	6085	6490	6850	7710	8485					
25.25	2095	2595	3020	3400	3740	4060	4355	5635	4900	5145	5390	5625	5840	6060	6275	6670	7040	7910						
25.50	2155	2665	3100	3490	3840	4160	4470	4750	5020	5280	5525	5760	6000	6210	6435	6850	7230	8110						
25.75	2210	2730	3180	3580	3940	4280	4590	4880	5165	5430	5685	5935	6160	6385	6610	7030	7420	8325						
26.00	2265	2810	3260	3670	4040	4390	4710	5010	5285	5560	5825	6080	6310	6550	6770	7210	7620	8550						
26.25	2315	2870	3335	3765	4145	4500	4825	5130	5420	5700	5970	6235	6490	6715	6950	7400	7820	8800						
26.50	2375	2950	3435	3860	4250	4615	4950	5265	5570	5860	6135	6400	6670	6910	7140	7610	8040	9050						
26.75	2440	3030	3525	3960	4360	4730	5080	5410	5720	6020	6300	6575	6840	7075	7310	7800	8260	9280						
27.00	2505	3100	3615	4070	4490	4855	5215	5550	5870	6180	6475	6780	7010	7280	7525	8020	8480	9530						
27.25	2570	3185	3710	4175	4600	4980	5345	5685	6015	6330	6625	6895	7180	7455	7705	8205	8675	9745						
27.50	2640	3270	3805	4280	4710	5105	5475	5820	6160	6480	6780	7060	6350	7630	7885	8390	8870	9960						
27.75	2710	3355	3900	4385	4825	5230	5610	5960	6305	6630	6935	7230	7525	7805	8065	8580	9070	10180						
28.00	2785	3445	4000	4490	4940	5355	5745	6100	6450	6780	7090	7400	7700	7980	8250	8770	9270	10400						
28.25	2845	3525	4090	4595	5055	5480	5880	6245	6605	6940	7260	7575	7880	8165	8445	8980	9495	106[illegible]						
28.50	2910	3605	4185	4700	5170	5605	6015	6390	6760	7105	7430	7750	8060	8350	8640	9190	9720	109[illegible]						
28.75	2975	3585	4280	4810	5285	5730	6150	6540	6915	7270	7605	7925	8240	8535	8835	9400	9945	11[illegible]50						
29.00	3045	3765	4375	4920	5405	5860	6290	6690	7075	7435	7780	8100	8420	8725	9030	9615	10170	11400						
29.25	3110	3850	4475	5030	5580	5995	6435	6845	7235	7605	7960	8295	8620	8935	9245	9840	10420							
29.50	3180	3935	4575	5140	5655	6130	6580	7000	7395	7775	8140	8490	8820	9145	9460	10070	10670							
29.75	3250	4025	4675	5255	5780	6270	6730	7155	7555	7945	8325	8685	9025	9355	9680	10300	10920							
30.00	3325	4115	4780	5370	5910	6410	6800	7310	7720	8120	.8510	8880	9230	9570	9900	10530	11170							
30.25	3400	4210	4890	5495	6050	6555	7035	7480	7900	8310	8705	9085	9440	9790	10120	10770	11425							
30.50	3480	4305	5000	5620	6190	6700	7190	7550	8080	8500	8900	9290	9655	10010	10340	11010	11680							
30.75	3560	4405	5115	5745	6330	6850	7345	7820	8265	8695	9100	9495	9870	10230	10565	11255	11940							
31.00	3640	4505	5230	5875	6470	7000	7500	7990	8450	8890	9300	9700	10085	10450	10790	11500	12200							
31.25	3720	4605	5350	6010	6615	7165	7675	8175	8645	9095	9520	9930	10320	10690	11040	11775	12470							
31.50	3805	4710	5470	6145	6760	7330	7855	8360	8840	9300	9740	10160	10560	10930	11290	12050	12740							
31.75	3890	4815	5595	6280	6910	7495	8035	8545	9035	9505	9960	10390	10800	11175	11545	12325	13070							
32.00	3975	4920	5720	6420	7060	7660	8215	8730	9230	9715	10180	10620	11040	11420	11800	12600	13280							
32.25	4060	5025	5845	6560	7215	7825	8390	8920	9425	9925	10395	10845	11270	11665	12050	12860	13565							
32.50	4145	5130	5970	6700	7370	7990	8570	9110	9625	10135	10610	11070	11[illegible]00	11910	12305	13120	13850							
32.75	4230	5240	6095	6845	7530	8160	8750	9305	9825	10345	10830	11295	11735	12155	12560	13384	14140							
33.00	4320	5350	6220	6890	7690	8330	8930	9500	10025	10560	11050	11520	11970	12400	12815	13650	14430							
33.25	4405	5455	6340	7125	7840	8495	9110	9585	10225	10760	11265	11745	12205	12650	13070	13925	14720							
33.50	4495	5560	6460	7260	7990	8660	9290	9870	10425	10965	11480	11970	12445	12900	13330	14200	15010							
33.75	4585	5665	6585	7395	8145	7830	9470	10060	10630	11170	11695	12200	12685	13150	13590	14475	15305							
34.00	4675	5770	6710	7535	8300	8000	9650	10250	10835	11375	11910	12430	12925	13400	13850	14750	15600							
34.25	4765	5885	6840	7680	8460	9175	9840	10460	11060	11610	12150	12680	13185	13675	14135	15050	15915							
34.50	4855	6000	6970	7825	8620	9350	10030	10670	11285	11845	12390	12930	13445	13950	14420	15350	16235							
34.75	4945	6115	7105	7910	8780	9525	10225	10885	11510	12080	12030	13185	13710	14225	14710	15650	16555							

750 1000 1500 2000 2500 Velocity in fpm

Reprinted with permission from ASHRAE, Systems Handbook, 1976

FIGURE 9-34 / Round duct capacities

Round Pipe Diam. In.	EQUIVALENT RECTANGULAR STACK AND DUCT SIZES																	Round Pipe Diam. In.
3.0		2½ x 3																
3.5		3½ x 3																
4.0		4½ x 3																
4.5	8 x 2¼	6 x 3																
5.0	10 x 2¼		8 x 3¼	5 x 4	4 x 5			3 x 8										
5.5	12 x 2¼		10 x 3¼	7 x 4	5 x 5			4 x 8										
6.0	14 x 2¼		10 x 3¼	8 x 4	6 x 5			4 x 8										
6.5			12 x 3¼	9 x 4	7 x 5	6 x 6		5 x 8										
7.0			14 x 3¼	11 x 4	8 x 5	7 x 6		5 x 8										
7.5				13 x 4	10 x 5	8 x 6	7 x 7	6 x 8										
8.0				15 x 4	11 x 5	9 x 6	8 x 7	7 x 8										
8.5				17 x 4	13 x 5	10 x 6	9 x 7	8 x 8										
9.0				20 x 4	15 x 5	12 x 6	10 x 7	8 x 8										
9.5				22 x 4	17 x 5	13 x 6	11 x 7	9 x 8	8 x 9									
10.0				25 x 4	19 x 5	15 x 6	12 x 7	11 x 8	9 x 9									
10.5					21 x 5	16 x 6	14 x 7	12 x 8	10 x 9	9 x 10								
11.0					23 x 5	18 x 6	15 x 7	13 x 8	11 x 9	10 x 10								
11.5					26 x 5	20 x 6	17 x 7	14 x 8	12 x 9	11 x 10								
12.0					29 x 5	22 x 6	18 x 7	16 x 8	14 x 9	12 x 10								
12.5					32 x 5	24 x 6	20 x 7	17 x 8	15 x 9	13 x 10	11 x 12							
13.0					35 x 5	27 x 6	22 x 7	18 x 8	16 x 9	14 x 10	12 x 12							
13.5						30 x 6	24 x 7	20 x 8	17 x 9	15 x 10	13 x 12							
14.0						33 x 6	26 x 7	22 x 8	19 x 9	17 x 10	14 x 12							
14.5						35 x 6	28 x 7	24 x 8	20 x 9	18 x 10	15 x 12							
15.0						38 x 6	31 x 7	26 x 8	22 x 9	19 x 10	16 x 12	14 x 14						15.0
15.5						41 x 6	33 x 7	28 x 8	24 x 9	21 x 10	17 x 12	14 x 14						15.5
16.0						45 x 6	36 x 7	30 x 8	25 x 9	22 x 10	18 x 12	15 x 14						16.0
16.5							38 x 7	32 x 8	27 x 9	24 x 10	19 x 12	16 x 14						16.5
17.0							41 x 7	34 x 8	29 x 9	25 x 10	21 x 12	17 x 14	15 x 16					17.0
17.5							44 x 7	37 x 8	31 x 9	27 x 10	22 x 12	18 x 14	16 x 16					17.5
18.0								39 x 8	33 x 9	29 x 10	23 x 12	20 x 14	17 x 16					18.0
18.5								42 x 8	36 x 9	31 x 10	25 x 12	21 x 14	18 x 16					18.5
19.0								45 x 8	38 x 9	33 x 10	26 x 12	22 x 14	19 x 16	17 x 18				19.0
19.5								47 x 8	41 x 9	35 x 10	28 x 12	23 x 14	20 x 16	18 x 18				19.5
20.0								51 x 8	43 x 9	37 x 10	29 x 12	25 x 14	21 x 16	19 x 18				20.0
20.5									46 x 9	39 x 10	31 x 12	26 x 14	22 x 16	20 x 18				20.5
21.0									48 x 9	42 x 10	33 x 12	27 x 14	23 x 16	21 x 18				21.0
21.5									51 x 9	44 x 10	34 x 12	29 x 14	25 x 16	22 x 18				21.5
22.0									54 x 9	47 x 10	36 x 12	30 x 14	26 x 16	23 x 18	20 x 20			22.0
22.5									56 x 9	49 x 10	38 x 12	31 x 14	27 x 16	24 x 18	21 x 20			22.5
23.0										52 x 10	40 x 12	33 x 14	28 x 16	25 x 18	22 x 20			23.0
23.5										54 x 10	42 x 12	35 x 14	30 x 16	26 x 18	23 x 20			23.5
24.0										57 x 10	44 x 12	36 x 14	31 x 16	27 x 18	24 x 20	22 x 22		24.0
24.5										60 x 10	46 x 12	38 x 14	32 x 16	28 x 18	25 x 20	23 x 22		24.5
25.00										63 x 10	49 x 12	40 x 14	34 x 16	29 x 18	26 x 20	24 x 22		25.00
25.25											50 x 12	41 x 14	34 x 16	30 x 18	27 x 20	24 x 22		25.25
25.50											51 x 12	41 x 14	35 x 16	31 x 18	28 x 20	25 x 22		25.50
25.75											52 x 12	42 x 14	36 x 16	31 x 18	28 x 20	25 x 22		25.75
26.00											54 x 12	44 x 14	37 x 16	32 x 18	29 x 20	26 x 22		26.00
26.25											55 x 12	45 x 14	38 x 16	33 x 18	29 x 20	26 x 22	24 x 24	26.25
26.50											56 x 12	45 x 14	38 x 16	33 x 18	30 x 20	27 x 22	25 x 24	26.50
26.75											57 x 12	46 x 14	39 x 16	34 x 18	30 x 20	27 x 22	25 x 24	26.75
27.00											59 x 12	47 x 14	40 x 16	35 x 18	31 x 20	28 x 22	26 x 24	27.00
27.25											60 x 12	48 x 14	41 x 16	36 x 18	31 x 20	28 x 22	26 x 24	27.25
27.50											61 x 12	49 x 14	42 x 16	36 x 18	32 x 20	29 x 22	27 x 24	27.50
27.75											63 x 12	51 x 14	43 x 16	37 x 18	33 x 20	29 x 22	27 x 24	27.75
28.00											64 x 12	52 x 14	43 x 16	38 x 18	33 x 20	30 x 22	28 x 24	28.00
28.25											66 x 12	53 x 14	44 x 16	38 x 18	34 x 20	31 x 22	28 x 24	28.25
28.50											67 x 12	54 x 14	45 x 16	39 x 18	35 x 20	31 x 22	29 x 24	28.50
28.75											68 x 12	55 x 14	46 x 16	40 x 18	35 x 20	32 x 22	29 x 24	28.75
29.00											70 x 12	57 x 14	47 x 16	41 x 18	36 x 20	32 x 22	30 x 24	29.00
29.25												58 x 14	48 x 16	42 x 18	37 x 20	33 x 22	30 x 24	29.25
29.50												59 x 14	49 x 16	42 x 18	37 x 20	34 x 22	31 x 24	29.50
29.75												60 x 14	50 x 16	43 x 18	38 x 20	34 x 22	31 x 24	29.75
30.00												61 x 14	51 x 16	44 x 18	39 x 20	35 x 22	32 x 24	30.00
30.25												62 x 14	52 x 16	45 x 18	39 x 20	35 x 22	32 x 24	30.25
30.50												64 x 14	53 x 16	46 x 18	40 x 20	36 x 22	33 x 24	30.50
30.75												65 x 14	54 x 16	47 x 18	41 x 20	37 x 22	33 x 24	30.75
31.00												66 x 14	55 x 16	47 x 18	41 x 20	37 x 22	34 x 24	31.00
31.25												67 x 14	56 x 16	48 x 18	42 x 20	38 x 22	35 x 24	31.25
31.50												68 x 14	57 x 16	48 x 18	43 x 20	38 x 22	35 x 24	31.50
31.75													58 x 16	50 x 18	44 x 20	39 x 22	36 x 24	31.75
32.00													59 x 16	51 x 18	44 x 20	40 x 22	36 x 24	32.00
32.25													60 x 16	52 x 18	45 x 20	40 x 22	37 x 24	32.25
32.50													62 x 16	52 x 14	46 x 20	41 x 22	37 x 24	32.50
32.75													63 x 16	53 x 18	47 x 20	42 x 22	38 x 24	32.75
33.00													64 x 16	54 x 18	48 x 20	43 x 22	39 x 24	33.00
33.25													65 x 16	55 x 18	48 x 20	43 x 22	39 x 24	33.25
33.50													66 x 16	56 x 18	49 x 20	44 x 22	40 x 24	33.50
33.75													67 x 16	57 x 18	50 x 20	45 x 22	40 x 24	33.75
34.00													69 x 16	58 x 18	51 x 20	45 x 22	41 x 24	34.00
34.25														59 x 18	52 x 20	46 x 22	42 x 24	34.25
34.50														60 x 18	53 x 20	47 x 22	42 x 24	34.50
34.75														61 x 18	53 x 20	48 x 22	43 x 24	34.75

Sizes shown in the above two columns are recommended minimum sizes of standard risers. More precise round and rectangular equivalents areas follows:

Round Pipe Diam. In.		
4.5	8 x 2¼	
4.7	9 x 2¼	
4.8		6 x 3¼
4.9	10 x 2¼	
5.0	11 x 2¼	
5.1		7 x 3¼
5.2	12 x 2¼	
5.4		8 x 3¼
5.6	14 x 2¼	
5.7		9 x 3¼
6.0		10 x 3¼
6.3		11 x 3¼
6.5		12 x 3¼
6.7		13 x 3¼
6.9		14 x 3¼

Reprinted with permission from ASHRAE, Systems Handbook, 1976

FIGURE 9-35 / Rectangular duct equivalents

Questions

9-1. What are the advantages of a forced air system as compared to hot water?

9-2. What types of materials are most commonly used for forced air ducts?

9-3. What can be done to be certain that the system will be as quiet as possible?

9-4. What is the purpose of putting dampers and vanes in the ductwork?

9-5. When is insulation around the ductwork recommended?

9-6. When heating is the predominant function of the forced air system, what are the recommended locations for supply and return?

9-7. What types of furnaces are available for use in forced air systems, and where might each type be located?

9-8. How may humidity be introduced into the forced air system?

9-9. What term is commonly used to refer to the cooling capacity of a cooling unit, and how does it relate to Btuh?

9-10. What does the term *EER* mean, and why is it important to check the EER of the cooling unit?

9-11. What type of equipment may be used when both heating and air conditioning are required?

9-12. What factors determine where the supplies and returns are located?

Chapter 10

Hot Water Heating Systems and Design

10-1   Types of Systems

For heat, the water is heated in a boiler to the preset temperature (180° to 210°F). Then a circulating pump is automatically cut on, and the hot water is circulated through the system of pipes, passing through any of a variety of convector types (Sec. 10-4). As it circulates, it gives off the heat, primarily through the convectors; then the pipes return the water to the boiler to be reheated and circulated again. Most of the convectors used can be regulated slightly by opening or closing adjustable dampers. A compression tank is included in the system to adjust for the varying pressure in the system since water expands as it is heated. Circulating hot water systems are also referred to as *hydronic* heating systems, and the four different hot water piping systems commonly used are series loop, one-pipe and two-pipe systems, and radiant panels.

Series Loop Systems

Most commonly used for residences and small buildings, the convectors in the series loop system are fed by a single pipe which goes through the convector and makes a loop around the building, or one portion of the building (Figs. 10-1 and

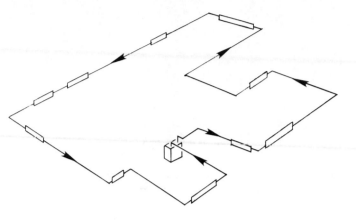

FIGURE 10-1   /   *Series loop isometric*

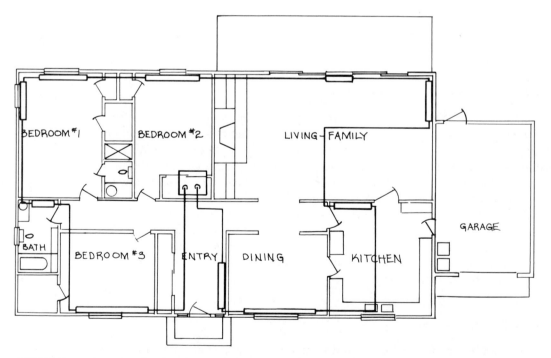

FIGURE 10-2   /   *Series loop plan*

10-2). The pipe acts as supply and return with the water getting cooler as it progresses through the system. To the designer this means that larger convectors are required to obtain the same amount of heat at the end of the loop as compared to convectors at the beginning because the water is cooler. Also, the longer the run of piping and the more convectors it serves, the cooler the water will become. For more even heat, the building may be broken into zones (Fig. 10-3), each with its own series loop system activated by its individual thermostat. It is economical to install, but any control of individual convectors is minimal. Only heating is supplied with this system.

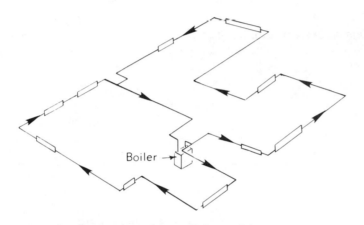

FIGURE 10-3   /   Series loop (zoned) isometric

One-Pipe Systems

As shown in Figs. 10-4 and 10-5, the one-pipe system has a single pipe going around the building, or a zone of the building. A portion of the hot water is diverted through a special tee at each convector so that a portion of the hot water is diverted through the convector where it gives off heat to the room, thereby cooling the water. Then the water is returned to the supply pipe. Upon entering the supply pipe, it will slightly reduce the temperature of the water in that pipe. The primary advantage of this system over the series loop is that each individual convector may be controlled by a valve to turn it on, off, or in between. The convectors may be placed above the pipe (upfeed) or below it (downfeed). The upfeed is more effective since the water tends to be diverted more easily in that direction. This system is more expensive than the series loop since it requires additional piping, fittings, and valves. It may also be zoned for larger buildings where the temperature drop over a long pipe run would be excessive.

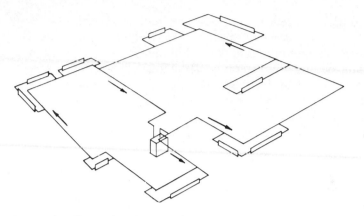

FIGURE 10-4 / One-pipe (zoned) isometric

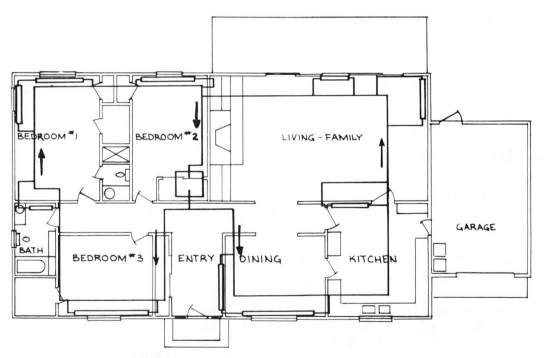

FIGURE 10-5 / One-pipe plan

Two-Pipe Systems

For large installations the supply of hot water needs to be kept separate from that water which has been cooled by passing through a convector. To accomplish this, one pipe is used to supply the hot water, which then empties into another pipe used for return. This type of system provides the water at as high a temperature as possible. The return may be classified as *reverse return* (Fig. 10-6) or *direct return* (Fig. 10-7). The reverse return results in a more even flow of water because the supply and return are of equal length, resulting in equal friction losses. The direct

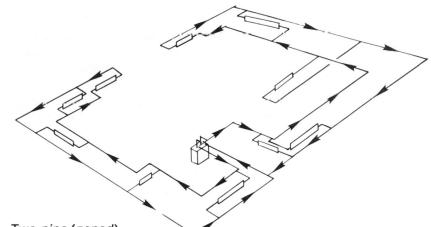

FIGURE 10-6 / Two-pipe (zoned) reverse return

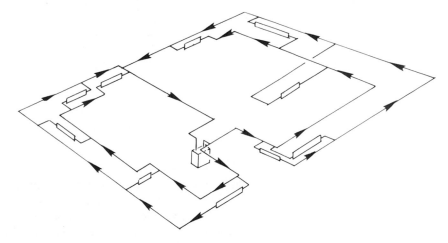

FIGURE 10-7 / Two-pipe (zoned) direct return

return requires slightly less piping. Individual convector control is available by the installation of valves. This is the best system available and also the most expensive. It would be unnecessary to put this system in a residence.

Radiant Panels

The hot water may be circulated through pipes located, usually, in the floor or ceiling of a building. The pipes are laid in a coil or grid arrangement (Fig. 10-8); for a floor system they are embedded in concrete, whereas for a ceiling they are attached to the framing and plastered or drywalled over. They may also be used on walls, but this is not common. The basic disadvantage with this type of system is that while it provides uniform heat over an entire room, heat is not uniformly lost; most of it is lost at exterior walls, usually at the window. This situation tends to cause drafts and a feeling of being cold near the windows. The floor panels have a tendency to make the occupant's feet hot and uncomfortable, while the heat coming down from the ceiling tends to stay high (since heat rises), and a person's legs under a table will probably feel cool. (This is also true of electric ceiling and wall radiant panels.)

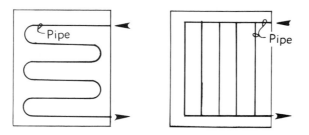

FIGURE 10-8   /   Radiant panels

10-2   Piping and Fittings

The piping used for hot water heating is usually copper, but steel pipe is sometimes used. Copper is preferred because it is lightweight and easy to work with—characteristics which are described in Sec. 2-4. The types of copper piping used for hot water heating systems are Type L pipe and tubing and Type M pipe.

The most commonly used fittings for the system are the same as those used in plumbing systems (Sec. 2-5, Figs. 2-3 through 2-5).

10-3 Boiler and System Controls

Boiler

The boiler furnace (Fig. 10-9) heats the water for circulation through the system. It may be rectangular or square (occasionally even round) and made of steel or cast iron. A boiler is rated by the amount of heat it can produce in an hour. The maximum amount of heat the system can put out is limited first by the size of the boiler selected. Boiler efficiency increases when the boiler runs for long periods of time, so the unit selected should not be oversized or it will run intermittently and thus be less efficient. Hot water boilers may use oil, gas, propane gas, coal, or electricity as fuel. In residences oil and gas boilers are most commonly used.

For a hot water heating system, the temperature that the water is heated to in the boiler is of prime importance since it has a direct relationship to the amount of heat which the radiation or convector units will give off. Typically, the thermostat should be set at about 180 °F but temperatures as high as 220 °F are possible. The thermostat which controls the water temperature (Fig. 10-10) is located somewhere on the boiler (usually in plain sight, sometimes behind a small sheet-metal cover plate) and should be checked, after installation, by the designer.

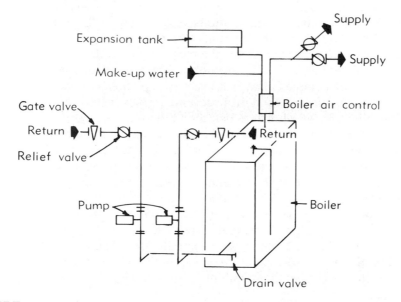

FIGURE 10-9 / Typical boiler installation

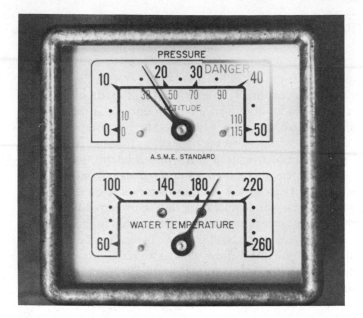

FIGURE 10-10   /   Boiler thermostat control

Thermostat

The thermostat which controls the air temperature in the space (Fig. 10-11) is placed in the building. With hot water heat, there will be one thermostat for each zone. The temperature desired is set on the thermostat, and when the temperature in the room falls below the desired temperature, the thermostat turns on the boiler and the circulating pump. When the desired temperature is reached, the thermostat will turn the boiler and the pump off. The thermostat has a temperature differential within which it will call for heat and then cut it off. Typically, this temperature differential is about 1 °F, which means that the thermostat will call for heat at 69 °F and shut it off at 70 °F. This differential may be adjusted on a small calibration setting inside the thermostat housing (Fig. 10-12). The less the differential, the more comfortable the space will feel. But it also means that the boiler will be turned on and off more frequently (to maintain a close tolerance of temperature) which will lower the efficiency of the boiler operation.

Thermostats used for hot water systems are usually either the single-setting thermostat (Fig. 10-11) or the day–night thermostat (Fig. 10-13).

The single-setting thermostat is the one most commonly used. The desired temperature is set and the thermostat will operate the cycles of the heating system. The temperature may be changed at any time by simply adjusting the temperature setting on the thermostat.

FIGURE 10-11   /   Thermostat

FIGURE 10-12   /   Thermostat calibration

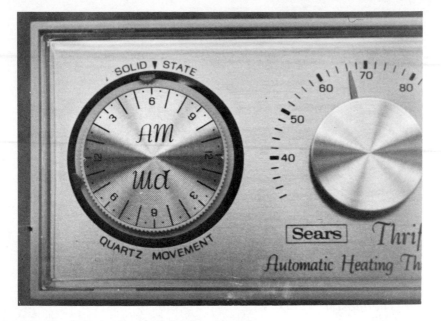

FIGURE 10-13   /   Day–night thermostat

A day–night thermostat permits the setting of one temperature for the daytime and another (usually lower) for nighttime. With this thermostat a clock is set for a given time (say, 8 A.M.) and at that time the temperature will go to the daytime setting (perhaps 72 °F); then at the other time set (say, 5 P.M.) the temperature will go to the nighttime setting (perhaps 60 °F). The times and temperatures are set on the thermostat and may be changed as desired.

The day–night thermostat is used in residences, stores, offices, apartments, institutions, and commercial and industrial projects. In a residence, the temperature differential may be 3 °F or 4 °F, set to begin to cool just before bedtime and to heat up as the occupants arise. In apartments where the heat is furnished and paid for by the apartment owner and not the renter, this type of thermostat is commonly used to control heat costs for the owner. In this case, the thermostat used would have two parts, one located in the apartments to sense the temperature and the second located in a place the renters cannot enter which controls the temperature desired and the times of operation. Since many stores and offices are open only limited hours, perhaps 8 A.M. to 5 P.M., it would be foolish to maintain the temperature needed during hours of operation through the hours in which the space is not in use. Rather than depend on someone to turn down the temperature before he leaves (which he may forget to do) and to turn up the temperature in the morning (no one will begin work until it warms up), the day–night thermostat takes care of these functions automatically. In locations where the possibility of people tampering with the thermostats is a problem, the unit may have a cover which locks it or may be designed so that the temperature settings can be changed only with a special keying device.

Thermostats are usually placed about 5 ft up on a wall. The location should be carefully checked to be certain that the thermostat will provide a true representation of the temperature in the spaces it serves. Guidelines used in thermostat location include the following:

1. Always mount it on an inside wall (on an outside wall, the cold air outside will affect the readings).

2. Keep it away from the cold air drafts (such as near a door or window), away from any possible warm air drafts (near a radiation unit, fireplace, or stove), and away from any direct sunlight.

Expansion Tank

The expansion tank (also called a *compression tank*) allows for the expansion of the water in the system as it is heated. It is located above the boiler.

Automatic Filler Valve

When the pressure in the system drops below 12 psi, this valve opens, allowing more water into the system; then the check valve automatically closes as the pressure increases. This maintains a minimum water level in the system.

Circulating Pump

The hot water is circulated from the boiler through the pipes and back to the boiler by a pump. The pump provides fast distribution of hot water through the system, thus delivering heat as quickly as possible. The circulating pump size is based on the delivery of water required, in gpm, and the amount of friction head allowed. Circulating pumps are not used on gravity systems.

Flow Control Valve

The flow control valve closes to stop the flow of hot water when the pump stops, so that the hot water will not flow through the system by gravity. Any gravity flow of the water would cause the temperature in the room to continue to rise.

Boiler Relief Valve

When the pressure in the system exceeds 30 psi, a spring-loaded valve opens, allowing some of the water to bleed out of the system and allowing the pressure to drop. The valve should be located where the discharge will not cause any damage.

Boiler Rating

Boiler manufacturers list both gross and net Btuh ratings of the boiler. The gross Btuh is the heat input to the boiler by the fuel, and the net Btuh is the usable heat output which is available for use in the hot water system.

10-4   Hot Water Heating Devices

Some type of heating device must be used to distribute the heat efficiently from the hot water to the room being heated. These devices are classified as *radiant* and *convector,* according to the way in which they transfer the heat.

Radiant heating units have the heat transfer surface exposed so that the heat is transferred by radiation to the surrounding objects and by natural convection to the surrounding air. A typical radiant device is shown in Fig. 10-14.

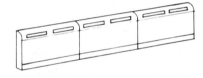

CAST   IRON   BASEBOARD

FIGURE 10-14   /   Radiant heating device

Convector heating units have the heat transfer surface enclosed in a cabinet or other enclosure (Fig. 10-15). The transfer of heat occurs primarily through convection as air flows through the enclosure, and past the heat transfer surface, by gravity. For institutional and commercial projects, the convectors used may have several rows of large finned-tube radiators in the cabinet (Fig. 10-16).

Unit heaters use a fan to distribute the air through the space. The unit usually consists of a heating coil and a fan enclosed in a cabinet (Fig. 10-17). The heat may be supplied by hot water or even steam when available. Often this type of unit is suspended from the ceiling in areas such as a warehouse, a storage area, or any large room situation, especially one with high ceilings. Such a unit is sized according to heat output, and the layout of these units to provide adequate coverage of the space with warm air must be carefully checked. This type of unit is also effective when the room is deep with a relatively small outside wall area for a convector or radiation unit. A typical situation would be that of a motel room (Fig. 10-18) where the unit heater is placed under the glass area in the exterior wall and the air is fan-blown through the room. Unit heaters may be recessed, surface mounted, or suspended from the ceiling or wall, or recessed or surface mounted on the floor (Fig. 10-19).

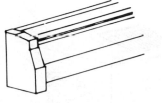
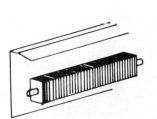

FIN TYPE BASEBOARD

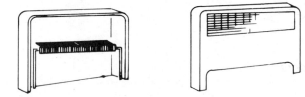

FIN TYPE RADIATOR

FIGURE 10-15 / Convector heating devices

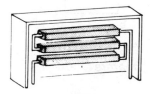

FIGURE 10-16 / High output convector

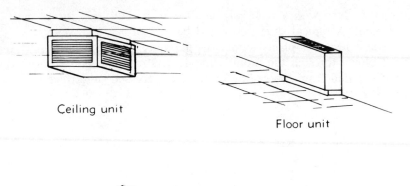

Ceiling unit

Floor unit

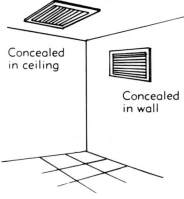

Concealed
in ceiling

Concealed
in wall

FIGURE 10-17 / Unit heaters

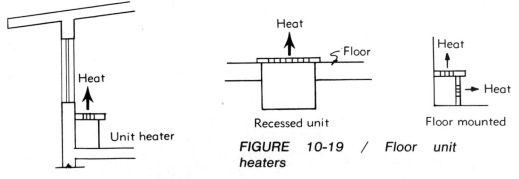

Heat

Unit heater

FIGURE 10-18 / Unit heater

Heat

Floor

Recessed unit

Heat

Heat

Floor mounted

FIGURE 10-19 / Floor unit
heaters

10-5 Heating Device Ratings

All radiant, convector, and unit heaters are rated in terms of the amount of heat they will give off in an hour; the capacity ratings are given in Btuh for small devices and in MBH (thousands of Btuh) for larger devices. The heating capacities vary, depending on the type of pipe, the size of the finned tube, the number of fins per foot of radiation, and the temperature of the water. Each manufacturer's specifications (or technical data report) should be checked for heating capacity of a particular unit.

Baseboard radiation units may be cast-iron radiation units or finned-tube convectors. A typical manufacturer's specification rating is shown in Fig. 10-20. The various types of elements available from this manufacturer are shown in the left column and the heat ratings, for the various water temperatures, on the right. Notice that the heating capacity of the unit increases as the water temperature increases. Comparing the copper–aluminum elements, the capacity for the 2¾-in. x 5-in. x 0.020 x 40/ft 1¼-in. tube element (the second entry on left) at 180°F is 850 Btuh, while at 200°F the capacity is 1030 Btuh. The capacity is increased by 180 Btuh simply by increasing the temperature of water that will flow through the element. This 180-Btuh increase represents a 21% gain in the heating capacity at no increase in the cost of boiler or heating device, only an increase in the temperature of the water. The effects of the fins and tube on the heating capacity of an element can be seen by comparing the first and third listings under the copper–aluminum elements. The smaller top element (2¾-in. x 3¾-in. x 0.011 x 50/ft 1-in. tube) has a capacity of 840 Btuh at 180°F, while the third listing (2¾-in. x 5-in. x 0.020 x 50/ft 1¼-in. tube) has a capacity of 910 Btuh. This is an increase of 70 Btuh or about 8.33%. The copper–aluminum elements may be compared with the steel elements by checking the second copper–aluminum listing against the second steel element listing. The second copper–aluminum listing (2¾-in. x 5-in. x 0.020 x 40/ft 1¼-in. tube) has a capacity of 850 Btuh at 180°F, and the second steel element listing has a capacity of 710 Btuh at 180°F. The copper–aluminum element capacity is 140 Btuh or 19.7% higher than that of the steel element.

As initial selections of heating devices are made, the various ratings must be checked. It may be necessary to use different sizes of heating devices in different rooms (usually depending on the amount of wall space available for mounting the devices), but once a basic decision is made as to type of material (steel or copper–aluminum), this will usually be used throughout.

To make an economical selection, the designer should also consider the relative costs of the devices per foot and then compare these costs to the heating capacities of the units. Prices vary considerably, but unless the steel elements, installed, cost about 20% less than the copper–aluminum elements, they will not be as economical to install. It is part of the designer's responsibility to provide the best system at the lowest cost.

Copper-Aluminum Elements	Hot Water Output* 1 gal. flow rate (for 5 gal. flow rate use factor 1.067)				
	220°	210°	200°	190°	180°
2¾" x 3¾" x .011 x 50/ft. 1" tube	1240	1120	1020	930	840
2¾" x 5" x .020 x 40/ft. 1¼" tube	1250	1120	1030	940	850
2¾" x 5" x .020 x 50/ft. 1¼" tube	1340	1200	1100	1000	910
Steel Elements					
2¾" x 5 x 24 ga. x 40/ft. 1" tube (IPS)	1020	920	840	770	690
2¾" x 5 x 24 ga. x 40/ft. 1¼" tube (IPS)	1040	940	860	780	710

*Based on 65° entering air.

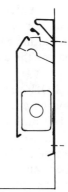

FIGURE 10-20   /   Finned tube ratings

10-6   Hot Water Heating System Design

The first thing which must be done is to decide whether the hot water heating system will be a series loop, one-pipe, two-pipe, or radiant panel system. The following step-by-step approach will work for any of the systems (except radiant panels) discussed in Sec. 10-1.

Step-by-Step Approach

1. Determine the heat loss of each room and list them.

2. Next, determine whether a series loop, a one-pipe, or a two-pipe system will be used.

3. Using a floor plan, locate the approximate position of the heating devices in each room.

4. Locate the boiler on the plan.

5. Determine how many zones will be used in the design.

6. Determine the actual length of the longest zone (circuit).

7. Assume an average pipe size for the system. *This pipe size is a preliminary selection which will be rechecked later.*

8. Determine the velocity of the water in the system from Fig. 10-21 for iron pipe, from Fig. 10-22 for copper tubing, and from Fig. 10-23 for steel pipe, based on the heat to be conveyed per hour in the zone or on gpm of hot water. Also, note the friction.

9. List the fittings which the hot water will pass through in the complete circuit [beginning with the heating unit and going through the longest circuit (zone) and back to the heating unit].

10. Determine the equivalent elbows for each fitting from Fig. 10-24. Each fitting is converted into the equivalent length of pipe by first converting the fitting into an equivalent number of 90° elbows and then converting the elbows into equivalent length.

11. Determine the total equivalent length of the fittings from Fig. 10-25. This table is based on the pipe size and the velocity in feet per second. The pipe was tentatively selected in step 7 and the velocity noted in step 8.

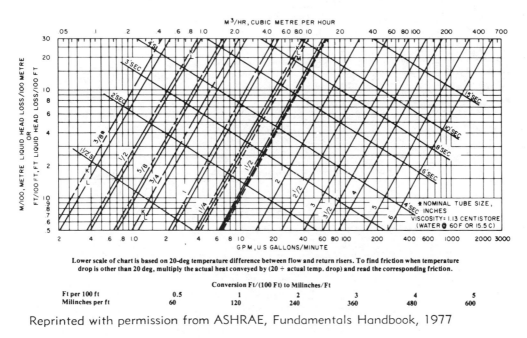

Reprinted with permission from ASHRAE, Fundamentals Handbook, 1977

FIGURE 10-21   /   Friction loss for iron pipe

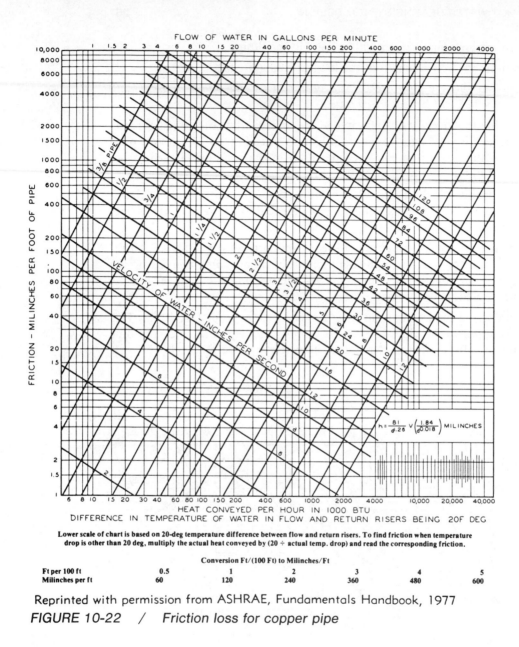

FLOW OF WATER IN GALLONS PER MINUTE

FRICTION – MILINCHES PER FOOT OF PIPE

VELOCITY OF WATER – INCHES PER SECOND

$$h = \frac{81}{d^{1.25}} V\left(\frac{1.84}{d^{0.018}}\right) \text{ MILINCHES}$$

HEAT CONVEYED PER HOUR IN 1000 BTU

DIFFERENCE IN TEMPERATURE OF WATER IN FLOW AND RETURN RISERS BEING 20F DEG

Lower scale of chart is based on 20-deg temperature difference between flow and return risers. To find friction when temperature drop is other than 20 deg, multiply the actual heat conveyed by (20 ÷ actual temp. drop) and read the corresponding friction.

Conversion Ft/(100 Ft) to Milinches/Ft

Ft per 100 ft	0.5	1	2	3	4	5
Milinches per ft	60	120	240	360	480	600

Reprinted with permission from ASHRAE, Fundamentals Handbook, 1977

FIGURE 10-22   /   Friction loss for copper pipe

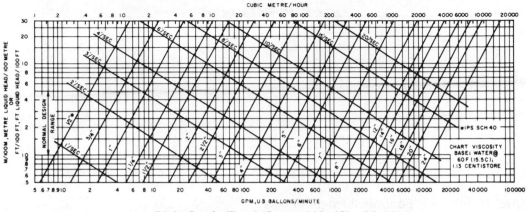

Friction Loss for Water in Commercial Steel Pipe (Schedule 40)

Reprinted with permission from ASHRAE, Fundamentals Handbook, 1977

FIGURE 10-23   /   Friction loss for steel pipe

Iron and Copper Elbow Equivalents

Fitting	Iron Pipe	Copper Tubing
Elbow, 90-deg	1.0	1.0
Elbow, 45-deg	0.7	0.7
Elbow, 90-deg long turn. . .	0.5	0.5
Elbow, welded, 90-deg. . . .	0.5	0.5
Reduced coupling	0.4	0:4
Open return bend.	1.0	1.0
Angle radiator valve.	2.0	3.0
Radiator or convector	3.0	4.0
Boiler or heater	3.0	4.0
Open gate valve	0.5	0.7
Open globe valve	12.0	17.0

Reprinted with permission from ASHRAE, Fundamentals Handbook, 1977

FIGURE 10-24   /   Elbow equivalents

Equivalent Length of Pipe for 90-Deg Elbows

Vel. Fps	Pipe Size														
	½	¾	1	1¼	1½	2	2½	3	3½	4	5	6	8	10	12
1	1.2	1.7	2.2	3.0	3.5	4.5	5.4	6.7	7.7	8.6	10.5	12.2	15.4	18.7	22.2
2	1.4	1.9	2.5	3.3	3.9	5.1	6.0	7.5	8.6	9.5	11.7	13.7	17.3	20.8	24.8
3	1.5	2.0	2.7	3.6	4.2	5.4	6.4	8.0	9.2	10.2	12.5	14.6	18.4	22.3	26.5
4	1.5	2.1	2.8	3.7	4.4	5.6	6.7	8.3	9.6	10.6	13.1	15.2	19.2	23.2	27.6
5	1.6	2.2	2.9	3.9	4.5	5.9	7.0	8.7	10.0	11.1	13.6	15.8	19.8	24.2	28.8
6	1.7	2.3	3.0	4.0	4.7	6.0	7.2	8.9	10.3	11.4	14.0	16.3	20.5	24.9	29.6
7	1.7	2.3	3.0	4.1	4.8	6.2	7.4	9.1	10.5	11.7	14.3	16.7	21.0	25.5	30.3
8	1.7	2.4	3.1	4.2	4.9	6.3	7.5	9.3	10.8	11.9	14.6	17.1	21.5	26.1	31.0
9	1.8	2.4	3.2	4.3	5.0	6.4	7.7	9.5	11.0	12.2	14.9	17.4	21.9	26.6	31.6
10	1.8	2.5	3.2	4.3	5.1	6.5	7.8	9.7	11.2	12.4	15.2	17.7	22.2	27.0	32.0

Reprinted with permission from ASHRAE, Fundamentals Handbook, 1977

FIGURE 10-25 / Equivalent length of pipe

12. Add the length of the longest circuit (zone), step 6, to the total equivalent length of fittings for the circuit, step 11.

13. Determine the pressure head, using the friction head selected, step 8, and the total equivalent length of pipe, step 12, and Fig. 10-23.

14. Select the rest of the pipe sizes required for the system, using the friction head selected and the heat it must supply, from Fig. 10-21.

15. Select the pump size required, using the gpm necessary with the required pressure head, from Fig. 10-26.

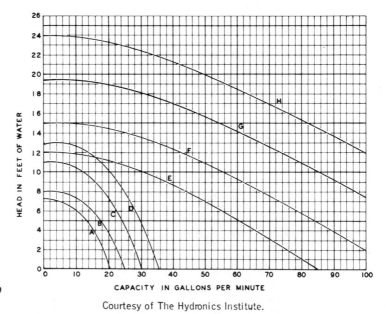

FIGURE 10-26 / Pump performance

Courtesy of The Hydronics Institute.

16. Find the temperature drop for the total circuit based on the total friction head in millinches (friction times total equivalent length) times the design temperature drop for the system divided by the pressure head (pressure head in millinches equals pressure head in feet times 12,000).

$$\frac{\text{Friction head (millinches)} \times \text{Total equivalent length (ft)} \times \text{Design temperature}}{\text{Pressure head (ft)} \times 12,000}$$

17. The next phase of the design is to determine how many lineal feet of exterior wall are available for radiation units of some type. In a room with little or no exterior wall available, it may be necessary to use interior wall space.

18. Calculate and record the temperature drop for each radiation unit served through the circuit. The formula used to calculate the temperature drop for each radiation unit(s) is:

$$\frac{\text{Radiation unit(s) heating capacity}}{\text{Circuit (zone) capacity}} \times \text{Temperature drop in total system}$$

19. Calculate and record the temperature in the circuit main, in a series loop or after the water returns from the radiation unit(s) served. *This is the entering temperature for each of the radiation units.*

    Note: If designing a series loop system, go directly to step 21a.

20. *Note:* This step is used only in the one-pipe system. For all other systems go to step 21.

    Calculate and record the temperature drop of the water which is diverted through the radiation unit(s) and through the fitting used. The amount of water diverted depends on the size of the fitting used and location of the main above or below the radiation unit; Fig. 10-27 is used for this percentage of diversion.

$$\text{Radiation unit(s) temp. drop} = \frac{\text{Temp. drop in circuit (zone)}}{\text{Percent diversion}} \times 100$$

    Note: The 100 is a constant and changes the percentage to a decimal equivalent.

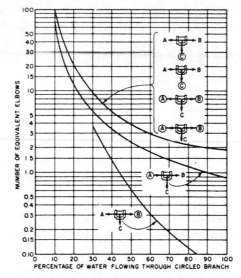

Notes: 1. The chart is based on straight tees, that is, branches A, B, and C are the same size.

2. Head loss in desired circuit is obtained by selecting proper curve according to illustrations, determining the flow at the circled branch, and multiplying the head loss for the same size elbow at the flow rate in the circled branch by the equivalent elbows indicated.

3. When the size of an outlet is reduced the equivalent elbows shown in the chart do not apply. The maximum loss for any circuit for any flow will not exceed 2 elbow equivalents at the maximum flow (gpm) occurring in any branch of the tee.

4. The top curve of the chart is the average of 4 curves, one for each of the tee circuits illustrated.

**Elbow Equivalents of Tees at
Various Flow Conditions**[1,4]

Reprinted with permission from ASHRAE,
Fundamentals Handbook, 1977

FIGURE 10-27   /   Elbow equivalents of tees

21. Calculate the average temperature.

  a. *Series loop only.* Calculate and record the average temperature in the radiation unit(s) by subtracting one-half of the temperature drop from the entering temperature of the circuit main.

  b. *All except series loop.* Calculate and record the average temperature in the radiation unit(s) by subtracting one-half of the temperature drop which occurs in the radiation units (from step 16) from the entering temperature of the circuit main.

22. Next, the heat emission rate of radiation required is determined by dividing the heat loss for each room by the available length of exterior wall.

23. Select the type of radiation unit(s) to be used based on the maximum emission rate required.

24. Determine the length or amount of radiation unit(s) required to evenly heat each room by dividing the heat loss of the room by the heat emission rate of the radiation unit(s) selected. Tabulate the lengths on the form.

25. Size the compression tank by determining the entire volume of water in the system and then finding the amount of expansion based on a temperature rise of 150 °F (from 50 °F entering to 200 °F heated) times $(0.0041t - 0.0466)$ the net coefficient of expansion of the water. The compression tank must be sized to accommodate this water expansion. The volume of water in the system is determined from the table in Fig. 10-28.

Volume of Water
in Standard Pipe and Tube

Nominal Pipe Size In.	Standard Steel Pipe			Type L Copper Tube	
	Schedule No.	Inside Dia In.	Gallons per Lin Ft	Inside Dia In.	Gallons per Lin Ft
⅜	—	—	—	0.430	0.0075
½	40	0.622	0.0157	0.545	0.0121
⅝	—	—	—	0.666	0.0181
¾	40	0.824	0.0277	0.785	0.0251
1	40	1.049	0.0449	1.025	0.0429
1¼	40	1.380	0.0779	1.265	0.0653
1½	40	1.610	0.106	1.505	0.0924
2	40	2.067	0.174	1.985	0.161
2½	40	2.469	0.249	2.465	0.248
3	40	3.068	0.384	2.945	0.354
3½	40	3.548	0.514	3.425	0.479
4	40	4.026	0.661	3.905	0.622
5	40	5.047	1.04	4.875	0.970
6	40	6.065	1.50	5.845	1.39
8	30	8.071	2.66	7.725	2.43
10	30	10.136	4.19	9.625	3.78
12	30	12.090	5.96	11.565	5.46

Reprinted with permission from ASHRAE, Fundamentals Handbook, 1977

FIGURE 10-28   /   Size expansion tank

10-7   Boilers

In residences the boiler (furnace) which provides the heat (either hot water or forced air) is commonly located in the basement or crawl space or in a first-floor utility room, but it may also be in the attic. Boilers are most commonly fired by natural gas or oil, and occasionally by electricity, coal, or bottled gas.

The boiler selected must be large enough to supply all of the heat loss in the spaces as calculated. The boiler must also have enough extra capacity to compensate for heat loss which will occur in the pipes which circulate the hot water through the system (called pipe loss or pipe tax). In addition, an extra reserve capacity is required so that the boiler can provide heat quickly to warm up a "cooled off" space. This "pickup" allowance also provides some extra heating capacity when it is necessary to increase the temperature of a space several degrees, not merely to maintain a temperature. For example, a store which closes at 5 P.M. may turn its thermostat back to 60 °F before closing. Then in the morning as the thermostat is raised to 68 ° or 70 °F, it is necessary to have some extra capacity in the boiler to provide this extra heat as quickly as possible. Many buildings have automatic, timed thermostats which are used to regulate the temperatures throughout the day.

Typically, the designer allows about 33⅓% for the heat loss in the pipes and an additional 15% to 20% as a pickup allowance, in addition to the calculated heat loss of the building. Spaces which are heated intermittently, such as a church or an auditorium, will have to have a much larger pickup allowance, perhaps as much as 50%. This is because the temperature will often be allowed to drop quite low (perhaps 50 °F) when the space is not in use, and then when the heat is raised to 70 °F, it must heat up quickly.

While most designers simply allow a certain percentage for piping loss, it can be calculated—but only after the piping layout is finalized and the installation decided upon and specified. From the piping layout it would be necessary to determine the length of pipe and the various temperatures of the air through which the pipe travels. Where the pipe travels through an unheated basement or attic, the heat loss would be much greater than the heat loss of the same pipe traveling through a heated space.

Once the piping loss and the pickup allowance have been taken into account, the boiler size may be selected. The boiler selected should be as close to the total Btuh as possible to provide the most efficient operation. Keep in mind that the outside design temperature used will not actually occur very often, that the boiler will be operating at less than full capacity during most of the time, and that the pickup allowance also gives a little extra capacity. Also, oversizing the boiler will probably be of little value during any unusually long cold spells (with temperatures well below the outside design temperature) unless the radiation or convector units selected are able to put out additional heat.

In large projects (institutional and commercial), two boilers are often used. Since boilers are more efficient the longer they operate, the first boiler would be designed to satisfy about 60% of the heat required, and the second would supply the balance. In this way, the first unit would come on and supply the heat required for about 75% of the days that heat is needed. Only during colder weather would the second unit turn on. The more efficient operation of the smaller first unit (when compared with the operation of a single boiler) pays for the added cost of a second unit. Also, this provides a backup unit in case one of the boilers requires repairs.

10-8 Installed and Existing Systems

No matter how carefully a system is designed and laid out, there is the possibility that at least a portion of the building is not being heated satisfactorily. This, of course, is also true of many existing systems. Quite often the problems in these systems can be corrected easily and relatively inexpensively after a careful analysis of the system.

First, carefully take notes as to exactly what the problem is, what time of day it is most noticeable, what the outside temperature is during the time that sufficient heat is not being properly distributed, and whether the boiler is running continuously or intermittently.

For example, in Fig. 10-29, note first that the general complaint is that the temperature of the entire house dropped to about 60° to 62°F during the night. During the day, it warmed up to the 70°F reading desired. The outside temperature that night reached a low of about −20°F, well below the design temperature of 0°F used for Albany, N.Y. (the location of the residence).

The first observation is that the outside temperature during the night was about 20°F below the outside design temperature and the inside temperature registers about 8°F below the thermostat setting. So, the problem is how to get more heat out of the baseboard convector radiators installed in the house. The first possibility is to check the temperature to which the boiler is heating the hot water. Each boiler has a thermostat which sets the highest temperature to which it can heat the water, and then the boiler will shut off while the circulating pumps continue to push hot water through the system.

It is most important to know whether or not the boiler was operating continuously or intermittently. Quite often the occupant confuses the fact that the pipes were hot and the hot water was being circulated with the actual boiler operation. It may be necessary to have the occupant obtain more information about the boiler operation before the system is corrected. If the boiler is operating continuously, it indicates that no matter how hard the boiler works, it cannot heat the water to the thermostat setting. When the boiler operates intermittently, it means that the boiler has heated the water to the thermostat setting and is waiting for

Complaint: Temperature in house 60° to 62°F during night, it raised to desired temperature during the day.

Heating equipment: hot water, working alright
Outside temperature —20°F
Wind: light
Boiler water temperature: 180°F

FIGURE 10-29 / Complaints

cooler water to circulate to it before starting again. Intermittent operation is most commonly found and will be discussed first.

Typically, the boiler thermostat is set at 170° or 180°F during installation. Keeping in mind that the amount of heat delivered by the convectors will increase with hotter water (Sec. 10-5, Fig. 10-20), the solution may be to increase the thermostat setting of the boiler. The hot water, in a closed heating system such as this, can be heated as high as 220°F. Generally, for every increase of 10°F in water temperature, the heat output of the radiation or convector units is increased about 10%. Intermittent operation is the most common problem and, fortunately, this is the most common solution.

If the temperature *is* set high and the boiler is operating intermittently, the next solution is to provide additional heat in each room by some means. In most rooms the length of finned-tube radiators may be increased, thus increasing the amount of heat which is put into the room. Many rooms have convector covers all along a wall, but check inside the cover; a great deal of that length may be plain tube and not finned-tube. In such a case a plumber can add some finned-tube element. It may be necessary to add extra lengths of finned-tube on an interior wall or to put a convector or unit heater up in a wall where baseboard space is not available. Any revision or addition of this type must be carefully planned and may be costly.

Questions

10-1. What are the differences between series loop and one-pipe hot water systems, and what are the advantages of each?

10-2. Discuss the two-pipe system, how it works, and its advantages and disadvantages.

10-3. Why are multiple heating circuits (zones) often used?

10-4. How does a radiant hot water heating panel work?

10-5. What types of heating devices are available to distribute heat to a space?

10-6. What is the one variable which affects the amount of heat given out by a finned-tube convector?

10-7. What type of system is most commonly used in a residence?

Chapter 11

Electric Heating Systems and Design

11-1   Types of Systems

The advantages of an electric heating system include low installation cost, individual room control, quiet operation, and cleanliness, as well as the fact that when cable or panels are used, there are no exposed heating units. The primary disadvantage of electric heat is its high cost of operation in almost all areas. A specialist is required to give honest figures for comparing electric heat costs with those of other types of fuels. Electrically operated boilers (furnaces) are not discussed in this chapter since they are not different systems but rather a different forced air unit with electricity as a fuel.

Most electric ratings are given in watts and Btuh. There are 3,413 Btuh for every 1,000 watts (1 kilowatt = 1,000 watts), and often the ratings will be given or noted as MBH (thousand Btuh's) and kW (kilowatts), such as 6.8 MBH and 2 kW.

Overall Systems

Baseboard   Electric board units have a heating element enclosed in a metal case. This system offers individual room control, but furniture arrangement and draperies must not interfere with the operation of the units by blocking the natural flow of air. This system is economical for a builder to install and is especially popular in low-cost housing and housing built for speculation (to try to sell), although the cost of operation is generally higher than most other fuels.

Resistance Cable   With this system, electric heating cable is stapled to the drywall in a grid pattern and covered with plaster or gypsum board. Individual thermostats control the heat in each room. However, since the cable is usually installed on the ceiling, the disadvantages of heat rising and cold feet must be considered.

Drawings are not usually done for this type of heating system; instead, the amount of heat required is noted for each space. The cable system allows complete freedom in furniture and drapery placement.

Panels   The prefabricated ceiling and wall panels used in this system have the heating wire sandwiched in rubber with an asbestos board backing. They are only ¼ in. thick and may be plastered, painted, or wallpapered over. The panels come in a standard size (usually 2 ft x 4 ft) and cannot be cut. They are often used in hung suspension ceilings. A panel system has the same basic advantages and disadvantages as a resistance cable system, including flexibility of furniture and drapery arrangement.

Unit Heaters

There are a variety of electric unit heaters available which may be used to supplement other heat sources in a space or to completely heat a room. In residences, such a unit heater is quite often installed in the bathroom, often to supplement other heat sources, since a temperature higher than 72 °F is necessary to feel comfortable when washing and after bathing. Unit heaters are also commonly installed in spaces where the heat is only used periodically, such as a basement, workshop or garage work area.

So that the warm air will be quickly spread throughout the area to be heated, unit heaters are equipped with a fan. It is preferable if the fan switch is the type which will not start until after the unit comes on and the air has warmed to a preset temperature; in this way, cold air is not pushed around the room.

Ceiling recessed units, as well as units recessed into the wall, are available.

System Combinations

Quite often in order to provide the best results, the design may incorporate more than one type of system. For example, a building may be predominantly heated with baseboard units, but in spaces where there is little free wall space, such as a kitchen, it may be desirable to use a unit heater in the ceiling or the wall under the cabinets. Another possibility for the kitchen might be to use resistance cables or panels in the ceiling. Bathrooms may be heated with unit heaters to provide added comfort.

Codes and Installation

While a hot water heating system is installed by the heating contractor, an electrical heating system is installed by an electrical contractor. ASHRAE publishes guides which discuss the use of the units for proper heating conditions and the installation, but the *National Electric Code* (NEC) also governs the installation of the resistance cable. The designer must have both the NEC code and ASHRAE guides available for reference.

11-2 Baseboard System Design

A baseboard electric system transfers heat to the space primarily by convection. It consists of baseboard units which may be mounted on the wall or recessed into the wall (Fig. 11-1). In selecting a baseboard unit, the designer must consider the direction in which the air will be discharged from the baseboard unit (Fig. 11-2).

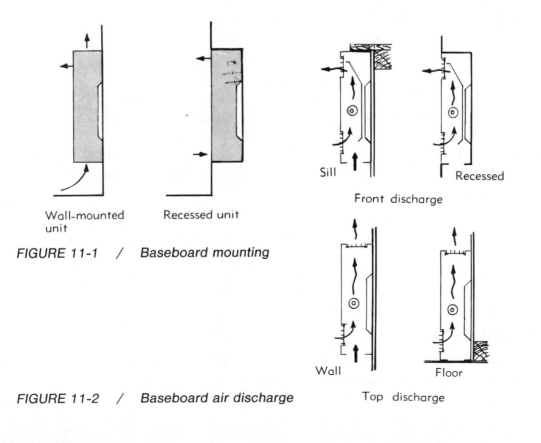

Wall-mounted unit   Recessed unit

FIGURE 11-1 / Baseboard mounting

Sill   Recessed

Front discharge

Wall   Floor

Top discharge

FIGURE 11-2 / Baseboard air discharge

Baseboard units are rated in watts and Btuh. These ratings, which may vary for different manufacturers, are given *for the length specified* and not per lineal foot. For example, in Fig. 11-3, the very first listing specifies a 36-in. (3-ft) length and a rating of 500 watts and 1,707 Btuh for the 3-ft length. The manufacturer often has several models, sizes, and ratings available, and the ratings will probably vary with other manufacturers. In Figs. 11-4 and 11-5, two separate series are listed; both have the same outside dimensions and the *B* series has a rating about 100% higher for each length than the *A* series. In addition, many manufacturers make larger units, with higher ratings, which are normally used in commercial, industrial, and institutional buildings. A 3-ft length of this style may range from 750 to 2,250 watts.

Length	Watts	Btuh
36″ (3′-0″)	500	1,707
52″ (4′-4″)	750	2,560
68″ (5′-8″)	1,000	3,413
100″ (8′-4″)	1,500	5,120

FIGURE 11-3 / Baseboard ratings

Length	Watts	Btuh
36″ (3′-0″)	750	2,560
48″ (4′-0″)	1,000	3,413
60″ (6′-0″)	1,250	4,269
72″ (6′-0″)	1,500	5,120
96″ (8′-0″)	2,000	6,830

A Series

FIGURE 11-4 / High output baseboard ratings

Length	Watts	Btuh
36″ (3′-0″)	1,500	5,120
48″ (4′-0″)	2,000	6,830
60″ (5′-0″)	2,500	8,538
72″ (6′-0″)	3,000	10,245
96″ (8′-0″)	4,000	13,660

B Series

FIGURE 11-5 / High output baseboard ratings

In designing an electric baseboard system, it may be necessary to use the larger units in some areas in order to provide the Btuh required.

Step-by-Step Approach

1. Do a heat loss calculation on each individual space, and tabulate them.

2. List the lineal feet of exterior wall that are available for baseboard convector units for each separate space, and tabulate them.

3. Using the manufacturer's ratings (Figs. 11-3 and 11-4 are typical), determine the length and corresponding rating that will be used to provide heat to each space.

4. Tabulate the baseboard convector units selected for each room; list their lengths, wattage ratings, and Btuh ratings.

> *Note:* Since exterior wall space for radiant baseboard units is likely to be limited in some areas, it may be desirable to use other units or devices to supplement or take the place of the radiant baseboards. The kitchen and bathrooms quite often have unit heaters recessed in the wall (Fig. 11-1). Kitchen heat may also be supplemented by a "kickspace" heater which is placed in the kickspace under the kitchen cabinets.

11-3   Resistance Cable System Design

The amount of heat given off by the cables will vary with the amount of heating cable used in the installation.

The electric cable used for ceiling installations comes in rolls; it is stapled to the ceiling and then covered with gypsum or plasterboard in accordance with the manufacturer's specifications and the code requirements. Basically, the cable must not be installed within 6 in. of any wall, within 8 in. of the edge of any junction box or outlet, or within 2 in. of any recessed lighting fixtures.

Cable assemblies are usually rated at 2.75 watts per lineal foot, with generally available ratings from 400- to 5,000-watt lengths in 200-watt increments, but the manufacturer's specifications should be checked to determine what is available. A typical list of available lengths, watts, and Btuh from one manufacturer is shown in Fig. 11-6. The cables have insulated coverings which are resistant to medium temperatures, water absorption, and the effects of aging and chemical reactions (concrete, plaster, etc.); a polyvinyl chloride covering with a nylon jacket is most commonly used. Each separate cable has an individual thermostat, providing flexible control throughout the building.

A typical cable installation in a plastered ceiling is shown in Fig. 11-7. The space between the rows of heating cable is generally limited to a minimum of 1.5 in., and some manufacturers recommend a 2-in. minimum spacing when drywall construction is used. Another limitation on the spacing of the cable is a 2.5-in. clearance required between cables under each joist (Fig. 11-8), and a review of the layout in Fig. 11-7 shows that the cable is installed parallel (in the same direction) as the joists.

To be certain the required amount of Btuh is obtained, it is sometimes desirable to specify the maximum spacing of heat cable allowed in a room. This maximum spacing may be determined by using the formula:

Btuh	Watts	Length Ft.
1365	400	145
2047	600	218
2730	800	292
3413	1000	362
4095	1200	436
5461	1600	582
6143	1800	654
6826	2000	728
7509	2200	800
8533	2500	910
10,239	3000	1090
11,287	3600	1310
15,700	4600	1672

FIGURE 11-6   /   Typical cable ratings

$$s = 12 \ (An/C)$$

where

s = cable spacing (in.)
An = net available area for heat cables (sq ft)
C = length of a cable required to deliver required Btuh (ft)
12 = constant (used to change ft to in.)

The net available area for heating cables is equal to the total ceiling area minus any area in which cable cannot be placed (due to borders, ceiling obstructions, cabinets, and any similar items). While a small lighting fixture may be neglected, if the ceiling has several, their area should be deducted.

Example

Given: Assume that bedroom 1 illustrated in Fig. 11-9 is about 18 ft–3 in. by 12 ft–3 in. and requires 4,024 Btuh. From the available cable lengths given in Fig. 11-6, a 1,200-watt, 4,095-Btuh, 436-ft cable is selected. Assume one ceiling fixture which is neglected in the calculation and a 6 in. border required between the cable and the intersection of wall.

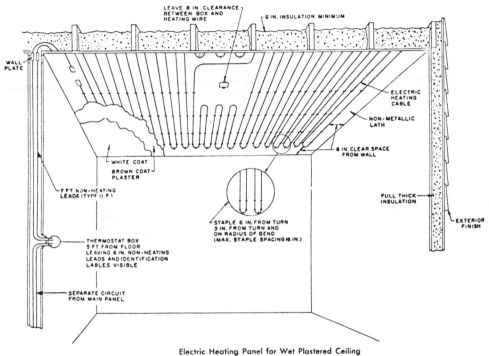

Electric Heating Panel for Wet Plastered Ceiling

Reprinted with permission from ASHRAE, Systems Handbook, 1976

FIGURE 11-7 / Cable heat installation

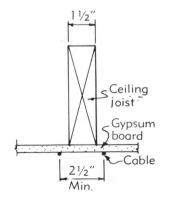

FIGURE 11-8 / Cable detail

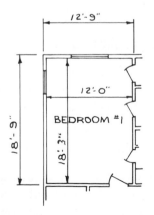

FIGURE 11-9 / Floor plan

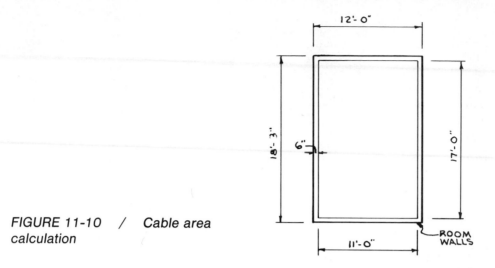

FIGURE 11-10   /   Cable area
calculation

Problem: Determine the net area available for heating cables and the maximum cable spacing.

$$An = 18 \text{ ft–3 in.} \times 12 \text{ ft–3 in.} - (6 \text{ in. around perimeter}$$
$$\text{of room}) \text{ (Fig. 11-10)}$$
$$17.25 \text{ ft} \times 11.25 \text{ ft} = 194 \text{ sq ft}$$
$$s = 12 \ (194 \text{ sq ft}/436 \text{ ft}) = 5.34 \text{ in. maximum spacing}$$

Bedroom 1 (Fig. 11-9) requires a maximum cable spacing of 5.34 in.

This is the procedure used to determine cable ceiling heat requirements for a building.

Step-by-Step Approach

1. Determine the heat loss of each individual room and tabulate them.

2. Select the cable required to provide the Btuh required for each room. Do not use a cable which will provide less Btuh than calculated.

3. Calculate the net ceiling area for each room.

4. Calculate the maximum cable spacing which can be used in each space.

The location of each thermostat must be shown on the drawing and may be put on the general construction (architectural) drawings; but often the information is put on the electrical drawings since the electrician will locate and install the thermostat and tie the cable circuit into the power panel which serves it.

11-4   Radiant Panel System Design

The heating rates for radiant ceiling panels are generally given in watts per panel, Btuh per panel, or both. As shown in Fig. 11-11, the ratings for a 2-ft x 4-ft panel may vary from about 500 to 750 watts per panel, depending on the panel selected and the manufacturer. Since 1 kW = 3,413 Btuh, 500 watts = 1,707 Btuh and 750 watts = 2,560 Btuh. It is important that the designer get accurate ratings by checking the engineering specifications for the type of panel which will actually be used on the project.

Watts	Btuh	Size
500	1707	2'-0"x4'-0"
750	2560	2'-0"x4'-0"
560	1911	2'-0"x4'-0"
700	3019	2'-0"x5'-0"
500	1707	2'-0"x3'-0"
750	2560	2'-0"x3'-0"
1000	4313	2'-0"x3'-0"

FIGURE 11-11   /   Radiant ceiling panel ratings

Step-by-Step Approach

To design ceiling panels for the residence for which the heat loss was calculated in Sec. 7-13:

1. The first step in the design is to tabulate the Btuh for each space as shown in Fig. 11-12.

2. Select the heating capacity in Btuh for the paneling being used.

3. Determine the number of ceiling panels required for each space.

4. List the square feet of ceiling area available for use in each space.

> Any space which does not have sufficient ceiling area for the panels must have supplemental heat provided by adding wall panels or electric baseboard or wall unit heaters. Another solution would be to use another type of system, such as baseboard or unit heaters, and not put any ceiling panels in the space.

It may be decided to put unit heaters in certain spaces where it is desirable to have a fan circulate the air through the space. Bathrooms are a typical example of where a unit heater might be used for this reason.

5. Determine the location of the thermostat, keeping in mind the location guides given in Sec. 10-3.

Room	Heat loss (Btuh)	Net ceiling area (s.f.)	Watts (Btuh ÷ 3413)	No. of panels
BEDROOM 1	4,085	194	1197	1-500W, 1-750W
BEDROOM 2	2,310	157	677	1-750W
LIVING	8,216	470	2407	1-500W, 1-1000W
KITCHEN	3,752	160	1100	1-500W, 1-750W
DINING	3,047	150	893	2-500W
ENTRY & HALL	3,364	170	986	2-500W
BEDROOM 3	3,008	150	881	2-500W
BATH	960	45	281	UNIT HEATER
INTERIOR BATH	198	14	58	UNIT HEATER

FIGURE 11-12   /   Radiant panel system design

Questions

11-1. Discuss the advantages and disadvantages of using electric heating systems.

11-2. What is the primary reason that electric heating systems are used?

11-3. What are the most common types of electric heat installations used?

11-4. Why is it important to have well-insulated construction when electric heat will be used?

Chapter 12
Solar Energy and Heat Pumps

12-1   Overview

The idea of harnessing the sun's energy for use in homes and factories is nothing new. Work began on solar furnaces more than two centuries ago—but with little success. In the United States solar hot water heaters were use in the early 1900's in Florida, Arizona, and California. The introduction of mass-produced hot water heaters which were low in cost and which used inexpensive oil, natural gas, and electricity all but stopped the further development of solar hot water heaters. The higher initial cost of the solar unit made it uneconomical except where the price of oil or electricity was high.

Since the 1930's limited experimentation continued in the application of solar energy, and interest increased markedly after World War II. But by 1960, the basic obstacle which had to be overcome was that the solar units were not "economically feasible" when compared with the low cost of other fuels. Not being "economically feasible" means that the amount of money saved on fuel costs is not sufficient to pay the increased cost of a solar system over a set period (say, 10 years).

In the 1970's, several major factors occurred to change the public's feelings toward solar systems.

1. The "oil embargo" of the early 1970's made the public aware that the flow of oil into the country was largely controlled by "others" and that the flow could be cut off at any time these "others" choose to do so.

2. The price increase of oil after the embargo caused the prices of other fuels dependent on oil (such as electricity) to skyrocket. Also, this rise in the cost of oil resulted in similar price rises for all other fuels (natural gas, propane gas, and coal).

3. The public realized, and the government admitted, that the supply of fuels used (oil, gas, and coal) is limited and that if the present use rate continues, one day we will "run out of gas." As a result the government has at least begun to put together a national energy policy while assuring the public that the energy crisis is real.

4. The energy crisis which occurred in the mid-1970's when natural gas was in short supply put thousands of people out of work due to a lack of natural gas to heat buildings and run machinery. While part of this crisis was brought on by the reluctance of firms to explore and produce natural gas, it made the government and the public face the fact that there is a limit to the amount of natural gas.

As a result of all this, suddenly solar energy systems were not priced too high to be economically feasible for use in hot water heaters and, in many areas, for heating and cooling as well. Also, many people are now willing to pay a little extra if it means that they can reduce the constantly increasing amount being paid for other fuels. The price of fuels will continue to go up, and cheap fuel is now gone forever.

12-2   Uses

Solar energy is being used to:

1. Heat hot water for use in the building.
2. Provide heating for the building.
3. Provide cooling for the building.
4. Provide heating and cooling for the building.
5. Provide heating and hot water for the building.
6. Provide heating, cooling, and hot water for the building (Fig. 12-1).

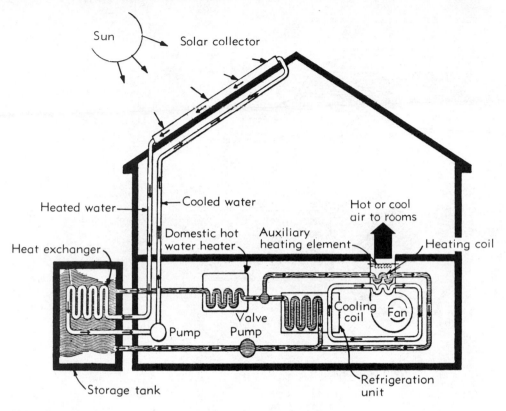

FIGURE 12-1 / *Solar heating and cooling system*

As outlined above, quite often the solar energy package will provide more than one service, usually at very little extra cost.

This chapter reviews some available solar systems, how they work, and what they have to offer.

12-3 Collectors and Storage

All systems are made up of two basic components—collectors and storage areas.

Collectors

First, all systems must have some type of collector. The flat-plate collector (shown in Fig. 12-2) is the collector most commonly used to gather in the heat from the sun. Basically, all collectors are similar in that they have a casing (or frame), in-

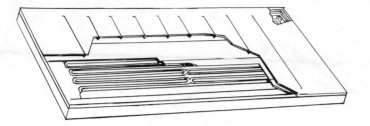

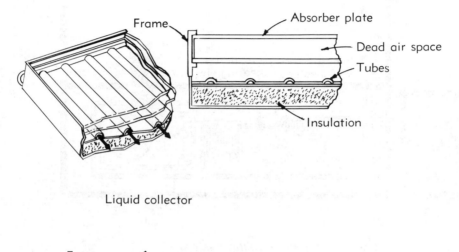

Liquid collector

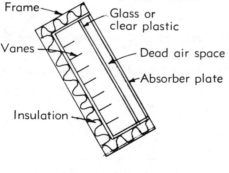

Air collector

FIGURE 12-2   /   *Flat plate collectors*

sulation, plate, heat transfer medium (liquid or gas), and glazing. There is no one design that is used, however, and several different collector designs are shown in Fig. 12-3. But it is important to note there are two basic types of heat transfer mediums—*liquid* and *air*—and this makes for two basic types of collectors—liquid and air.

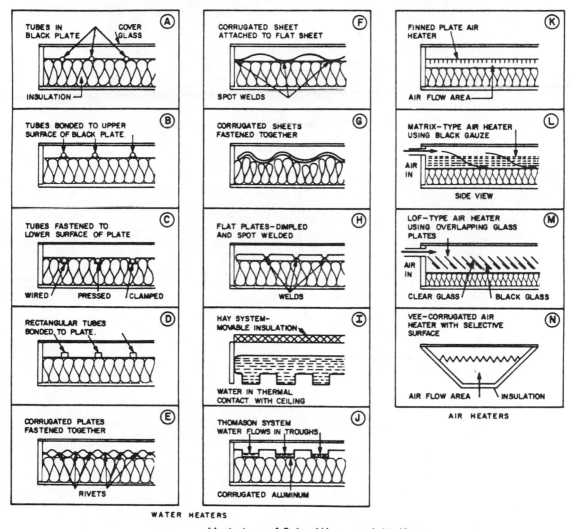

WATER HEATERS

AIR HEATERS

Variations of Solar Water and Air Heaters

Reprinted with permission from ASHRAE, Applications Handbook, 1974

FIGURE 12-3 / Collector designs

The collector is located outside and is angled to receive the maximum amount of sunshine possible (Fig. 12-4). To increase the amount of the sun's rays which hit the collector, some systems even use a reflective surface in front of the collector (Fig. 12-5), with the reflective panel placed either on an adjoining flat roof or in front of the collector. The collector is commonly located on the roof, and many units are also designed to be placed on the ground.

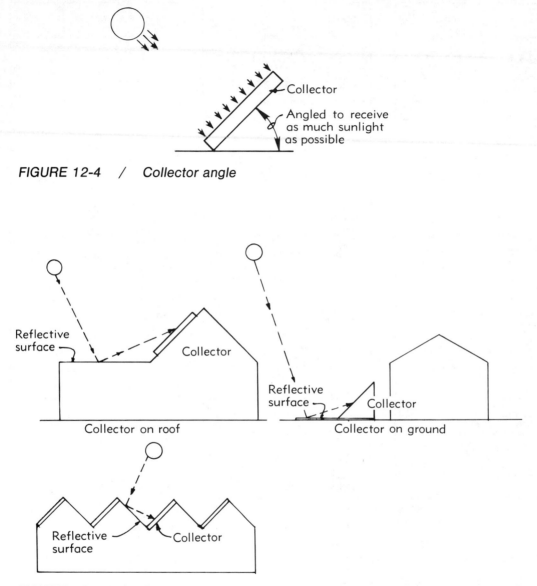

FIGURE 12-4   /   Collector angle

FIGURE 12-5   /   Reflection to collector

Storage Mediums

Once the heat exchange medium (liquid or air) is warmed in the collector, the heat it absorbs is transferred to a storage medium for future use. The storage mediums most commonly used are coarse aggregates (clean, washed rock), water, and a combination of the coarse aggregates and water (Fig. 12-6).

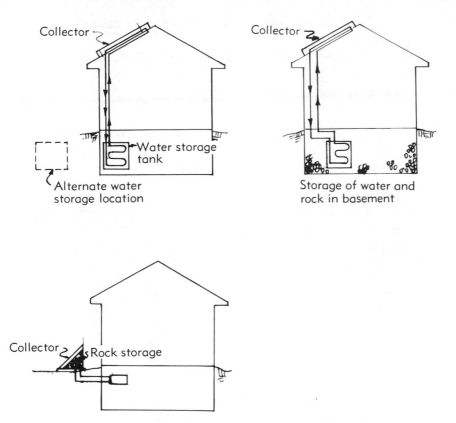

FIGURE 12-6 / Storage medium

12-4 Heating, Cooling, and Hot Water

The system shown in Fig. 12-1 utilizes a liquid heat transfer medium (water or water and anti-freeze), a collector on the roof, and water as the heat storage medium. Such a system is the most versatile, providing the most benefits to the owner. The system shown has auxiliary units for heating, cooling, and hot water for the time when the solar system cannot provide sufficient heat (or cooling).

Heating

The heat transfer medium is heated in the collector and is then circulated through the storage tank, transferring its heat to the storage medium—in this case, water. This heated water then circulates through the hot water heater tank to heat all or part of the hot water required for the building. The heated water then passes a fan which forces air past the hot water coils. The air passing the coils is warmed and circulates through the building.

There are many variations on the design; in Fig. 12-1, the water from the storage tank passes first through the fan and forced air and then through the hot water tank. A hot water heating system is shown in Fig. 12-7 and discussed in Sec. 12-5.

Cooling

To provide cooling for the building, the system is, in effect, reversed. While the collectors used to gather the heat ideally face south, the radiators used to give off heat to the exterior face north. (Although some systems utilize the collectors already on the south, it is not as effective.)

In order to use the system for cooling, the storage medium must be made as low in temperature (cool) as possible; then it circulates past the refrigerant in the refrigeration unit which then circulates past the fan to blow cool air into the building. One method used is to have the heat pump transfer heat from the house to the heat storage medium and into the storage tank where the temperature of the entire storage medium slowly increases. Then at night, the radiation system turns on and the heat transfer medium cools the storage medium by absorbing the heat as it passes through the tank. Circulating it up through the night radiator collectors facing north, the collectors radiate the heat to the surrounding atmosphere and then the medium goes back to the storage tank to constantly repeat the process of lowering the water temperature in the storage tank so it can be used for cooling.

Another method used with a system of this type is to connect to a well; then if the water in the storage tank reaches a certain temperature (about 65 °F), the system will automatically switch to the well as its source of cool water. Since many of the same controls (valves and pumps) are utilized in both the heating and the cooling operations, it is often this dual feature that makes the system economically feasible.

Another method used converts the sun's energy into the energy source used to power the cooling equipment. In this type of installation, storage batteries are charged during the daytime hours to operate a heat pump.

The use of solar energy for cooling is not nearly as advanced as its use for heating. A great deal more research is required before economical, dependable solar cooling is available.

12-5   Hot Water Heating

Hot water solar systems are similar to the system described (in Sec. 12-4) except that the storage medium (water) is used to heat the hot water which is then circulated through the system (Fig. 12-7). An auxiliary heat source is still required to supplement the solar system. This system could also be used for cooling (similar to Fig. 12-1) if the devices in the building are selected to effectively handle chilled

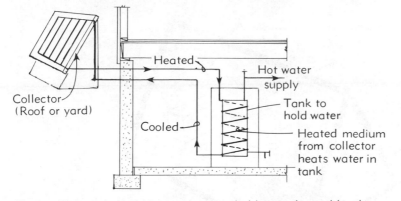

Tank—This tank could be used to just hold water heated by the collector medium or it could be a direct hot water heater used to supplement the collector during times when the collector cannot provide all of the hot water required.

FIGURE 12-7 / Hot water system

water. Realistically, this is rarely the case in residential work. Chilled water systems are discussed in Sec. 8-1. Solar hot water is also discussed in Sec. 2-16.

12-6 Hot Air System (Heating)

A hot air heating system uses air as the heat transfer medium and rocks as the heat storage medium. As the diagram in Fig. 12-5 shows, the collector may be located on the ground. The air in the collector is heated as it is pulled across the vanes in the collector, and it is then pushed over the rocks in the storage medium, transferring much of the heat collected to the rocks. This continuous flow of air is constantly warmed in the collector and then cooled as it transfers its heat to the rocks (Fig. 12-8).

When the thermostat in the building calls for heat, the distribution fans come on and circulate the cooler air from the building over the rocks in the storage area, and this warmed air is then circulated back through the building (Fig. 12-9).

When both the collection and the distribution are on, the air flow from the building passes through the collector to provide heat directly from the collector. This commonly occurs when the building thermostat calls for heat during the daytime while the collector is also activated to gather the heat from the sun. With a system of this type, it is usually recommended that there be continuous air circulation in the building. A solar system of this type is designed to continuously

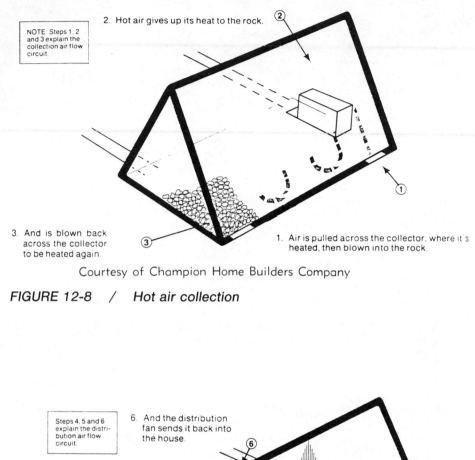

2. Hot air gives up its heat to the rock.

NOTE: Steps 1, 2 and 3 explain the collection air flow circuit.

3. And is blown back across the collector to be heated again.

1. Air is pulled across the collector, where it s heated, then blown into the rock.

Courtesy of Champion Home Builders Company

FIGURE 12-8   /   Hot air collection

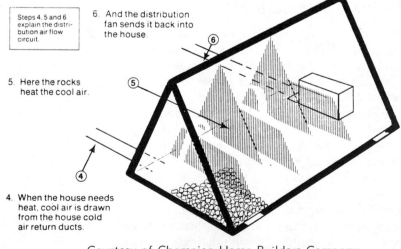

Steps 4, 5 and 6 explain the distribution air flow circuit.

6. And the distribution fan sends it back into the house.

5. Here the rocks heat the cool air.

4. When the house needs heat, cool air is drawn from the house cold air return ducts.

Courtesy of Champion Home Builders Company

FIGURE 12-9   /   Hot air storage and transfer

286

circulate air that is relatively cooler than that from the forced air system using a furnace. In the solar system, the air will usually feel just slightly warm, or perhaps even a little cool to the touch since the air temperature will be lower than your body temperature. Studies of systems using continuous air circulation show that less heat is required when such a system is used.

The fact that this system is easily adaptable to existing forced air systems is significant. In such an installation, the collector could be set on the ground.

12-7 Supplementary Heat

Almost all solar systems are more expensive to install than conventional boiler or furnace systems. As discussed in Chapter 7, the conventional system is sized to deliver all of the heat required down to a particular design temperature ($-10\,°F$ in Rutland, Vt., and $20\,°F$ in Raleigh, N.C.). It is quite inexpensive to size the boiler or furnace to provide all of the heat required to meet those demands, even with an extra 10% pickup load added on. But keep in mind two things:

1. During most of the heating season, the temperatures are well above the design temperature used. (Many times it might reach the low during the night, but it warms up $15\,°$ to $25\,°F$ during the day.)

2. The solar system costs much more for the materials used.

This means that providing all of the heat required to keep a house warm in a northern city on *the coldest day ever recorded there* would require a solar unit about four times as large as one that would provide 90% of the heat required during the entire heating season.

For these reasons many of the solar systems have auxiliary or supplemental heating systems along with the solar system. In this situation the solar system would provide a certain percentage of the heat required (perhaps 40%, 50%, 60% or more) and the supplemental heating boiler or furnace would provide the rest. In this manner the most economically feasible installation can be obtained, and the problem of allocating huge areas to contain the storage medium is overcome.

A solar system with supplemental heat can be designed to save a significant amount of the total heat bill, but it is important to realize that it is the *total annual fuel bill* being discussed, that the savings will be highest in the milder months, and that the heat bills will increase in the colder months. So it is the "average" being discussed, as illustrated in Fig. 12-10.

While this type of system may not satisfy the "purist" in terms of total solar systems, it provides a very "cost effective" system which will save large amounts of fuel. In addition, it makes solar systems easily adaptable to existing installations where the existing system may be used as the supplemental system. It is most

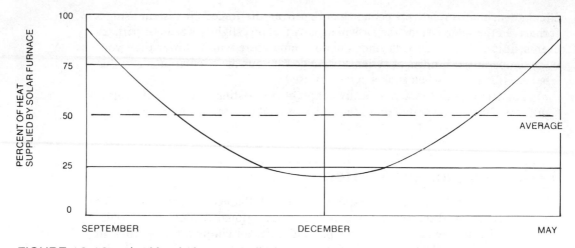

FIGURE 12-10   /   Yearly heat supplied

important not only that fuels be conserved in new construction but also that systems be developed that are adaptable to existing heating systems (hot water and air).

12-8   Heat Pumps

Use of refrigeration to provide cooling is discussed in Sec. 8-4, as are the basic principles which apply to such use. The use of refrigeration to provide both heating and cooling for a space is accomplished with a device called a *heat pump*. This increasingly popular form of heating and cooling a space requires explanation of the principles involved and its advantages and disadvantages.

First, the discussion of the cooling principles of refrigerants in Sec. 8-4 must be carefully read and understood. In effect, it states that the refrigerant can take heat from one place (air or water) and move it to another by use of an evaporator, compressor, and condenser.

Now, using those basic cooling principles and a valve control, it is possible to reverse the cycle, causing the refrigerant to absorb heat from an outside surrounding medium (usually air, but water is sometimes used) and to release this heat inside the building (in the air or water being used to heat the building).

The reversing valve control allows the refrigerant to be used to provide cooling or heating, depending on the direction of flow after it leaves the compressor. If the refrigerant flows to the condenser, it provides cooling; if it flows toward the evaporator section, it provides heating.

The most commonly used surrounding mediums are the outside air and the forced air in the ductwork. Outside air is the surrounding medium most likely to be used to draw heat from in the winter for heating and to release heat to in the summer for cooling. The temperature of this outside air affects the efficiency of the unit in providing heating and cooling Btuh. Typically, as the outside air temperature goes down in the winter, the amount of heat which the heat pump will produce goes down also. In effect, the more heat needed in the space, the less Btuh the unit will provide.

At this point, it is important to realize that a heat pump is not electric heat. Actually, it is a type of solar heating which draws heat from the surrounding air. It requires electrical power to run the equipment, but it is more efficient than electric heat. The efficiency of the heat pump can be determined from the manufacturer's engineering data. While there are many sizes and capacities of units available, we will review the typical data for a 3-ton (36,000-Btuh) cooling capacity unit. Since each manufacturer's units vary, so will their data; and as more efficient units are developed, the result will be higher values from the heat pump.

Note in Fig. 12-11 that at a 60°F outside temperature, the unit will provide 41,000 Btuh for heating. As the temperature goes down to 40°F, the unit will supply 32,000 Btuh, and yet more heat is required inside the space at 40°F than at 60°F. When it gets cold—say, 20°F—outside, the unit will provide 21,000 Btuh. It is obvious that as the temperature goes down, so does the ability of the heat pump to produce heat.

It is when the heat pump alone is producing the heat that the unit is economical to operate. The coefficient of performance [(Btuh/watts) × 3.14] is not generally given by the manufacturer, but it has been calculated for the 3-ton unit in Fig. 12-11. This coefficient of performance offers a comparison of the heat pump and electric resistance heat. The table shows a COP of 2.46 at 60°F, dropping to 2.17 at 40°F and to 1.71 at 20°F. Due to this fluctuation, it is difficult to give an actual comparison with other fuels and systems. It depends very much on the geographic area in which it is being used and how many hours it operates at the different temperatures.

For comparison, electric heat has a COP of 1.0. Electric heat tends to cost about twice as much as oil or natural gas. So, for the heat pump to be competitive, it needs to operate at a COP of about 2.0, and at 40°F it does this. But at lower temperatures, it becomes less and less efficient.

Since the heat pump puts out 21,000 Btuh at 20°F, the rest of the heat is supplied by electric heat resistance units, which mount inside the evaporator blower discharge area; or else electric duct heaters, which are placed right in the ductwork, are used to supplement the heat pump. These supplemental units run on electricity and provide the standard 3,413 Btuh per 1,000 W (watts) (1 kW). These electric resistance units are generally available in increments of 3, 5, 10, 15, and 20 kW, depending on the manufacturer. Many of the smaller heat pump units have space to install only the smaller sizes, perhaps to a limit of 10 kW, and the manufacturer's information must be checked. The large units, such as the 3-ton unit being discussed here, will take the 15-kW unit.

Typical 3-ton (36,000 Btuh) heat pump
Cooling capacity, 62° outside wet bulb,
85° air temperature entering evaporator.

Outside air temperature db°F	Cooling Btuh	Watts	EER
85	36,000	5,250	6.85
95	34,000	5,400	6.30
105	32,000	5,750	5.56

Heating capacity

Outside air temperature	Heating Btuh	Watts	COP
60	41,000	5,300	2.46
50	38,000	5,100	2.37
45	35,000	4.900	2.37
40	32,000	4,700	2.17
30	26,000	4,300	1.92
20	21,000	3,900	1.71
10	15,000	3,500	1.36
0	10,000	3,100	1.02

FIGURE 12-11   /   Typical 3-ton heat pump

The 15-kW unit would be made up of three 5-kW elements which would operate at three different stages set to provide the required heat to the space. The
first stage is controlled by the room thermostat, and it operates on a 2°F differential from the setting on the room thermostat. This means that if the room thermostat is set, say, at 70°F, as the thermostat calls for heat, the heat pump goes on and
begins to send heat to the space. If the temperature of the room falls below 68°F,
then the first 5-kW unit would come on and begin to provide additional heat to
supplement the heat pump. The second and third stages of electrical resistance
heat are activated by outdoor thermostat settings which are adjustable (from 50°
to 0°F).

This differential of 2°F between the thermostat setting and the room temperature, which activates the first stage, may mean that in cold weather the room
temperature may stabilize at 68°F. This is because 68°F is the temperature at
which the first stage shuts off; to get a 70°F reading on those days, it may be necessary to raise the thermostat reading to about 72°F.

The cooling efficiency of the heat pump should also be checked. Many times
the less expensive units have much lower efficiency ratings than the individual

cooling units discussed in Sec. 10-2. It is important that the most efficient model be selected. For example, the 3-ton unit being discussed in this section has its engineering data shown in Fig. 12-11. As the temperature goes up, the cooling Btuh provided goes down; at 85 °F it produces 36,000 Btuh for cooling and 5,250 W, while at 95 °F it produces 34,000 Btuh and 5,450 W. Its EER ranges from 6.85 to 5.56 as listed in the table. The EER most commonly used for comparison of cooling units is based on its performance at a 95 °F temperature; based on that, this unit's EER would be 6.24.

In reviewing the operation and efficiency of the heat pump, the following points should be considered:

1. The heat pump is more efficient in warmer climates than in cooler areas. In Florida and southern California, for example, heat pumps are reasonably efficient. As you approach "mid-South" states, those states in a band from North Carolina and Virginia on the east to northern California on the west, the efficiency begins to fall off. In nothern states these units would depend on the electric resistance heat for so much of the time that efficiency is minimal.

2. Technology will continue to improve the efficiency of the heat pump. It is part of the designer's responsibility to keep abreast of developments in the field that will provide increased efficiency.

3. A comparison of the heat pump with other fuels and systems must be made for each geographical area, and its complexity suggests that a computer be used. This type of analysis is available in many areas now. However, the designer should be aware that it is being made available by the same people who are selling heat pumps and perhaps by those who sell the electricity to run the unit. This is not to infer that it would not be "technically accurate"; only that the utmost caution should always be used when using calculations, analyses, claims, and the like from any interested party (such as the company selling the unit). The best idea is to check actual installations and compare the costs with those of comparable installations. But be certain that they are comparable installations, that the thermostats are set at about the same temperatures, and that the actual electrical and fuel bills are available (don't rely on word of mouth).

4. While heat pumps are more efficient than electric resistance heat, in northern and mid-South states actual use has shown that it is not less expensive to heat with a heat pump than with oil and natural gas fuels.

5. While the currently available heat pump is a solar unit, it will probably soon be available with a solar collector panel which can be attached to it to provide greater efficiency. This may be one of the first practical, small and mid-sized solar system projects. Currently, at least one manufacturer is working on its development.

6.   The shortage of fuel oil due to the embargo in the early 1970's, the shortage
      of natural gas available to the user, and the general uncertainty over future
      supplies and prices of these fuels have caused many owners and designers to
      consider using the heat pump in many areas where it might not ordinarily be
      considered. In effect, most people feel that, one way or another, at least with
      the heat pump, the fuel (the electricity) will be available to run the unit and
      provide the heating and cooling required.

7.   It is more efficient and generally less expensive, especially during the heat-
      ing season, to use one large unit instead of two smaller units, unless one sec-
      tion of the house (or building) will be closed off. For example, based on the
      data in Fig. 12-12, if a building requires a 4-ton cooling unit at 20°F, the
      heat pump will provide 28,000 Btuh for heating while using 4,800 W. Using
      two 2-ton units, at 20°F each unit will provide 14,000 Btuh using 2,700 W,
      for a total of 28,000 Btuh using 5,400 W. Again, this is the type of analysis
      that the designer must consider. Now, if part of the building were to be
      closed off—say, a large bedroom wing—with the temperature set quite low
      (about 50°F), it might be more economical to have two units—in this case,
      one unit to serve the bedrooms and one for the rest of the building.

4-ton heat pump, heating capacity

Outside air temperature db°F	Heating Btuh	Watts
60	52,000	5,900
40	41,000	5,300
20	28,000	4,800
0	20,000	4.300

2-ton heat pump, heating capacity

Outside air temperature db°F	Heating Btuh	Watts
60	31,000	3,850
40	22,000	3,300
20	14,000	2,700
0	8,200	2,200

FIGURE 12-12   /   4-ton and 2-ton heat pumps

Questions

12-1. What factors have made solar energy more attractive in recent years?

12-2. What may solar energy be used for in a building?

12-3. Briefly describe what a *collector* is and how it works.

12-4. What are the two basic types of heat transfer mediums?

12-5. What are the basic components of a collector?

12-6. What are the commonly used storage mediums, and what is the function of a storage medium in the solar energy system?

12-7. Sketch a schematic of a solar energy system providing heating and hot water only; label all the parts.

12-8. Sketch a schematic of a solar energy system providing heating, cooling, and hot water; label all the parts.

12-9. Why is supplementary heat often *required* in solar heating systems?

12-10. Why might it be *desirable* to have supplemental heat with a solar heating system?

12-11. Describe briefly how a heat pump operates.

12-12. What happens to the heating and cooling outputs of a heat pump as the temperature varies?

Chapter 13

Electrical Systems and Design

13-1 Codes

All buildings require electrical systems to provide power for the lights and to run various appliances and equipment. The safety of the system is of prime importance, and minimum requirements are included in building codes. Most applicable codes have separate electrical sections, or else completely separate electrical codes are prepared. In addition, many local codes make reference to the *National Electric Code* (NEC) or are based on the national code. The designer must first determine what code is applicable to the locale in which the building will be built, and then be certain that the electrical design is in accordance with the code. The *National Electric Code* is used as a basis for this portion of the text. Generally, these codes place limitations on the type and size of the wiring to be used, the circuit size, outlet spacings, conduit requirements, and the like. The tables used in this text are from the 1981 NEC. Be certain that you always have a copy of the latest edition available for your use.

FIGURE 13-1 / Typical Underwriters Laboratories seal

13-2 Underwriters Laboratories (UL)

UL is an independent organization that tests various electrical fixtures and devices to determine if they meet minimum specifications as set up by UL. The device to be tested is furnished by the manufacturer, and if the test shows that it meets the minimum specifications, it will be put on the UL official published list, referred to as "listed by Underwriters Laboratories, Inc." The approved device may then have a UL label on it. A typical UL seal is shown in Fig. 13-1, and many consumers will not buy any electrical device which does not have a UL label.

13-3 Licenses

Most municipalities have laws requiring that any person who wishes to engage in the business of installing electrical systems must be licensed (usually by the state or the province). This generally means that the person must have a minimum number of years of experience working with a licensed electrician and must pass a written test which deals primarily with the electrical code being used and with methods of installation.

By requiring a license, it is assured that the electrician knows, at a minimum, the code requirements and installation procedures. In areas where no laws require that only licensed electricians may install electrical systems, there is no protection for the consumer against an unskilled electrician. Always insist on licensed electricians for all installations.

13-4 Permits

Many municipalities require a permit before any electrical installations may be made on the project. Depending on the municipality, a complete electrical drawing may be required and may even be reviewed by the municipality before installation may begin, while others may require no drawings at all. In general, most municipalities that require electrical permits also require licensed electricians.

In addition, these municipalities will probably have electrical inspectors, trained personnel who check the project during regularly scheduled visits. Typically, they will want to inspect the installation after the rough wiring is in and before it is concealed in the construction, and again when all of the fixtures and devices are installed and wired back to the panel and the service and meter installed.

On large projects many electrical inspections may be necessary since the work may be done in stages. For example, conduit which will be encased in concrete may have to be checked before the concrete is poured, and conduit to be built into the masonry walls will have to be checked before the walls are begun. These types of covering up will occur throughout the project. Be certain that the installer and the designer are aware of when inspections are required and of what will be inspected. Also, it is important that close coordination and cooperation be maintained with the inspector since he could slow down the progress of the work if he does not make his inspections promptly. Whenever possible, he will need to know as early as possible when inspections will be necessary.

13-5   Terminology

Circuit: Two or more wires that carry electricity from the source to an electrical device and back.

Circuit Breaker: A switch that automatically stops the flow of electricity in a particular circuit when the circuit is overloaded.

Conductor: The wire used to carry electricity.

Conduit: A channel or tube designed to carry the conductors in locations where the conductors need protection.

Convenience Outlet: An outlet that receives the plugs of electrical devices such as lamps, radios, clocks, etc. Also referred to as a *receptacle.*

Fixtures: The lighting fixtures used. They may be wall or ceiling mounted, recessed or surface mounted. Also included are table and floor lighting fixtures.

Ground: To minimize injuries from shock and possible damage from lightning, the electrical system should be equipped with a wire (called a ground) that connects to the earth.

Service Entrance: The wires, fittings, and equipment that bring the electricity into the building.

Service Panel: The main panel that receives the electricity at the service entrance, breaks it down, and distributes it through the various circuits.

Switch: The control used to turn the flow of electricity on or off to the electrical device to which it is connected.

13-6   Amps, Ohms, Volts

The design of electrical systems in a building requires that the designer have a "working familiarity" with amperes, ohms, and volts. These three electrical terms are often used by the designer to determine the total electrical load requirements of the building, and they are all related.

Ampere (Amp, Amperage—A):   A unit (or measure) of the flow of electrons passing through a circuit (current).

Volt (Voltage—V):   The unit of electrical pressure required to push the amperage through the circuit.

Ohm (Ω):   The unit of electrical resistance that resists the flow of electrons through the circuit. Ohm's law states that the current in an electrical circuit is equal to the pressure divided by the resistance.

$$\text{Amps} = \frac{\text{Volts}}{\text{Ohms}}$$

Watt (W):   The unit of electrical energy or electrical power. It indicates how much power has been used.

$$\text{Watts} = \text{Amps} \times \text{Volts}$$

Kilowatt (kW):   1,000 watts; for example, 9,500 W equals 9.5 kW.

13-7   Service Entrance

The service entrance furnishes electricity to a house; a three-wire service bringing in 120/240 volt, single-phase power is generally standard. These three wires attach to the house at a mast (Fig 13-2), or are installed underground (Fig. 13-3), and run through a metal conduit through the meter and into the service panel. The meter and service panel should be placed as close to the mast as possible. This will place the main breaker as close to the meter as possible.

The location of the service entrance is generally controlled by economics. Often the service is located near the point of greatest power usage (in a house, this is usually the kitchen) since larger wires are needed where high usage is indicated, and the closer the entrance to the high-usage area, the less of the larger, more expensive wiring is required (Fig. 13-4).

Electric meters are weatherproof and should be located on the outside of the house so readings can be taken by the power company without disturbing anyone or when no one is at home.

In many locales service is brought to the buildings in electrical wires below ground (Fig. 13-3). In this manner, unsightly wires, masts, and fittings are concealed. When the entire community is served by underground service, the power poles and lines are never missed. However, this is more expensive than running services above ground.

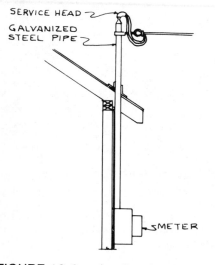

FIGURE 13-2   /   Overhead service

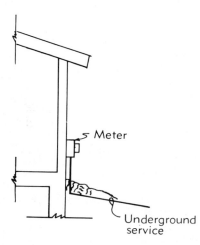

FIGURE 13-3   /   Underground service

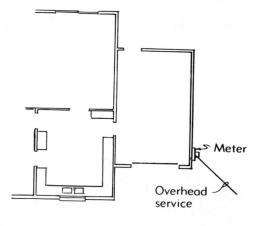

FIGURE 13-4   /   Service location

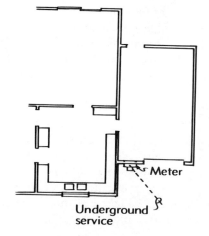

Alternate location

The sizing of the service entrance, based on the amount of power it must supply, should be guided by the following information:

100 amperes: Adequate power to provide general-purpose circuits, water heater, electric laundry, and cooking.

150 amperes: Adequate power to provide general-purpose circuits, water heater, electric laundry and cooking, and, for a small house, the air conditioning and heating.

200 amperes: Adequate power to provide general-purpose circuits, water heater, electric laundry and cooking, air conditioning, and heating.

Once all of the circuits, fixtures, appliances, and type of heating are determined, the size of the service entrance may be calculated by experienced personnel. It is best to anticipate a little high when selecting the size of the service entrance. It is much more expensive to increase the size later than when the building is being built.

13-8   Service Panel

This distribution box is the main panel (Fig. 13-5) that receives the service electricity, breaks it down, and distributes it through branch circuits to the places where the electricity is needed. Inside the panel is a main disconnect switch that cuts off power to the entire building, and the circuit breakers (or fuses) that control the power to the individual circuits serving the house.

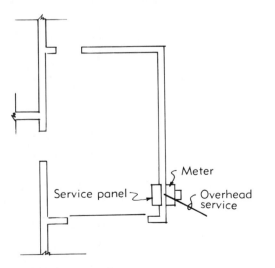

FIGURE 13-5   /   Service panel

The circuit breakers (or fuses) are protective devices which will automatically cut off power to any circuit that is overloaded or short-circuited. The circuit breaker may be turned back on by flipping its surface-mounted switch; if the circuit is still overloaded, the switch will immediately flip off again. Fuses burn out when the circuit is overloaded and must be replaced to activate the circuit again. Circuit breakers and fuses are sized as to the amperage they will carry, and when replaced, the replacement should have the same rating.

The service panel is sized to match the service coming in, commonly 100, 150, or 200 amps. The number of circuits required in the building will determine the size of the panel. Panels are rated in amperage and poles, the poles being how many circuits it will handle. All 120-volt circuits, as required for most lighting, convenience outlets, and appliances, require one pole each. All appliances such as ranges, clothes dryers, hot water heaters, large air conditioners, and many motors require 240 volts, and two poles are required. The panel selected should have extra poles so that additional circuits may be run if and when they are desired.

The panel may be surface mounted or recessed and should be conveniently located for easy servicing and resetting of circuit breakers and fuses as required. It should not be placed in a location where there is a possibility of water being on the panel or on the floor around it. Typically, it is located in a garage, corridor, basement, or utility room of the building.

13-9   Feeder Circuits

On large buildings where the wiring for circuits would have long runs, a feeder circuit may be run from the service panel to a subdistribution panel (Fig. 13-6 and 13-7). Locating the subdistribution panel conveniently to service the larger feeder

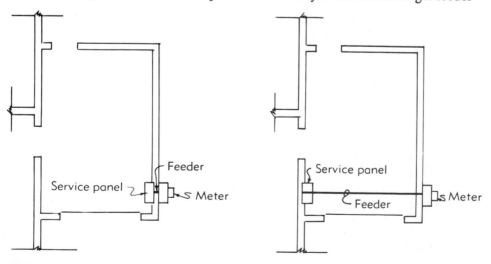

FIGURE 13-6   /   Feeder circuit

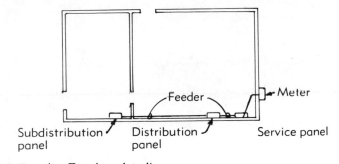

FIGURE 13-7 / Feeder circuit

conductors (wires) will allow a minimal voltage drop when compared with the excessive voltage drop that occurs when branch circuits are in excess of 75 to 100 ft long.

13-10 Branch Circuits

The branch circuit connects the service panel to the electrical device it supplies (Fig. 13-8). It may supply power to a single device such as a water heater, range, or air conditioner, or it may service a group or series of devices such as convenience outlets and lights. The branch circuit may have a variety of capacities, such as 15, 20, 30, 40, or 50 amps, depending on the requirements of the electrical devices serviced. The general-purpose circuits for lights and convenience outlets are usually sized at 15 or 20 amps. One general-purpose branch circuit will provide a maximum of 20 amps × 120 volts = 2,400 watts, of which the Code allows 80%. There is a tendency for people to put higher wattage bulbs (luminaires) in lighting fixtures as they need replacing; a group of light fixtures totaling 1,200 to 1,600 watts may be placed on a circuit and still allow for additional future usage. The same is true with convenience outlets; generally no more than six should be on a circuit.

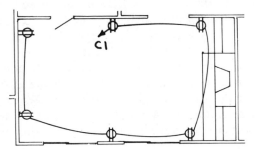

FIGURE 13-8 / Typical branch circuit

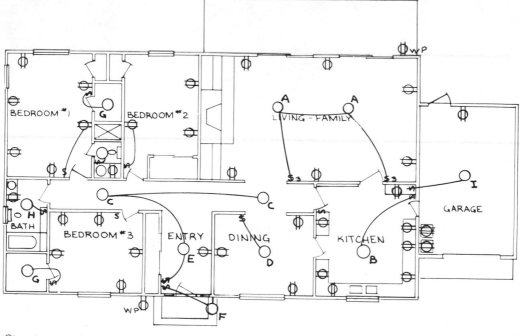

Circuits not shown

FIGURE 13-9 / Circuit labeling

The wiring layout for most buildings shows the branch circuit arrangements. If not shown on the layout, it will be left to the electrical contractor to decide on groupings (Fig. 13-9).

13-11   Receptacles

Receptacles, also referred to as convenience outlets (Fig. 13-10) are used to plug in lights and small appliances around the house. Each room should be laid out with no less than one outlet per wall and with outlets no more than 10 ft apart. The amount, location, and type will vary with the room, depending on both the design of the room and the furniture layout. Duplex outlets (two receptacles) are most commonly used, but single and triple receptacles are also used. In addition, strips that allow movement of the receptacle to any desired location are available in 3-ft and 6-ft lengths and may even be used around the entire room. When specified, one of the receptacles may be controlled by a wall switch. This is particularly desirable in rooms where portable fixtures are used. Typical room layouts are shown in Fig. 13-11.

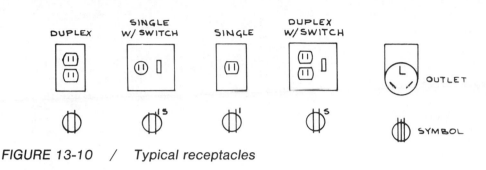

FIGURE 13-10 / Typical receptacles

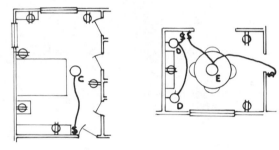

FIGURE 13-11 /
Typical room layouts

Some room designs make it difficult to locate the outlets on the walls. Plans such as Fig. 13-12 require that furniture be located out from the wall and the space between the furniture and the wall used for pedestrian traffic out to the deck. If the outlets were placed on the exterior wall, the cords from lamps to the outlets would cross the traffic area, creating a safety hazard. Floor outlets may be used in this situation; these outlets may be located anywhere desired in the floor. A note of caution—they should be carefully planned so they will not interfere with furniture arrangement.

Ranges, dryers, large air conditioners, and other such electrical devices which require 240-volt service need special outlets. These special three-prong outlets (Fig. 13-10) are designed so that conventional 120-volt devices cannot be plugged into them. The symbol used will vary only slightly from that used for 120-volt convenience outlets in that there are three straight lines through the circle instead of two. Typically each one of these special outlets is on a circuit itself.

Two commonly used specialty outlets are the split-wired outlet and the weatherproof outlet. A split-wired outlet (Fig. 13-13) is any outlet which has the top outlet on a different circuit from the bottom or which has one outlet that may be switched off and on from a wall switch. The weatherproof outlet is used in all exterior locations because it resists damage from weather. It is noted on the plan by use of the standard outlet symbol and the letters WP next to it.

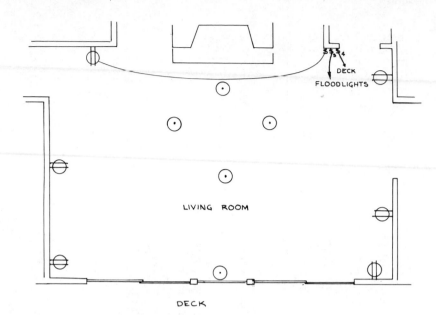

FIGURE 13-12   /   Floor receptacles

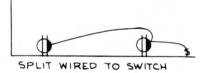

SPLIT WIRED TO SWITCH

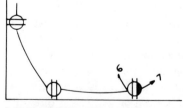

SPLIT WIRED TO DIFFERENT
CIRCUIT

FIGURE 13-13   /   Split-wired outlets

13-12   Luminaires (Lighting Fixtures)

The luminaires used in a residence must be carefully selected with the client. Lighting of some type will be required throughout the house, and quite often exterior lighting will also be required. The size, type, and location of fixtures throughout must be coordinated with the style of the house and the client's preferences. The lighting may come from built-in and surface-mounted ceiling and wall luminaires; floor and table lamps may be used as a supplement, or they may be preferred throughout. The living areas of the house are where the client might prefer various types of accent and indirect lighting to achieve the lighting effects desired.

Fluorescent lighting (tubes) is more efficient than incandescent lighting (bulbs), and it is effective as indirect lighting in valances and coves around rooms and also where high lighting levels are desired such as in bathrooms, work areas in the kitchen, and workshop areas. Objections to fluorescent lighting include its higher initial cost, slow starting, and a tendency to flicker.

Many clients prefer a permanent ceiling fixture that can be turned on from the wall switch, while others prefer that the wall switch activate a convenience outlet to which a table or floor lamp is connected. Small rooms frequently have one central ceiling fixture activated by a wall switch. This provides the general illumination required and may be supplemented by wall, floor, and table fixtures. Shallow closets generally don't require fixtures if there is average room illumination. However, many clients want fixtures in the closets, and, if so, a ceiling fixture may be used. The closet fixture may be operated by a pull chain, but, again, many clients prefer either a wall switch just outside the door or a door-operated switch that turns the light on when the door is opened and shuts it off when the door is closed. The lighting symbols used are shown in Fig. 13-14. For those fixtures activated by a switch, a line must be shown connecting the switch and the fixtures it controls.

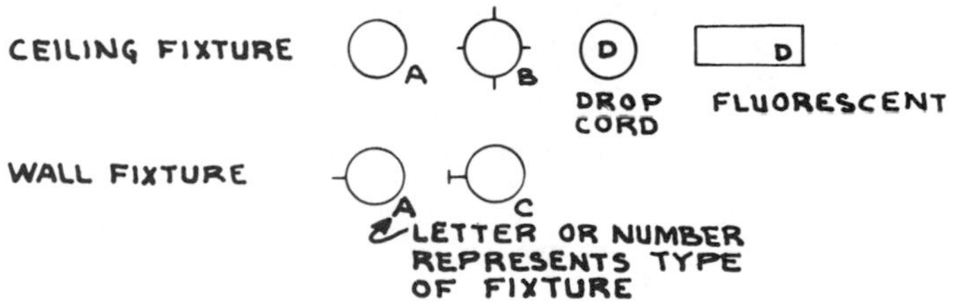

FIGURE 13-14   /   Fixture symbols

13-13   Switches

Wall switches are used to control lighting fixtures in the various rooms of the house, and they may also be used to control convenience outlets. The switch most commonly used is the *toggle switch* which has a small arm that is pushed up and down. Also used is the *mercury switch,* a completely noiseless switch which has mercury in a sealed tube; when the switch is turned on, the mercury completes the circuit.

Wall switches are located 4 ft above the floor and a few inches in from the door frame on the latch side (doorknob side) of the entry door into a room. Generally, they are located just inside the room.

Rooms with two entrances often have two switches controlling the fixture, referred to as 3-way switches. When the fixture is to be controlled from three locations, it will require the use of two 3-way switches and one 4-way switch (Fig. 13-15).

A dimmer control is used when it is desirable to vary the intensity of the light being given off from very low to bright. A delayed action switch is used when it is desirable to have the lights go out about a minute after the switch is turned off.

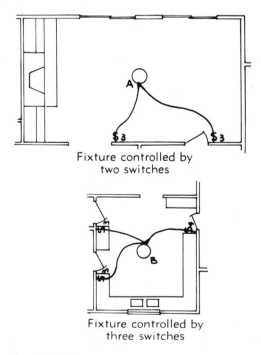

Fixture controlled by
two switches

Fixture controlled by
three switches

FIGURE 13-15   /   Switches

Low-Voltage Switching

The flexibility desired in home lighting systems has led to the development of low-voltage wiring which allows flexibility in the control of fixtures through the use of centrally located remote-control switches that control any or all of the lights in the house.

Low-voltage wiring (about the size of wiring used to wire a door chime) connects the wall switch to a relay center. When the switch is turned on, it sends a low voltage (usually 24 V) to the relay center; this triggers a relay switch which activates the line voltage (120 V) at the light. The savings in wiring costs, the convenience of a centrally located remote-control selector switch, and the elimination of any possible electric shocks at the switch make this increasingly popular in homes.

13-14 Conductors

The wires used to supply electricity throughout the system are called *conductors*. Copper has traditionally been used as the conductor material, and the wiring practices developed over the years have been based on its use. Aluminum conductors are also available and are allowed in many, but not all, codes. Further engineering study is now going on to be certain that all aluminum conductor installations will be as safe as possible. One of the major reasons for using aluminum conductors is that their costs range from one-third to one-half those of copper conductors. Aluminum conductors must be larger than copper conductors that carry the same amperage. This means that for installations requiring that the conductors be placed in conduit, the larger aluminum conductors may require larger conduits. (Conduits are discussed in Sec. 13-15).

The various types of insulation which are placed on the conductor wires have been standardized and are listed in Fig. 13-16. The types of conductors are referred to by the type letter assigned to the insulation used. For example, RHW conductor has a moisture- and heat-resistant rubber insulation, with a maximum operating temperature of 75 °C (167 °F), and it may be used in both dry and wet locations. The maximum operating temperature has an effect on the allowable ampacities which the NEC will allow for the conductor (Fig. 13-40); the higher the maximum operating temperature, the higher the allowable ampacity. All individual conductors must be protected by raceways. Individual conductors in raceways are used extensively in commercial and industrial installations where changes in the electrical requirements are likely to occur.

When two or more conductors, each insulated separately, are grouped together in one common covering, they are referred to as *cables* (Fig. 13-17). These cables are used extensively in electrical wiring, particularly in residences. They are designated according to type of insulation used and where they are used; generally, they do not have to be protected by raceways.

Trade Name	Type Letter	Max. Operating Temp.	Application Provisions	Insulation
Heat-Resistant Rubber	RH	75°C 167°F	Dry locations.	Heat-Resistant Rubber
Heat-Resistant Rubber	RHH	90°C 194°F	Dry locations.	
Moisture and Heat-Resistant Rubber	RHW	75°C 167°F	Dry and wet locations. For over 2000 volts insulation shall be ozone-resistant.	Moisture and Heat-Resistant Rubber
Heat-Resistant Latex Rubber	RUH	75°C 167°F	Dry locations.	90% Un-milled, Grainless Rubber
Moisture-Resistant Latex Rubber	RUW	60°C 140°F	Dry and wet locations.	90% Un-milled, Grainless Rubber
Thermoplastic	T	60°C 140°F	Dry locations.	Flame-Retardant, Thermoplastic Compound
Moisture-Resistant Thermoplastic	TW	60°C 140°F	Dry and wet locations.	Flame-Retardant, Moisture-Resistant Thermoplastic
Heat-Resistant Thermoplastic	THHN	90°C 194°F	Dry locations.	Flame-Retardant, Heat-Resistant Thermoplastic

For insulated aluminum and copper-clad aluminum conductors, the minimum size shall be No. 12.

FIGURE 13-16 / Conductor insulation

Trade Name	Type Letter	Max. Operating Temp.	Application Provisions	Insulation
Moisture- and Heat-Resistant Thermoplastic	THW	75°C 167°F 90°C 194°F	Dry and wet locations. Special applications within electric discharge lighting equipment. Limited to 1000 open-circuit volts or less. (Size 14-8 only as permitted in Section 410-31.)	Flame-Retardant, Moisture- and Heat-Resistant Thermoplastic
Moisture- and Heat-Resistant Thermoplastic	THWN	75°C 167°F	Dry and wet locations.	Flame-Retardant, Moisture- and Heat-Resistant Thermoplastic
Moisture- and Heat-Resistant Cross-Linked Synthetic Polymer	XHHW	90°C 194°F 75°C 167°F	Dry locations. Wet locations.	Flame-Retardant Cross-Linked Synthetic Polymer
Moisture-, Heat- and Oil-Resistant Thermoplastic	MTW	60°C 140°F 90°C 194°F	Machine tool wiring in wet locations as permitted in NFPA Standard No. 79. (See Article 670.) Machine tool wiring in wet locations as permitted in NFPA Standard No. 79. (See Article 670.)	Flame-Retardant, Moisture-, Heat- and Oil-Resistant Thermoplastic
Silicone-Asbestos	SA	90°C 194°F 125°C 257°F	Dry locations. For special application.	Silicone Rubber
Fluorinated Ethylene Propylene	FEP or FEPB	90°C 194°F 200°C 392°F	Dry locations. Dry locations — special applications.	Fluorinated Ethylene Propylene Fluorinated Ethylene Propylene
Modified Fluorinated Ethylene Propylene	FEPW	75°C 90°C	Wet locations. Dry locations.	Modified Fluorinated Ethylene Propylene
Modified Ethylene Tetrafluoro-ethylene	Z	90°C 194°F 150°C 302°F	Dry locations. Dry locations — special applications.	Modified Ethylene Tetrafluoro-ethylene
Modified Ethylene Tetrafluoro-ethylene	ZW	75°C 167°F 90°C 194°F 150°C 302°F	Wet locations. Dry locations. Dry locations — special applications.	Modified Ethylene Tetrafluoro-ethylene

FIGURE 13-16 / Conductor insulation (continued)

Trade Name	Type Letter	Max. Operating Temp.	Application Provisions	Insulation
Varnished Cambric	V	85°C 185°F	Dry locations only. Smaller than No. 6 by special permission.	Varnished Cambric
Asbestos and Varnished Cambric	AVA	110°C 230°F	Dry locations only.	Impregnated Asbestos and Varnished Cambric
Asbestos and Varnished Cambric	AVL	110°C 230°F	Dry and wet locations.	
Asbestos and Varnished Cambric	AVB	90°C 194°F	Dry locations only.	Impregnated Asbestos and Varnished Cambric

Trade Name	Type Letter	Max. Operating Temp.	Application Provisions	Insulation
Asbestos	A	200°C 392°F	Dry locations only. Only for leads within apparatus or within raceways connected to apparatus. Limited to 300 volts.	Asbestos
Asbestos	AA	200°C 392°F	Dry locations only. Only for leads within apparatus or within raceways connected to apparatus or as open wiring. Limited to 300 volts.	Asbestos
Asbestos	AI	125°C 257°F	Dry locations only. Only for leads within apparatus or within raceways connected to apparatus. Limited to 300 volts.	Impregnated Asbestos
Asbestos	AIA	125°C 257°F	Dry locations only. Only for leads within apparatus or within raceways connected to apparatus or as open wiring.	Impregnated Asbestos
Paper		85°C 185°F	For underground service conductors, or by special permission.	Paper

For insulated aluminum and copper-clad aluminum conductors, the minimum size shall be No. 12.

Reproduced by permission from the National Electrical Code, NFPA 70-81, 1981 edition, Copyright National Fire Protection Association, 470 Atlantic Avenue, Boston, Mass. 02210, 1981

FIGURE 13-16 / Conductor insulation (continued)

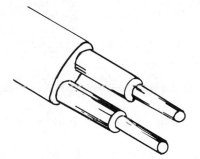

FIGURE 13-17 / Cable

All conductor sizes are given by an AWG or MCM number. Standard available conductor sizes are given in Fig. 13-40. Those conductor sizes based on the American Wire Gauge (from No. 16 to No. 4/0) are listed as AWG—for example, No. 12 AWG. The larger the AWG number, the smaller the conductor. The cross-sectional area of any conductor is listed in *circular* mils, with a circular mil defined as the area of a circle one mil in diameter; then the area is the square of the diameter (in mils). All conductors larger than 4/0 AWG are sized in direct relation to the circular mil and are labeled MCM or one thousand (M) circular mils. A wire with an area of 500,000 circular mils would be called 500 MCM.

13-15 Raceways

A channel which is designed exclusively, and used solely, for holding wires, cables, or bus bars is called a *raceway*. The raceway may be made of metal or insulating material. Metal raceways include rigid and flexible metal conduits, electrical metallic tubing (EMT), and cellular metal raceways, and all may be concealed in the construction or exposed in the space. The most popular insulating raceways are made of cement, asbestos, or impregnated fiber, all of which are commonly used in underground exposures since they are corrosion resistant.

Types

Rigid metal conduit is usually steel (ferrous) or aluminum (nonferrous). The steel conduit has its outside surface coated in zinc to galvanize it, making it resistant to rusting, and zinc is applied to the interior surface of the conduit to make it easier to pull the conductors through it. Steel conduit is also available dipped in a clear, elastic enamel. The enamel coating makes it easier to pull the conductors and provides some resistance to corrosion, but it should not be used outside or where severe corrosive conditions may be present. Rigid metal conduit is extensively used throughout the building and may be placed in the walls, ceiling, and floors of the construction. In addition, corrosion-resistant metal conduit may also be used outside.

Flexible metal conduit is made of a continuous length of galvanized, spirally wound steel strip. It is used primarily when it is necessary to make connections from a junction box to machinery and to go around obstructions. Only the water-proof type may be used in wet locations.

Use of liquid-tight flexible metal conduit is restricted to connections of motors or portable equipment when the connections must be flexible. Further, its use is not allowed where it may be subjected to physical damage, where it may be in contact with rapidly moving parts, where temperatures exceed 60 °C (140 °F), and in hazardous locations.

Plastic-coated galvanized steel conduit is available for locations where the conduit will be subjected to the highly corrosive actions of fumes, gases, or chemicals. Polyvinyl chloride is extruded over the conduit, and all connections are taped with a vinyl, pressure-sensitive electrical insulating tape.

Also available for installations requiring high corrosion-resistance and high strength is an alloy of a mild carbon steel with 2% nickel and 1% copper. This provides a highly corrosion-resistant conduit which is available galvanized or enameled.

Electrical metallic tubing (EMT) is a thin-walled metallic conduit weighing about one-third less than rigid metal conduits. It may be used anywhere except where it will be subject to severe physical damage during or after installation, in cinder concrete or fill underground, or in any hazardous locations. This type of conduit connects to its fittings with set screws, saving the time often required to put screw threads on rigid metal conduits.

Surface metal raceways (Fig. 13-18) must be installed in dry locations and must not be concealed in the construction. This type of raceway is used extensively with metal partitions (Fig. 13-19) where the raceway has a backplate which attaches to the metal stud and a snap-on cover. The NEC limits conductor sizes used in this type of raceway to No. 6 AWG and smaller. The number of conductors allowed must be taken from the raceway manufacturer's data sheet and is based on the amount which Underwriters Laboratories will allow. This type of installation is used extensively when remodeling, adding to existing systems, and building new additions where room arrangements will be subject to changes.

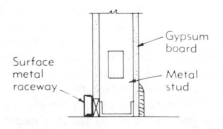

FIGURE 13-18   /   Surface race-way shapes

FIGURE 13-19   /   Surface metal raceway

Underfloor raceways, made of metal or fiber, are commonly used in any building where periodic remodeling or a change in the occupancy may occur. This includes most office buildings and many institutional and industrial buildings. While the size and number of conductors used will depend on the size of the raceway and is controlled by UL, it may also be found in the manufacturer's data. Some typical underfloor raceways are shown in Fig. 13-20. The NEC states that for raceways less than 4 in. wide, a minimum of ¾ in. of wood or concrete must cover the raceway. Raceways are 4 to 8 in. wide, at least 1 in. apart (Fig. 13-21) and must have at least a 1-in. concrete cover. When they are less than 1 in. apart, raceways must have a 1½-in. concrete cover. Also available are *flush raceways* with removable covers (Fig. 13-22).

Cellular metal raceways are installed when the hollow spaces in cellular metal floors are used for the distribution of conductors through the building (Fig. 13-23). The NEC limits conductor size to No. 1 AWG or less, and the number of conductors which may be put in an individual cell (single, enclosed tubular space) is limited to 40% of the cross-sectional cell area, except that the limit does not apply to type AC metal-clad cable or to nonmetallic sheathed cable.

Wireways are sheet-metal troughs with hinged or removable covers. Wireways are used primarily for exposed inside work; if they are used outside, they must be of rain-tight construction. Conductor size is limited to 500 MCM, and the number of conductors is limited to a maximum of 30. The total area of all conductors installed in the wireway is limited to 20% of the interior cross-sectional area of the wireway.

Busways (also called bus ducts) are factory-assembled conductors mounted in a steel housing. They have high current-carrying capacities and are often used as service-entrance conductors, feeders, and subfeeders, and even as branch circuits where large service loads are required. The NEC allows the use of busways only where they will be exposed. They may not be concealed in the construction or installed where they may be subjected to severe physical damage or corrosive vapors.

Installation

Rigid nonmetallic conduit used below ground must be moisture resistant and, when used above ground, also flame retardant and resistant to impact. When used for direct burial, not encased in concrete, the material must be strong enough to withstand any loads which may be placed on it after installation. Typical materials used below ground are fiber, asbestos cement, soapstone, rigid polyvinyl chloride, and high-density polyethylene. Rigid polyvinyl chloride is used above ground.

This type of conduit should *not* be used:

1. Less than 8 ft above the ground, outdoors, unless protected from any possible physical damage.

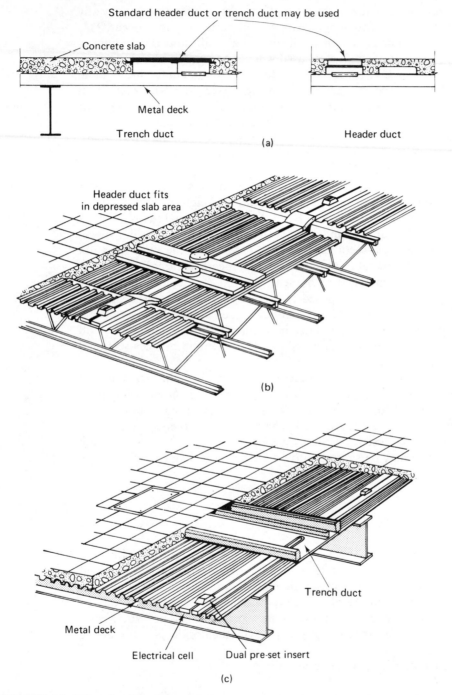

Standard header duct or trench duct may be used

Concrete slab

Metal deck

Trench duct

Header duct

(a)

Header duct fits
in depressed slab area

(b)

Trench duct

Metal deck

Electrical cell

Dual pre-set insert

(c)

FIGURE 13-20 / Raceways

314

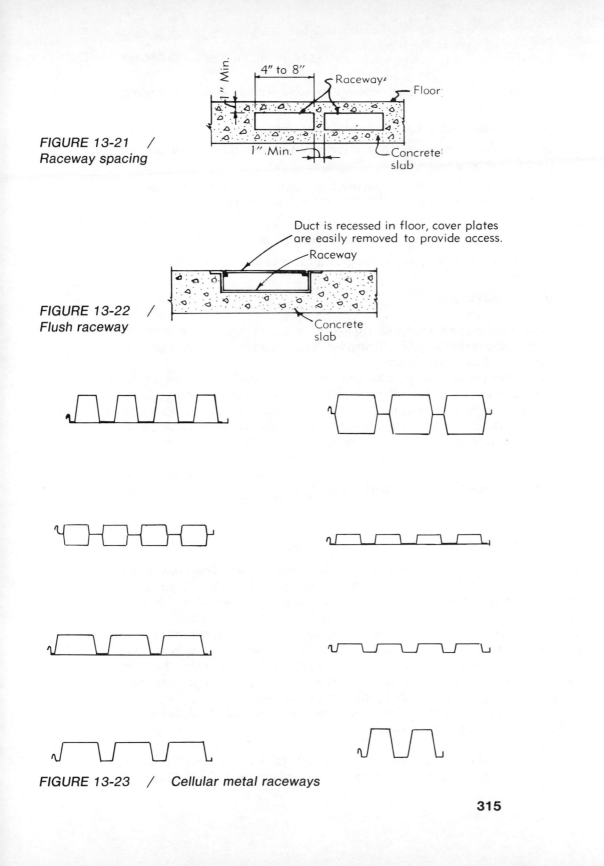

FIGURE 13-21 / Raceway spacing

FIGURE 13-22 / Flush raceway

FIGURE 13-23 / Cellular metal raceways

315

2.   In combustible construction where it is concealed (built into the walls, floors, ceilings).

3.   In any location where it might be subject to physical damage.

4.   In any location where the temperature may be higher than that which the conduit has been tested for.

5.   Where the conductor's maximum insulation temperature is higher than that of the conduit being used.

6.   If there is any possibility that the electrical service running through it may exceed 600 V, unless encased in a minimum of 2 in. of concrete.

7.   In sunlight, unless the conduit being used has been tested and approved for such use.

8.   In hazardous locations.

Rigid metal conduits are connected to their fittings by screwing the threaded fittings onto the threaded conduits. Whenever the conduit has been cut, it must be rethreaded to make the connection.

The number of conductors which may be put in a rigid metal conduit depends on the conductor and conduit sizes. The sizes are selected from Fig. 13-41 and typical examples are shown in Sec. 13-18. The number of conductors which may be put in electrical metallic tubing again depends on the conductor and conduit sizes. The sizes are also selected from Fig. 13-41.

13-16   Electrical System Design

Preliminary Information

Ideally, the electrical designer should be involved from the very beginning in the design of the project. It would be best, in some situations, if he could even be involved in the selection of the site for the project. On a large project it may be necessary to extend high-voltage lines to the project site. This will take time and the owner may have to pay part of the cost. The designer is the person who could best discuss the situation with the power company. All of the utilities (whether sewer, water storm sewer, natural gas lines, etc.) must be checked to determine if they are near the property and whether they can be brought to the property economically or not. Such information is needed early in the design stage.

Before actually beginning the design layout of the project, the designer will need to accumulate certain information:

1.   Determine whether electrical service is available. If it is not, arrangements must be made with the power company to extend service to the building site.

Large projects may require more voltage or more wattage than existing service can supply. Each of these situations requires coordination with the power company as early in the design stage as possible. Costs which may have to be paid by the owner should be thoroughly discussed, written, and given to the owner.

2. Obtain a list from the owner of all the types of equipment, appliances, etc., to be used in the building and which will require electricity. While the electrical designer will know the electrical requirements of much of the equipment, it may be necessary to find the manufacturer's specifications for certain items, such as motor sizes and power required.

3. Working with the architectural designer, locate all of the equipment and appliances on the floor plan. In commercial projects this sometimes takes many meetings with the architects, owners, and manufacturer's representatives. There are times when the type of equipment used and its location must be approved by governmental agencies.

4. Review with the architect where the basic mechanical equipment, such as the service entrance, the power and lighting panels, and the conduit or cable, will be located.

5. Discuss with the owners any future plans for adding to the building, remodeling, constructing other buildings, increasing future equipment requirements, or anything else that could affect the size and location of the electrical service. Many times the service entrance must be sized to anticipate future expansion as well as present building plans. Once the basic information has been gathered, the designer can begin to design the system itself.

Step-by-Step Approach

The system is designed by first drawing, or having a print made, of the floor plan of the building.

1. The receptacles are located first, as discussed in Sec. 13-11. The various types of receptacles available are shown in Fig. 13-10, along with the symbols used to represent each. All switching, sizing of wire, and circuit layout will be done later.

2. Locate on the floor plan all connections to be made for appliances and equipment. This calls for close coordination with the architectural designer since each appliance and piece of equipment must be known in order to locate the receptacles properly. Many times the plans do not show everything which must be connected. For example, a garbage disposal must be connected to power and may even have a switch on the wall to turn it on and off; yet it is seldom shown on the floor plan. Specifically, the electrical designer should ask the architectural designer to list all appliances and equip-

ment in a letter or on the drawing for complete coordination. In addition, the electrical designer will need to know the voltage and amperage required. Typical requirements for various appliances are shown in Fig. 13-24, but these may vary among different manufacturers and should be checked.

The number of appliances or equipment should also be noted. For example, quite often two water heaters are used in residences and both will need connections. In some residences and many commercial buildings, more than one heating and/or cooling unit may be used.

Device	Watts
Air conditioner, central	3,000 to 5,000
Air conditioner, room	800 to 1,500
Clothes dryer	4,000 to 8,000
Garbage disposal	300 to 500
Heat pump	3,000 to 6,000
Humidifier	80 to 200
Iron, hand	600 to 1,200
Lamp, incandescent	10 to 250
Lamp, fluorescent	15 to 60
Radio	40 to 150
Range	8,000 to 14,000
Range, oven	4,000 to 6,000
Range, top	4,000 to 8,000
Television	200 to 400
Water heaters	2,000 to 5,000

FIGURE 13-24   /   *Residential appliance checklist*

3.   Locate the lighting fixtures.

At the same time, the designer must make a list of what types of fixtures will be used throughout and how many watts each will use. This list will be used later when grouping circuits, and it must also be included in the specifications or on the drawings as a "Fixture Schedule" (Fig. 13-25). The list is also used by the electrical estimator when he is determining the cost to be charged for the work, then by the electrical purchasing agent when he orders the material for the project, and finally by the electrician who actually installs the work. Many times the architectural designer decides what fixtures are to be used, often in coordination with the electrical designer.

When a minimum amount of illumination is required, the electrical designer may have to calculate the number and types of lighting fixtures which should be used. A complete discussion of this subject is given in Chapter 14.

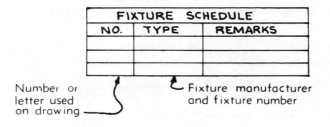

FIGURE 13-25 / Fixture schedule

4. The circuit layout may be an *individual branch circuit* which feeds only one receptacle, light, appliance, or piece of equipment, or a *branch circuit* which supplies power to two or more receptacles, lights, appliances, or equipment. An example of an individual branch circuit would be the circuit to a clothes dryer (240 V) and back to the electrical panel. The NEC states that an individual branch circuit should supply any load required to service that single item.

15 and 20-ampere branch circuits are used for receptacles, light fixtures, and small appliances. They are limited according to what will be connected to them.

a. When the circuit serves fixed appliances and light fixtures or portable appliances, the total of the fixed appliances shall be no more than 50% of the branch circuit rating. Assuming a 15-amp, 120-V branch circuit, it would have a maximum rating of 15 amps × 120 V = 1,800 W (refer to Sec. 13-6 for formula explanation). In this case, the fixed appliances would be limited to 900 W, leaving the other 900 W available to supply the light fixtures or portable appliances also served by the branch circuit. A 20-amp, 120-V branch circuit would have a maximum of 2,400 W.

b. When the load on the circuit will be a continuous operating load, such as for store lights, the total load should not exceed 80% of the circuit rating. The lighting load must include any ballasts, transformers, or auto-transformers which are part of the lighting system. Since a 15-amp branch has a full rating of 1,800 W, the limit would be 80% or 12 amps and 1,440 W. A 20-amp, 2,400-W branch would be limited to 16 amps and 1,920 W of connected load.

c.   When portable appliances will be used on a circuit, the limit for any one portable appliance is 80% of the branch circuit rating.

d.   Receptacles are computed at a load of 1½ amps each and limited to 80% of the rating. This limits a branch circuit serving only receptacles to its rating divided by 1½ amps. For example, a 15-amp circuit is limited to a maximum of 8 outlets and a 20-amp circuit to 10 outlets.

e.   A minimum of two 20-amp circuits is required for small appliances in the kitchen, laundry, dining room, family room, and breakfast or dinette area. These are in addition to the other receptacles required, and no lights or fixed appliances should be connected to these circuits. A typical layout of the two circuits is shown in Fig. 13-26.

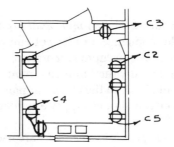

FIGURE 13-26   /   Typical kitchen circuit layout

f.   A minimum of one 20-amp circuit is required as an individual branch to the laundry room receptacle. Any other special requirements, such as an electric clothes dryer requiring 240-V service, must also be added.

   The designer must be certain that he doesn't exceed the code requirements. In actual practice, the designer tends to be a little more conservative, generally limiting a 15-amp branch to 1,000 to 1,200 W and a 20-amp branch to 1,300 to 1,600 W. Receptacles are generally limited to about six on a circuit. This allows the circuit to take additional loads, such as when higher wattage bulbs are used to replace those originally installed and calculated. In addition, more and more small appliances and equipment are being purchased and connected to receptacles (for example, air purifiers, humidifiers, stereos, and the like). The designer must also try to anticipate any future requirements. Such a layout allows for the extension of a circuit if it is necessary to add a light or a receptacle instead of adding a whole new circuit from the panel. If it is possible that the occupant will want to install individual air conditioners, an individual branch circuit to each receptacle required may be desired.

30-, 40-, 50-, and 60-ampere branch circuits will be used for fixed appliances, equipment, and heavy-duty lampholders (in other than residential occupancies). Generally, the electrical requirements of the connected load must be determined, and the total load connected to the branch circuit should be limited to 80% of the branch circuit rating.

The code states that any branch circuit serving a single motor shall have an ampacity (amperage rating) of not less than 125% of the motor's full-load current rating (this is the same as saying that no motor can exceed 80% of the branch circuit rating).

For example, if the motor to operate the air conditioner requires 22 amps, it will require a minimum branch circuit of 22 amps × 1.25% = 27.5 amperes, and a 30-ampere branch circuit will be used. This means that the electrical designer will need the manufacturers' data for all equipment and appliances selected to be certain the proper branch circuit sizes are used. Many times the fuse sizes required for individual branch circuits are listed in the manufacturers' data.

5.   Lay out the switches required to control the lights, appliances, equipment, and any desired receptacles. The discussion of switches in Section 13-13 generally outlines where they are most commonly used, as well as the symbols by which they are identified.

6.   Calculate the electrical load, the total of all general lighting, appliance, and equipment loads in the building.

   a.   *The general lighting load* is calculated for all types of occupancies (Fig. 13-27) based on the unit load given in the table (in watts) times the square footage of the building.

   The square footage shall be determined using the outside dimensions of the building involved and the number of stories. For dwellings, do not include any open porches, garages, or carports. Any unfinished or unused spaces do not have to be included in the square footage *unless* they are adaptable for future use.

   b.   *The appliance and laundry circuit load* is calculated next.

   Since the code requires two 20-amp branch circuits, the load would be based on 1,500 W (from the code) for each branch circuit. In addition, one 20-amp circuit is required for laundry room appliances. This results in a total of three 20-amp branch circuits for appliances.

   c.   Subtotal the general lighting, appliance, and laundry branch circuit loads.

   d.   *The demand load* allowed by the code takes into account the fact that all of the electrical connections will not be in use at one time. While there are limits to this reduction for certain types of occupancies, in a dwelling the first 3,000 W are taken as 100%, and from 3,000 to 120,000

Type of Occupancy	Unit Load per Sq. Ft. (Watts)
Armories and Auditoriums	1
Banks	3½**
Barber Shops and Beauty Parlors	3
Churches	1
Clubs	2
Court Rooms	2
*Dwelling Units	3
Garages — Commercial (storage)	½
Hospitals	2
*Hotels and Motels, including apartment houses without provisions for cooking by tenants	2
Industrial Commercial (Loft) Buildings	2
Lodge Rooms	1½
Office Buildings	3½**
Restaurants	2
Schools	3
Stores	3
Warehouses (storage)	¼
In any of the above occupancies except one-family dwellings and individual dwelling units of multifamily dwellings: Assembly Halls and Auditoriums Halls, Corridors, Closets Storage Spaces	1 ½ ¼

For SI units: one square foot = 0.093 square meter.

* All receptacle outlets of 20-ampere or less rating in one-family and multifamily dwellings and in guest rooms of hotels and motels [except those connected to the receptacle circuits specified in Section 220-3(b)] shall be considered as outlets for general illumination, and no additional load calculations shall be required for such outlets.

** In addition a unit load of 1 watt per square foot shall be included for general purpose receptacle outlets when the actual number of general purpose receptacle outlets is unknown.

Reproduced by permission from the National Electrical Code, NFPA 70-81, 1981 edition, Copyright National Fire Protection Association, 470 Atlantic Avenue, Boston, Mass. 02210, 1981

FIGURE 13-27 / *General lighting loads*

W, only 35% of the load is calculated (from Fig. 13-28). The loads of all other appliances and equipment (motors) must be added to this demand load in order to determine the total service load on the system.

e. To determine the *appliance and equipment load,* all appliances and equipment which will not be on the lines discussed above must be listed along with their electrical requirements. It is most important that the manufacturer's data be used in the design.

The demand load for an *electric range,* consisting of an oven and a countertop cooking unit, is taken from Fig. 13-29. The demand load for a *clothes dryer* is the total amount of power required according to the manufacturer's data. The demand for *fixed appliances* (other than the range, clothes dryer, and air conditioning and space heating equipment) is taken as 100% of the total amount they require; *except* that when there are four or more of these fixed appliances (other than those omitted), the demand load can be taken as 75% of the fixed appliance load.

Lighting Load Feeder Demand Factors

Type of Occupancy	Portion of Lighting Load to Which Demand Factor Applies (wattage)	Demand Factor Percent
Dwelling Units	First 3000 or less at	100
	Next 3001 to 120,000 at	35
	Remainder over 120,000 at	25
*Hospitals	First 50,000 or less at	40
	Remainder over 50,000 at	20
*Hotels and Motels — Including Apartment Houses without Provision for Cooking by Tenants	First 20,000 or less at	50
	Next 20,001 to 100,000 at	40
	Remainder over 100,000 at	30
Warehouses (Storage)	First 12,500 or less at	100
	Remainder over 12,500 at	50
All Others	Total Wattage	100

* The demand factors of this table shall not apply to the computed load of feeders to areas in hospitals, hotels, and motels where the entire lighting is likely to be used at one time; as in operating rooms, ballrooms, or dining rooms.

Reproduced by permission from the National Electrical Code, NFPA 70-81, 1981 edition, Copyright National Fire Protection Association, 470 Atlantic Avenue, Boston, Mass. 02210, 1981

FIGURE 13-28 / Demand factors

Motors, such as those used in *central air conditioners,* have their demand loads calculated as 125% of the motor rating.

The demand load for all of the lighting and appliances has now been calculated, and should be tabulated.

7. Size the minimum service entrance based on the demand load from step 6. Service entrances and the typical sizes used for residential work are discussed in Sec. 13-7. The service entrance size is found by dividing the demand load for the building by the voltage serving the building. Most commonly 240-V service is used.

8. Sizing the feeder (the circuit conductors between the service equipment and the branch overcurrent device—circuit breaker or fuse) is the next step. The feeder size is based on the total demand load calculated. The size is then selected from the table in Fig. 13-40. The table lists the size of the conductor in the left column and the different insulation temperature ratings across the top. Generally, conductors with insulation ratings of 60°, 75°, and 95 °C (140°, 167°, and 185 °F) are most commonly used.

For example a No. 6 copper conductor, 60 °C insulation, will carry 55 amps without subjecting the insulation to damaging heat. The same No. 6 conductor with 75 °C insulation can safely carry 65 amps. These values must be adjusted using a correction factor from the lower portion of the table if the room temperatures are within certain ranges. For example, if the No. 6 conductor with 60 °C insulation will carry 55 amps and if the room temperature is 45 °C (113 °F), the load-carrying capacity would be corrected by a factor of 0.58; 55 amps × 0.58 = 31 amps, the maximum safe allowable amperage.

Reproduced by permission from the National Electrical Code, NFPA 70-81, 1981 edition, Copyright National Fire Protection Association, 470 Atlantic Avenue, Boston, Mass. 02210, 1981

Note 1. Over 12 kW through 27 kW ranges all of same rating. For ranges individually rated more than 12 kW but not more than 27 kW, the maximum demand in Column A shall be increased 5 percent for each additional kW of rating or major fraction thereof by which the rating of individual ranges exceeds 12 kW.

Note 2. Over 12 kW through 27 kW ranges of *unequal ratings*. For ranges individually rated more than 12 kW and of different ratings but none exceeding 27 kW an average value of rating shall be computed by adding together the ratings of all ranges to obtain the total connected load (using 12 kW for any range rated less than 12 kW) and dividing by the total number of ranges; and then the maximum demand in Column A shall be increased 5 percent for each kW or major fraction thereof by which this average value exceeds 12 kW.

Note 3. Over 1¾ kW through 8¾ kW. In lieu of the method provided in Column A, it shall be permissible to add the nameplate ratings of all ranges rated more than 1¾ kW but not more than 8¾ kW and multiply the sum by the demand factors specified in Column B or C for the given number of appliances.

Note 4. Branch-Circuit Load. It shall be permissible to compute the branch-circuit load for one range in accordance with Table 220-19. The branch-circuit load for one wall-mounted oven or one counter-mounted cooking unit shall be the nameplate rating of the appliance. The branch-circuit load for a counter-mounted cooking unit and not more than two wall-mounted ovens, all supplied from a single branch circuit and located in the same room, shall be computed by adding the nameplate rating of the individual appliances and treating this total as equivalent to one range.

Note 5. This table also applies to household cooking appliances rated over 1¾ kW and used in instructional programs.

See Table 220-20 for commercial cooking equipment.

Demand Loads for Household Electric Ranges, Wall-Mounted Ovens, Counter-Mounted Cooking Units, and Other Household Cooking Appliances over 1¾ kW Rating. Column A to be used in all cases except as otherwise permitted in Note 3 below.

NUMBER OF APPLIANCES	Maximum Demand (See Notes) COLUMN A (Not over 12 kW Rating)	Demand Factors Percent (See Note 3) COLUMN B (Less than 3½ kW Rating)	COLUMN C (3½ kW to 8¾ kW Rating)
1	8 kW	80%	80%
2	11 kW	75%	65%
3	14 kW	70%	55%
4	17 kW	66%	50%
5	20 kW	62%	45%
6	21 kW	59%	43%
7	22 kW	56%	40%
8	23 kW	53%	36%
9	24 kW	51%	35%
10	25 kW	49%	34%
11	26 kW	47%	32%
12	27 kW	45%	32%
13	28 kW	43%	32%
14	29 kW	41%	32%
15	30 kW	40%	32%
16	31 kW	39%	28%
17	32 kW	38%	28%
18	33 kW	37%	28%
19	34 kW	36%	28%
20	35 kW	35%	28%
21	36 kW	34%	26%
22	37 kW	33%	26%
23	38 kW	32%	26%
24	39 kW	31%	26%
25	40 kW	30%	26%
26-30	15 kW plus 1 kW for each range	30%	24%
31-40		30%	22%
41-50	25 kW plus ¾ kW for each range	30%	20%
51-60		30%	18%
61 & over		30%	16%

FIGURE 13-29 / Demand for electric ranges

The size of the *neutral feeder conductor* may be determined as 70% of the demand load calculated for the range (step 6) plus all other demand loads on the system.

Now size the feeder conduit. The minimum conduit size is determined for new work by using the table in Fig. 13-41. The conductor sizes are listed in the left column, and conduit (or tubing) sizes across the top. The numbers within the body of the table indicate the maximum number of conductors of any given size which can be put in the conduit in accordance with the NEC. First, find the conductor size being used in the left column. Then move to the right until the number shown is the same as, or larger than, the number of conductors to be placed in the conduit. Then move vertically upward and read the conduit size.

9. Determine the minimum number of lighting circuits by dividing the general lighting load by the voltage, finding the amperage required, and dividing the amperage into circuits.

10. Lay out all branch circuits on the drawing. The branch circuits for receptacles and switching are discussed in Sec. 13-10 and 13-16. The symbols used for the circuits are shown in Fig. 13-13. Remember that all of these general-use receptacles and all lighting will use 120-V service.

11. Select the lighting panel based on the number of circuits and the required amperage. Be certain that all the pole space is not taken up so there is room for expansion. Remember that each 120-V circuit takes up one pole, while each 240-V circuit takes up two poles.

12. Lay out the panel circuits, either on the drawing or in tabulated form as shown in Fig. 13-30. In large designs, with more than one panel, this provides the electrician with a schedule of what circuits will be served from what box. It is also used to note the size of the conductors used for circuits (step 8).

   While a lighting panel layout is not often done for a residence, it is helpful to both the electrician and the designer if one is included. For commercial projects, a panel layout is almost always included. A typical commercial application is shown in Fig. 13-31. The panel drawing for the residence is shown in Fig. 13-34 with each of the branch circuits, and the circuit numbers, noted.

13. Size the conductors for all of the branch circuits, and note them on the panel drawing or in the tabulation. The conductors are sized just as the feeder conductor was sized in step 8.

   Branch circuit conductors to general-purpose receptacles and light fixtures must be a minimum of No. 14 AWG when used with a 15-amp overcurrent device (circuit breaker or fuse). Because No. 14 AWG conductors are limited to a maximum load of 1,725 W and a maximum circuit length of 30 ft, most designers use 20-amp breakers and No. 12 AWG conductors.

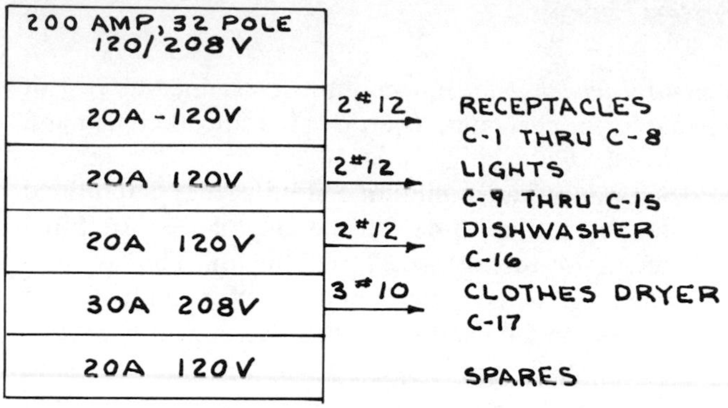

200 AMP, 32 POLE 120/208V

20A - 120V	2 #12	RECEPTACLES C-1 THRU C-8
20A 120V	2 #12	LIGHTS C-9 THRU C-15
20A 120V	2 #12	DISHWASHER C-16
30A 208V	3 #10	CLOTHES DRYER C-17
20A 120V		SPARES

FIGURE 13-30 / Circuits and panels

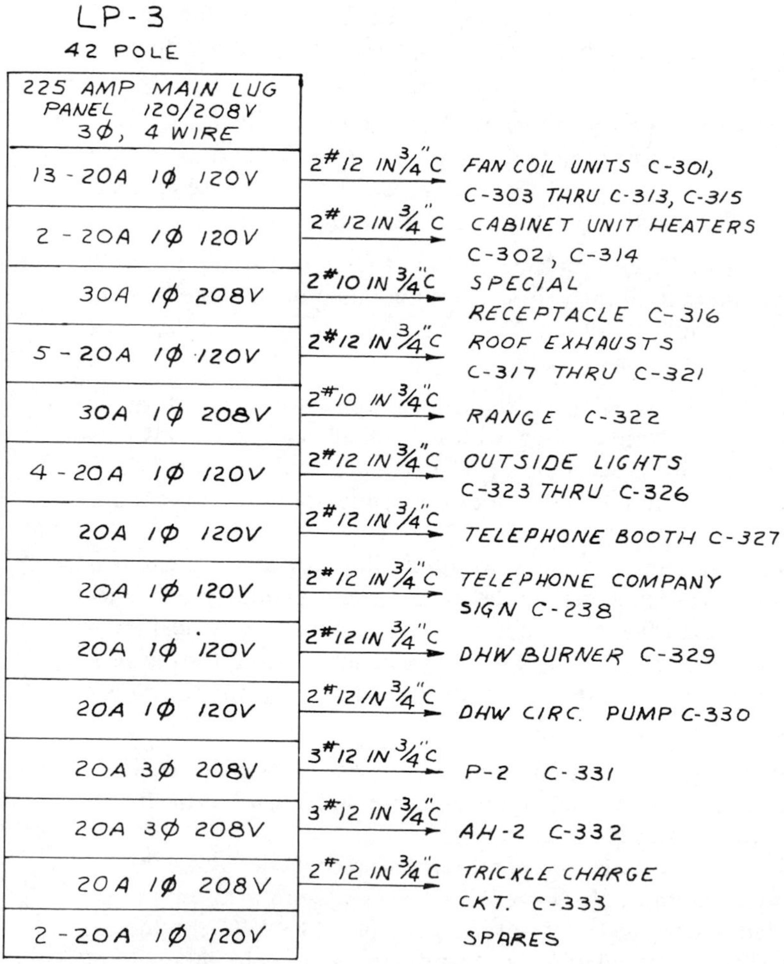

LP-3
42 POLE

225 AMP MAIN LUG PANEL 120/208V 3Φ, 4 WIRE

13 - 20A 1Φ 120V	2 #12 IN 3/4"C	FAN COIL UNITS C-301, C-303 THRU C-313, C-315
2 - 20A 1Φ 120V	2 #12 IN 3/4"C	CABINET UNIT HEATERS C-302, C-314
30A 1Φ 208V	2 #10 IN 3/4"C	SPECIAL RECEPTACLE C-316
5 - 20A 1Φ 120V	2 #12 IN 3/4"C	ROOF EXHAUSTS C-317 THRU C-321
30A 1Φ 208V	2 #10 IN 3/4"C	RANGE C-322
4 - 20A 1Φ 120V	2 #12 IN 3/4"C	OUTSIDE LIGHTS C-323 THRU C-326
20A 1Φ 120V	2 #12 IN 3/4"C	TELEPHONE BOOTH C-327
20A 1Φ 120V	2 #12 IN 3/4"C	TELEPHONE COMPANY SIGN C-238
20A 1Φ 120V	2 #12 IN 3/4"C	DHW BURNER C-329
20A 1Φ 120V	2 #12 IN 3/4"C	DHW CIRC. PUMP C-330
20A 3Φ 208V	3 #12 IN 3/4"C	P-2 C-331
20A 3Φ 208V	3 #12 IN 3/4"C	AH-2 C-332
20A 1Φ 208V	2 #12 IN 3/4"C	TRICKLE CHARGE CKT. C-333
2 - 20A 1Φ 120V		SPARES

FIGURE 13-31 / Commercial panels and circuits

In this design, the conductors for the 20-amp branch circuits serving the receptacles and light fixtures are sized first. The conductor size selected from the table in Fig. 13-40 is No. 12 AWG, RHW, copper. This is noted on the panel drawing as shown (Fig. 13-32):

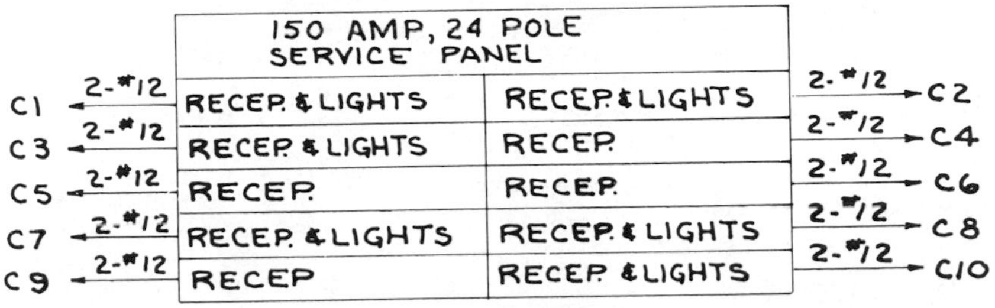

FIGURE 13-32 / Conductor notation

Next, the conductor for each branch circuit is sized, based on the amperage required and the type of conductor being used. The Code requires limiting of such loads to 80% of the ratings. To allow for this, the calculated amperage is multiplied by 1.25.

Example

Air conditioner—11,250 W:

$$11,250 \text{ W} \div 240 \text{ V} = 46.9 \text{ amps}$$
$$46.9 \times 1.25 = 58.7 \text{ amps}$$

From Fig. 13-40, use No. 6 AWG, RHW, copper.
Water heater—3,800 W:

$$3,800 \text{ W} \div 240 \text{ V} = 15.8 \text{ amps}$$
$$15.8 \times 1.25 = 19.75 \text{ amps}$$

From Fig. 13-40, use No. 12 AWG, RHW, copper.
Note the conductor sizes for each branch circuit on the panel drawing as shown in Fig. 13-33.

Whenever there will be more than three conductors in a raceway, the allowable ampacity of each conductor must be reduced. The amount of reduction required is shown in Fig. 13-40, note 8.

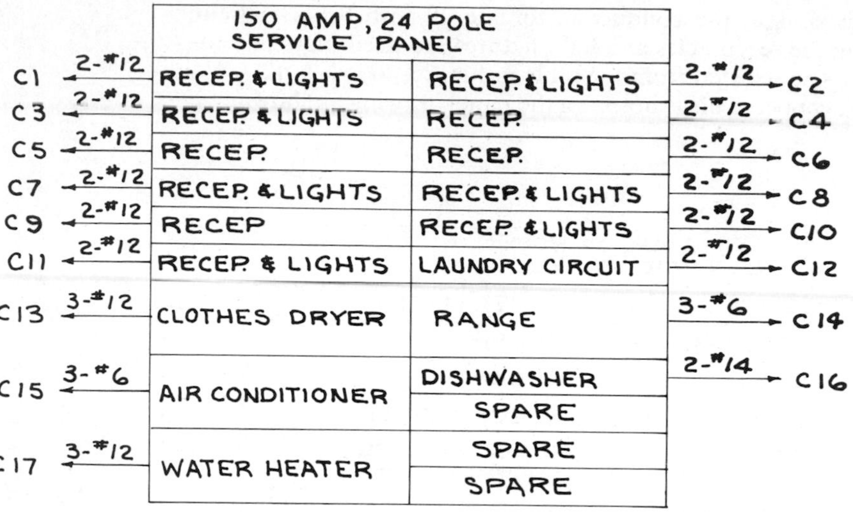

150 AMP, 24 POLE SERVICE PANEL	
C1 2-#12 RECEP. & LIGHTS	RECEP. & LIGHTS 2-#12 C2
C3 2-#12 RECEP. & LIGHTS	RECEP. 2-#12 C4
C5 2-#12 RECEP.	RECEP. 2-#12 C6
C7 2-#12 RECEP. & LIGHTS	RECEP. & LIGHTS 2-#12 C8
C9 2-#12 RECEP.	RECEP. & LIGHTS 2-#12 C10
C11 2-#12 RECEP. & LIGHTS	LAUNDRY CIRCUIT 2-#12 C12
C13 3-#12 CLOTHES DRYER	RANGE 3-#6 C14
C15 3-#6 AIR CONDITIONER	DISHWASHER 2-#14 C16
	SPARE
C17 3-#12 WATER HEATER	SPARE
	SPARE

FIGURE 13-33 / Conductor notation

For example, if six No. 10 AWG copper conductors are placed in a 1-in. conduit, according to reduction values in Fig. 13-40, the allowable ampacity will be reduced to 80% of the allowable values given in Fig. 13-40. The allowable ampacity for No. 10 AWG copper conductors is 30. Since this must be reduced by 80%:

$$30 \times 0.80 = 24 \text{ amps (allowed ampacity)}$$

14. On commercial, industrial, and institutional projects, the electrical supply feeds into several panels, often broken up into *lighting panels* (to serve light fixtures and general-purpose receptacles) and *power panels* (to supply the electricity to all appliances and equipment in the project). Quite often there are several of each type of panel.

In such a design, the circuits are labeled with a circuit number and a panel number. For example, C-3, LP-1 would be circuit 3 from lighting panel 1. Typical examples of this type of notation are shown in Fig. 13-34.

FIGURE 13-34 / Typical commercial notation

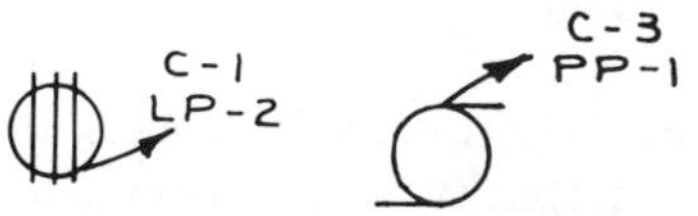

In such a design it is also necessary to have a feeder from the service entrance to the main distribution panel which is in turn connected to the lighting and power panels by feeders (Fig. 13-35). Each of the feeders must be sized in accordance with the code.

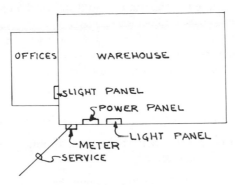

FIGURE 13-35   /   Typical commercial panel layout

13-17   Optional Calculation for a One-Family Residence

There is an optional method of calculating the demand load for a residence, based on percentages of the loads listed in Fig. 13-36. Under the optional method of calculating the demand load for a one-family residence, a much smaller service is required (117.6 amps compared with 143 amps), and a 150-amp service would still be used. Based on amps, the feeder required (from Fig. 13-40) is a No. 1 AWG, RHW, copper conductor.

Neutral feeder calculations are the same as for the feeder *except* for the reduced range load.

Optional Calculation for Dwelling Unit

Load (in kW or kVA)	Demand Factor Percent
Air conditioning and cooling, including heat pump compressors	100
Central electric space heating	65
Less than four separately controlled electric space heating units	65
First 10 kW of all other load	100
Remainder of other load	40

Reproduced by permission from the National Electrical Code, NFPA 70-81, 1981 edition, Copyright National Fire Protection Association, 470 Atlantic Avenue, Boston, Mass. 02210, 1981

FIGURE 13-36   /   Optional residential demand load

13-18   Conduit Sizing

Conduits and raceways are discussed in Sec. 13-15, and in this section, the sizing of rigid metal conduit and electrical metallic tubing is covered. The size of the conduit is directly related to the number and size of the conductors which will be placed in it.

All of the tables to be used are based on the NEC's maximum percentages of the conduit that can be filled with conductors. Based on these percentages, the table in Fig. 13-41 gives the maximum number of conductors which can be placed in the trade (standard) sizes of conduit or tubing listed. For example:

1.   What size conduit is required to run three No. 3 AWG conductors in?

From Fig. 13-41, 1¼-in. conduit or tubing is required for three No. 3 AWG conductors.

2.   How many No. 1 AWG conductors may be placed in 2-in. conduit or tubing?

A maximum of five No. 1 AWG conductors may be placed in 2-in. conduit or tubing.

Remember that when more than three conductors are placed in any raceway (including conduit or tubing), the allowable ampacity of each conductor is derated (reduced) in accordance with note 8 for Fig. 13-40.

13-19   Voltage Drop

The NEC limits the amount of voltage drop (the loss of voltage due to resistance in the conductors) for power, heating, and lighting (or any combination of these loads) to 3%. In addition, the maximum total voltage drop for feeders and branch circuits should be no more than 5%, leaving 2% for branch circuit loss. In most residences, and small buildings, the voltage drop in the feeder is small because the length of the conductor is short. The voltage drop can be calculated by using the formula:

$$\text{Voltage drop} = \frac{I \times L \times R}{1,000}$$

where

I = current carried in the conductor (amps)

L = length of current-carrying conductor (ft)

R = resistance of conductor (ohms per 1,000 ft)

1,000 = constant (converting R per 1,000 ft to R per ft)

Example

Given: The commercial building shown in Fig. 13-37.

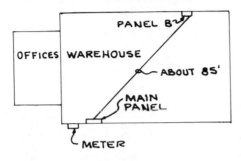

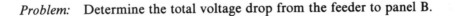

FIGURE 13-37   /   Voltage drop

Problem: Determine the total voltage drop from the feeder to panel B.

The feeder to panel B has an I of 93 amps, and the conductor is No. 3 AWG copper. The length of the conductor from the main distribution panel to panel B is about 85 ft. Resistances for the various sizes of copper and aluminum conductors are given in Fig. 13-38. This table lists the DC resistances in ohms per M (1,000) ft at 25 °C (77 °F), which are then converted to AC resistances by multiplying by the factors also given in Fig. 13-39. For a No. 3 conductor, there is no revision; but note that as the conductors get larger, so do the factors. From Fig. 13-38, the resistance for a No. 3 conductor is 0.169 ohms per 1,000 ft.

The total voltage drop for the feeder to panel B is:

$$\frac{93 \text{ amps} \times 85 \text{ ft} \times 0.169 \text{ ohms}}{1,000} = 1.34 \text{ V}$$

The percentage of voltage drop, in this case, would be 1.34 V (voltage drop) divided by 240 (voltage), or less than 1%.

Example

Given: A residence.

Problem: Check the voltage drop in the branch circuit to the farthest circuit from the panel, 90 ft away.

Properties of Conductors

Size AWG, MCM	Area Cir. Mils	Concentric Lay Stranded Conductors			Bare Conductors		DC Resistance Ohms/M Ft. At 25°C, 77°F.		
		No. Wires	Diam. Each Wire Inches		Diam. Inches	*Area Sq. Inches	Copper		Aluminum
							Bare Cond.	Tin'd. Cond.	
18	1620	Solid	.0403		.0403	.0013	6.51	6.79	10.7
16	2580	Solid	.0508		.0508	.0020	4.10	4.26	6.72
14	4110	Solid	.0641		.0641	.0032	2.57	2.68	4.22
12	6530	Solid	.0808		.0808	.0051	1.62	1.68	2.66
10	10380	Solid	.1019		.1019	.0081	1.018	1.06	1.67
8	16510	Solid	.1285		.1285	.0130	.6404	.659	1.05
8	16510	7	.0486		.1458	.0167	.653	.679	1.07
6	26240	7	.0612		.184	.027	.410	.427	.674
4	41740	7	.0772		.232	.042	.259	.269	.424
3	52620	7	.0867		.260	.053	.205	.213	.336
2	66360	7	.0974		.292	.067	.162	.169	.266
1	83690	19	.0664		.332	.087	.129	.134	.211
0	105600	19	.0745		.372	.109	.102	.106	.168
00	133100	19	.0837		.418	.137	.0811	.0843	.133
000	167800	19	.0940		.470	.173	.0642	.0668	.105
0000	211600	19	.1055		.528	.219	.0509	.0525	.0836
250	250000	37	.0822		.575	.260	.0431	.0449	.0708
300	300000	37	.0900		.630	.312	.0360	.0374	.0590
350	350000	37	.0973		.681	.364	.0308	.0320	.0505
400	400000	37	.1040		.728	.416	.0270	.0278	.0442
500	500000	37	.1162		.813	.519	.0216	.0222	.0354
600	600000	61	.0992		.893	.626	.0180	.0187	.0295
700	700000	61	.1071		.964	.730	.0154	.0159	.0253
750	750000	61	.1109		.998	.782	.0144	.0148	.0236
800	800000	61	.1145		1.030	.833	.0135	.0139	.0221
900	900000	61	.1215		1.090	.933	.0120	.0123	.0197
1000	1000000	61	.1280		1.150	1.039	.0108	.0111	.0177
1250	1250000	91	.1172		1.289	1.305	.00863	.00888	.0142
1500	1500000	91	.1284		1.410	1.561	.00719	.00740	.0118
1750	1750000	127	.1174		1.526	1.829	.00616	.00634	.0101
2000	2000000	127	.1255		1.630	2.087	.00539	.00555	.00885

* Area given is that of a circle having a diameter equal to the overall diameter of a stranded conductor.

The values given in the table are those given in Handbook 100 of the National Bureau of Standards except that those shown in the 8th column are those given in Specification B33 of the American Society for Testing and Materials, and those shown in the 9th column are those given in Standard No. S-19-81 of the Insulated Power Cable Engineers Association and Standard No. WC3-1969 of the National Electrical Manufacturers Association.

The resistance values given in the last three columns are applicable only to direct current. When conductors larger than No. 4/0 are used with alternating current, the multiplying factors in Table 9 compensate for skin effect.

Reproduced by permission from the National Electrical Code, NFPA 70-81, 1981 edition, Copyright National Fire Protection Association, 470 Atlantic Avenue, Boston, Mass. 02210, 1981

FIGURE 13-38 / Properties of conductors

The circuit has four receptacles on it, and its load is about 1,440 (4 duplex outlets at 180 W each = 4 × 2 × 180 = 1,440 W). This 1,440 W gives an amperage of 1,440 W ÷ 120 V = 12.0 amps. The approximate length of the branch circuit is 90 ft, and the resistance of a No. 12 AWG conductor is 1.68 ohms per 1,000 ft.

$$\frac{12.0 \text{ amps} \times 90 \text{ ft} \times 0.168 \text{ ohms}}{1,000} = 1.81 \text{ V}$$

The percentage of voltage drop, in this case, would be 1.81 V (voltage drop) divided by 120 (voltage) or about 1.5%, well within the 2% drop that is considered good design practice.

**Multiplying Factors for Converting DC
Resistance to 60-Hertz AC Resistance**

Size	Multiplying Factor			
	For Nonmetallic-Sheathed Cables in Air or Nonmetallic Conduit		For Metallic-Sheathed Cables or all Cables in Metallic Raceways	
	Copper	Aluminum	Copper	Aluminum
Up to 3 AWG	1.	1.	1.	1.
2	1.	1.	1.01	1.00
1	1.	1.	1.01	1.00
0	1.001	1.000	1.02	1.00
00	1.001	1.001	1.03	1.00
000	1.002	1.001	1.04	1.01
0000	1.004	1.002	1.05	1.01
250 MCM	1.005	1.002	1.06	1.02
300 MCM	1.006	1.003	1.07	1.02
350 MCM	1.009	1.004	1.08	1.03
400 MCM	1.011	1.005	1.10	1.04
500 MCM	1.018	1.007	1.13	1.06
600 MCM	1.025	1.010	1.16	1.08
700 MCM	1.034	1.013	1.19	1.11
750 MCM	1.039	1.015	1.21	1.12
800 MCM	1.044	1.017	1.22	1.14
1000 MCM	1.067	1.026	1.30	1.19
1250 MCM	1.102	1.040	1.41	1.27
1500 MCM	1.142	1.058	1.53	1.36
1750 MCM	1.185	1.079	1.67	1.46
2000 MCM	1.233	1.100	1.82	1.56

Reproduced by permission from the National Electrical Code, NFPA 70-81, 1981 edition, Copyright National Fire Protection Association, 470 Atlantic Avenue, Boston, Mass. 02210, 1981

FIGURE 13-39 / *Multiplying factors*

Allowable Ampacities of Insulated Conductors
Rated 0-2000 Volts, 60° to 90°C

Not More Than Three Conductors in Raceway or Cable or Earth
(Directly Buried), Based on Ambient Temperature of 30°C (86°F)

Size	Temperature Rating of Conductor, See Table 310-13								Size
	60°C (140°F)	75°C (167°F)	85°C (185°F)	90°C (194°F)	60°C (140°F)	75°C (167°F)	85°C (185°F)	90°C (194°F)	
AWG MCM	TYPES †RUW, †T, †TW, †UF	TYPES †FEPW, †RH, †RHW, †RUH, †THW, †THWN, †XHHW, †USE, †ZW	TYPES V, MI	TYPES TA, TBS, SA, AVB, SIS, †FEP, †FEPB, †RHH, †THHN, †XHHW*	TYPES †RUW, †T, †TW, †UF	TYPES †RH, †RHW, †RUH, †THW, †THWN, †XHHW, †USE	TYPES V, MI	TYPES TA, TBS, SA, AVB, SIS, †RHH, †THHN, †XHHW*	AWG MCM
	COPPER				ALUMINUM OR COPPER-CLAD ALUMINUM				
18	. . . .	. . . .	. . . .	14	. . . .	. . . .	. . . .	. . . .	. . . .
16	. . . .	. . . .	18	18	. . . .	. . . .	. . . .	. . . .	. . . .
14	20†	20†	25	25†	. . . .	. . . .	. . . .	. . . .	. . . .
12	25†	25†.	30	30†	20†	20†	25	25†	12
10	30†	35†	40	40†	25†	30†	30	35†	10
8	40	50	55	55	30	40	40	45	8
6	55	65	70	75	40	50	55	60	6
4	70	85	95	95	55	65	75	75	4
3	85	100	110	110	65	75	85	85	3
2	95	115	125	130	75	90	100	100	2
1	110	130	145	150	85	100	110	115	1
0	125	150	165	170	100	120	130	135	0
00	145	175	190	195	115	135	145	150	00
000	165	200	215	225	130	155	170	175	000
0000	195	230	250	260	150	180	195	205	0000
250	215	255	275	290	170	205	220	230	250
300	240	285	310	320	190	230	250	255	300
350	260	310	340	350	210	250	270	280	350
400	280	335	365	380	225	270	295	305	400
500	320	380	415	430	260	310	335	350	500
600	355	420	460	475	285	340	370	385	600
700	385	460	500	520	310	375	405	420	700
750	400	475	515	535	320	385	420	435	750
800	410	490	535	555	330	395	430	450	800
900	435	520	565	585	355	425	465	480	900
1000	455	545	590	615	375	445	485	500	1000
1250	495	590	640	665	405	485	525	545	1250
1500	520	625	680	705	435	520	565	585	1500
1750	545	650	705	735	455	545	595	615	1750
2000	560	665	725	750	470	560	610	630	2000
CORRECTION FACTORS									
Ambient Temp. °C	For ambient temperatures over 30°C, multiply the ampacities shown above by the appropriate correction factor to determine the maximum allowable load current.								Ambient Temp. °F
31-40	.82	.88	.90	.91	.82	.88	.90	.91	86-104
41-45	.71	.82	.85	.87	.71	.82	.85	.87	105-113
46-50	.58	.75	.80	.82	.58	.75	.80	.82	114-122
51-60	. . . .	.58	.67	.71	. . . .	.58	.67	.71	123-141
61-70	. . . .	.35	.52	.58	. . . .	.35	.52	.58	142-158
71-80	. . . .	. . . .	.30	.41	. . . .	. . . .	.30	.41	159-176

† The load current rating and the overcurrent protection for conductor types marked with an obelisk (†) shall not exceed 15 amperes for 14 AWG, 20 amperes for 12 AWG, and 30 amperes for 10 AWG copper; or 15 amperes for 12 AWG and 25 amperes for 10 AWG aluminum and copper-clad aluminum.

* For dry locations only. See 75°C column for wet locations.

Reproduced by permission from the National Electrical Code, NFPA 70-81, 1981 edition, Copyright National Fire Protection Association, 470 Atlantic Avenue, Boston, Mass. 02210, 1981

FIGURE 13-40   /   Allowable ampacities of insulated conductors

Allowable Ampacities of Insulated Conductors
Rated 0-2000 Volts, 60° to 90°C

Single conductors in free air, based on ambient temperature of 30°C (86°F).

Size	Temperature Rating of Conductor, See Table 310-13								Size
	60°C (140°F)	75°C (167°F)	85°C (185°F)	90°C (194°F)	60°C (140°F)	75°C (167°F)	85°C (185°F)	90°C (194°F)	
AWG MCM	TYPES †RUW, †T, †TW	TYPES †FEPW, †RH, †RHW, †RUH, †THW, †THWN, †XHHW, †ZW	TYPES V, MI	TYPES TA, TBS, SA, AVB, SIS, †FEP, †FEPB, †RHH †THHN, †XHHW*	TYPES †RUW, †T, †TW	TYPES †RH, †RHW, †RUH, †THW, †THWN, †XHHW	TYPES V, MI	TYPES TA, TBS, SA, AVB, SIS, |RHH, †THHN, †XHHW*	AWG MCM
	COPPER				ALUMINUM OR COPPER-CLAD ALUMINUM				
18	. . . .	. . . .	. . . .	18	. . . .	. . . .	. . . .	. . . .	. . . .
16	. . . .	. . . .	23	24	. . . .	. . . .	. . . .	. . . .	. . . .
14	25†	30†	30	35†	. . . .	. . . .	30	35†	. . . .
12	30†	35†	40	40†	25†	30†	40	40†	12
10	40†	50†	55	55†	35†	40†	60	60	10
8	60	70	75	80	45	55	60	60	8
6	80	95	100	105	60	75	80	80	6
4	105	125	135	140	80	100	105	110	4
3	120	145	160	165	95	115	125	130	3
2	140	170	185	190	110	135	145	150	2
1	165	195	215	220	130	155	165	175	1
0	195	230	250	260	150	180	195	205	0
00	225	265	290	300	175	210	225	235	00
000	260	310	335	350	200	240	265	275	000
0000	300	360	390	405	235	280	305	315	0000
250	340	405	440	455	265	315	345	355	250
300	375	445	485	505	290	350	380	395	300
350	420	505	550	570	330	395	430	445	350
400	455	545	595	615	355	425	465	480	400
500	515	620	675	700	405	485	525	545	500
600	575	690	750	780	455	540	595	615	600
700	630	755	825	855	500	595	650	675	700
750	655	785	855	885	515	620	675	700	750
800	680	815	885	920	535	645	700	725	800
900	730	870	950	985	580	700	760	785	900
1000	780	935	1020	1055	625	750	815	845	1000
1250	890	1065	1160	1200	710	855	930	960	1250
1500	980	1175	1275	1325	795	950	1035	1075	1500
1750	1070	1280	1395	1445	875	1050	1145	1185	1750
2000	1155	1385	1505	1560	960	1150	1250	1335	2000
CORRECTION FACTORS									
Ambient Temp. °C	For ambient temperatures over 30°C, multiply the ampacities shown above by the appropriate correction factor to determine the maximum allowable load current.								Ambient Temp. °F
31-40	.82	.88	.90	.91	.82	.88	.90	.91	86-104
41-45	.71	.82	.85	.87	.71	.82	.85	.87	105-113
46-50	.58	.75	.80	.82	.58	.75	.80	.82	114-122
51-60	. . . .	.58	.67	.71	. . . .	.58	.67	.71	123-141
61-70	. . . .	.35	.52	.58	. . . .	.35	.52	.58	142-158
71-80	. . . .	. . . .	.30	.41	. . . .	. . . .	.30	.41	159-176

† The load current rating and the overcurrent protection for conductor types marked with an obelisk (†) shall not exceed 20 amperes for 14 AWG, 25 amperes for 12 AWG, and 40 amperes for 10 AWG copper, or 20 amperes for 12 AWG and 30 amperes for 10 AWG aluminum and copper-clad aluminum.
* For dry locations only. See 75°C column for wet locations.

Reproduced by permission from the National Electrical Code, NFPA 70-81, 1981 edition, Copyright National Fire Protection Association, 470 Atlantic Avenue, Boston, Mass. 02210, 1981

FIGURE 13-40 / Allowable ampacities of insulated conductors (continued)

Notes to Tables

1. **Explanation of Tables.** For explanation of Type Letters, and for recognized size of conductors for the various conductor insulations, see Section 310-13. For installation requirements, see Sections 310-1 through 310-10, and the various articles of this Code. For flexible cords, see Tables 400-4 and 400-5.

2. **Application of Tables.** For open wiring on insulators and for concealed knob-and-tube wiring, the allowable ampacities of Tables 310-17 and 310-19 shall be used. For all other recognized wiring methods, the allowable ampacities in Tables 310-16 and 310-18 shall be used, unless otherwise provided in this Code.

3. **Three-Wire, Single-Phase Dwelling Services.** In dwelling units, conductors, as listed below, shall be permitted to be utilized as three-wire, single-phase, service-entrance conductors and the three-wire, single-phase feeder that carries the total current supplied by that service.

Conductor Types and Sizes
RH-RHH-RHW-THW-THWN-THHN-XHHW

Copper	Aluminum and Copper-Clad AL	Service Rating in Amps
AWG	AWG	
4	2	100
3	1	110
2	1/0	125
1	2/0	150
1/0	3/0	175
2/0	4/0	200

4. **Type MC Cable.** The ampacities of Type MC cables are determined by the temperature limitation of the insulated conductors incorporated within the cable. Hence the ampacities of Type MC cable may be determined from the columns in Tables 310-16 and 310-18 applicable to the type of insulated conductors employed within the cable.

5. **Bare Conductors.** Where bare conductors are used with insulated conductors, their allowable ampacities shall be limited to that permitted for the insulated conductors of the same size.

6. **Mineral-Insulated, Metal-Sheathed Cable.** The temperature limitation on which the ampacities of mineral-insulated, metal-sheathed cable are based is determined by the insulating materials used in the end seal. Termination fittings incorporating unimpregnated, organic, insulating materials are limited to 85°C operation.

7. **Type MTW Machine Tool Wire.** The ampacities of Type MTW wire are specified in Table 200-B of the Standard for Electrical Metalworking Machine Tools and Plastics Processing Machinery (NFPA 79-1980).

8. **More than Three Conductors in a Raceway or Cable.** Where the number of conductors in a raceway or cable exceeds three, the ampacity shall be as given in Tables 310-16 and 310-18, but the maximum allowable load current of each conductor shall be reduced as shown in the following table:

Number of Conductors	Percent of Values in Tables 310-16 and 310-18
4 thru 6	80
7 thru 24	70
25 thru 42	60
43 and above	50

Where single conductors or multiconductor cables are stacked or bundled without maintaining spacing and are not installed in raceways, the maximum allowable load current of each conductor shall be reduced as shown in the above table.

Exception No. 1: When conductors of different systems, as provided in Section 300-3, are installed in a common raceway the derating factors shown above shall apply to the number of power and lighting (Articles 210, 215, 220, and 230) conductors only.

Exception No. 2: The derating factors of Sections 210-22(c), 220-2(a) and 220-10(b) shall not apply when the above derating factors are also required.

Exception No. 3: For conductors installed in cable trays, the provisions of Section 318-10 shall apply.

9. **Overcurrent Protection.** Where the standard ratings and settings of overcurrent devices do not correspond with the ratings and settings allowed for conductors, the next higher standard rating and setting shall be permitted.

Exception: As limited in Section 240-3.

10. **Neutral Conductor.**

(a) A neutral conductor which carries only the unbalanced current from other conductors, as in the case of normally balanced circuits of three or more conductors, shall not be counted when applying the provisions of Note 8.

(b) In a 3-wire circuit consisting of 2-phase wires and the neutral of a 4-wire, 3-phase wye-connected system, a common conductor carries approximately the same current as the other conductors and shall be counted when applying the provisions of Note 8.

(c) On a 4-wire, 3-phase wye circuit where the major portion of the load consists of electric-discharge lighting, data processing, or similar equipment, there are harmonic currents present in the neutral conductor and the neutral shall be considered to be a current-carrying conductor.

11. **Grounding Conductor.** A grounding conductor shall not be counted when applying the provisions of Note 8.

12. **Voltage Drop.** The allowable ampacities in Tables 310-16 through 310-19 are based on temperature alone and do not take voltage drop into consideration.

FIGURE 13-40 / Allowable ampacities of insulated conductors (continued)

Reproduced by permission from the National Electrical Code, NFPA 70-81, 1981 edition, Copyright National Fire Protection Association, 470 Atlantic Avenue, Boston, Mass. 02210, 1981.

Maximum Number of Conductors in Trade Sizes of Conduit or Tubing

(Based on Table 1, Chapter 9)

Type Letters	Conductor Size AWG, MCM	½	¾	1	1¼	1½	2	2½	3	3½	4	4½	5	6
RHW,	14	3	6	10	18	25	41	58	90	121	155			
	12	3	5	9	15	21	35	50	77	103	132			
	10	2	4	7	13	18	29	41	64	86	110	138		
	8	1	2	4	7	9	16	22	35	47	60	75	94	137
RHH	6	1	1	2	5	6	11	15	24	32	41	51	64	93
	4	1	1	1	3	5	8	12	18	24	31	39	50	72
(with	3	1	1	1	3	4	7	10	16	22	28	35	44	63
outer	2		1	1	1	4	6	9	14	19	24	31	38	56
covering)	1		1	1	1	3	5	7	11	14	18	23	29	42
	0		1	1	1	2	4	6	9	12	16	20	25	37
	00			1	1	1	3	5	8	11	14	18	22	32
	000			1	1	1	3	4	7	9	12	15	19	28
	0000						2	4	6	8	10	13	16	24
	250				1	1	1	3	5	6	8	11	13	19
	300				1	1	1	3	4	5	7	9	11	17
	350				1	1	1	2	4	5	6	8	10	15
	400				1		1	1	3	4	6	7	9	14
	500				1	1	1	1	3	4	5	6	8	11
	600					1	1	1	2	3	4	5	6	9
	700					1	1	1	1	3	3	4	6	8
	750						1	1	1	3	3	4	5	8

Reproduced by permission from the National Electrical Code, NFPA 70-81, 1981 edition, Copyright National Fire Protection Association, 470 Atlantic Avenue, Boston, Mass. 02210, 1981.

FIGURE 13-41 / Conductors in conduit

Questions

13-1. Briefly describe what the Underwriters Laboratories does.

13-2. What does it mean when an electric fixture has a UL tag on it?

13-3. Define the following terms:
   a. Service entrance
   b. Service panel
   c. Feeder circuits
   d. Branch circuits
   e. Receptacles
   f. Luminaires

13-4. When is a *split-wired outlet* used?

13-5. What is the difference between conductors and cable?

13-6. When are raceways used, and what are three commonly used types?

13-7. Show, in a formula, the relationship of amps, volts, and ohms; then briefly describe each.

13-8. What type of information will the designer need to accumulate before actually beginning to design the electrical system?

13-9. What is an *individual branch circuit,* and when is it used?

13-10. How many circuits are required to accommodate kitchen appliances?

13-11. What is meant by the *demand load* in reference to the electrical load of the building?

13-12. When selecting the panel size, what considerations for the future should be taken into account?

13-13. How is the general lighting load for a building determined?

13-14. How is the minimum service entrance determined?

13-15. In selecting the service entrance size, what should be considered?

Chapter 14

Lighting Systems and Design

14-1 Overview

The basic reasons for providing light in a space are to make the objects in the space visible and to allow the conduct of activities within the space. Part of the light required may be provided by windows and skylights which allow sunlight to enter the space. Many times this sunlight is sufficient to provide all the light required on sunny days. However, as the sun moves, it shines first on the east portion of the building, and then moves toward the west as the day progresses. This means that windows facing the east are subjected to the strong rays of the sun in the morning, but must count on reflected light later in the day. Windows facing north get no direct sun, while windows facing south get a considerable amount. And on cloudy days, no direct sunlight is available. In effect, while natural light from windows and skylights can be counted on to provide some general light, it does not provide a controlled light source by which to perform activities.

Therefore, in most projects, at least some electric lighting must be introduced to provide a constant, controlled amount of light so that the space can be used whenever necessary, whether sunny or cloudy, day or night. This chapter discusses the terminology and procedures used to arrive at a lighting design that will provide the required amount of light.

Since lighting should be an integral part of the building, the lighting designer must work closely with the architect to achieve a lighting solution which blends with and becomes a part of the architectural design.

14-2   Terminology

Light: That radiant energy which has a wavelength that the human eye can see. Light from the sun may be *sunlight* or it may be *skylight.* Light which is produced electrically should be referred to as *electric light* and not artificial light (as it is commonly called). This is because, even though it is there because of our technology, it is not "artificial."

Luminous Flux: The term used to refer to that portion of the radiant energy which the human eye can see (it produces the sensation of light in the human eye).

Lumen (lm):   A quantity of light used to express the total output of a light source. It is the unit of measure for luminous flux and for light. One lumen is the amount of light which falls on 1 sq ft of surface area when all points on the surface are 1 ft from a standard candle (Fig. 14-1).

Footlambert (fl):   The unit of measure for brightness for any perfectly diffused (spread out) surface which emits or reflects light. Footlamberts are expressed in lumens per square foot; 1 footlambert equals 1 lumen per sq ft. When lumens are measured from a light source (such as a light fixture or a reflecting wall or ceiling), they are referred to as footlamberts. (See *Footcandle* below.)

Reflectance: The ability of a surface to reflect light. It is expressed as the ratio of the light reflected by a surface to the amount of light which strikes the surface.

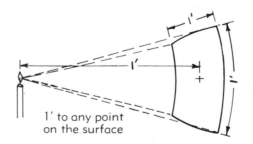

1' to any point
on the surface

One lumen is the amount of light which falls on 1 sq. ft. of surface area which is located 1' from a standard candle.

FIGURE 14-1   /   Lumen

Transmission Factor: The ability of a surface or object to allow the light to transmit (pass through it). It is expressed as the ratio of the light transmitted through a body to the amount of light which strikes the surface.

Illumination: The density of light (luminous flux) on a surface. The amount of illumination is found by dividing the amount of luminous flux (in lumens) by the area over which the flux is distributed. The unit of measure for illumination is the footcandle.

Footcandle (fc): The unit of measure for illumination, expressed in lumens per square foot, indicating how much light is actually on a surface. When lumens are measured at the surface where they will be "used," such as a desk top, they are referred to as footcandles. (See *Footlambert* above.) The number of footcandles for a given surface is found by dividing the number of lumens on a surface by the area of surface in square feet. One footcandle is the equivalent of 1 lumen distributed uniformly over 1 sq ft of surface located 1 ft from a standard candle (Fig. 14-2). The number of footcandles required varies considerably with the use of the space or area being lit; some typical footcandle requirements are given in Fig. 14-3.

Brightness: The property of a surface. For example, the surface of a wall either absorbs or reflects light, exhibiting a certain amount of brightness. Technically, it is the luminous intensity of any surface in a given direction per unit of projected area of the surface viewed from that direction.

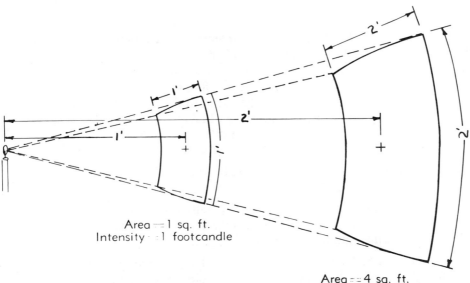

Area = 1 sq. ft.
Intensity = 1 footcandle

Area = 4 sq. ft.
Intensity = 1/4 footcandle

FIGURE 14-2 / Footcandle

Recommended illumination levels (footcandles)

Schools		Industrial	
corridors	20	general lighting	30-50
auditorium	20-30	laundries	30-50
study halls	70-80	locker rooms	30
classrooms	70	machines, rough	40-50
chalkboard area	150	machines, fine	80-100
drafting rooms	80-100	intricate work	150-400
laboratories	80	assembly areas	50-100
art	100	Theaters	
sewing	120-150	entrance, lobby	30-40
shop	100	foyer	30-40
gymnasium	50	auditorium	10
Stores		Post office	
circulation area	30	lobby	30
merchandise	100-150	mail sorting	100
showcases	150-200	corridors, storage	30

FIGURE 14-3   /   Typical footcandle requirements

Candlepower (cp):   A measurement of the luminous intensity of the source of light, stated in terms of candles. The amount of candlepower from any light source varies with the direction from the source in which the measurement is taken. This is because different types of light sources give off their light in different directions, some aiming up to the ceiling and others toward the floor. Manufacturers have available a candlepower distribution curve which shows in what direction the light will go and how much. The typical candlepower distribution of various luminaires is shown in Fig. 14-19.

Lamp: A man-made source of light, commonly referred to as a bulb (for incandescent lamps) and a tube (fluorescent lamps).

Reflector: A device which redirects the light of a lamp by reflecting it to the desired location. As the light leaves the source, it hits the reflector (Fig. 14-4) and is directed in the direction that the reflector is aimed.

Globe: An enclosing device which covers all or part of the lamp. It may protect the lamp, diffuse the light, redirect the light or modify the color of the light.

Luminaire: A complete lighting unit consisting of a light source, globe, reflector, housing, wiring and any supporting brackets that are a part of the housing.

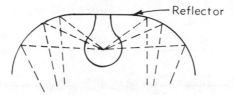

FIGURE 14-4 / Reflector

14-3 Electric Lamps

Available electric light sources are grouped into two classes:

1. Incandescent light sources (which use a tungsten filament).
2. Gaseous discharge light sources (such as fluorescent, mercury vapor, sodium, and neon).

For general lighting purposes inside residences and commercial, industrial, and institutional projects, the incandescent and fluorescent lamps are used. Mercury vapor, quartz, and sodium lamps are predominantly used outside to light large areas such as parking lots and to serve as flood lights.

Incandescent lamps have three main parts: the filament, the base, and the hollow-glass bulb that encloses the filament. The filament is made of tungsten and is connected by lead-in wires to the base. When the base is screwed into a socket and the power turned on, the circuit is complete. As the tungsten filament heats, the lamp gives off light. The bulb bases most commonly used are the *medium* (usually up to 200 W) and the mogul (over 200 W). But other bases are also used, depending on the type and the size of the lamp. The glass bulb is available with clear or frosted glass, coated inside or outside with a diffusing or reflecting material, or etched on the inside.

The typical luminous characteristics of an incandescent lamp with a frosted bulb are listed in Fig. 14-5. Among the advantages of incandescent lamps are:

1. They operate directly from the standard electrical distribution circuits.
2. A wide range of lighting distribution characteristics is available.
3. The standard sockets make them easily interchangeable.
4. Surrounding air temperature does not affect their performance.
5. Their radiation characteristics are good within the luminous range.
6. They can be easily equipped with a dimmer that can control the amount of light the lamp gives off from none to full outlet.

General Service Lamps for 115, 120, and 125 Volt Circuits
(Will Operate in Any Position but Lumen Maintenance is Best for 40 to 1500 Watts
When Burned Vertically Base-Up)

Watts	Bulb and Other Description	Base (see Fig. 8–9)	Filament (see Fig. 8–7)	Rated Average Life (hours)	Maximum Over-All Length (inches)	Average Light Center Length (inches)	Approximate Initial Filament Temperature (K)	Maximum Bare Bulb Temperature* (°F)	Base Temperature† (°F)	Approximate Initial Lumens	Rated Initial Lumens Per Watt‡	Lamp Lumen Depreciation** (per cent)
10	S-14 inside frosted or clear	Med.	C-9	1500	3½	2½	2420	106	106	80	8.0	89
15	A-15 inside frosted	Med.	C-9	2500	3½	2⅜	—	—	—	126	8.4	83
25	A-19 inside frosted	Med.	C-9	2500	3⅞	2½	2550	110	108	230	9.2	79
40	A-19 inside frosted and white¶	Med.	C-9	1500	4¼	2¹⁵⁄₁₆	2650	260	221	455	11.4	87.5
40	S-11 clear	Inter-med.	CC-2V or C-7A	350 500	2⁵⁄₁₆	1⅝	2800	570	390	477	11.9	—
50	A-19 inside frosted	Med.	CC-6	1000	4⁷⁄₁₆	3⅛	—	—	—	680	13.6	—
60	A-19 inside frosted and white¶	Med.	CC-6	1000	4⁷⁄₁₆	3⅛	2790	255	200	860	14.3	93
75	A-19 inside frosted and white¶	Med.	CC-6	750	4⁷⁄₁₆	3⅛	2840	275	205	1180	15.7	92
100	A-19 inside frosted and white¶	Med.	CC-8	750	4⁷⁄₁₆	3⅛	2905	300	208	1740	17.4	90.5
100§	A-19 inside frosted and white	Med.	CC-8	1000	4⁷⁄₁₆	3⅛	—	—	—	1680	16.8	—
100	A-21 inside frosted	Med.	CC-6	750	5¼	3⅞	2880	260	194	1690	16.9	90
100§	A-23 inside frosted or clear	Med.	C-9	1000	5¹⁵⁄₁₆	4⁷⁄₁₆	—	—	—	1480	14.8	—
150	A-21 inside frosted	Med.	CC-8	750	5½	4	2960	—	—	2880	19.2	89
150	A-21 white	Med.	CC-8	750	5½	4	2930	—	—	2790	18.6	89
150	A-23 inside frosted or clear or white	Med.	CC-6	750	6³⁄₁₆	4⅝	2925	280	210	2780	18.5	89
150	PS-25 clear or inside frosted	Med.	C-9	750	6¹⁵⁄₁₆	5¼	2910	290	210	2660	17.7	87.5
200	A-23 inside frosted white or clear	Med.	CC-8	750	6⁵⁄₁₆	4⅝	2980	345	225	4000	20.0	89.5
200	PS-25 clear or inside frosted	Med.	CC-6	750	6¹⁵⁄₁₆	5¼	—	—	—	3800	19.0	—
200	PS-30 clear or inside frosted	Med.	C-9	750	8¹⁄₁₆	6	2925	305	210	3700	18.5	85
300	PS-25 clear or inside frosted	Med.	CC-8	750	6¹⁵⁄₁₆	5³⁄₁₆	3015	401	234	6360	21.2	87.5
300	PS-30 clear or inside frosted	Med.	C-9	750	8¹⁄₁₆	6	3000	275	175	6100	20.3	82.5
300	PS-30 clear or inside frosted	Mog.	CC-8	1000	8⅝	7	—	—	—	5960	19.8	—
300	PS-35 clear or inside frosted	Mog.	C-9	1000	9⅜	7	2980	330	215	5860	19.6	86
500	PS-35 clear or inside frosted	Mog.	CC-8	1000	9⅜	7	3050	415	175	10600	21.2	89
500	PS-40 clear or inside frosted	Mog.	C-9	1000	9¾	7	2945	390	215	10140	20.3	—
750	PS-52 clear or inside frosted	Mog.	C-7A	1000	13¹⁄₁₆	9½	2990	—	—	15660	20.9	—
750	PS-52 clear or inside frosted	Mog.	CC-8 or 2CC-8	1000	13¹⁄₁₆	9½	3090	—	—	17000	22.6	89
1000	PS-52 clear or inside frosted	Mog.	C-7A	1000	13¹⁄₁₆	9½	2995	480	235	21800	21.8	—
1000	PS-52 clear or inside frosted	Mog.	CC-8 or 2CC-8	1000	13¹⁄₁₆	9½	3110	—	—	23600	23.6	89
1500	PS-52 clear or inside frosted	Mog.	C-7A	1000	13¹⁄₁₆	9½	3095	510	265	34000	22.6	78

* Lamp burning base up in ambient temperature of 77°F.
† At junction of base and bulb.
‡ For 120-volt lamps.
§ Used mainly in Canada.
¶ Lumen and lumen per watt values of white lamps are generally lower than for inside frosted.
** Per cent initial light output at 70 per cent of rated life.

Reprinted with permission from IES, IES Lighting Handbook, Fifth Edition 1972.

FIGURE 14-5 / Incandescent lamp characteristics

The incandescent lamp is used extensively in residences in ceiling, wall, floor and table luminaires. In commercial applications, it is primarily for specialty usage, such as spotlighting.

Fluorescent lamps are devices which convert invisible ultraviolet radiation into visible radiation. This conversion is made by the chemical phosphorus which is distributed over the inside of the tube.

The fluorescent lamp is used extensively in commercial, industrial and institutional projects. The typical fluorescent lamp has a cylindrical, sealed, glass tube which contains a mixture of low-pressure mercury vapor and an inert gas— usually argon (and phosphorus on the inside of the tube). Each end of the fluorescent tube has a cathode built in to supply the electrons which start, and maintain, the mercury arc. This mercury arc is absorbed by the phosphorus which re-radiates it as visible radiation.

The typical fluorescent lamp is available with straight tubes, for most commercial uses, and with circular, square, or U-shaped tubes, for specialty uses. Lamp lengths are given in inches. A range of lighting "colors" is available from the lamps; they may be referred to as "daylight" and "white," and some manufacturers use terms such as "cool white," "soft white," and "warm white." The "deluxe" lamp produces a warmer, more lifelike light for flesh tones by adding more red to the phosphor. This deluxe type of lamp is used extensively in retail stores.

The cathodes commonly used in fluorescent lamps are:

1. Instant-start (Fig. 14-20).
2. Rapid-start (Fig. 14-6).

The instant-start fluorescent lamp, of which the slimline lamp is the best known, makes use of a high-voltage transformer which strikes an arc without any of the cathode preheating that was necessary in early lamp designs. This type of lamp has only one pin at each end of the tube. While more expensive and slightly less efficient than the rapid-start lamp, it is manufactured in some lengths and currents which are not available with the rapid-start. Since it will operate at lower temperatures (below 50°F) than the rapid-start lamp, it is often used in outdoor situations or in any location where the temperature may be low (such as in many manufacturing facilities, outdoor loading docks, and covered parking areas).

The rapid-start fluorescent lamp is the more popular of the two since it has a higher light output per foot and is slightly less expensive than the instant-start. This type of lamp has about a 1-sec starting time and operates on a cathode current which flows continuously from a separate ballast; no starter is needed. Typical fluorescent lamp data are given in Fig. 14-6.

The advantages of fluorescent lamps are as follows:

1. They provide more light (lumens) for less operating cost than incandescent lamps.
2. Since they provide more light (lumens) per watt, less wattage is required, resulting in fewer branch circuits.
3. Less heat is given off by fluorescent lamps.

Typical Hot-Cathode Fluorescent Lamps (Rapid Starting)

Lightly Loaded Lamps (Circline, U-Shaped, Lightly Loaded, Medium Loaded)

	Circline			U-Shaped	Lightly Loaded Lamps					Medium Loaded Lamps					
Nominal length (inches)	8¼ dia.	12 dia.	16 dia.	24	24	36	48	48	48	24	30	36	42	48	60
Bulb	T-9	T-10	T-10	T-12	T-12	T-12	T-12	T-12	T-10	T-12	T-12	T-12	T-12	T-12	T-12
Base	4-Pin	4-Pin	4-Pin	Med. Bipin	Med. Bipin	Med. Bipin	Med. Bipin	Med. Bipin	Med. Bipin	Recess D.C.	Recess D.C.	Recess D.C.	Recess D.C.	Recess D.C.	Recess D.C.
Approx. lamp amperes	0.39	0.435	0.42	0.42		0.43	0.43		0.43	0.8 / 1.0	0.8 / 1.0	0.8 / 1.0	0.8 / 1.0	0.8 / 1.0	0.8 / 1.0
Approx. lamp volts	62	80	109	103		81	100		101	39.5 / 38		58 / 55	67 / 63	76 / 71	94 / 88
Approx. lamp watts[a]	22.5	33	41.5	40		32.4	40.7		41	35.5 / 41		47.5 / 54.5	56 / 64	61 / 70	74 / 85
Rated life (hours)[b]	7500	7500	7500	12000	7500	15000	18000	18000	18000	9000 / 7500	9000	9000 / 7500	9000 / 7500	12000 / 7500	12000 / 7500
Lamp lumen depreciation (LLD)[c]	72	82	77	84		81	84		79	77 / 72		77 / 72	77 / 72	82 / 72	82 / 72
Initial lumens[d]															
Cool White	980	1750	2450	2900	1230	2300	3200	3350	3200	1650 / 1800	2290 / 2500	2810 / 3060	3520 / 3840	4150 / 4520	5300 / 5780
Deluxe Cool White	800	1250	1780			1560	2220		2270					2880	
Warm White[e]	980	1800	2500	2950		2260	3250		3250	1690		2850		4200	5400
Deluxe Warm White	745	1240	1760			1530	2190							2920	
White		1810	2300			2260	3250		3250					4200	
Daylight	875	1525	2100	2950		1850	2660		2700	1385 / 1510		2330 / 2850	2970 / 3150	3500 / 3850	4300 / 4920

Medium Loaded Lamps and Highly Loaded Lamps

	Medium Loaded Lamps						Highly Loaded Lamps										
Nominal length (inches)	64	72	72	72	84	96	48	72	96	48	60	72	96	48	72	96	96
Bulb	T-12	T-12	T-12	T-12	T-12	T-12	T-10	T-10	T-10	T-12	T-12	T-12	T-12	PG-17	PG-17	PG-17	T11-17
Base	Recess D.C.	Mog. Bipin[j]	Recess D.C.	Recess D.C.	Recess D.C.	Recess D.C.	Rec. D.C.[k]	Rec. D.C.[k]	Rec. D.C.[k]	Rec. D.C.[m]	Rec. D.C.	Rec. D.C.[m]	Rec. D.C.[m]	Rec. D.C.	Rec. D.C.	Rec. D.C.	Rec. D.C.
Approx. lamp amperes	0.8 / 1.0	1.0	0.8 / 1.0		0.8 / 1.0	0.8 / 1.0	1.5	1.5	1.5	1.5	1.5	1.5	1.5	1.5	1.5	1.5	1.5
Approx. lamp volts	100 / 93	104	112 / 104		132 / 121	149 / 142	80	120	160	80		120	155	85	120	175	
Approx. lamp watts[a]	78 / 89.5	98.5	86 / 98		98 / 111	111 / 128	105[i]	150[i]	205[i]	110		165	215	110	165	215	
Rated life (hours)[b]	12000 / 7500	7500	12000 / 7500		12000 / 7500	12000 / 7500	9000	9000	9000	9000	9000	9000	9000	9000	9000	9000	15000
Lamp lumen depreciation (LLD)[c]	82 / 72	72	82 / 72		82 / 72	82 / 79	66	66	66	69		72	72	69	69	69	
Initial lumens[d]																	
Cool White	5650 / 6150	6900	6150 / 7040		7700 / 8400	9150 / 9980	6000[i]	9500[i]	13000[i]	6800	9150	11000	15300	7000	11500	16000	16500
Deluxe Cool White			4500 / 5050			6350	4400[i]	7100[i]	9700[i]	4300		7200	10800	4800	8000	11000	
Warm White[e]			6500 / 7300			9150 / 9800				6500		11000	15300	6400	10600	15000	
Deluxe Warm White			4500 / 5000			6350											
White			6500 / 7300			9150				7200		10900	15750	6600	10900	15500	
Daylight	4650		5450 / 6100		6500 / 7100	7650 / 8500				5700		9300	13000	5600	9300	13300	

Reprinted with permission from IES, IES Lighting Handbook, Fifth Edition 1972.

FIGURE 14-6 / Fluorescent lamp characteristics

14-4 Lighting Systems

The luminaire may project *direct, indirect,* or *semi-indirect* light on the surface or in the area to be lit. *Direct* lighting (Fig. 14-7) projects light directly onto the surface or object, and there is little reflection of the light rays. *Indirect* lighting projects all of its light onto a surface (usually a ceiling), and the light is reflected from that surface onto the object (Fig. 14-8). *Semi-indirect* lighting projects part of the light onto a surface to be reflected onto the object, and part of the light travels directly to the object (Fig. 14-9). Even when a direct lighting system is used, the light that falls onto an object or surface is usually a combination of light reflected from the walls, ceiling, and even floors as well as the direct light.

The use of diffusers below fluorescent lamps makes possible an even distribution of lighting without causing any glare. Thus, the tremendous selection and availability of such diffusers has made the direct lighting system the most popular in commercial, industrial, and institutional projects.

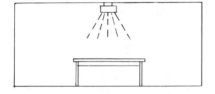

FIGURE 14-7   /   Direct lighting

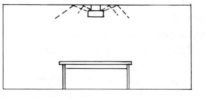

FIGURE 14-8   /   Indirect lighting

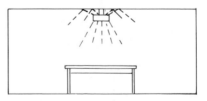

FIGURE 14-9   /   Semi-indirect lighting

14-5 Methods of Lighting

The three methods of providing light to any space are localized, general, and a combination of localized and general.

Localized lighting (Fig. 14-10) provides light only at the point where it is needed. This is accomplished primarily by providing individual luminaires in spe-

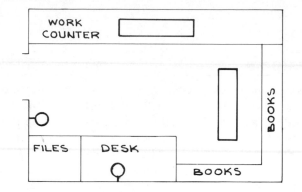

FIGURE 14-10   /   Localized lighting

cific locations. For example, to provide the localized lighting necessary for reading a paper in a chair, a floor, ceiling, or table luminaire would probably be used. Localized lighting generally produces pools or areas of light among larger areas of shadow. It is used primarily in residences and apartments, and to some extent in industrial plants.

General lighting (Fig. 14-11) provides a uniform level of lighting over an entire area. In this type of design, the luminaires are evenly distributed within the space. The luminaires may use various types of diffusing covers to spread the light. General lighting is often used in stores, classrooms, markets, factories, and other such general-use spaces.

Combination lighting (Fig. 14-12) provides enough general illumination for the entire space with additional localized lighting in areas where such things as desks, showcases, drafting tables, or machinery are located. With this type of lighting, the general lighting level would be lower than when only general lighting is used. Combination lighting is used in almost all types of buildings.

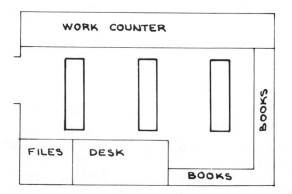

FIGURE 14-11   /   General and local lighting

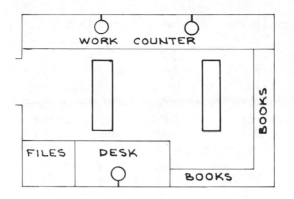

FIGURE 14-12 /
Combined lighting

14-6 Principles of Design

Several basic principles of lighting design should be discussed before the actual design is begun.

General lighting *requirements* must be determined for the surface; that is, the number of footcandles (lumens per square foot) must be determined for the use of the surface. The number of *footcandles* required for a variety of common uses is shown in Fig. 14-3. Selecting the required number of footcandles is among the first steps in the lighting design. Next, the designer will have to take into account the room area, the light loss due to room proportions, the color of the walls, the coefficient of utilization, and the maintenance factor.

The *room area* in square feet is then determined, taking the room dimensions from the drawings.

The *coefficient of utilization* is a measure of the amount of the total lumens put out by a luminaire that will actually reach the working plane, or the surface being lit. The higher the percentage of lumens that reach the surface, the higher the coefficient. The coefficient is a function of the room dimensions, the reflection factors of walls and ceilings, and the characteristics of any particular luminaire. For any particular luminaire (such as those shown in Fig. 14-19), the two variables become the room ratio and the reflection factors of walls and ceilings.

Reflection factors of the floor, ceiling, and walls must also be considered. The reflection factors of the surface finish materials, such as paints, ceiling tile, carpet, and wood, are easily found in the manufacturers' data sheets.

Ceiling reflection factors are usually taken as the reflection factor of the ceiling finish. When the ceiling has more than one finish, each finish must be considered in relation to the area it covers. Most ceiling factors are listed in manufacturers' brochures as 50%, 70%, and 80%.

Wall reflection factors must take into consideration not only the finish on the wall but also the other vertical reflection surfaces including doors, curtains (or other window coverings), windows (when they are not covered), cabinets, and any other items which may be on the walls such as a chalkboard or bulletin board.

The wall factors listed in the manufacturers' material are 10%, 30%, and 50%. Average rooms have wall reflection factors of 30%, and it would be unlikely that any room would have a factor exceeding 50%.

Floor reflection factors must be based on the reflection factor not only of the floor but also of all horizontal surfaces, including furniture such as desks, chairs, couches, files, and so on. A conservative factor of 10% is often used, but the increased use of lighter floor colors has caused many designers to use a floor value of 30%. Many manufacturers list both 10% and 30% floor reflection factors. As a compromise value, an effective floor cavity reflectance (p_{FC}) of 20% is used in the CU tables in Fig. 14-19. When the actual value of the floor cavity reflectance is more or less than the 20%, the CU values in Fig. 14-19 are adjusted by the appropriate factor from Fig. 14-18.

Since the lighting design is usually done before all the room finishes are selected, the designer must have a "feeling" for what will be done in the space. Many times paint colors, ceiling and floor tiles, and the other finishes will not be actually selected (as to color and style) until the project is well under construction. The designer will have to check carefully as to what each space will be used for and what colors and finishes the architect, owner, and decorator may use. From this information, the lighting designer must make an "educated guess," and when in doubt, he should use lower values to be on the safe side.

The *maintenance factor* takes into consideration all of the reasons that would cause a luminaire (with its lamp) to operate at less than 100% of its design and test capabilities after it is installed. Reasons for such decreased performance include:

1. The output of the luminaire decreases with age.

2. The voltage at the luminaire is generally less than the voltage at which it is rated.

3. Longtime chemical changes and discolorations affect the reflecting surface and diffusing grilles.

4. Dust and dirt affect the lamp, its reflecting surface, and its diffusing grilles.

These loss of performance factors are grouped into:

LLD = Lamp Lumen Depreciation Factor

LDD = Luminaire Dirt Depreciation Factor

These two factors are combined (multiplied by each other) to obtain the maintenance factor. This maintenance factor may be kept to a minimum by regularly cleaning the entire luminaire and periodically replacing the lamp, but it cannot be eliminated.

Values of lamp lumen depreciation (LLD) for various lamps are given in Figs. 14-5 and 14-20. The values are listed as the percentage of initial lumens produced at 70% of life for the various types of lamps in common use.

The luminaire dirt depreciation (LDD) categories range from I through VI and are listed in Figs. 14-16 and 14-17. Each category applies to certain types of luminaire and lamp situations. The appropriate LDD category classification to be used for each type is listed in the typical luminaire listings in Fig. 14-19.

The selection for cleanliness (very clean through very dirty) is a judgment factor based on the designer's anticipation of the quality of maintenance and housekeeping to which the luminaire will be subjected.

LDD values are listed as the percentage of initial lumens produced by the specific luminaire type.

> *Caution:* Care must be used in selecting both the surface reflection factors and the maintenance factor. Many designers (and architects/engineers) have a tendency to use values which are too high so they will have to use fewer luminaires, saving money on the number of luminaires bought, the wiring, the circuits, and so on. This becomes false economy since the lighting system will not provide the light required in the space.

The breakdown of a space into the room cavities used to determine the coefficient of utilization is shown in Fig. 14-13. The cavity ratios are used to determine how the proportions of a room will affect the characteristics of light flux. For example, a room that is narrow in relation to its height will allow less flux to reach the working plane (surface) than one that is wide.

The ceiling and floor cavity ratios (CCR and FCR respectively) are used in conjunction with the wall, ceiling, and floor reflectances. The ratios are used to combine separate wall and ceiling reflectances into a single effective ceiling cavity reflectance, p_{CC}, or to combine separate wall and floor reflectances into a single effective floor cavity reflectance, p_{FC}.

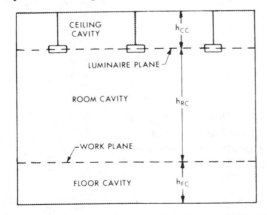

Reprinted with permission from IES, IES Lighting Handbook, Fifth Edition 1972.

FIGURE 14-13 / Cavities

The RCR, CCR, and FCR may be calculated by use of the equation:

$$\text{Cavity ratio} = \frac{5h \,(\text{Room length} + \text{Room width})}{\text{Room length} \times \text{Room width}}$$

Where:

$$h = h_{RC} \text{ for the room cavity ratio (RCR)}$$
$$= h_{CC} \text{ for the ceiling cavity ratio (CCR)}$$
$$= h_{FC} \text{ for the floor cavity ratio (FCR)}$$

When the luminaire is surface mounted or recessed, the CCR = 0 and the ceiling reflectance is used as the p_{CC}. Many cavity ratios are given in Fig. 14-14.

To determine the coefficient of utilization (CU) for a particular room size and luminaire, it is necessary to:

1. Determine the RCR, CCR, and FCR, either by calculating the ratio or by using Fig. 14-14.

2. Determine the effective ceiling cavity reflectance p_{CC} and the effective floor cavity reflectance p_{FC} (Fig. 14-15).

3. Determine the coefficient of utilization (CU) based on the RCR, p_{CC}, p_{FC}, and wall reflectance (referred to as p_{WC}). The CU's for many typical luminaires are shown in Fig. 14-19. When the exact ratios and reflectances are not given in the tables, they may be interpolated (averaged from the values given).

4. When the effective floor cavity reflectance varies greatly from the 20% *value* used in Fig. 14-19, a multiplying factor is found in Fig. 14-18 by which the CU is adjusted.

Example

Given:

Room: 40 ft × 50 ft
Fixture mounting height: 6 ft (above working plane)
Working plane: 2 ft–6 in. above finished floor
Footcandles desired: 100 fc (store, merchandise)
Ceiling reflectance: 80%
Wall reflectance: 50%
Floor reflectance: 10%
Maintenance factor: Fair
Luminaires: Fluorescent, 40-W, rapid-start, white (type 22, Fig. 14-19),
        mounted 1 ft–0 in. from the ceiling

Problem: Find the total lumens and the number of luminaires required and the number of footcandles they provide.

1. Determine the heights (h) of the zonal cavities.

$$h_{CC} = 1.0$$
$$h_{RC} = 6.0$$
$$h_{FC} = 2.5$$

2. Determine the cavity ratios, using the formula or taking them directly from Fig. 14-15.

$$CCR = 0.4$$
$$RCR = 2.5$$
$$FCR = 1.0$$

3. Determine the effective ceiling and floor cavity reflectances from Fig. 14-15 by use of the given reflectances and the calculated cavity ratios.

$$\rho_{CC} = 74\%$$
$$\rho_{WC} = 50\% \text{ (the given value)}$$
$$\rho_{FC} = 11\%$$

4. Determine the CU from the manufacturer's specifications or from Fig. 14-19. The RCR, ρ_{FC}, and ρ_{CC} must be interpolated (averaged) from the values given. From Fig. 14-19, the values are:

ρ_{CC}	80	70
RCR = 2.0	0.72	0.69
3.0	0.65	0.62

Interpolate the RCR: RCR = 2.5.

$$\rho_{CC} \ 80 = 0.72 - 0.07 \ (0.5) = 0.685$$
$$\rho_{CC} \ 70 = 0.69 - 0.07 \ (0.5) = 0.655$$

Interpolate the ρ_{CC}, using RCR = 2.5, ρ_{WC} = 50, and ρ_{CC} = 74:

ρ_{CC}	80	70
CU	0.685	0.655

$$CU \ (\rho_{CC} = 74) = 0.685 - \text{}^{6}\!/\!_{10} \ (0.03) = 0.667$$

Determine the ρ_{FC} factor, using $CU = 0.6$ and $\rho_{FC} = 0.11$ and the ρ_{FC} factor from Fig. 14-18:

$$CU = 0.667 \times 0.946 \ (\text{from Fig. 14-18}) = 0.631$$

5. Determine the lamp lumen depreciation (LLD) from the table in Fig. 14-20. Based on fluorescent lamps, instant start, 425 ma, deluxe cool white:

$$LLD = 83\%$$

6. Determine the luminaire dirt depreciation (LDD) from Fig. 14-17. The luminaire selected (type 22, Fig. 14-19) lists an LDD maintenance category of II. Assuming a dirty maintenance with a 24-month interval, the LDD from Fig. 14-17 is 80%.

7. Determine the total lumens required for the space:

$$\text{Total lumens} = \frac{\text{Footcandles} \times \text{Room area}}{CU \times LLD \times LDD}$$

$$\text{Total lumens} = \frac{100 \ (20 \times 30)}{0.631 \times 0.83 \times 0.80} = 143{,}203 \text{ lumens}$$

8. Determine the minimum number of lamps required by dividing the number of lumens per lamp into the total amount of lumens required. Since 40-W, instant start, deluxe cool white fluorescent lamps are used, from Fig. 14-20 the lumens per lamp are 1,980.

9. Determine the number of lamps required by dividing the total number of lumens required by the lumens per lamp:

$$\text{Lamps} = \frac{143{,}203}{1{,}980} = 72.3 = 73 \text{ lamps}$$

10. Determine the number of luminaires required by dividing the number of lamps required by the number of lamps in the luminaire selected.

$$\text{Luminaires} = \frac{73}{2} = 36.5 = 37 \text{ luminaires}$$

The designer has several choices in luminaire placement. Using a 4-ft luminairc, a maximum of 12 luminaires could be placed end to end in a row. To install the luminaires required in this manner would require 3.08 rows. The luminaires could also be placed 10 per row using 4 rows (and a total of 40 luminaires). This would provide slightly more fc than required.

The spacing used should be checked against spacing–mounting-height ratios in Fig. 14-19. In this design, the mounting height above the working plane is 6 ft. Using Fig. 14-19, the maximum spacing (S) should be no more than the mounting height times 1.0:

$$\frac{Max\ S}{MH_{WP}} = 1.0$$

or

$$Max\ S = MH_{WP} \times 1.0$$

In this design, the maximum spacing should be 6.0 ft.

To calculate the number of footcandles, the original formula

$$Lumens = \frac{Footcandles \times Room\ area}{Coefficient\ of\ utilization\ (cu) \times Maintenance\ factor\ (mf)}$$

is rewritten:

$$Footcandles = \frac{Lumens \times cu \times mf}{Room\ area}$$

$$= \frac{2{,}100\ (74) \times 0.606 \times 0.83 \times 0.80}{600}$$

$$= 104.2\ fc$$

Since 100 fc are desired, the design is complete.

Cavity Depth / **Room Dimensions**

Width	Length	1.0	1.5	2.0	2.5	3.0	3.5	4.0	5.0	6.0	7.0	8	9	10	11	12	14	16	20	25	30
8	8	1.2	1.9	2.5	3.1	3.8	4.4	5.0	6.2	7.5	8.8	10.0	11.2	12.5	—	—	—	—	—	—	—
	10	1.1	1.7	2.2	2.8	3.4	3.9	4.5	5.6	6.8	7.9	9.0	10.1	11.2	12.4	—	—	—	—	—	—
	14	1.0	1.5	2.0	2.5	2.9	3.4	3.9	4.9	5.9	6.9	7.9	8.8	9.8	10.8	11.8	—	—	—	—	—
	20	0.9	1.3	1.8	2.2	2.6	3.1	3.5	4.4	5.2	6.1	7.0	7.9	8.8	9.6	10.5	12.2	—	—	—	—
	30	0.8	1.2	1.6	2.0	2.4	2.8	3.2	4.0	4.8	5.5	6.3	7.1	7.9	8.7	9.5	11.1	—	—	—	—
	40	0.8	1.1	1.5	1.9	2.2	2.6	3.0	3.8	4.5	5.2	6.0	6.8	7.5	8.2	9.0	10.5	12.0	—	—	—
10	10	1.0	1.5	2.0	2.5	3.0	3.5	4.0	5.0	6.0	7.0	8.0	9.0	10.0	11.0	12.0	—	—	—	—	—
	14	0.9	1.3	1.7	2.1	2.6	3.0	3.4	4.3	5.1	6.0	6.9	7.7	8.6	9.4	10.3	12.0	—	—	—	—
	20	0.8	1.1	1.5	1.9	2.2	2.6	3.0	3.8	4.5	5.2	6.0	6.8	7.5	8.2	9.0	10.5	12.0	—	—	—
	30	0.7	1.0	1.3	1.7	2.0	2.3	2.7	3.3	4.0	4.7	5.3	6.0	6.7	7.3	8.0	9.3	10.7	—	—	—
	40	0.6	0.9	1.2	1.6	1.9	2.2	2.5	3.1	3.8	4.4	5.0	5.6	6.2	6.9	7.5	8.8	10.0	12.5	—	—
	60	0.6	0.9	1.2	1.5	1.8	2.0	2.3	2.9	3.5	4.1	4.7	5.2	5.8	6.4	7.0	8.2	9.3	11.7	—	—
12	12	0.8	1.2	1.7	2.1	2.5	2.9	3.3	4.2	5.0	5.8	6.7	7.5	8.3	9.2	10.0	11.7	—	—	—	—
	16	0.7	1.1	1.5	1.8	2.2	2.6	2.9	3.6	4.4	5.1	5.8	6.6	7.3	8.0	8.8	10.2	11.7	—	—	—
	24	0.6	0.9	1.2	1.6	1.9	2.2	2.5	3.1	3.8	4.4	5.0	5.6	6.2	6.9	7.5	8.8	10.0	12.5	—	—
	36	0.6	0.8	1.1	1.4	1.7	1.9	2.2	2.8	3.3	3.9	4.4	5.0	5.6	6.1	6.7	7.8	8.9	11.1	—	—
	50	0.5	0.8	1.0	1.3	1.6	1.8	2.1	2.6	3.1	3.6	4.1	4.6	5.2	5.7	6.2	7.2	8.3	10.3	—	—
	70	0.5	0.7	1.0	1.2	1.5	1.7	2.0	2.4	2.9	3.4	3.9	4.4	4.9	5.4	5.9	6.8	7.8	9.8	12.2	—
14	14	0.7	1.1	1.4	1.8	2.1	2.5	2.9	3.6	4.3	5.0	5.7	6.4	7.1	7.9	8.6	10.0	11.4	—	—	—
	20	0.6	0.9	1.2	1.5	1.8	2.1	2.4	3.0	3.6	4.2	4.9	5.5	6.1	6.7	7.3	8.5	9.7	12.1	—	—
	30	0.5	0.8	1.0	1.3	1.6	1.8	2.1	2.6	3.1	3.7	4.2	4.7	5.2	5.8	6.3	7.3	8.4	10.5	—	—
	42	0.5	0.7	1.0	1.2	1.4	1.7	1.9	2.4	2.9	3.3	3.8	4.3	4.8	5.2	5.7	6.7	7.6	9.5	11.9	—
	60	0.4	0.7	0.9	1.1	1.3	1.5	1.8	2.2	2.6	3.1	3.5	4.0	4.4	4.8	5.3	6.2	7.0	8.8	11.0	—
	90	0.4	0.6	0.8	1.0	1.2	1.4	1.7	2.1	2.5	2.9	3.3	3.7	4.1	4.5	5.0	5.8	6.6	8.3	10.3	12.4
17	17	0.6	0.9	1.2	1.5	1.8	2.1	2.4	2.9	3.5	4.1	4.7	5.3	5.9	6.5	7.1	8.2	9.4	11.8	—	—
	25	0.5	0.7	1.0	1.2	1.5	1.7	2.0	2.5	3.0	3.5	4.0	4.4	4.9	5.4	5.9	6.9	7.9	9.9	12.4	—
	35	0.4	0.7	0.9	1.1	1.3	1.5	1.7	2.2	2.6	3.1	3.5	3.9	4.4	4.8	5.2	6.1	7.0	8.7	10.9	—
	50	0.4	0.6	0.8	1.0	1.2	1.4	1.6	2.0	2.4	2.8	3.2	3.5	3.9	4.3	4.7	5.5	6.3	7.9	9.9	11.8
	80	0.4	0.5	0.7	0.9	1.1	1.2	1.4	1.8	2.1	2.5	2.9	3.2	3.6	3.9	4.3	5.0	5.7	7.1	8.9	10.7
	120	0.3	0.5	0.7	0.8	1.0	1.2	1.3	1.7	2.0	2.4	2.7	3.0	3.4	3.7	4.0	4.7	5.4	6.7	8.4	10.1
20	20	0.5	0.8	1.0	1.2	1.5	1.8	2.0	2.5	3.0	3.5	4.0	4.5	5.0	5.5	6.0	7.0	8.0	10.0	12.5	—
	30	0.4	0.6	0.8	1.0	1.2	1.5	1.7	2.1	2.5	2.9	3.3	3.8	4.2	4.6	5.0	5.8	6.7	8.3	10.4	12.5
	45	0.4	0.5	0.7	0.9	1.1	1.3	1.4	1.8	2.2	2.5	2.9	3.2	3.6	4.0	4.3	5.1	5.8	7.2	9.0	10.8
	60	0.3	0.5	0.7	0.8	1.0	1.2	1.3	1.7	2.0	2.3	2.7	3.0	3.3	3.7	4.0	4.7	5.3	6.7	8.3	10.0
	90	0.3	0.5	0.6	0.8	0.9	1.1	1.2	1.5	1.8	2.1	2.4	2.8	3.1	3.4	3.7	4.3	4.9	6.1	7.6	9.2
	150	0.3	0.4	0.6	0.7	0.8	1.0	1.1	1.4	1.7	2.0	2.3	2.6	2.8	3.1	3.4	4.0	4.5	5.7	7.1	8.5
24	24	0.4	0.6	0.8	1.0	1.2	1.5	1.7	2.1	2.5	2.9	3.3	3.8	4.2	4.6	5.0	5.8	6.7	8.3	10.4	12.5
	32	0.4	0.5	0.7	0.9	1.1	1.3	1.5	1.8	2.2	2.6	2.9	3.3	3.6	4.0	4.4	5.1	5.8	7.3	9.1	10.9
	50	0.3	0.5	0.6	0.8	0.9	1.1	1.2	1.5	1.8	2.2	2.5	2.8	3.1	3.4	3.7	4.3	4.9	6.2	7.7	9.2
	70	0.3	0.4	0.6	0.7	0.8	1.0	1.1	1.4	1.7	2.0	2.2	2.5	2.8	3.1	3.4	3.9	4.5	5.6	7.0	8.4
	100	0.3	0.4	0.5	0.6	0.8	0.9	1.0	1.3	1.6	1.8	2.1	2.3	2.6	2.8	3.1	3.6	4.1	5.2	6.5	7.8
	160	0.2	0.4	0.5	0.6	0.7	0.8	1.0	1.2	1.4	1.7	1.9	2.2	2.4	2.6	2.9	3.4	3.8	4.8	6.0	7.2

FIGURE 14-14 / Cavity ratios

Room Dimensions		Cavity Depth																			
Width	Length	1.0	1.5	2.0	2.5	3.0	3.5	4.0	5.0	6.0	7.0	8	9	10	11	12	14	16	20	25	30
30	30	0.3	0.5	0.7	0.8	1.0	1.2	1.3	1.7	2.0	2.3	2.7	3.0	3.3	3.7	4.0	4.7	5.4	6.7	8.4	10.0
	45	0.3	0.4	0.6	0.7	0.8	1.0	1.1	1.4	1.7	1.9	2.2	2.5	2.7	3.0	3.3	3.9	4.4	5.5	6.9	8.2
	60	0.2	0.4	0.5	0.6	0.7	0.9	1.0	1.2	1.5	1.7	2.0	2.2	2.5	2.7	3.1	3.6	4.0	4.5	6.2	7.4
	90	0.2	0.3	0.4	0.6	0.6	0.7	0.9	1.1	1.3	1.6	1.6	1.8	2.2	2.2	2.4	2.8	3.2	4.5	5.6	6.7
	150	0.2	0.3	0.4	0.5	0.6	0.7	0.8	1.0	1.1	1.4	1.6	1.7	2.0	2.2	2.4	2.8	3.2	4.0	5.0	5.9
	200	0.2	0.3	0.4	0.5	0.6	0.7	0.8	1.0	1.1	1.3	1.5	1.7	1.9	2.0	2.2	2.6	3.0	3.7	4.7	5.6
36	36	0.3	0.4	0.6	0.7	0.8	1.0	1.1	1.4	1.7	1.9	2.2	2.5	2.8	3.0	3.3	3.9	4.4	5.5	6.9	8.3
	50	0.3	0.4	0.5	0.6	0.7	0.8	1.0	1.2	1.4	1.7	1.9	2.1	2.5	2.6	2.9	3.3	3.8	4.8	5.9	7.2
	75	0.2	0.3	0.4	0.5	0.6	0.7	0.8	1.0	1.2	1.4	1.6	1.8	2.0	2.1	2.3	2.6	2.6	3.8	5.1	6.1
	100	0.2	0.3	0.4	0.5	0.6	0.7	0.8	0.9	1.1	1.3	1.5	1.7	1.9	2.1	2.3	2.4	3.0	3.8	4.7	5.7
	150	0.2	0.3	0.3	0.4	0.5	0.6	0.7	0.9	1.0	1.2	1.4	1.6	1.7	1.9	2.1	2.3	2.8	3.3	4.3	5.2
	200	0.1	0.2	0.3	0.4	0.5	0.5	0.7	0.8	1.0	1.1	1.3	1.5	1.6	1.8	2.0	2.3	2.6	3.3	4.1	4.9
42	42	0.2	0.4	0.5	0.6	0.7	0.8	1.0	1.2	1.4	1.6	1.9	2.1	2.4	2.6	2.8	3.3	3.8	4.7	5.9	7.1
	60	0.2	0.3	0.4	0.5	0.6	0.7	0.8	1.0	1.2	1.4	1.6	1.8	2.0	2.2	2.4	2.8	3.2	4.0	5.0	6.0
	90	0.2	0.3	0.3	0.4	0.5	0.6	0.6	0.8	1.0	1.1	1.2	1.4	1.5	1.7	1.9	2.2	2.5	3.1	4.4	4.6
	140	0.1	0.2	0.3	0.4	0.4	0.5	0.6	0.7	0.9	1.1	1.1	1.3	1.4	1.5	1.7	2.0	2.3	2.8	3.6	4.3
	200	0.1	0.2	0.3	0.3	0.4	0.5	0.5	0.7	0.9	0.9	1.1	1.3	1.4	1.5	1.6	1.9	2.1	2.7	3.5	4.2
	300	0.1	0.2	0.2	0.3	0.3	0.4	0.5	0.7	0.8	0.9	1.1	1.3	1.4	1.3	1.4	1.9	2.2	2.3	3.5	4.2
50	50	0.2	0.4	0.5	0.5	0.6	0.7	0.8	1.0	1.2	1.4	1.6	1.8	2.0	2.2	2.4	2.8	3.2	4.0	5.0	6.0
	70	0.2	0.3	0.4	0.4	0.5	0.6	0.7	0.7	1.0	1.2	1.4	1.5	1.7	1.9	2.0	2.4	2.7	3.4	3.7	5.1
	100	0.2	0.2	0.3	0.3	0.4	0.5	0.5	0.7	0.9	0.9	1.1	1.3	1.3	1.5	1.6	1.9	2.1	3.0	3.3	4.0
	150	0.1	0.2	0.3	0.3	0.4	0.4	0.5	0.6	0.8	0.9	1.1	1.2	1.3	1.5	1.6	1.9	2.1	2.7	3.3	4.0
	200	0.1	0.2	0.3	0.2	0.3	0.3	0.4	0.5	0.5	0.6	0.7	0.8	1.1	1.1	1.4	1.6	2.1	2.3	3.3	3.5
	300	0.1	0.1	0.2	0.2	0.2	0.3	0.3	0.4	0.4	0.6	0.6	0.7	0.7	0.9	1.2	1.4	1.9	2.0	2.9	3.0
60	60	0.2	0.2	0.3	0.4	0.5	0.6	0.7	0.8	1.0	1.2	1.3	1.5	1.7	1.8	2.0	2.3	2.7	3.3	4.2	5.0
	100	0.2	0.2	0.3	0.3	0.4	0.4	0.5	0.6	0.7	0.8	1.1	1.0	1.2	1.3	1.6	1.9	2.1	2.7	3.3	4.0
	150	0.1	0.2	0.2	0.3	0.3	0.4	0.5	0.5	0.6	0.7	0.8	1.0	1.2	1.3	1.2	1.6	1.6	2.3	2.9	3.5
	300	0.1	0.1	0.2	0.2	0.3	0.3	0.4	0.5	0.6	0.7	0.8	0.9	1.0	1.1	1.2	1.4	1.6	2.0	2.5	3.0
75	75	0.1	0.2	0.3	0.3	0.4	0.5	0.5	0.7	0.8	0.9	1.1	1.2	1.3	1.5	1.6	1.9	2.1	2.7	3.3	4.3
	120	0.1	0.2	0.2	0.3	0.3	0.4	0.4	0.5	0.7	0.8	0.9	1.0	1.1	1.2	1.0	1.5	1.7	2.2	2.7	3.3
	200	0.1	0.1	0.2	0.2	0.3	0.3	0.4	0.5	0.6	0.7	0.7	0.8	1.2	1.0	1.1	1.3	1.5	1.8	2.3	2.7
	300	0.1	0.1	0.2	0.2	0.2	0.3	0.3	0.4	0.5	0.5	0.7	0.7	0.8	0.9	1.0	1.4	1.6	1.7	2.1	2.5
100	100	0.1	0.1	0.2	0.2	0.3	0.3	0.4	0.5	0.6	0.7	0.8	0.9	1.0	1.1	1.2	1.4	1.6	2.0	2.5	3.0
	200	0.1	0.1	0.1	0.2	0.2	0.3	0.3	0.4	0.4	0.5	0.6	0.7	0.7	0.8	0.9	1.3	1.3	1.5	1.9	2.2
	300	0.1	0.1	0.1	0.2	0.2	0.2	0.3	0.3	0.4	0.5	0.5	0.7	0.7	0.7	0.8	0.9	1.1	1.3	1.7	2.0
150	150	0.1	0.1	0.1	0.2	0.2	0.2	0.3	0.3	0.4	0.5	0.6	0.6	1.0	1.1	1.2	1.4	1.6	1.3	1.7	2.0
	300	0.1	0.1	0.1	0.1	0.1	0.2	0.2	0.2	0.4	0.5	0.5	0.7	0.7	0.7	0.8	0.9	1.1	1.0	1.2	1.5
200	200	0.1	0.1	0.1	0.1	0.1	0.2	0.2	0.2	0.3	0.3	0.4	0.5	0.5	0.6	0.6	0.7	0.8	1.0	1.2	1.5
	300	—	0.1	0.1	0.1	0.1	0.1	0.2	0.2	0.2	0.3	0.3	0.4	0.4	0.5	0.5	0.6	0.7	0.8	1.0	1.2
300	300	—	—	0.1	0.1	0.1	0.1	0.1	0.2	0.2	0.2	0.3	0.3	0.3	0.4	0.4	0.5	0.5	0.6	0.7	0.8
500	500	—	—	—	—	0.1	0.1	0.1	0.1	0.1	0.2	0.2	0.2	0.2	0.2	0.2	0.3	0.3	0.4	0.5	0.6

Reprinted with permission from IES, IES Lighting Handbook, Fifth Edition 1972.

FIGURE 14-14 / Cavity ratios (continued)

Per Cent Effective Ceiling or Floor Cavity Reflectances for Various Reflectance Combinations

Per Cent Base* Reflectance →	90										80										70										50										30									
Per Cent Wall Reflectance / Cavity Ratio	90	80	70	60	50	40	30	20	10	0	90	80	70	60	50	40	30	20	10	0	90	80	70	60	50	40	30	20	10	0	90	80	70	60	50	40	30	20	10	0	90	80	70	60	50	40	30	20	10	0
0.2	89	88	87	86	85	85	85	84	84	82	79	78	78	77	77	76	76	75	74	72	70	69	68	68	67	67	66	66	65	64	50	50	49	49	48	48	48	46	46	44	31	31	30	30	30	29	29	29	28	27
0.4	88	87	86	85	84	83	81	80	79	76	79	77	76	75	74	73	72	71	70	68	69	68	67	66	65	64	63	62	61	58	50	49	48	47	46	45	45	44	44	42	31	31	30	30	30	29	28	28	27	25
0.6	87	86	84	82	80	79	77	76	74	73	78	76	75	73	71	70	68	66	65	63	69	67	65	64	63	61	59	58	57	54	50	48	47	46	44	43	42	41	41	38	32	31	30	29	28	27	26	26	25	23
0.8	87	85	82	80	77	75	73	71	69	67	78	75	73	71	69	67	65	63	61	57	68	66	64	62	60	58	56	55	53	50	50	48	47	44	42	40	39	38	37	36	32	31	30	29	28	26	25	25	23	22
1.0	86	83	80	77	75	72	69	66	64	62	77	74	72	69	67	65	62	60	57	55	68	65	62	60	58	55	53	52	50	47	50	48	46	44	43	41	38	37	36	34	33	32	30	29	27	25	24	23	22	20
1.2	85	82	78	75	72	69	66	63	60	57	76	73	70	67	64	61	58	55	53	51	67	64	61	59	57	54	50	48	46	44	50	47	45	41	39	36	35	34	34	29	33	32	30	28	27	25	23	22	21	19
1.4	85	80	77	73	69	65	62	59	57	52	76	72	68	65	62	59	55	53	50	48	67	63	60	58	55	51	47	45	44	41	50	47	45	42	40	38	35	34	32	27	34	32	30	28	26	24	22	21	19	18
1.6	84	79	75	71	67	63	59	56	53	48	75	71	67	63	60	57	53	50	47	44	67	62	59	56	53	47	45	43	41	38	50	47	44	41	39	36	33	32	30	26	34	33	30	27	25	23	22	20	18	17
1.8	83	78	73	69	64	60	56	53	50	47	75	70	66	62	58	54	50	47	44	41	66	61	58	54	51	46	42	40	38	35	50	46	43	40	38	35	31	30	28	25	35	33	29	27	25	23	21	19	17	16
2.0	83	77	72	67	62	56	53	50	47	43	74	69	64	60	56	52	48	45	41	38	66	60	56	52	49	45	40	38	36	33	50	46	43	40	37	34	30	28	26	24	35	33	29	26	24	22	20	18	16	14
2.2	82	76	70	65	59	54	50	47	44	40	74	68	63	58	54	49	45	42	38	35	66	60	55	51	48	43	38	36	34	32	50	46	42	38	36	33	29	27	24	22	36	32	29	26	24	22	19	17	15	13
2.4	82	75	69	64	58	53	48	45	41	37	73	67	61	56	52	47	43	40	36	33	65	60	54	50	46	41	37	35	32	30	50	46	42	37	35	31	27	25	23	21	36	32	29	26	24	22	19	16	14	12
2.6	81	74	67	62	56	51	46	42	38	35	73	66	60	55	50	45	41	38	34	31	65	59	54	49	45	40	35	33	30	28	50	46	41	37	34	30	26	23	21	20	36	32	29	25	23	21	18	16	14	12
2.8	81	73	66	60	54	49	44	40	36	34	73	65	59	53	48	43	39	36	32	29	65	59	53	48	43	38	33	30	28	26	50	46	41	36	33	29	25	22	20	19	37	33	29	25	23	21	17	15	13	11
3.0	80	72	64	58	52	47	42	38	34	30	72	65	58	52	47	42	37	34	30	27	64	58	52	47	42	37	32	29	27	24	50	45	40	36	32	28	24	21	19	17	37	33	29	25	22	20	17	15	12	10
3.2	79	71	63	56	50	45	40	36	32	28	72	65	57	51	45	40	35	33	28	25	64	58	51	46	40	36	31	28	25	23	50	44	39	35	31	27	23	20	18	16	37	33	29	24	22	19	16	14	12	10
3.4	79	70	62	54	48	43	38	34	30	27	71	64	56	49	44	39	34	32	27	24	64	57	50	45	39	35	29	27	24	22	50	44	39	35	30	26	22	19	17	15	37	33	29	24	21	19	16	14	11	09
3.6	78	69	61	53	47	42	36	32	28	25	71	63	54	48	43	38	32	30	25	23	63	56	49	44	38	33	28	25	22	20	50	44	39	34	30	26	22	19	16	14	38	33	29	24	21	18	15	13	10	08
3.8	78	69	60	51	45	40	35	31	27	23	70	62	53	47	41	36	31	28	24	22	63	56	49	43	37	32	27	24	21	19	50	44	38	33	29	25	21	18	15	13	38	33	28	24	21	18	15	13	10	08
4.0	77	68	58	51	44	39	33	29	25	22	70	61	53	46	40	35	30	26	22	20	63	55	48	42	36	31	26	23	20	17	50	44	38	33	28	24	20	17	15	12	38	33	28	24	21	18	14	12	09	07
4.2	77	62	57	50	43	37	32	28	24	21	69	60	52	45	39	34	29	25	21	18	62	55	47	41	35	30	25	22	19	16	50	43	37	32	28	24	20	17	14	12	38	33	28	24	20	17	14	12	09	07
4.4	76	61	56	49	42	36	31	27	23	20	69	60	51	44	38	33	28	24	20	17	62	54	46	40	34	29	24	21	18	15	50	43	37	32	27	23	19	16	13	11	39	33	28	24	20	17	14	11	09	06
4.6	76	60	55	47	40	35	30	26	22	19	69	59	50	43	37	32	27	23	19	15	62	53	45	39	33	28	24	21	17	14	50	43	36	31	26	22	18	15	13	10	39	33	28	24	20	17	13	10	08	06
4.8	75	59	54	46	39	34	28	25	21	18	68	58	49	42	36	31	26	22	18	14	62	53	45	38	32	27	23	20	16	13	50	43	36	31	26	22	18	15	12	09	39	33	28	23	20	17	13	10	08	05
5.0	75	59	53	45	38	33	28	24	21	16	68	58	48	41	35	30	25	21	18	14	61	52	44	36	31	26	22	19	16	12	50	42	35	30	25	21	17	14	12	09	39	33	28	23	19	16	13	10	08	05
6.0	73	61	49	41	34	29	24	20	16	11	66	55	44	38	31	27	22	19	15	10	60	51	41	35	28	24	19	16	13	09	50	42	34	29	23	18	15	13	10	06	39	33	27	23	18	15	11	09	06	04
7.0	70	58	45	38	30	27	21	18	14	08	64	53	41	35	28	24	19	16	12	07	58	48	38	32	26	22	17	14	11	06	49	41	32	27	21	17	14	11	08	05	40	33	26	22	17	14	10	08	05	03
8.0	68	55	42	35	27	23	18	15	12	06	62	50	38	32	25	21	17	14	11	05	57	46	35	29	23	19	15	13	10	05	49	40	30	25	19	16	12	10	07	03	40	33	26	21	16	13	09	07	04	02
9.0	66	52	38	31	25	21	16	14	11	05	61	49	36	30	23	19	15	13	10	04	55	45	33	29	24	18	15	12	09	04	48	39	29	24	18	15	11	09	07	03	40	32	25	20	15	12	09	07	04	02
10.0	65	51	36	29	22	19	15	11	09	04	59	46	33	27	21	18	14	11	08	03	55	43	31	25	19	16	12	10	08	03	47	37	27	22	17	14	11	08	06	02	40	32	24	19	14	11	08	06	03	01

*Ceiling, floor, or floor of cavity.

Reprinted with permission from IES, IES Lighting Handbook, Fifth Edition 1972.

Maintenance Category	Top Enclosure	Bottom Enclosure
I	1. None.	1. None
II	1. None 2. Transparent with 15 per cent or more uplight through apertures. 3. Translucent with 15 per cent or more uplight through apertures. 4. Opaque with 15 per cent or more uplight through apertures.	1. None 2. Louvers or baffles
III	1. Transparent with less than 15 per cent upward light through apertures. 2. Translucent with less than 15 per cent upward light through apertures. 3. Opaque with less than 15 per cent uplight through apertures.	1. None 2. Louvers or baffles
IV	1. Transparent unapertured. 2. Translucent unapertured. 3. Opaque unapertured.	1. None 2. Louvers
V	1. Transparent unapertured. 2. Translucent unapertured. 3. Opaque unapertured.	1. Transparent unapertured 2. Translucent unapertured
VI	1. None. 2. Transparent unapertured. 3. Translucent unapertured. 4. Opaque unapertured.	1. Transparent unapertured 2. Translucent unapertured 3. Opaque unapertured

Reprinted with permission from IES, IES Lighting Handbook, Fifth Edition 1972.

FIGURE 14-16   /   Lamp lumen depreciation

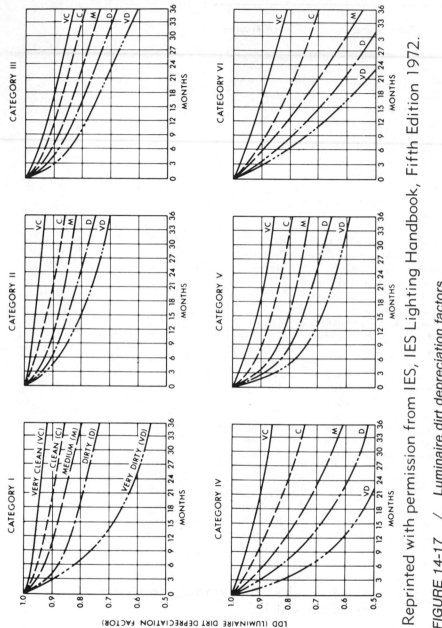

Reprinted with permission from IES, IES Lighting Handbook, Fifth Edition 1972.

FIGURE 14-17 / Luminaire dirt depreciation factors

Multiplying Factors for Other than 20 Per Cent Effective Floor Cavity Reflectance

% Effective Ceiling Cavity Reflectance, ρ_{CC}	80				70				50			30			10		
% Wall Reflectance, ρ_W	70	50	30	10	70	50	30	10	50	30	10	50	30	10	50	30	10

For 30 Per Cent Effective Floor Cavity Reflectance (20 Per Cent = 1.00)

Room Cavity Ratio	70	50	30	10	70	50	30	10	50	30	10	50	30	10	50	30	10
1	1.092	1.082	1.075	1.068	1.077	1.070	1.064	1.059	1.049	1.044	1.040	1.028	1.026	1.023	1.012	1.010	1.008
2	1.079	1.066	1.055	1.047	1.068	1.057	1.048	1.039	1.041	1.033	1.027	1.026	1.021	1.017	1.013	1.010	1.006
3	1.070	1.054	1.042	1.033	1.061	1.048	1.037	1.028	1.034	1.027	1.020	1.024	1.017	1.012	1.014	1.009	1.005
4	1.062	1.045	1.033	1.024	1.055	1.040	1.029	1.021	1.030	1.022	1.015	1.022	1.015	1.010	1.014	1.009	1.004
5	1.056	1.038	1.026	1.018	1.050	1.034	1.024	1.015	1.027	1.018	1.012	1.020	1.013	1.008	1.014	1.009	1.004
6	1.052	1.033	1.021	1.014	1.047	1.030	1.020	1.012	1.024	1.015	1.009	1.019	1.012	1.006	1.014	1.008	1.003
7	1.047	1.029	1.018	1.011	1.043	1.026	1.017	1.009	1.022	1.013	1.007	1.018	1.010	1.005	1.014	1.008	1.003
8	1.044	1.026	1.015	1.009	1.040	1.024	1.015	1.007	1.020	1.012	1.006	1.017	1.009	1.004	1.013	1.007	1.003
9	1.040	1.024	1.014	1.007	1.037	1.022	1.014	1.006	1.019	1.011	1.005	1.016	1.009	1.004	1.013	1.007	1.002
10	1.037	1.022	1.012	1.006	1.034	1.020	1.012	1.005	1.017	1.010	1.004	1.015	1.009	1.003	1.013	1.007	1.002

For 10 Per Cent Effective Floor Cavity Reflectance (20 Per Cent = 1.00)

Room Cavity Ratio	70	50	30	10	70	50	30	10	50	30	10	50	30	10	50	30	10
1	.923	.929	.935	.940	.933	.939	.943	.948	.956	.960	.963	.973	.976	.979	.989	.991	.993
2	.931	.942	.950	.958	.940	.949	.957	.963	.962	.968	.974	.976	.980	.985	.988	.991	.995
3	.939	.951	.961	.969	.945	.057	.966	.973	.967	.975	.981	.978	.983	.988	.988	.992	.996
4	.944	.958	.969	.978	.950	.963	.973	.980	.972	.980	.986	.980	.986	.991	.987	.992	.996
5	.949	.964	.976	.983	.954	.968	.978	.985	.975	.983	.989	.981	.988	.993	.987	.992	.997
6	.953	.969	.980	.986	.958	.972	.982	.989	.977	.985	.992	.982	.989	.995	.987	.993	.997
7	.957	.973	.983	.991	.961	.975	.985	.991	.979	.987	.994	.983	.990	.996	.987	.993	.998
8	.960	.976	.986	.993	.963	.977	.987	.993	.981	.988	.995	.984	.991	.997	.987	.994	.998
9	.963	.978	.987	.994	.965	.979	.989	.994	.983	.990	.996	.985	.992	.998	.988	.994	.999
10	.965	.980	.989	.995	.967	.981	.990	.995	.984	.991	.997	.986	.993	.998	.988	.994	.999

For 0 Per Cent Effective Floor Cavity Reflectance (20 Per Cent = 1.00)

Room Cavity Ratio	70	50	30	10	70	50	30	10	50	30	10	50	30	10	50	30	10
1	.859	.870	.879	.886	.873	.884	.893	.901	.916	.923	.929	.948	.954	.960	.979	.983	.987
2	.871	.887	.903	.919	.886	.902	.916	.928	.926	.938	.949	.954	.963	.971	.978	.983	.991
3	.882	.904	.915	.942	.898	.918	.934	.947	.936	.950	.964	.958	.969	.979	.976	.984	.993
4	.893	.919	.941	.958	.908	.930	.948	.961	.945	.961	.974	.961	.974	.984	.975	.985	.994
5	.903	.931	.953	.969	.914	.939	.958	.970	.951	.967	.980	.964	.977	.988	.975	.985	.995
6	.911	.940	.961	.976	.920	.945	.965	.977	.955	.972	.985	.966	.979	.991	.975	.986	.996
7	.917	.947	.967	.981	.924	.950	.970	.982	.959	.975	.988	.968	.981	.993	.975	.987	.997
8	.922	.953	.971	.985	.929	.955	.975	.986	.963	.978	.991	.970	.983	.995	.976	.988	.998
9	.928	.958	.975	.988	.933	.959	.980	.989	.966	.980	.993	.971	.985	.996	.976	.988	.998
10	.933	.962	.979	.991	.937	.963	.983	.992	.969	.982	.995	.973	.987	.997	.977	.989	.999

Reprinted with permission from IES, IES Lighting Handbook, Fifth Edition 1972.

FIGURE 14-18 / Multiplying factors for other than 20 percent effective floor cavity reflectance

In some cases, luminaire data in this table are based on an actual typical luminaire; in other cases, the data represent a composite of generic luminaire types. Therefore, whenever possible, specific luminaire data should be used in preference to this table of typical luminaires.

The polar intensity sketch (candlepower distribution curve) and the corresponding spacing-to-mounting-height guide are representative of many luminaires of each type shown. A specific luminaire may differ in perpendicular plane (crosswise) and parallel plane (lengthwise) intensity distributions and in S/MH guide from the values shown. However, the various coefficients depend only on the average intensity at each polar angle from nadir. The tabulated coefficients can be applied to any luminaire whose average intensity distribution matches the values used to generate the coefficients. The average intensity values used to generate the coefficients are given at the end of the table, normalized to a per thousand lamp lumen basis.

The various coefficients below depend on the shape of the average intensity distribution curve and are linearly related

Typical Luminaire	Maint. Cat.	Maximum S/MH Guide[d]	RCR[c]	80, pw 50	30	10	70, pw 50	30	10	50, pw 50	30	10	30, pw 50	30	10	10, pw 50	30	10	0, pw 0	WDRC[e]
				Coefficients of Utilization for 20 Per Cent Effective Floor Cavity Reflectance ($\rho_{FC} = 20$)																
1 Pendant diffusing sphere with incandescent lamp (35½%↑, 45%↓)	V	1.5	0	.87	.87	.87	.81	.81	.81	.69	.69	.69	.59	.59	.59	.49	.49	.49	.44	
			1	.71	.67	.63	.66	.62	.59	.56	.53	.50	.47	.45	.43	.39	.37	.35	.31	.35
			2	.61	.54	.49	.56	.50	.46	.47	.43	.39	.39	.36	.33	.32	.29	.27	.23	.27
			3	.52	.45	.39	.48	.42	.37	.41	.36	.31	.34	.30	.26	.27	.24	.22	.18	.22
			4	.46	.38	.33	.42	.36	.30	.36	.30	.26	.30	.26	.22	.24	.21	.18	.15	.19
			5	.40	.33	.27	.37	.30	.25	.32	.26	.22	.26	.22	.19	.21	.18	.15	.12	.16
			6	.36	.28	.23	.33	.26	.21	.28	.23	.19	.23	.19	.16	.19	.15	.13	.10	.14
			7	.32	.25	.20	.29	.23	.18	.25	.20	.16	.21	.16	.13	.17	.13	.11	.09	.13
			8	.29	.22	.17	.27	.20	.16	.23	.17	.14	.19	.15	.12	.15	.12	.09	.07	.12
			9	.26	.19	.15	.24	.18	.14	.20	.15	.12	.17	.13	.10	.14	.11	.08	.06	.11
			10	.23	.17	.13	.22	.16	.12	.19	.14	.10	.16	.12	.09	.13	.09	.07	.05	.10
2 Concentric ring unit with incandescent silvered-bowl lamp (83%↑, 3½%↓)	II	1.5	0	.83	.83	.83	.71	.71	.71	.49	.49	.49	.30	.30	.30	.12	.12	.12	.03	
			1	.72	.69	.66	.62	.60	.57	.43	.42	.40	.26	.25	.25	.10	.10	.10	.03	.02
			2	.63	.58	.54	.54	.50	.47	.38	.36	.33	.23	.22	.21	.09	.09	.08	.02	.01
			3	.55	.49	.45	.48	.43	.39	.33	.30	.28	.20	.19	.17	.08	.08	.07	.02	.01
			4	.48	.42	.37	.42	.37	.33	.29	.26	.24	.18	.16	.15	.07	.07	.06	.02	.01
			5	.43	.36	.32	.37	.32	.28	.26	.23	.20	.16	.14	.13	.06	.06	.05	.01	.01
			6	.38	.32	.27	.33	.28	.24	.23	.20	.17	.14	.12	.11	.06	.05	.04	.01	.01
			7	.34	.28	.23	.30	.24	.21	.21	.17	.15	.13	.11	.09	.05	.04	.04	.01	.01
			8	.31	.25	.20	.27	.21	.18	.19	.15	.13	.12	.10	.08	.05	.04	.03	.01	.01
			9	.28	.22	.18	.24	.19	.16	.17	.14	.11	.10	.09	.07	.04	.03	.03	.01	.01
			10	.25	.20	.16	.22	.17	.14	.16	.12	.10	.10	.08	.06	.04	.03	.03	.01	.01
3 Porcelain-enameled ventilated standard dome with incandescent lamp (0%↑, 83½%↓)	IV	1.3	0	.99	.99	.99	.97	.97	.97	.92	.92	.92	.88	.88	.88	.85	.85	.85	.83	
			1	.88	.85	.82	.86	.83	.81	.83	.80	.78	.79	.78	.76	.77	.75	.73	.72	.29
			2	.78	.73	.68	.76	.72	.67	.73	.69	.66	.71	.67	.64	.68	.65	.63	.61	.28
			3	.69	.62	.57	.67	.61	.57	.65	.60	.56	.63	.58	.55	.61	.57	.54	.52	.26
			4	.61	.54	.49	.60	.53	.48	.58	.52	.48	.56	.51	.47	.54	.50	.46	.45	.24
			5	.54	.47	.41	.53	.46	.41	.51	.45	.41	.50	.44	.40	.48	.43	.40	.38	.23
			6	.48	.41	.35	.47	.40	.35	.46	.39	.35	.44	.39	.34	.43	.38	.34	.32	.21
			7	.43	.35	.30	.42	.35	.30	.41	.34	.30	.39	.34	.30	.38	.33	.29	.28	.20
			8	.38	.31	.26	.38	.31	.26	.37	.30	.26	.36	.30	.26	.35	.30	.26	.24	.19
			9	.35	.28	.23	.34	.27	.23	.33	.27	.23	.33	.27	.23	.32	.27	.23	.21	.17
			10	.31	.25	.20	.31	.24	.20	.30	.24	.20	.29	.24	.20	.29	.23	.20	.18	.16
4 Prismatic square surface drum (18½%↑, 60½%↓)	V	1.3	0	.89	.89	.89	.85	.85	.85	.77	.77	.77	.70	.70	.70	.63	.63	.63	.60	
			1	.78	.75	.72	.74	.72	.69	.68	.66	.64	.62	.60	.58	.56	.55	.54	.51	.24
			2	.69	.65	.61	.66	.62	.58	.61	.57	.54	.56	.53	.50	.51	.49	.47	.44	.20
			3	.62	.57	.52	.60	.55	.50	.55	.51	.47	.50	.47	.44	.46	.44	.41	.39	.18[*]
			4	.56	.50	.46	.54	.49	.44	.50	.45	.42	.46	.42	.39	.42	.39	.37	.35	.16
			5	.51	.45	.40	.49	.43	.39	.45	.41	.37	.42	.38	.35	.39	.36	.33	.31	.15
			6	.46	.40	.36	.45	.39	.35	.42	.37	.33	.39	.35	.31	.36	.32	.30	.28	.13
			7	.42	.36	.32	.41	.35	.31	.38	.33	.29	.35	.31	.28	.33	.29	.27	.25	.13
			8	.39	.32	.28	.37	.32	.28	.35	.30	.26	.32	.28	.25	.30	.27	.24	.22	.12
			9	.35	.29	.25	.34	.29	.25	.32	.27	.24	.30	.26	.23	.28	.24	.22	.20	.11
			10	.32	.27	.23	.31	.26	.22	.29	.25	.21	.27	.23	.20	.26	.22	.20	.18	.11

[a] ρ_{CC} = per cent effective ceiling cavity reflectance.

[b] ρ_w = per cent wall reflectance.

[c] RCR = Room Cavity Ratio.

[d] Maximum S/MH guide — ratio of maximum luminaire spacing to mounting or ceiling height above work-plane.

FIGURE 14-19 / Coefficients of utilization

Figure 14-19 — Coefficients of Utilization

	Typical Distribution and Per Cent Lamp Lumens		ρcc →	80			70			50			30			10			0	WDRC
Typical Luminaire	Maint. Cat.	Maximum S/MH Guide[d]	ρw →	50	30	10	50	30	10	50	30	10	50	30	10	50	30	10	0	
			RCR[c]	Coefficients of Utilization for 20 Per Cent Effective Floor Cavity Reflectance (ρFC = 20)																

20 — Porcelain-enameled reflector with 35°CW shielding (Maint. Cat. II, Max S/MH Guide 1.3; 22½%↑, 65%↓)

RCR	80-50	80-30	80-10	70-50	70-30	70-10	50-50	50-30	50-10	30-50	30-30	30-10	10-50	10-30	10-10	0	WDRC
0	.99	.99	.99	.94	.94	.94	.84	.84	.84	.76	.76	.76	.68	.68	.68	.65	
1	.88	.85	.82	.84	.81	.78	.76	.74	.72	.69	.67	.66	.62	.61	.60	.57	.21
2	.78	.73	.68	.74	.70	.66	.68	.64	.61	.62	.59	.56	.56	.54	.52	.49	.20
3	.69	.63	.58	.66	.61	.56	.61	.56	.53	.56	.52	.49	.51	.48	.46	.43	.19
4	.62	.55	.50	.60	.53	.49	.55	.50	.46	.50	.46	.43	.46	.43	.40	.37	.17
5	.55	.48	.43	.53	.47	.42	.49	.44	.39	.45	.41	.37	.41	.38	.35	.32	.16
6	.50	.43	.38	.48	.41	.37	.44	.39	.35	.41	.36	.33	.37	.34	.31	.29	.15
7	.45	.38	.33	.43	.37	.32	.40	.34	.30	.37	.32	.29	.34	.30	.27	.25	.14
8	.40	.34	.29	.39	.32	.28	.36	.30	.27	.33	.28	.25	.31	.27	.24	.22	.14
9	.36	.30	.25	.35	.29	.24	.32	.27	.23	.30	.25	.22	.28	.24	.21	.19	.13
10	.33	.27	.22	.32	.26	.22	.29	.24	.20	.27	.23	.19	.25	.21	.18	.17	.12

21 — Diffuse aluminum reflector with 35°CW shielding (Maint. Cat. II, Max S/MH Guide 1.5/1.3; 17%↑, 66%↓)

RCR	80-50	80-30	80-10	70-50	70-30	70-10	50-50	50-30	50-10	30-50	30-30	30-10	10-50	10-30	10-10	0	WDRC
0	.94	.94	.94	.90	.90	.90	.82	.82	.82	.75	.75	.75	.69	.69	.69	.66	
1	.85	.82	.80	.82	.79	.77	.75	.73	.72	.69	.68	.66	.64	.63	.62	.59	.18
2	.76	.72	.68	.74	.70	.66	.68	.65	.62	.63	.61	.58	.58	.56	.55	.52	.17
3	.69	.63	.59	.66	.61	.57	.62	.58	.54	.57	.54	.51	.53	.51	.48	.46	.17
4	.62	.56	.51	.60	.54	.50	.56	.51	.47	.52	.48	.45	.48	.45	.43	.41	.16
5	.55	.49	.44	.53	.48	.43	.50	.45	.41	.47	.43	.39	.44	.40	.38	.36	.15
6	.50	.43	.39	.48	.42	.38	.45	.40	.36	.42	.38	.35	.40	.36	.33	.31	.15
7	.45	.38	.34	.43	.37	.33	.41	.36	.32	.38	.34	.30	.36	.32	.29	.27	.14
8	.40	.34	.29	.39	.33	.29	.37	.31	.28	.34	.30	.26	.32	.28	.25	.24	.13
9	.36	.30	.25	.35	.29	.25	.33	.28	.24	.31	.26	.23	.29	.25	.22	.20	.13
10	.33	.26	.22	.32	.26	.22	.30	.25	.21	.28	.23	.20	.26	.22	.19	.18	.12

22 — Porcelain-enameled reflector with 30°CW x 30°LW shielding (Maint. Cat. II, Max S/MH Guide 1.0; 23½%↑, 57%↓)

RCR	80-50	80-30	80-10	70-50	70-30	70-10	50-50	50-30	50-10	30-50	30-30	30-10	10-50	10-30	10-10	0	WDRC
0	.90	.90	.90	.85	.85	.85	.76	.76	.76	.68	.68	.68	.60	.60	.60	.57	
1	.81	.78	.76	.77	.74	.72	.69	.67	.66	.62	.61	.60	.56	.55	.54	.51	.16
2	.72	.68	.64	.69	.65	.62	.62	.59	.57	.56	.54	.52	.51	.49	.47	.45	.16
3	.65	.59	.55	.62	.57	.53	.56	.52	.49	.51	.48	.46	.46	.44	.42	.39	.15
4	.58	.52	.48	.56	.50	.46	.51	.46	.43	.46	.43	.40	.42	.39	.37	.35	.14
5	.52	.46	.41	.50	.44	.40	.46	.41	.38	.42	.38	.35	.38	.35	.33	.30	.13
6	.47	.41	.36	.45	.39	.35	.41	.37	.33	.38	.34	.31	.35	.31	.29	.27	.13
7	.43	.36	.32	.41	.35	.31	.38	.33	.29	.34	.30	.27	.32	.28	.26	.24	.12
8	.38	.32	.28	.37	.31	.27	.34	.29	.26	.31	.27	.24	.29	.25	.23	.21	.11
9	.35	.29	.24	.33	.28	.24	.31	.26	.22	.28	.24	.21	.26	.22	.20	.18	.11
10	.32	.26	.22	.30	.25	.21	.28	.23	.20	.26	.22	.19	.24	.20	.18	.16	.10

23 — Diffuse aluminum reflector with 35°CW x 35°LW shielding (Maint. Cat. II, Max S/MH Guide 1.5/1.1; 17%↑, 56½%↓)

RCR	80-50	80-30	80-10	70-50	70-30	70-10	50-50	50-30	50-10	30-50	30-30	30-10	10-50	10-30	10-10	0	WDRC
0	.83	.83	.83	.79	.79	.79	.71	.71	.71	.65	.65	.65	.59	.59	.59	.56	
1	.75	.72	.70	.72	.69	.68	.65	.64	.62	.60	.59	.58	.55	.54	.53	.50	.15
2	.67	.63	.60	.65	.61	.58	.59	.57	.54	.55	.53	.51	.50	.49	.47	.45	.14
3	.61	.56	.52	.58	.54	.51	.54	.50	.48	.50	.47	.45	.46	.44	.42	.40	.14
4	.55	.49	.45	.53	.48	.44	.49	.45	.42	.45	.42	.40	.42	.39	.37	.36	.13
5	.49	.44	.40	.47	.42	.39	.44	.40	.37	.41	.38	.35	.38	.35	.33	.31	.12
6	.45	.39	.35	.43	.38	.34	.40	.36	.33	.37	.34	.31	.35	.32	.30	.28	.12
7	.40	.35	.31	.39	.34	.30	.36	.32	.29	.34	.30	.27	.32	.29	.26	.25	.11
8	.36	.31	.27	.35	.30	.26	.33	.28	.25	.31	.27	.24	.29	.25	.23	.21	.11
9	.33	.27	.23	.32	.26	.23	.29	.25	.22	.28	.24	.21	.26	.22	.20	.19	.10
10	.30	.24	.21	.29	.24	.20	.27	.22	.19	.25	.21	.19	.23	.20	.18	.16	.10

24 — Metal or dense diffusing sides with 45°CW x 45°LW shielding (Maint. Cat. II, Max S/MH Guide 1.1; 39%↑, 32%↓)

RCR	80-50	80-30	80-10	70-50	70-30	70-10	50-50	50-30	50-10	30-50	30-30	30-10	10-50	10-30	10-10	0	WDRC
0	.75	.75	.75	.68	.68	.68	.57	.57	.57	.46	.46	.46	.36	.36	.36	.31	
1	.67	.64	.62	.61	.59	.57	.51	.50	.49	.42	.41	.40	.34	.33	.32	.29	.08
2	.59	.55	.52	.55	.51	.49	.46	.44	.42	.38	.36	.35	.31	.30	.29	.25	.08
3	.53	.48	.45	.49	.45	.42	.41	.39	.36	.35	.33	.31	.28	.27	.26	.23	.08
4	.47	.42	.39	.44	.40	.36	.37	.34	.32	.31	.29	.27	.26	.24	.23	.20	.07
5	.43	.37	.33	.40	.35	.31	.34	.30	.28	.28	.26	.24	.23	.22	.20	.18	.07
6	.39	.33	.29	.36	.31	.28	.31	.27	.25	.26	.23	.21	.22	.20	.18	.16	.07
7	.35	.30	.26	.33	.28	.25	.28	.24	.22	.24	.21	.19	.20	.18	.16	.15	.06
8	.32	.27	.23	.30	.25	.22	.25	.22	.19	.22	.19	.17	.18	.16	.15	.13	.06
9	.29	.24	.20	.27	.22	.19	.23	.20	.17	.20	.17	.15	.16	.15	.13	.12	.06
10	.26	.21	.18	.25	.20	.17	.21	.18	.15	.18	.15	.14	.15	.13	.12	.10	.05

[a] ρcc = per cent effective ceiling cavity reflectance.
[b] ρw = per cent wall reflectance.
[c] RCR = Room Cavity Ratio.
[d] Maximum S/MH guide—ratio of maximum luminaire spacing to mounting or ceiling height above work-plane.

FIGURE 14-19 / Coefficients of utilization (continued)

Typical Luminaire	Maint. Cat.	Maximum S/MH Guide	RCR	ρcc→ 80 / 50	80 / 30	80 / 10	70 / 50	70 / 30	70 / 10	50 / 50	50 / 30	50 / 10	30 / 50	30 / 30	30 / 10	10 / 50	10 / 30	10 / 10	0 / 0	WDRC
30 2 lamp prismatic wraparound—multiply by 0.95 for 4 lamps	V	1.5/1.2	0	.80	.80	.80	.77	.77	.77	.71	.71	.71	.66	.66	.66	.60	.60	.60	.58	
			1	.71	.69	.66	.69	.66	.64	.64	.62	.60	.59	.58	.56	.55	.54	.53	.50	.20
			2	.64	.59	.56	.61	.58	.54	.57	.54	.51	.53	.51	.49	.49	.48	.46	.44	.18
			3	.57	.52	.48	.55	.50	.47	.51	.48	.45	.48	.45	.42	.45	.42	.40	.38	.17
			4	.51	.46	.41	.49	.44	.40	.46	.42	.39	.43	.40	.37	.41	.38	.35	.34	.16
			5	.46	.40	.36	.44	.39	.35	.41	.37	.34	.39	.35	.32	.37	.33	.31	.29	.15
			6	.41	.35	.31	.40	.35	.31	.38	.33	.30	.35	.31	.28	.33	.30	.27	.26	.14
			7	.37	.31	.27	.36	.31	.27	.34	.29	.26	.32	.28	.25	.30	.27	.24	.23	.13
			8	.33	.28	.24	.32	.27	.23	.30	.26	.22	.29	.25	.22	.27	.24	.21	.19	.12
			9	.30	.24	.20	.29	.24	.20	.27	.23	.19	.26	.22	.19	.24	.21	.18	.17	.12
			10	.27	.22	.18	.26	.21	.18	.25	.20	.17	.23	.19	.16	.22	.18	.16	.15	.11
31 2 lamp prismatic wraparound—multiply by 0.95 for 4 lamps	V	1.2	0	.82	.82	.82	.77	.77	.77	.68	.68	.68	.60	.60	.60	.53	.53	.53	.49	
			1	.71	.68	.65	.67	.65	.62	.60	.58	.56	.53	.51	.50	.47	.45	.44	.41	.22
			2	.63	.58	.54	.59	.55	.52	.53	.50	.47	.47	.45	.42	.42	.40	.38	.35	.18
			3	.56	.50	.46	.53	.48	.44	.47	.44	.40	.42	.39	.37	.38	.35	.33	.31	.16
			4	.50	.44	.40	.48	.42	.38	.43	.39	.35	.38	.35	.32	.34	.32	.29	.27	.14
			5	.45	.39	.34	.43	.37	.33	.38	.34	.31	.35	.31	.28	.31	.28	.26	.24	.13
			6	.41	.34	.30	.39	.33	.29	.35	.30	.27	.32	.28	.25	.28	.25	.23	.21	.12
			7	.37	.31	.27	.35	.30	.26	.32	.27	.24	.29	.25	.22	.26	.23	.20	.19	.11
			8	.33	.27	.23	.32	.26	.23	.29	.24	.21	.26	.22	.20	.23	.20	.18	.16	.10
			9	.30	.24	.20	.29	.23	.20	.26	.22	.18	.24	.20	.17	.21	.18	.16	.14	.10
			10	.27	.22	.18	.26	.21	.18	.24	.19	.16	.22	.18	.15	.19	.16	.14	.13	.09
32 2 lamp white diffuse wraparound—multiply by 0.90 for 4 lamps	V	1.3	0	.52	.52	.52	.50	.50	.50	.46	.46	.46	.42	.42	.42	.39	.39	.39	.37	
			1	.45	.43	.41	.43	.41	.39	.40	.38	.37	.36	.35	.34	.34	.33	.32	.30	.18
			2	.39	.35	.33	.37	.34	.32	.34	.32	.30	.32	.30	.28	.29	.28	.26	.25	.16
			3	.34	.30	.27	.33	.29	.26	.30	.27	.25	.28	.25	.23	.26	.24	.22	.21	.14
			4	.30	.26	.23	.29	.25	.22	.27	.24	.21	.25	.22	.20	.23	.21	.19	.18	.12
			5	.26	.22	.19	.25	.21	.19	.23	.20	.18	.22	.19	.17	.20	.18	.16	.15	.11
			6	.23	.19	.16	.22	.18	.16	.21	.18	.15	.19	.17	.14	.18	.16	.14	.13	.10
			7	.21	.17	.14	.20	.16	.14	.19	.16	.13	.17	.15	.13	.16	.14	.12	.11	.10
			8	.19	.15	.12	.18	.14	.12	.17	.14	.11	.16	.13	.11	.15	.12	.10	.09	.09
			9	.17	.13	.10	.16	.13	.10	.15	.12	.10	.14	.11	.09	.13	.11	.09	.08	.08
			10	.15	.12	.09	.15	.11	.09	.14	.11	.09	.13	.10	.08	.12	.10	.08	.07	.08
33 2 lamp, 1′ wide troffer with 45° plastic louver—multiply by 0.90 for 3 lamps	IV	1.0	0	.54	.54	.54	.53	.53	.53	.51	.51	.51	.48	.48	.48	.46	.46	.46	.45	
			1	.49	.48	.46	.48	.47	.46	.46	.45	.44	.45	.44	.43	.43	.42	.42	.41	.13
			2	.44	.42	.40	.43	.41	.39	.42	.40	.38	.40	.39	.37	.39	.38	.37	.36	.13
			3	.40	.37	.34	.39	.36	.34	.38	.36	.34	.37	.35	.33	.36	.34	.33	.32	.12
			4	.36	.33	.30	.36	.32	.30	.35	.32	.30	.34	.31	.29	.33	.31	.29	.28	.11
			5	.33	.29	.26	.32	.29	.26	.31	.28	.26	.30	.28	.26	.30	.27	.26	.25	.11
			6	.30	.26	.24	.29	.26	.24	.29	.26	.24	.28	.25	.23	.27	.25	.23	.22	.10
			7	.27	.24	.21	.27	.23	.21	.26	.23	.21	.26	.23	.21	.25	.22	.21	.20	.09
			8	.25	.21	.19	.24	.21	.19	.24	.21	.19	.23	.21	.18	.23	.20	.18	.18	.09
			9	.22	.19	.17	.22	.19	.17	.22	.19	.17	.21	.18	.16	.21	.18	.16	.16	.08
			10	.21	.17	.15	.20	.17	.15	.20	.17	.15	.20	.17	.15	.19	.17	.15	.14	.08
34 2 lamp, 1′ wide troffer with 45° white metal louver—multiply by 0.90 for 3 lamps	IV	0.9	0	.50	.50	.50	.49	.49	.49	.47	.47	.47	.45	.45	.45	.43	.43	.43	.42	
			1	.46	.45	.44	.45	.44	.43	.43	.42	.42	.42	.41	.40	.40	.40	.39	.38	.11
			2	.42	.40	.38	.41	.39	.37	.40	.38	.36	.38	.37	.36	.37	.36	.35	.34	.11
			3	.38	.35	.33	.37	.35	.33	.36	.34	.32	.35	.33	.32	.34	.33	.31	.31	.10
			4	.35	.32	.29	.34	.31	.29	.33	.31	.29	.32	.30	.28	.31	.30	.28	.27	.10
			5	.31	.28	.26	.31	.28	.26	.30	.28	.26	.29	.27	.25	.29	.27	.25	.24	.09
			6	.29	.26	.23	.29	.26	.23	.28	.25	.23	.27	.25	.23	.27	.24	.23	.22	.09
			7	.27	.23	.21	.26	.23	.21	.26	.23	.21	.25	.23	.21	.24	.22	.21	.20	.08
			8	.24	.21	.19	.24	.21	.19	.23	.21	.19	.23	.20	.19	.22	.20	.19	.18	.08
			9	.22	.19	.17	.22	.19	.17	.21	.19	.17	.21	.19	.17	.21	.18	.17	.16	.07
			10	.20	.17	.15	.20	.17	.15	.21	.17	.15	.19	.17	.15	.19	.17	.15	.14	.07

Coefficients of Utilization for 20 Per Cent Effective Floor Cavity Reflectance ($\rho_{FC} = 20$)

[a] ρ_{CC} = per cent effective ceiling cavity reflectance.
[b] ρ_W = per cent wall reflectance.
[c] RCR = Room Cavity Ratio.
[d] Maximum S/MH guide—ratio of maximum luminaire spacing to mounting or ceiling height above work-plane.

FIGURE 14-19 / *Coefficients of utilization* (*continued*). *Note:* Select luminaires are included here. Contact luminaire manufacturer for exact specifications.

Reprinted with permission from IES, IES Lighting Handbook, Fifth Edition 1972.

Typical Luminaires	ρ_{CC} →	80			70			50			30			10			0
	ρ_W →	50	30	10	50	30	10	50	30	10	50	30	10	50	30	10	0
	RCR ↓	Coefficients of Utilization for 20 Per Cent Effective Floor Cavity Reflectance, ρ_{FC}															

45

Single row fluorescent lamp cove without reflector, mult. by 0.93 for 2 rows and by 0.85 for 3 rows.

RCR									
1	.42	.40	.39	.36	.35	.33	.25	.24	.23
2	.37	.34	.32	.32	.29	.27	.22	.20	.19
3	.32	.29	.26	.28	.25	.23	.19	.17	.16
4	.29	.25	.22	.25	.22	.19	.17	.15	.13
5	.25	.21	.18	.22	.19	.16	.15	.13	.11
6	.23	.19	.16	.20	.16	.14	.14	.12	.10
7	.20	.17	.14	.17	.14	.12	.12	.10	.09
8	.18	.15	.12	.16	.13	.10	.11	.09	.08
9	.17	.13	.10	.15	.11	.09	.10	.08	.07
10	.15	.12	.09	.13	.10	.08	.09	.07	.06

Coves are not recommended for lighting areas having low reflectances.

46

ρ_{CC} from below ~65%

Diffusing plastic or glass
1) Ceiling efficiency ~60%; diffuser transmittance ~50%; diffuser reflectance ~40%. Cavity with minimum obstructions and painted with 80% reflectance paint—use $\rho_c = 70$.
2) For lower reflectance paint or obstructions—use $\rho_c = 50$.

RCR						
1	.60	.58	.56	.58	.56	.54
2	.53	.49	.45	.51	.47	.43
3	.47	.42	.37	.45	.41	.36
4	.41	.36	.32	.39	.35	.31
5	.37	.31	.27	.35	.30	.26
6	.33	.27	.23	.31	.26	.23
7	.29	.24	.20	.28	.23	.20
8	.26	.21	.18	.25	.20	.17
9	.23	.19	.15	.23	.18	.15
10	.21	.17	.13	.21	.16	.13

47

ρ_{CC} from below ~60%

Prismatic plastic or glass.
1) Ceiling efficiency ~67%; prismatic transmittance ~72%; prismatic reflectance ~18%. Cavity with minimum obstructions and painted with 80% reflectance paint—use $\rho_c = 70$.
2) For lower reflectance paint or obstructions—use $\rho_c = 50$.

RCR									
1	.71	.68	.66	.67	.66	.65	.65	.64	.62
2	.63	.60	.57	.61	.58	.55	.59	.56	.54
3	.57	.53	.49	.55	.52	.48	.54	.50	.47
4	.52	.47	.43	.50	.45	.42	.48	.44	.42
5	.46	.41	.37	.44	.40	.37	.43	.40	.36
6	.42	.37	.33	.41	.36	.32	.40	.35	.32
7	.38	.32	.29	.37	.31	.28	.36	.31	.28
8	.34	.28	.25	.33	.28	.25	.32	.28	.25
9	.30	.25	.22	.30	.25	.21	.29	.25	.21
10	.27	.23	.19	.27	.22	.19	.26	.22	.19

48

ρ_{CC} from below ~45%

Louvered ceiling.
1) Ceiling efficiency ~50%; 45° shielding opaque louvers of 80% reflectance. Cavity with minimum obstructions and painted with 80% reflectance paint—use $\rho_c = 50$.
2) For other conditions refer to Fig. 9-55.

RCR						
1	.51	.49	.48	.47	.46	.45
2	.46	.44	.42	.43	.42	.40
3	.42	.39	.37	.39	.38	.36
4	.38	.35	.33	.36	.34	.32
5	.35	.32	.29	.33	.31	.29
6	.32	.29	.26	.30	.28	.26
7	.29	.26	.23	.28	.25	.23
8	.27	.23	.21	.26	.23	.21
9	.24	.21	.19	.24	.21	.19
10	.22	.19	.17	.22	.19	.17

49

3' x 3' fluorescent troffer with 48" lamps mounted along diagonals—use units 38, 41, or 43 as appropriate

50

2' x 2' fluorescent troffer with two "U" lamps—use units 38, 41, or 43 as appropriate

b RCR = Room Cavity Ratio.
c ρ_{CC} = Per cent effective ceiling cavity reflectance.
d ρ_W = Per cent wall reflectance.

FIGURE 14-19 / Coefficients of utilization (continued)

Typical Hot-Cathode Fluorescent Lamps (Instant Starting)*

Nominal length (inches)	42	64	72	96	48	60	24	36	42	48	60	64	72	84	96
Bulb	T-6	T-6	T-8	T-8	T-12	T-17	T-12	T-12	T-12	T-12	T-12	T-12	T-12	T-12	T-12
Base	Single Pin	Single Pin	Single Pin	Single Pin	Medium Bipin	Mogul Bipin	Single Pin	Single Pin	Single Pin	Single Pin	Single Pin	Single Pin	Single Pin	Single Pin	Single Pin
Lamp amperes	0.200	0.200	0.200	0.200	0.425	0.425	0.425	0.425	0.425	0.425	0.425	0.425	0.425	0.425	0.425
Approx. lamp volts	147	227	215	290	104	107.5	53	77	88	100	123	131	147	172	200
Approx. lamp watts	25	38	37.5	50	41	41.5	21.5	30	34.5	39	48	50.5	57.5	66.5	75
Rated life[a] (hours)	7500	7500	7500	7500	7500–12000	7500–9000	7500–9000	7500–9000	7500–9000	9000–12000	7500–12000	7500–12000	9000–12000	7500–12000	12000
Lamp lumen depreciation (LLD)[b]	76	77	83	89	83	89	81	82	80	82	78	78	89	91	89
Initial lumens[c]															
Cool White	1800	2900	3000	4125	2850	2900	1150	1975	2325	2950	3450	3700	4500	5200	6200
Deluxe Cool White	1250	2020	2085	2870	1980	2020	800	1370	1615	2050	2400	2570	3130	3615	4310
Warm White[f]	1830	2945	3045	4190	2890	2940	1170	2000	2360	2995	3505	3760	4570	5280	6300
Deluxe Warm White[e]	1230	1990	2055	2825	1950	1990	790	1350	1590	2020	2365	2540	3085	3560	4250
White	1830	2945	3045	4190	2890	2940	1170	2000	2360	2995	3505	3760	4570	5280	6300
Daylight	1495	2410	2495	3430	2370	2410	955	1640	1930	2450	2865	3075	3740	4320	5150

* The life and light output ratings of fluorescent lamps are based on their use with ballasts that provide proper operating characteristics. Ballasts that do not provide proper electrical values may substantially reduce either lamp life, or light output, or both.

[a] Rated life under specified test conditions with three hours per start. At longer burning intervals per start, longer life can be expected.

[b] Per cent of initial light output at 70 per cent rated life at 3 hours per start. Average for cool white lamps. Approximate values.

[c] At 100 hours. Where color is made by more than one manufacturer, lumens and footlamberts represent average of manufacturers.

[d] Chroma 50, Optima, Magnalux, Ultima, Color Classer 50, Color-Matcher 50, Color Rater 50.

[e] Chroma 75, Color Classer 75, Color-Matcher 75, Color Rater 75.

[f] Also called Candelite, Charm-Tone, Ember Glo.

Note: All electrical and lumen values apply only under standard photometric conditions.

Reprinted with permission from IES, IES Lighting Handbook, Fifth Edition 1972.

FIGURE 14-20 / Raceways

Questions

14-1. Why are fluorescent lamps used extensively in industrial and commercial projects?

14-2. What are the three types of light which may be projected by a luminaire onto a surface?

14-3. What is the difference between *localized* and *generalized lighting*, and where would you consider using each of them?

14-4. What is meant by the terms *room index* and *room ratio?*

14-5. How do the reflection factors of the space affect the number of luminaires required?

14-6. What must be considered when determining wall reflection factors?

14-7. What is meant by the *maintenance factor* when considering luminaires?

14-8. What does *coefficient of utilization* mean with regard to luminaires?

Design Exercises

14-9. Determine the total lumens and the number of luminaires required for the following problem:

Room: 24 ft × 48 ft
Fixture mounting height: 9 ft (above working plane), 1 ft–0 in. below ceiling
Working plane: 3 ft–0 in. above finished floor
Use: Laboratory, 120 fc
Ceiling reflectance: 70%
Wall reflectance: 50%
Floor reflectance: 30%
Maintenance factor: Clean, 12 months
Luminaires: Fluorescent, 40-W, instant-start, white, type 29 (Fig. 14-19), 12 hours per start

14-10. Determine the total lumens and the number of luminaires required for the following problem:

Room: 18 ft × 24 ft
Fixture mounting height: 6 ft (above working plane), flush to ceiling
Working plane: 2 ft–6 in. above finished floor
Footcandles desired: 75 fc, study hall
Ceiling reflectance: 80%
Wall reflectance: 50%
Floor reflectance: 30%
Maintenance factor: Dirty, 24 months
Luminaires: Fluorescent, 40-W, instant-start, deluxe cool white, type a 34 (Fig. 14-19), 12 hours per start

Chapter 15

System Installation

15-1 Overview

Too often a building is designed with little or no concern for its plumbing, heating, and electrical systems. Many projects also have special requirements in terms of communications (telephones, nursing stations, etc.) or security that must be considered.

The materials and assemblies used in the construction of the building have an important impact on the ease of installation and cost of the mechanicals. The materials and assemblies most commonly used and the integration of the mechanicals into them are discussed in this chapter. The major areas of coordination between contractors are listed at the end of the chapter.

When considering the space required to run the mechanicals, the two primary considerations will be the size of the pipe connections, particularly of cast iron, and whether mechanicals cross each other, one in a horizontal direction and one in a vertical direction (the space required may be greater at that point than at any other).

15-2   Poured Concrete

If the concrete is poured on the job, it is often required that the mechanicals be embedded in the concrete. The conduit and boxes for electrical work, the pipes for heating and plumbing, and the various inserts, sleeves, and straps are placed by the mechanicals in the area or form to be filled with concrete. Coordination is required with the general contractor since some of the mechanicals' materials should be installed before the reinforcing bars are positioned and some must be installed after.

Sleeves and inserts are often installed before the re-bars; therefore they must be securely fastened so they will not be disturbed by the bar-setter or by the concrete when it is placed. Sleeves are the holes left in the concrete so that pipes or other material may pass through. The sleeve is easily formed by nailing a metal cup to the form, placing a fiber cylinder over it and inserting a metal closure on the top of the cylinder. These fiber cylinders are available in a wide range of diameters. The fewer the number of nails required to attach materials to the form, the less chance of damaging the concrete surface. Wooden forms are used to block out chases and rectangular or square sleeves. An adhesive tape about ⅛ in. thick is available that will hold the inserts in place against the form. The insert and form must be clean and dry for the tape to stick properly, and when they are, it is very effective, it leaves no nail holes, and the form is easily stripped.

Embedding conduit in concrete presents no problem except that care must be taken in placing the concrete so that the conduit is not damaged, allowing moisture to enter. The wiring is then easily pulled through the conduit when convenient.

All water, waste, and vent pipes should be tested before they are covered—in this case, embedded—to determine if the entire system is watertight. Tests commonly run for water piping require that it be watertight under a hydrostatic water pressure of 125 psi for a minimum of 1 hr; any leaks that appear must be repaired with the joint compound used originally. Sanitary (waste) drainage and vent piping should be tested before any fixtures are installed and before connection is made to the sewer. The test consists of capping or plugging the opening, filling the entire system with water, and allowing it to stand for 3 hr, during which time any leaks are repaired. The testing times must be coordinated with the general contractor, so they may be completed while the piping is completely exposed. Once the concrete is poured and the pipes embedded, it is very time-consuming and expensive to remove the concrete so that repairs to the pipe may be made.

Inserts and hangers are often embedded in concrete slabs to provide support for pipes running horizontally below them. Some typical inserts and hangers are shown in Fig. 15-1. These inserts eliminate or reduce the amount of piping embedded in the concrete; at the same time, the pipes installed below the concrete deck are either exposed to view, concealed by a suspended ceiling, or enclosed in a soffit. Mechanicals exposed to view are acceptable in some areas, such as storage and some work areas, but not in most offices or public areas.

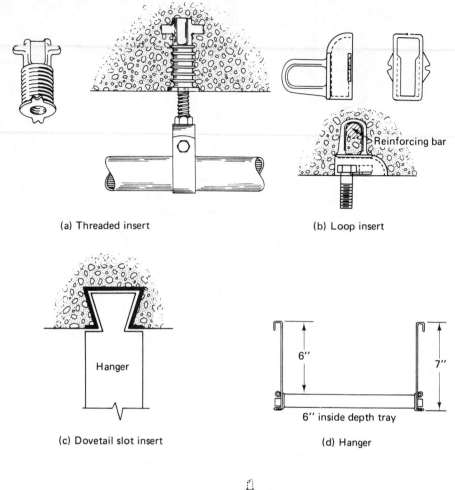

(a) Threaded insert

(b) Loop insert

Reinforcing bar

Hanger

(c) Dovetail slot insert

6"

7"

6" inside depth tray

(d) Hanger

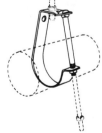

(e) Pipe hanger

FIGURE 15-1 / Typical inserts and hangers

Poured concrete walls may be furred out to allow for the passage of mechanicals so that they need not be embedded in the concrete. The most commonly used types of furring are the wetwall and the drywall systems (Fig. 15-2), but any material may be used as long as sufficient space is left between the materials for all the mechanicals which must be placed. The space required is determined by the largest mechanical passing through (usually the pipes), the direction of its run, and whether it crosses any other mechanicals.

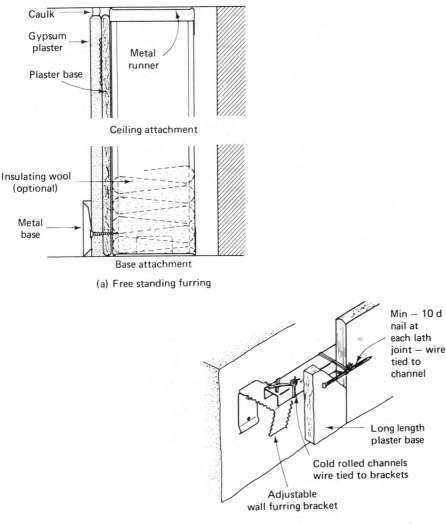

(a) Free standing furring

(b) Adjustable wall furring bracket and attachment of plaster base

FIGURE 15-2 / Wall furring

Metal raceways may be installed in a poured concrete floor (Fig. 15-3) to allow for the passage of electrical and telephone wires and conduit. In this manner, changes may be made and wires added with a minimum of cost and time. The raceways may be either level with or below the surface of the concrete. The manufacturers of metal decking for floors have been most resourceful in adapting their systems to electrical and even distribution systems.

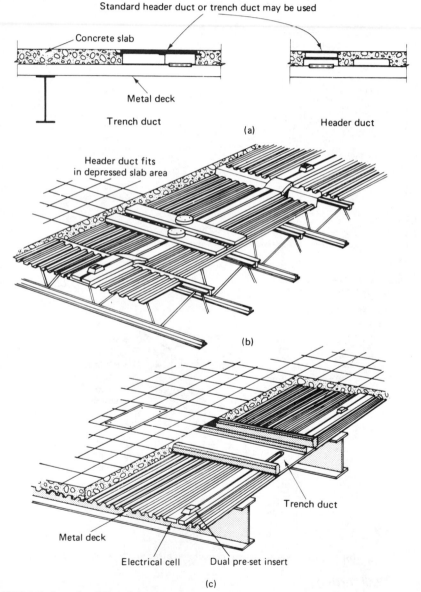

Standard header duct or trench duct may be used

Concrete slab

Metal deck

Trench duct   Header duct

(a)

Header duct fits
in depressed slab area

(b)

Trench duct

Metal deck

Electrical cell   Dual pre-set insert

(c)

FIGURE 15-3   /   Metal raceways

15-3   Precast Concrete

Either the mechanicals are placed on top of the precast concrete and embedded in a concrete topping, or they are placed below the concrete structural member.

Electrical work below the precast concrete is usually attached to it by a clip and an insert, while pipes are suspended by hangers. The hangers may either be fitted into the joints between the precast members, or the inserts may be cast into the members. The conduit may sometimes be placed inconspicuously, although any pipes, ducts, junction boxes, and terminals would be unsightly in most areas, and either a suspended ceiling or soffit is used to conceal the mechanicals (as in Fig. 15-10, which also relates to poured concrete). The double tee may have a soffit area right in the recessed area of the tee to house mechanicals running in the direction of the span (Fig. 15-4).

Mechanicals required for the space above the precast concrete may be run in concrete topping, or an entire elevated floor area may be used. Junction boxes and conduit may be placed in the forms and precast in the concrete. When entire walls are precast, the conduit and boxes are often cast right into the wall.

Holes may be cut into the precast concrete to allow the vertical passage of mechanicals. The holes may be cast circular or rectangular or may be field cut with a diamond core drill. The sizes of the holes must be coordinated with the manufacturer's recommendations. The width of the holes in the tees cannot exceed the distance between the stems (Fig. 15-5). Hollow core slab manufacturers have steel header pieces available to allow for a variety of cutout sizes (Fig. 15-6).

When double walls (partitions) are used to allow vertical passage of mechanicals, it may be possible for each of the structural elements to bear (rest) on one of the walls, allowing the easy and economical passage of mechanicals; of course, the cost of constructing two bearing walls must be considered (Fig. 15-7). This approach may also be used for poured-in-place concrete.

15-4   Wood

A wood deck over laminated wood beams and arches easily allows the passage of pipes through the roof. When conduit runs for lighting fixtures are needed on the ceiling, the decking may be routed (grooved) parallel to the edge to conceal the electrical conduit. Either the conduit is laid in one of the grooves (Fig. 15-8), left in the top of the laminated section, or a wiremold may be run in the corner at the juncture of the decking and the laminated section. No concealed space is available for the running of ducts or pipes.

Wooden trusses, similar to the bowstring type shown in Fig. 15-9, are very adaptable, allowing the passage of mechanicals through the decking and throughout the space. Ducts and pipes may run horizontally and only large ducts may present any problems. A ceiling is usually applied to the bottom of the trusses.

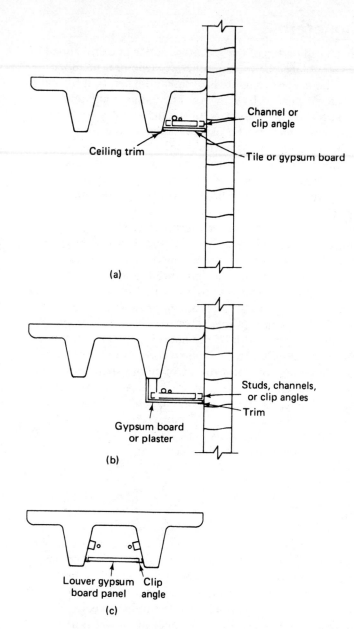

Channel or clip angle

Ceiling trim

Tile or gypsum board

(a)

Studs, channels, or clip angles

Trim

Gypsum board or plaster

(b)

Louver gypsum board panel   Clip angle

(c)

FIGURE 15-4   /   Double tee soffit

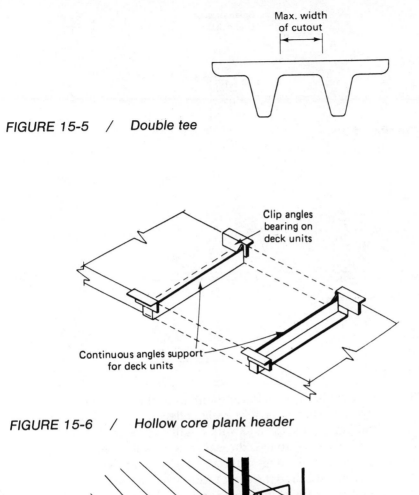

FIGURE 15-5   /   Double tee

FIGURE 15-6   /   Hollow core plank header

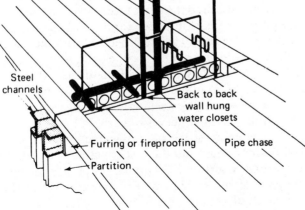

FIGURE 15-7   /   Double bearing walls

Beam or arch
channeled to
receive
electrical
conduit

FIGURE 15-8   /   *Channeled beam*

FIGURE 15-9   /   *Bowstring truss*

15-5   Steel Joists

Steel joist assemblies offer some of the most economical solutions to the problem of placing mechanicals. The space available in the joist design offers flexibility in installing the electrical wiring and piping, and the ductwork installation is limited only by the clear space available for the ducts to pass through. Suspended ceilings are then required to conceal the mechanicals running through the space, but this system may still be economical in comparison to the cost of using precast concrete without suspended ceilings. The portion of assembly used for the ceiling structure (between the finished ceiling and the floor above) is often specified with mechanical considerations in mind. For large ductwork, a soffit may be built, or the ceiling may be suspended a sufficient amount to allow passage of the ducts. Holes for mechanicals running vertically are easily cut in the decking and sleeves placed in the concrete. When gypsum decks are used on the steel joists, openings are left by providing supports between the purlins and the sleeves or curb.

A suspended ceiling allows freedom in the mechanical layout in terms of directions, shortest distances, and diagonal runs, but the cost of suspended ceilings must be considered. Soffit areas, usually constructed of drywall or plaster, are economical if mechanicals are designed to run within confined areas; however, this will require more materials—extra lengths of pipe, extra couplings, etc.—since diagonal runs may be uneconomical. A typical soffit installation is shown in Fig. 15-10.

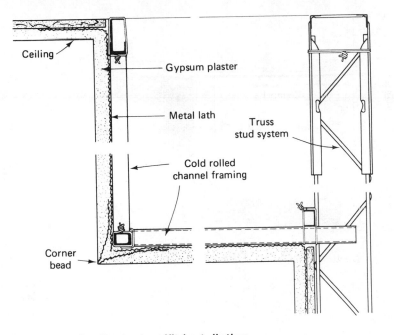

Ceiling

Gypsum plaster

Metal lath

Truss
stud system

Cold rolled
channel framing

Corner
bead

FIGURE 15-10 / Typical soffit installation

15-6 Pipe Tunnels

The use of a pipe tunnel (Fig. 15-11) provides concealed space for the passage of mechanicals at ground level and from building to building. Hangers from the top or from a side attachment may be used. When a large amount of mechanicals must be moved inconspicuously, the pipe tunnel is an excellent, though relatively expensive, approach. Each tunnel should be large enough that a person can pass through to check it or to make repairs when required. Access may be from the ends, or access doors may be built in.

15-7 Partitions

The partitions through which the mechanicals run horizontally and vertically must also be considered. The solution will vary depending on the type of wall.

Masonry walls can be cut out to receive vertical electrical wiring and some piping, but cutting these units is expensive. When a large amount of piping is required, such as for bathrooms, the most common solution is the double or furred-out wall which leaves space for the mechanicals. This solution allows great free-

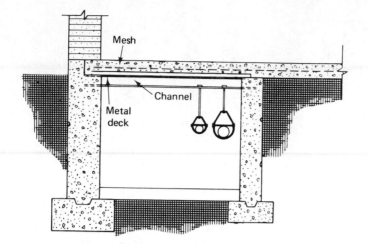

FIGURE 15-11   /   Pipe tunnel

dom in installing the mechanicals in both horizontal and vertical directions. If only a few vertical pipes are involved, such as roof drains, either the masonry may be broken or cut, or smaller units may be used to allow space. Be certain that the wall is thick enough to conceal the pipe and that an interior finish is placed over the masonry. For exposed masonry walls, an opening is left for the pipe, and thin pieces of masonry are placed around it. The core holes of two-core blocks can be lined up to allow vertical passage of the conduit and pipes; be sure to check the core's size at its smallest end to determine size limitations.

With metal stud drywall and wetwall construction, the type of stud used and the clear wall space must be considered. For mechanicals running horizontally, solid metal studs are available with knockouts 24 in. o.c. (this may vary with the manufacturer) or with prepunched holes. Truss-type studs (Fig. 15-12) are also available; they offer the most flexibility and may allow installation of slightly larger sized pipe. Where horizontal mechanicals are such that they cannot pass through the studs, double or core walls are used. This type of construction is often used where there is a large concentration of mechanicals, such as for bathrooms. For vertical runs, the width of the stud may provide sufficient space for the mechanicals, or the double or core wall may be used (Fig. 15-13). Solid plaster walls have only enough space for electrical conduits.

Poured and precast concrete walls are discussed above is Secs. 15-2 and 15-3. Such walls may be furred out with wetwall or drywall construction similar to that used for masonry walls, and vertical runs may be accommodated by blocking out that portion of the form where the pipe, conduit, or duct would run.

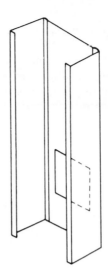

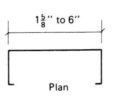

$1\frac{5}{8}''$ to $6''$

Plan

(a) Metal stud

$1\frac{5}{8}''$ to $6''$

Plan

(b) Truss type
stud

FIGURE 15-12 / Truss-type studs

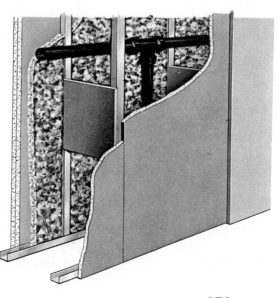

FIGURE 15-13 / Vertical runs

379

15-8   Coordination Requirements

Coordination among the various contractors (general plumbing, electrical, and HVAC) is important in the understanding of: Who is responsible for what? Why? When? Listed below are the major areas of coordination required between the electrical and general contractors.

ITEM	COORDINATION REQUIREMENTS
1. Underground Utilities	Location, size, excavation by whom, from where?
2. Equipment	Recessed depth, size of access openings, method of feed, supports, by whom, size limitations.
3. Distribution	Outlet locations, materials, method of feed, chases, in walls, under floor, overhead, special considerations.
4. Terminal Fixtures and Devices	Location, method of support, finish, color and material.
5. Mounting Surfaces	What is mounting surface? Can it work?
6. Specialty Equipment	Field provisions, storage.
7. Scheduling	Work to be done? When required? Job to be completed on time— who—why—when?

Listed below are the major areas of coordination required between the plumbing and general contractors.

ITEM	COORDINATION REQUIREMENTS
1. Underground Utilities	Location, size, excavation by whom, from where?
2. Building Entrance	Floor sleeves, supports.
3. Mechanical Room Equipment	Supports required, location, anchors, by whom?
4. Distribution	Wall sleeves, hangers, chases, in wall, roof vents, access doors.

ITEM	COORDINATION REQUIREMENTS
5. Fixtures	Method of support, feed, outlets, built-in, floor drains, vents.
6. Finishes	Factory or field.
7. Specialty Equipment	Field provisions, storage.
8. Scheduling	Work to be done, when required? Job to be completed on time— who—why—when?

Listed below are the major areas of coordination required between the HVAC and general contractors.

ITEM	COORDINATION REQUIREMENT
1. Underground Utilities	Location, size, excavation by whom, from where?
2. Equipment	Method of support, location, by whom, anchors, access for receiving and installing, size limitations, flues, roof curbs.
3. Piping	Wall sleeves, size limitations, chases, in walls, under floors, floor sleeves, expansion compensators, access doors.
4. Ductwork	Sizes, support, access doors, drops, outlet sizes, chases, outside air louvers, roof curbs, lintels.
5. Terminal Equipment	Recesses for CUH, RC, FC, etc., size of radiation, method of concealing, grille fastenings.
6. Mechanical-Electrical Responsibility	Who is doing what?
7. Finishes	Field or factory?
8. Scheduling	Who? Why? When?

Questions

15-1. What are the primary considerations when determining the size of the space required to run the mechanicals?

15-2. What is the *sleeve*, as the term applies to concrete construction?

15-3. Why is coordination between the mechanical systems designer and draftsmen and the architectural designer and draftsmen so important?

15-4. Why is coordination between the mechanical contractor and the general construction contractor so important?

15-5. What limitations are there on holes when precast-concrete double tees are involved?

15-6. What limitations are there on duct sizes when steel trusses are used?

15-7. What are *pipe tunnels,* and when are they used.

15-8. What type of masonry wall construction may be used for the partition wall housing the plumbing between back-to-back bathrooms?

15-9. When might double or core walls of drywall or wetwall construction be used?

15-10. What problems may occur when mechanicals are embedded in concrete?

APPENDIX A

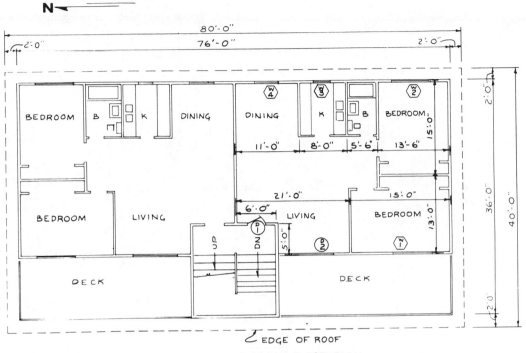

N

TYPICAL FLOOR PLAN

EDGE OF ROOF

Design data
Apartment building, 4 story
Floor to floor height: 10'-0"
3-in. service main
Street main pressure: 50 psi
2 exterior hose bibs
Street main to riser distance: 60 ft.
Flat roof
Occupancy: 2.5 persons per apartment
Heat loss values (U)
  walls   0.13
  roof   0.71
  windows and doors   0.61
Cooling values (HTM)
  walls   3.1
  roof   2.9

SCHEDULE		
NO.	SIZE	TYPE
D1	3'-0" x 6'-8"	1¼" WOOD
D2	6'-0" x 6'-8"	ALUM.- SLIDING
W1	5'-0" x 4'-0"	WOOD - D.H.
W2	5'-0" x 3'-0"	''
W3	3'-0" x 4'-0"	''
W4	4'-0" x 4'-0"	''

SINGLE GLASS

APPENDIX B

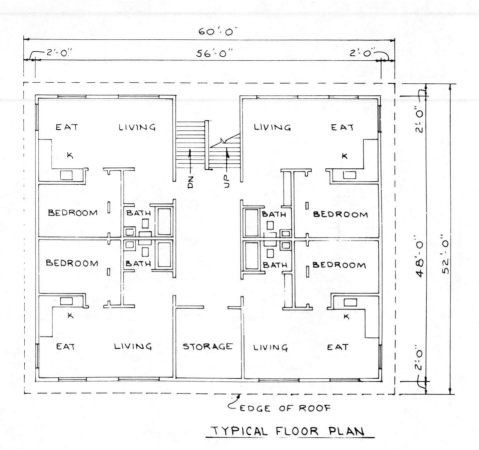

TYPICAL FLOOR PLAN

Design data
Apartment building, 3 story
Floor to floor height: 9'-0"
3-in. service main
Street main pressure: 55 psi
3 exterior hose bibs
Street main to riser distance: 85 ft.
Flat roof
Occupancy: 1.5 persons per apartment

Index

About the Author:

Frank R. Dagostino, formerly on the staff at Hudson Valley Community College in New York and Sandhills Community College in Southern Pines, North Carolina, has his bachelor's degree in Architecture from the University of Florida. A registered architect, Frank R. Dagostino is also an architectural and construction consultant, and has written several books published by Reston Publishing Company.